THE
HARVARD CLASSICS

Registered Edition

◆

The Sin of Anger — Purgatory, Canto XV

THE HARVARD CLASSICS
EDITED BY CHARLES W. ELIOT, LL.D.

The Divine Comedy *of* Dante Alighieri

Hell · Purgatory
Paradise

TRANSLATED BY HENRY F. CARY

With Introduction *and* Notes

P. F. Collier & Son Corporation
NEW YORK

CONTENTS

2

CONTENTS

INTRODUCTORY NOTE

MUCH of the life of Dante Alighieri is obscure, and the known facts are surrounded by a haze of legend and conjecture. He was born in Florence in 1265, of a family noble but not wealthy. His early education is a matter of inference, but we know that he learned the art of writing verse from the poets of France and Provence, and that after he reached manhood he devoted much time to study and became profoundly learned. As a young man he saw military service and shared in the recreations of his contemporaries; and he married some time before he was thirty-two. In Dante's day politics in Florence were exciting and dangerous; and after a few years of participation in public affairs he was condemned to death by his political enemies in 1302. He saved himself by exile, and never returned to his native town. The rest of his life was mainly spent wandering about the north of Italy, in Verona, Bologna, Pisa, Lucca, and finally Ravenna, where he died in 1321. During the years of his exile he found generous patrons in men like the heads of the Scala family in Verona and Guido Novello da Polenta in Ravenna; and at Bologna and elsewhere he was welcomed as a teacher.

In the early part of the century in which Dante was born, the literary language of Tuscany was still Latin, and not the least of his services to his country was his influence in finally establishing the dignity of Italian as a medium for great literature. He himself used Latin in at least three works: his lecture "De Aqua et Terra"; his "De Monarchia," in which he expounded his political theory of the relation of the Empire and the Papacy; and his unfinished "De Vulgari Eloquentia," containing his defense of the use of Italian. More important, however, were his two great works in the vernacular, the "Vita Nuova," a series of poems with prose commentary, on his love for Beatrice, and the "Divina Commedia."

The Beatrice, real or ideal, who plays so important a part in the poetry of Dante, is stated by Boccaccio to have been the daughter of Folco Portinari, a rich Florentine, and wife of the banker Simone dei Bardi. With this actual person Dante's acquaintance seems to have been of the slightest; but, after the fashion of the chivalric lovers of the day, he took her as the object of his ideal devotion. She became for him, especially after her death in 1290, the center of a mystical devotion of extraordinary intensity, and appears in his masterpiece as the personification of heavenly enlightenment.

The "Divine Comedy" was entitled by Dante himself merely "Com-

3

media," "meaning a poetic composition in a style intermediate between the sustained nobility of tragedy, and the popular tone of elegy." The word had no dramatic implication at that time, though it did involve a happy ending. The poem is the narrative of a journey down through Hell, up the mountain of Purgatory, and through the revolving heavens into the presence of God. In this aspect it belongs to the two familiar medieval literary types of the Journey and the Vision. It is also an allegory, representing under the symbolism of the stages and experiences of the journey, the history of a human soul, painfully struggling from sin through purification to the Beatific Vision. Other schemes of interpretation have been worked out and were probably intended, for Dante granted the medieval demand for a threefold and even fourfold signification in this type of writing.

But the "Divine Comedy" belongs to still other literary forms than those mentioned. Professor Grandgent has pointed out that it is also an encyclopedia, a poem in praise of Woman, and an autobiography. It contains much of what Dante knew of theology and philosophy, of astronomy and cosmography, and fragments of a number of other branches of learning, so that its encyclopedic character is obvious. In making it a monument to Beatrice, he surpassed infinitely all the poetry devoted to the praise of women in an age when the deification of women was the commonplace of poetry. And finally he made it an autobiography —not a narrative of the external events of his life, but of the agony of his soul.

Thus, in an altogether unique way, Dante summarizes the literature, the philosophy, the science, and the religion of the Middle Ages. Through the intensity of his capacity for experience, the splendor of his power of expression, and the depth of his spiritual and philosophic insight, he at once sums up and transcends a whole era of human history.

THE DIVINE COMEDY

INFERNO [HELL]

CANTO I

ARGUMENT.—The writer, having lost his way in a gloomy forest, and being
hindered by certain wild beasts from ascending a mountain, is met by Virgil, who
promises to show him the punishments of Hell, and afterward of Purgatory; and
that he shall then be conducted by Beatrice into Paradise. He follows the Roman poet.

IN the midway[1] of this our mortal life,
    I found me in a gloomy wood, astray
    Gone from the path direct: and e'en to tell,
It were no easy task, how savage wild
That forest, how robust and rough its growth,
Which to remember only, my dismay
Renews, in bitterness not far from death.
Yet, to discourse of what there good befel,
All else will I relate discover'd there.

    How first I enter'd it I scarce can say,
Such sleepy dulness in that instant weigh'd
My senses down, when the true path I left;
But when a mountain's foot I reach'd, where closed
The valley that had pierced my heart with dread,
I look'd aloft, and saw his shoulders broad
Already vested with that planet's beam,[2]
Who leads all wanderers safe through every way.

    Then was a little respite to the fear,
That in my heart's recesses deep had lain
All of that night, so pitifully past:
And as a man, with difficult short breath,
Forespent with toiling, 'scaped from sea to shore,
Turns to the perilous wide waste, and stands

---

[1] "In the midway." The era of the
poem is intended by these words to be
fixed to the thirty-fifth year of the poet's
age, A.D. 1300. In his Convito, human
life is compared to an arch or bow, the
highest point of which is, in those well
framed by nature, at their thirty-fifth
year.

[2] "That planet's beam." The sun.

At gaze; e'en so my spirit, that yet fail'd,
Struggling with terror, turn'd to view the straits
That none hath passed and lived. My weary frame
After short pause recomforted, again
I journey'd on over that lonely steep,
The hinder foot[3] still firmer. Scarce the ascent
Began, when, lo! a panther,[4] nimble, light,
And cover'd with a speckled skin, appear'd;
Nor, when it saw me, vanish'd; rather strove
To check my onward going; that oft-times,
With purpose to retrace my steps, I turn'd.

    The hour was morning's prime, and on his way
Aloft the sun ascended with those stars,[5]
That with him rose when Love Divine first moved
Those its fair works: so that with joyous hope
All things conspired to fill me, the gay skin
Of that swift animal, the matin dawn,
And the sweet season. Soon that joy was chased.
And by new dread succeeded, when in view
A lion came, 'gainst me as it appear'd,
With his head held aloft and hunger-mad,
That e'en the air was fear-struck. A she-wolf
Was at his heels, who in her leanness seem'd
Full of all wants, and many a land hath made
Disconsolate ere now. She with such fear
O'erwhelm'd me, at the sight of her appall'd,
That of the height all hope I lost. As one,
Who, with his gain elated, sees the time
When all unawares is gone, he inwardly
Mourns with heart-griping anguish; such was I,
Haunted by that fell beast, never at peace,
Who coming o'er against me, by degrees
Impell'd me where the sun in silence rests.

    While to the lower space with backward step
I fell, my ken discern'd the form of one
Whose voice seem'd faint through long disuse of speech.
When him in that great desert I espied,

---

[3] "The hinder foot." In ascending a hill the weight of the body rests on the hinder foot.

[4] "A panther." Pleasure or luxury.

[5] "With those stars." The sun was in Aries, in which sign he supposes it to have begun its course at the creation.

"Have mercy on me," cried I out aloud,
"Spirit! or living man! whate'er thou be."
    He answered: "Now not man, man once I was,
And born of Lombard parents, Mantuans both
By country, when the power of Julius yet
Was scarcely firm. At Rome my life was past,
Beneath the mild Augustus, in the time
Of fabled deities and false. A bard
Was I, and made Anchises' upright son
The subject of my song, who came from Troy,
When the flames prey'd on Ilium's haughty towers.
But thou, say wherefore to such perils past
Return'st thou? wherefore not this pleasant mount
Ascendest, cause and source of all delight?"
"And art thou then that Virgil, that well-spring,
From which such copious floods of eloquence
Have issued?" I with front abash'd replied.
"Glory and light of all the tuneful train!
May it avail me, that I long with zeal
Have sought thy volume, and with love immense
Have conn'd it o'er. My master thou, and guide!
Thou he from whom alone I have derived
That style, which for its beauty into fame
Exalts me. See the beast, from whom I fled.
O save me from her, thou illustrious sage!
For every vein and pulse throughout my frame
She hath made tremble." He, soon as he saw
That I was weeping, answer'd, "Thou must needs
Another way pursue, if thou wouldst 'scape
From out that savage wilderness. This beast,
At whom thou criest, her way will suffer none
To pass, and no less hinderance makes than death:
So bad and so accursed in her kind,
That never sated is her ravenous will,
Still after food more craving than before.
To many an animal in wedlock vile
She fastens, and shall yet to many more,
Until that greyhound[6] come, who shall destroy

[6] This passage has been commonly understood as a eulogium on the liberal spirit of his Veronese patron, Can Grande della Scala.

Her with sharp pain. He will not life support
By earth nor its base metals, but by love,
Wisdom, and virtue; and his land shall be
The land 'twixt either Feltro.[7] In his might
Shall safety to Italia's plains arise,
For whose fair realm, Camilla, virgin pure,
Nisus, Euryalus, and Turnus fell.
He, with incessant chase, through every town
Shall worry, until he to hell at length
Restore her, thence by envy first let loose.
I, for thy profit pondering, now devise
That thou mayst follow me; and I, thy guide,
Will lead thee hence through an eternal space,
Where thou shalt hear despairing shrieks, and see
Spirits of old tormented, who invoke
A second death;[8] and those next view, who dwell
Content in fire,[9] for that they hope to come,
Whene'er the time may be, among the blest,
Into whose regions if thou then desire
To ascend, a spirit worthier[10] than I
Must lead thee, in whose charge, when I depart,
Thou shalt be left: for that Almighty King,
Who reigns above, a rebel to His law
Adjudges me; and therefore hath decreed
That, to His city, none through me should come.
He in all parts hath sway; there rules, there holds
His citadel and throne. O happy those,
Whom there He chuses!" I to him in few:
"Bard! by that God, whom thou didst not adore,
I do beseech thee (that this ill and worse
I may escape) to lead me where thou said'st,
That I Saint Peter's gate[11] may view, and those
Who, as thou tell'st, are in such dismal plight."
     Onward he moved, I close his steps pursued.

---

[7] Verona, the country of Can della Scala, is situated between Feltro, a city in the Marca Trivigiana, and Monte Feltro, a city in the territory of Urbino.

[8] "A second death." "And in these days men shall seek death, and shall not find it; and shall desire to die, and death shall flee from them." Rev. ix. 6.

[9] The spirits in Purgatory.

[10] "A spirit worthier." Beatrice, who conducts the Poet through Paradise.

[11] The gate of Purgatory, which the Poet feigns to be guarded by an angel placed there by St. Peter.

CANTO II

ARGUMENT.—After the invocation, which poets are used to prefix to their works, he shows that, on a consideration of his own strength, he doubted whether it sufficed for the journey proposed to him, but that, being comforted by Virgil, he at last took courage, and followed him as his guide and master.

NOW was the day departing, and the air,
    Imbrown'd with shadows, from their toils released
    All animals on earth; and I alone
Prepared myself the conflict to sustain,
Both of sad pity, and that perilous road,
Which my unerring memory shall retrace.
    O Muses! O high genius! now vouchsafe
Your aid. O mind! that all I saw hast kept
Safe in a written record, here thy worth
And eminent endowments come to proof.
    I thus began: "Bard! thou who art my guide,
Consider well, if virtue be in me
Sufficient, ere to this high enterprise
Thou trust me. Thou hast told that Silvius' sire,[1]
Yet clothed in corruptible flesh, among
The immortal tribes had entrance, and was there
Sensibly present. Yet if Heaven's great Lord,
Almighty foe to ill, such favor show'd
In contemplation of the high effect,
Both what and who from him should issue forth,
It seems in reason's judgment well deserved;
Sith he of Rome and of Rome's empire wide,
In Heaven's empyreal height was chosen sire:
Both which, if truth be spoken, were ordain'd
And stablish'd for the holy place, where sits
Who to great Peter's sacred chair succeeds.
He from this journey, in thy song renown'd,
Learn'd things, that to his victory gave rise
And to the papal robe. In after-times
The Chosen Vessel[2] also travel'd there,
To bring us back assurance in that faith
Which is the entrance to salvation's way.
But I, why should I there presume? or who
Permits it? not Æneas I, nor Paul.

1 "Silvius' sire." Æneas.   2 "The Chosen Vessel." St. Paul.

Myself I deem not worthy, and none else
Will deem me. I, if on this voyage then
I venture, fear it will in folly end.
Thou, who art wise, better my meaning know'st,
Than I can speak." As one, who unresolves
What he hath late resolved, and with new thoughts
Changes his purpose, from his first intent
Removed; e'en such was I on that dun coast,
Wasting in thought my enterprise, at first
So eagerly embraced. "If right thy words
I scan," replied that shade magnanimous,
"Thy soul is by vile fear assail'd, which oft
So overcasts a man, that he recoils
From noblest resolution, like a beast
At some false semblance in the twilight gloom.
That from this terror thou mayst free thyself,
I will instruct thee why I came, and what
I heard in that same instant, when for thee
Grief touch'd me first. I was among the tribe,
Who rest suspended,[3] when a dame, so blest
And lovely I besought her to command,
Call'd me; her eyes were brighter than the star
Of day; and she, with gentle voice and soft,
Angelically tuned, her speech address'd:
'O courteous shade of Mantua! thou whose fame
Yet lives, and shall live long as nature lasts!
A friend, not of my fortune but myself,
On the wide desert in his road has met
Hindrance so great, that he through fear has turn'd.
Now much I dread lest he past help have stray'd,
And I be risen too late for his relief,
From what in heaven of him I heard. Speed now,
And by thy eloquent persuasive tongue,
And by all means for his deliverance meet,
Assist him. So to me will comfort spring.
I, who now bid thee on this errand forth,
Am Beatrice;[4] from a place I come

---

[3] The spirits in Limbo, neither admitted to a state of glory nor doomed to punishment.

[4] "Beatrice." The daughter of Folco Portinari, who is here invested with the character of celestial wisdom or theology.

Revisited with joy. Love brought me thence,
Who prompts my speech. When in my Master's sight
I stand, thy praise to him I oft will tell.'
  "She then was silent, and I thus began:
'O Lady! by whose influence alone
Mankind excels whatever is contain'd
Within that heaven which hath the smallest orb,
So thy command delights me, that to obey,
If it were done already, would seem late.
No need hast thou further to speak thy will:
Yet tell the reason, why thou art not loth
To leave that ample space, where to return
Thou burnest, for this centre here beneath.'
  "She then: 'Since thou so deeply wouldst inquire,
I will instruct thee briefly why no dread
Hinders my entrance here. Those things alone
Are to be fear'd whence evil may proceed;
None else, for none are terrible beside.
I am so framed by God, thanks to His grace!
That any sufferance of your misery
Touches me not, nor flame of that fierce fire
Assails me. In high Heaven a blessed Dame[5]
Resides, who mourns with such effectual grief
That hindrance, which I send thee to remove,
That God's stern judgment to her will inclines.'
To Lucia,[6] calling, her she thus bespake:
'Now doth thy faithful servant need thy aid,
And I commend him to thee.' At her word
Sped Lucia, of all cruelty the foe,
And coming to the place, where I abode
Seated with Rachel, her of ancient days,
She thus address'd me: "Thou true praise of God!
Beatrice! why is not thy succour lent
To him, who so much loved thee, as to leave
For thy sake all the multitude admires?
Dost thou not hear how pitiful his wail,
Nor mark the death, which in the torrent flood,
Swoln mightier than a sea, him struggling holds?"

[5] "A blessed Dame." The Divine
Mercy.

[6] "Lucia." The enlightening Grace of
Heaven; as it is commonly explained.

Ne'er among men did any with such speed
Haste to their profit, flee from their annoy,
As, when these words were spoken, I came here,
Down from my blessed seat, trusting the force
Of thy pure eloquence, which thee, and all
Who well have mark'd it, into honor brings.'
   "When she had ended, her bright beaming eyes
Tearful she turn'd aside; whereat I felt
Redoubled zeal to serve thee. As she will'd,
Thus am I come: I saved thee from the beast,
Who thy near way across the goodly mount
Prevented. What is this comes o'er thee then?
Why, why dost thou hang back? why in thy breast
Harbour vile fear? why hast not courage there,
And noble daring; since three maids,[7] so blest,
Thy safety plan, e'en in the court of Heaven;
And so much certain good my words forebode?"
   As florets, by the frosty air of night
Bent down and closed, when day has blanch'd their leaves,
Rise all unfolded on their spiry stems;
So was my fainting vigor new restored,
And to my heart such kindly courage ran,
That I as one undaunted soon replied:
"O full of pity she, who undertook
My succour! and thou kind, who didst perform
So soon her true behest! With such desire
Thou hast disposed me to renew my voyage,
That my first purpose fully is resumed.
Lead on: one only will is in us both.
Thou art my guide, my master thou, and lord."
   So spake I; and when he had onward moved,
I enter'd on the deep and woody way.

[7] "Three maids." The Divine Mercy, Lucia and Beatrice.

CANTO III

ARGUMENT.—Dante, following Virgil, comes to the gate of Hell; where, after having read the dreadful words that are written thereon, they both enter. Here, as he understands from Virgil, those were punished who had passed their time (for living it could not be called) in a state of apathy and indifference both to good and evil. Then, pursuing their way, they arrive at the river Acheron; and there find the old ferryman Charon, who takes the spirits over to the opposite shore; which, as soon as Dante reaches, he is seized with terror, and falls into a trance.

"THROUGH me you pass into the city of woe:
  Through me you pass into eternal pain:
  Through me among the people lost for aye.
Justice the founder of my fabric moved:
To rear me was the task of Power divine,
Supremest Wisdom, and primeval Love.[1]
Before me things create were none, save things
Eternal, and eternal I endure.
All hope abandon, ye who enter here."
  Such characters, in color dim, I mark'd
Over a portal's lofty arch inscribed.
Whereat I thus: "Master, these words import
Hard meaning." He as one prepared replied:
"Here thou must all distrust behind thee leave;
Here be vile fear extinguish'd. We are come
Where I have told thee we shall see the souls
To misery doom'd, who intellectual good
Have lost." And when his hand he had stretch'd forth
To mine, with pleasant looks, whence I was cheer'd,
Into that secret place he led me on.
  Here sighs, with lamentations and loud moans,
Resounded through the air pierced by no star,
That e'en I wept at entering. Various tongues,
Horrible languages, outcries of woe,
Accents of anger, voices deep and hoarse,
With hands together smote that swell'd the sounds,
Made up a tumult, that forever whirls
Round through that air with solid darkness stain'd,
Like to the sand that in the whirlwind flies.
  I then, with horror yet encompast, cried:
"O master! what is this I hear? what race
Are these, who seem so overcome with woe?"

---

[1] "Power," "Wisdom," "Love," the three Persons of the Blessed Trinity.

He thus to me: "This miserable fate
Suffer the wretched souls of those, who lived
Without or praise or blame, with that ill band
Of angels mix'd, who nor rebellious proved,
Nor yet were true to God, but for themselves
Were only. From his bounds Heaven drove them forth
Not to impair his lustre; nor the depth
Of Hell receives them, lest the accursed tribe
Should glory thence with exultation vain."
    I then: "Master! what doth aggrieve them thus,
That they lament so loud?" He straight replied:
"That will I tell thee briefly. These of death
No hope may entertain: and their blind life
So meanly passes, that all other lots
They envy. Fame of them the world hath none,
Nor suffers; Mercy and Justice scorn them both.
Speak not of them, but look, and pass them by."
    And I, who straightway look'd, beheld a flag,
Which whirling ran around so rapidly,
That it no pause obtain'd: and following came
Such a long train of spirits, I should ne'er
Have thought that death so many had despoil'd.
    When some of these I recognized, I saw
And knew the shade of him, who to base fear[2]
Yielding, abjured his high estate. Forthwith
I understood, for certain, this the tribe
Of those ill spirits both to God displeasing
And to His foes. These wretches, who ne'er lived,
Went on in nakedness, and sorely stung
By wasps and hornets, which bedew'd their cheeks
With blood, that, mix'd with tears, dropp'd to their feet,
And by disgustful worms was gather'd there.
    Then looking further onwards, I beheld

[2] This is commonly understood of Celestine V, who abdicated the papal power in 1294. Venturi mentions a work written by Innocenzio Barcellini, of the Celestine order, and printed at Milan in 1701, in which an attempt is made to put a different interpretation on this passage. Lombardi would apply it to some one of Dante's fellow-citizens, who, refusing, through avarice or want of spirit, to support the party of the Bianchi at Florence, had been the main occasion of the miseries that befell them. But the testimony of Fazio degli Uberti, who lived so near the time of our author, seems almost decisive on this point. He expressly speaks of the Pope Celestine as being in Hell.

A throng upon the shore of a great stream:
Whereat I thus: "Sir! grant me now to know
Whom here we view, and whence impell'd they seem
So eager to pass o'er, as I discern
Through the blear light?" He thus to me in few:
"This shalt thou know, soon as our steps arrive
Beside the woful tide of Acheron."
    Then with eyes downward cast, and fill'd with shame,
Fearing my words offensive to his ear,
Till we had reach'd the river, I from speech
Abstain'd. And lo! toward us in a bark
Comes on an old man, hoary white with eld,
Crying, "Woe to you, wicked spirits! hope not
Ever to see the sky again. I come
To take you to the other shore across,
Into eternal darkness, there to dwell
In fierce heat and in ice. And thou, who there
Standest, live spirit! get thee hence, and leave
These who are dead." But soon as he beheld
I left them not, "By other way," said he,
"By other haven shalt thou come to shore,
Not by this passage; thee a nimbler boat
Must carry." Then to him thus spake my guide:
"Charon! thyself torment not: so 'tis will'd,
Where will and power are one: ask thou no more."
    Straightway in silence fell the shaggy cheeks
Of him, the boatman o'er the livid lake,
Around whose eyes glared wheeling flames. Meanwhile
Those spirits, faint and naked, color changed,
And gnash'd their teeth, soon as the cruel words
They heard. God and their parents they blasphemed,
The human kind, the place, the time, and seed,
That did engender them and give them birth,
    Then all together sorely wailing drew
To the curst strand, that every man must pass
Who fears not God. Charon, demoniac form,
With eyes of burning coal, collects them all,
Beckoning, and each, that lingers, with his oar
Strikes. As fall off the light autumnal leaves
One still another following, till the bough

Strews all its honours on the earth beneath;
E'en in like manner Adam's evil brood
Cast themselves, one by one, down from the shore,
Each at a beck, as falcon at his call.[3]
   Thus go they over through the umber'd wave;
And ever they on the opposing bank
Be landed, on this side another throng
Still gathers. "Son," thus spake the courteous guide,
"Those who die subject to the wrath of God
All here together come from every clime
And to o'erpass the river are not loth:
For so Heaven's justice goads them on, that fear
Is turn'd into desire. Hence ne'er hath past
Good spirit. If of thee Charon complain,
Now mayst thou know the import of his words."
   This said, the gloomy region trembling shook
So terribly, that yet with clammy dews
Fear chills my brow. The sad earth gave a blast,
That, lightening, shot forth a vermilion flame,
Which all my senses conquer'd quite, and I
Down dropp'd, as one with sudden slumber seized.

CANTO IV

ARGUMENT.—The Poet, being roused by a clap of thunder, and following his guide onward, descends into Limbo, which is the first circle of Hell, where he finds the souls of those, who, although they have lived virtuously and have not to suffer for great sins, nevertheless, through lack of baptism, merit not the bliss of Paradise. Hence he is led on by Virgil to descend into the second circle.

BROKE the deep slumber in my brain a crash
   Of heavy thunder, that I shook myself,
   As one by main force roused. Risen upright,
My rested eyes I moved around, and search'd
With fixed ken, to know what place it was
Wherein I stood. For certain, on the brink
I found me of the lamentable vale,
The dread abyss, that joins a thundrous sound
Of plaints innumerable. Dark and deep,

---

[3] "As a falcon at his call." This is Vellutello's explanation, and seems preferable to that commonly given: "as a bird that is enticed to the cage by the call of another."

And thick with clouds o'erspread, mine eye in vain
Explored its bottom, nor could aught discern.
"Now let us to the blind world there beneath
Descend," the bard began, all pale of look:
"I go the first, and thou shalt follow next."
Then I, his alter'd hue perceiving, thus:
"How may I speed, if thou yieldest to dread,
Who still art wont to comfort me in doubt?"
He then: "The anguish of that race below
With pity stains my cheek, which thou for fear
Mistakest. Let us on. Our length of way
Urges to haste." Onward, this said, he moved;
And entering led me with him, on the bounds
Of the first circle that surrounds the abyss.

    Here, as mine ear could note, no plaint was heard
Except of sighs, that made the eternal air
Tremble, not caused by tortures, but from grief
Felt by those multitudes, many and vast,
Of men, women, and infants. Then to me
The gentle guide: "Inquirest thou not what spirits
Are these which thou beholdest? Ere thou pass
Farther, I would thou know, that these of sin
Were blameless; and if aught they merited,
It profits not, since baptism was not theirs,
The portal[1] to thy faith. If they before
The Gospel lived, they served not God aright;
And among such am I. For these defects,
And for no other evil, we are lost;
Only so far afflicted, that we live
Desiring without hope." Sore grief assail'd
My heart at hearing this, for well I knew
Suspended in that Limbo many a soul
Of mighty worth. "O tell me, sire revered!
Tell me, my master!" I began, through wish
Of full assurance in that holy faith
Which vanquishes all error; "say, did e'er
Any, or through his own or other's merit,

---

[1] "Portal." "*Porta della fede.*" This was an alteration made in the text by the Academicians della Crusca, on the authority, as it would appear, of only two manuscripts. The other reading is, "*parte della fede,*" "part of the faith."

Come forth from thence, who afterward was blest?"
Piercing the secret purport[2] of my speech,
He answer'd: "I was new to that estate
When I beheld a puissant one[3] arrive
Amongst us, with victorious trophy crown'd.
He forth the shade of our first parent drew,
Abel, his child, and Noah righteous man,
Of Moses lawgiver for faith approved,
Of patriarch Abraham, and David king,
Israel with his sire and with his sons,
Nor without Rachel whom so hard he won,
And others many more, whom He to bliss
Exalted. Before these, be thou assured,
No spirit of human kind was ever saved."
    We, while he spake, ceased not our onward road,
Still passing through the wood; for so I name
Those spirits thick beset. We were not far
On this side from the summit, when I kenn'd
A flame, that o'er the darken'd hemisphere
Prevailing shined. Yet we a little space
Were distant, not so far but I in part
Discover'd that a tribe in honour high
That place possess'd. "O thou, who every art
And science valuest! who are these, that boast
Such honor, separate from all the rest?"
    He answer'd: "The renown of their great names,
That echoes through your world above, acquires
Favor in Heaven, which holds them thus advanced."
Meantime a voice I heard: "Honor the bard
Sublime! his shade returns, that left us late!"
No sooner ceased the sound, than I beheld
Four mighty spirits toward us bend their steps,
Of semblance neither sorrowful nor glad.
    When thus my master kind began: "Mark him,
Who in his right hand bears that falchion keen,
The other three preceding, as their lord.

This is that Homer, of all bards supreme:
Flaccus the next, in satire's vein excelling;
The third is Naso; Lucan is the last.
Because they all that appellation own,
With which the voice singly accosted me,
Honouring they greet me thus, and well they judge."
    So I beheld united the bright school
Of him the monarch of sublimest song,[4]
That o'er the others like an eagle soars.
    When they together short discourse had held,
They turn'd to me, with salutation kind
Beckoning me; at the which my master smiled:
Nor was this all; but greater honour still
They gave me, for they made me of their tribe;
And I was sixth amid so learn'd a band.
    Far as the luminous beacon on we pass'd,
Speaking of matters, then befitting well
To speak, now fitter left untold. At foot
Of a magnificent castle we arrived,
Seven times with lofty walls begirt, and round
Defended by a pleasant stream. O'er this
As o'er dry land we pass'd. Next, through seven gates,
I with those sages enter'd, and we came
Into a mead with lively verdure fresh.
    There dwelt a race, who slow their eyes around
Majestically moved, and in their port
Bore eminent authority: they spake
Seldom, but all their words were tuneful sweet.
    We to one side retired, into a place
Open and bright and lofty, whence each one
Stood manifest to view. Incontinent,
There on the green enamel of the plain
Were shown me the great spirits, by whose sight
I am exalted in my own esteem.
    Electra[5] there I saw accompanied
By many, among whom Hector I knew,
Anchises' pious son, and with hawk's eye
Cæsar all arm'd, and by Camilla there

---

[4] "The monarch of sublimest song."
Homer.

[5] Daughter of Atlas, and mother of
Dardanus, founder of Troy.

Penthesilea. On the other side,
Old King Latinus seated by his child
Lavinia, and that Brutus I beheld
Who Tarquin chased, Lucretia, Cato's wife
Marcia, with Julia[6] and Cornelia there;
And sole apart retired, the Soldan fierce.[7]
    Then when a little more I raised my brow,
I spied the master of the sapient throng,[8]
Seated amid the philosophic train.
Him all admire, all pay him reverence due.
There Socrates and Plato both I mark'd
Nearest to him in rank, Democritus,
Who sets the world at chance,[9] Diogenes,
With Heraclitus, and Empedocles,
And Anaxagoras, and Thales sage,
Zeno, and Dioscorides well read
In nature's secret lore. Orpheus I mark'd
And Linus, Tully and moral Seneca,
Euclid and Ptolemy, Hippocrates,
Galenus, Avicen, and him who made
That commentary vast, Averroes.[10]
    Of all to speak at full were vain attempt;
For my wide theme so urges, that oft-times
My words fall short of what bechanced In two
The six associates part. Another way
My sage guide leads me, from that air serene,
Into a climate ever vex'd with storms:
And to a part I come, where no light shines.

[6] "Julia." The daughter of Julius Cæsar, and wife of Pompey.

[7] "The Soldan fierce." Saladin, or Salaheddin, the rival of Richard Cœur de Lion.

[8] "The master of the sapient throng." *"Maestro di color che sanno."* Aristotle.

[9] "Who sets the world at chance." Democritus, who maintained the world to have been formed by the fortuitous concourse of atoms.

[10] Averroes, called by the Arabians Ibn Roschd, translated and commented on the works of Aristotle.

CANTO V

ARGUMENT.—Coming into the second circle of Hell, Dante at the entrance beholds Minos the Infernal Judge, by whom he is admonished to beware how he enters those regions. Here he witnesses the punishment of carnal sinners, who are tossed about ceaselessly in the dark air by the most furious winds. Among these, he meets with Francesca of Rimini, through pity at whose sad tale he falls fainting to the ground.

FROM the first circle I descended thus
  Down to the second, which, a lesser space
  Embracing, so much more of grief contains,
Provoking bitter moans. There Minos stands,
Grinning with ghastly feature: he, of all
Who enter, strict examining the crimes,
Gives sentence, and dismisses them beneath,
According as he foldeth him around:
For when before him comes the ill-fated soul,
It all confesses; and that judge severe
Of sins, considering what place in Hell
Suits the transgression, with his tail so oft
Himself encircles, as degrees beneath
He dooms it to descend. Before him stand
Always a numerous throng; and in his turn
Each one to judgment passing, speaks, and hears
His fate, thence downward to his dwelling hurl'd.
"O thou! who to this residence of woe
Approachest!" when he saw me coming, cried
Minos, relinquishing his dread employ,
"Look how thou enter here; beware in whom
Thou place thy trust; let not the entrance broad
Deceive thee to thy harm." To him my guide:
"Wherefore exclaimest? Hinder not his way
By destiny appointed; so 'tis will'd,
Where will and power are one. Ask thou no more."
 Now 'gin the rueful wailings to be heard.
Now am I come where many a plaining voice
Smites on mine ear. Into a place I came
Where light was silent all. Bellowing there groan'd
A noise, as of a sea in tempest torn
By warring winds. The stormy blast of Hell
With restless fury drives the spirits on,
Whirl'd round and dash'd amain with sore annoy.

When they arrive before the ruinous sweep,
There shrieks are heard, there lamentations, moans,
And blasphemies 'gainst the good Power in Heaven.
I understood, that to this torment sad
The carnal sinners are condemn'd, in whom
Reason by lust is sway'd. As, in large troops
And multitudinous, when winter reigns,
The starlings on their wings are borne abroad;
So bears the tyrannous gust those evil souls.
On this side and on that, above, below,
It drives them: hope of rest to solace them
Is none, nor e'en of milder pang. As cranes,
Chanting their dolorous notes, traverse the sky,
Stretch'd out in long array; so I beheld
Spirits, who came loud wailing, hurried on
By their dire doom. Then I: "Instructor! who
Are these, by the black air so scourged?" "The first
'Mong those, of whom thou question'st," he replied,
"O'er many tongues was empress. She in vice
Of luxury was so shameless, that she made
Liking be lawful by promulged decree,
To clear the blame she had herself incurr'd.
This is Semiramis, of whom 'tis writ,
That she succeeded Ninus her espoused;
And held the land, which now the Soldan rules.
The next in amorous fury slew herself,
And to Sichæus' ashes broke her faith:
Then follows Cleopatra, lustful queen."
    There mark'd I Helen, for whose sake so long
The time was fraught with evil; there the great
Achilles, who with love fought to the end.
Paris I saw, and Tristan; and beside,
A thousand more he show'd me, and by name
Pointed them out, whom love bereaved of life.
    When I had heard my sage instructor name
Those dames and knights of antique days, o'erpower'd
By pity, well-nigh in amaze my mind
Was lost; and I began: "Bard! willingly
I would address those two together coming,
Which seem so light before the wind." He thus:

"Note thou, when nearer they to us approach.
Then by that love which carries them along,
Entreat; and they will come." Soon as the wind
Sway'd them towards us, I thus framed my speech:
"O wearied spirits! come, and hold discourse
With us, if by none else restrain'd." As doves
By fond desire invited, on wide wings
And firm, to their sweet nest returning home,
Cleave the air, wafted by their will along;
Thus issued, from that troop where Dido ranks,
They, through the ill air speeding: with such force
My cry prevail'd, by strong affection urged.
        "O gracious creature and benign! who go'st
Visiting, through this element obscure,
Us, who the world with bloody stain imbrued;
If, for a friend, the King of all, we own'd,
Our prayer to him should for thy peace arise,
Since thou hast pity on our evil plight.
Of whatsoe'er to hear or to discourse
It pleases thee, that will we hear, of that
Freely with thee discourse, while e'er the wind,
As now, is mute. The land,[1] that gave me birth,
Is situate on the coast, where Po descends
To rest in ocean with his sequent streams.
        "Love, that in gentle heart is quickly learnt,
Entangled him by that fair form, from me
Ta'en in such cruel sort, as grieves me still:
Love, that denial takes from none beloved,
Caught me with pleasing him so passing well,
That, as thou seest, he yet deserts me not.
Love brought us to one death: Caïna[2] waits
The soul, who spilt our life." Such were their words;
At hearing which, downward I bent my looks,
And held them there so long, that the bard cried:
"What art thou pondering?" I in answer thus:
"Alas! by what sweet thoughts, what fond desire
Must they at length to that ill pass have reach'd!"
        Then turning, I to them my speech address'd,

----

[1] "The land." Ravenna.   [2] "Caïna." The place to which murderers are doomed.

And thus began: "Francesca![3] your sad fate
Even to tears my grief and pity moves.
But tell me; in the time of your sweet sighs,
By what, and how Love granted, that ye knew
Your yet uncertain wishes?" She replied:
"No greater grief than to remember days
Of joy, when misery is at hand. That kens
Thy learn'd instructor. Yet so eagerly
If thou art bent to know the primal root,
From whence our love gat being, I will do
As one, who weeps and tells his tale. One day,
For our delight we read of Lancelot,[4]
How him love thrall'd. Alone we were, and no
Suspicion near us. Oft-times by that reading
Our eyes were drawn together, and the hue
Fled from our alter'd cheek. But at one point
Alone we fell. When of that smile we read,
The wished smile so rapturously kiss'd
By one so deep in love, then he, who ne'er
From me shall separate, at once my lips
All trembling kiss'd. The book and writer both
Were love's purveyors. In its leaves that day
We read no more." While thus one spirit spake,
The other wail'd so sorely, that heart-struck
I, through compassion fainting, seem'd not far
From death, and like a corse fell to the ground.

---

[3] "Francesca." Francesca, the daughter of Guido da Polenta, Lord of Ravenna, was given by her father in marriage to Gianciotto, son of Malatesta, Lord of Rimini, a man of extraordinary courage, but deformed in his person. His brother Paolo, who unhappily possessed those graces which the husband of Francesca wanted, engaged her affections; and being taken in adultery, they were both put to death by the enraged Gianciotto.

[4] "Lancelot." One of the Knights of the Round Table, and the lover of Ginevra, or Guinever, celebrated in romance. The incident alluded to seems to have made a strong impression on the imagination of Dante, who introduces it again, in the Paradise, Canto xvi.

CANTO VI

ARGUMENT.—On his recovery, the Poet finds himself in the third circle, where the gluttonous are punished. Their torment is, to lie in the mire, under a continual and heavy storm of hail, snow, and discolored water; Cerberus, meanwhile barking over them with his threefold throat, and rending them piecemeal. One of these, who on earth was named Ciacco, foretells the divisions with which Florence is about to be distracted. Dante proposes a question to his guide, who solves it; and they proceed toward the fourth circle.

MY sense reviving, that erewhile had droop'd
With pity for the kindred shades, whence grief
O'ercame me wholly, straight around I see
New torments, new tormented souls, which way
Soe'er I move, or turn, or bend my sight.
In the third circle I arrive, of showers
Ceaseless, accursed, heavy and cold, unchanged
For ever, both in kind and in degree.
Large hail, discolor'd water, sleety flaw
Through the dun midnight air stream'd down amain:
Stank all the land whereon that tempest fell.

Cerberus, cruel monster, fierce and strange,
Through his wide threefold throat, barks as a dog
Over the multitude immersed beneath.
His eyes glare crimson, black his unctuous beard,
His belly large, and claw'd the hands, with which
He tears the spirits, flays them, and their limbs
Piecemeal disparts. Howling there spread, as curs,
Under the rainy deluge, with one side
The other screening, oft they roll them round,
A wretched, godless crew. When that great worm[1]
Descried us, savage Cerberus, he oped
His jaws, and the fangs show'd us; not a limb
Of him but trembled. Then my guide, his palms
Expanding on the ground, thence fill'd with earth
Raised them, and cast it in his ravenous maw.
E'en as a dog, that yelling bays for food
His keeper, when the morsel comes, lets fall
His fury, bent alone with eager haste

[1] "When that great worm, descried us   "The abhorred worm,
. . . he opened his jaws." In Canto   that boreth through the world."
xxxiv. Lucifer is called

To swallow it; so dropp'd the loathsome cheeks
Of demon Cerberus, who thundering stuns
The spirits, that they for deafness wish in vain.
　　We, o'er the shades thrown prostrate by the brunt
Of the heavy tempest passing, set our feet
Upon their emptiness, that substance seem'd.
　　They all along the earth extended lay,
Save one, that sudden raised himself to sit,
Soon as that way he saw us pass. "O thou!"
He cried, "who through the infernal shades art led,
Own, if again thou know'st me. Thou wast framed
Or ere my frame was broken." I replied:
"The anguish thou endurest perchance so takes
Thy form from my remembrance, that it seems
As if I saw thee never. But inform
Me who thou art, that in a place so sad
Art set, and in such torment, that although
Other be greater, none disgusteth more."
He thus in answer to my words rejoin'd:
"Thy city, heap'd with envy to the brim,
Aye, that the measure overflows its bounds,
Held me in brighter days. Ye citizens
Were wont to name me Ciacco.[2] For the sin
Of gluttony, damned vice, beneath this rain,
E'en as thou seest, I with fatigue am worn:
Nor I sole spirit in this woe: all these
Have by like crime incurr'd like punishment."
　　No more he said, and I my speech resumed:
"Ciacco! thy dire affliction grieves me much,
Even to tears. But tell me, if thou know'st,
What shall at length befall the citizens
Of the divided city;[3] whether any
Just one inhabit there: and tell the cause,
Whence jarring Discord hath assail'd it thus."
　　He then: "After long striving they will come

---

[2] "Ciacco." So called from his inordinate appetite; "ciacco," in Italian, signifying a pig. The real name of this glut-
ton has not been transmitted to us.

[3] "The divided city." The city of Florence, divided into the Bianchi and Neri
factions.

Contrary in kind disparts them. To the Church
Were separate those, that with no hairy cowls
Are crowned, both Popes and Cardinals, o'er whom
Avarice dominion absolute maintains."

I then: " 'Mid such as these some needs must be,
Whom I shall recognize, that with the blot
Of these foul sins were stain'd." He answering thus:
"Vain thought conceivest thou. That ignoble life,
Which made them vile before, now makes them dark,
And to all knowledge indiscernible.
For ever they shall meet in this rude shock:
These from the tomb with clenched grasp shall rise,
Those with close-shaven locks. That ill they gave,
And ill they kept, hath of the beauteous world
Deprived, and set them at this strife, which needs
No labor'd phrase of mine to set it off.
Now mayst thou see, my son! how brief, how vain,
The goods committed into Fortune's hands,
For which the human race keep such a coil!
Not all the gold that is beneath the moon,
Or ever hath been, of these toil-worn souls
Might purchase rest for one." I thus rejoin'd:
"My guide! of these this also would I learn;
This Fortune, that thou speak'st of, what it is,
Whose talons grasp the blessings of the world."

He thus: "O beings blind! what ignorance
Besets you! Now my judgment hear and mark.
He, whose transcendent wisdom passes all,
The heavens creating, gave them ruling powers
To guide them; so that each part shines to each,
Their light in equal distribution pour'd.
By similar appointment he ordain'd,
Over the world's bright images to rule,
Superintendence of a guiding hand
And general minister, which, at due time,
May change the empty vantages of life
From race to race, from one to other's blood,
Beyond prevention of man's wisest care:
Wherefore one nation rises into sway,
Another languishes, e'en as her will

To hinder down this rock thy safe descent."
Then to that swoln lip turning, "Peace!" he cried,
"Curst wolf! thy fury inward on thyself
Prey, and consume thee! Through the dark profound,
Not without cause, he passes. So 'tis will'd
On high, there where the great Archangel pour'd
Heaven's vengeance on the first adulterer proud."
    As sails, full spread and bellying with the wind,
Drop suddenly collapsed, if the mast split;
So to the ground down dropp'd the cruel fiend.
    Thus we, descending to the fourth steep ledge,
Gain'd on the dismal shore, that all the woe
Hems in of all the universe. Ah me!
Almighty Justice! in what store thou heap'st
New pains, new troubles, as I here beheld.
Wherefore doth fault of ours bring us to this?
    E'en as a billow, on Charybdis rising,
Against encounter'd billow dashing breaks;
Such is the dance this wretched race must lead,
Whom more than elsewhere numerous here I found.
From one side and the other, with loud voice,
Both roll'd on weights, by main force of their breasts,
Then smote together, and each one forthwith
Roll'd them back voluble, turning again;
Exclaiming these, "Why holdest thou so fast?"
Those answering, "And why castest thou away?"
So, still repeating their despiteful song,
They to the opposite point, on either hand,
Traversed the horrid circle; then arrived,
Both turn'd them round, and through the middle space,
Conflicting met again. At sight whereof
I, stung with grief, thus spake: "O say, my guide!
What race is this. Were these, whose heads are shorn,
On our left hand, all separate to the Church?"
    He straight replied: "In their first life, these all
In mind were so distorted, that they made,
According to due measure, of their wealth
No use. This clearly from their words collect,
Which they howl forth, at each extremity
Arriving of the circle, where their crime

This said, his fixed eyes he turn'd askance,
A little eyed me, then bent down his head,
And 'midst his blind companions with it fell.

When thus my guide: "No more his bed he leaves,
Ere the last angel-trumpet blow. The Power
Adverse to these shall then in glory come,
Each one forthwith to his sad tomb repair,
Resume his fleshly vesture and his form,
And hear the eternal doom re-echoing rend
The vault." So pass'd we through that mixture foul
Of spirits and rain, with tardy steps; meanwhile
Touching, though slightly, on the life to come.
For thus I question'd: "Shall these tortures, Sir!
When the great sentence passes, be increased,
Or mitigated, or as now severe?"

He then: "Consult thy knowledge; that decides,
That, as each thing to more perfection grows,
It feels more sensibly both good and pain.
Though ne'er to true perfection may arrive
This race accurst, yet nearer then, than now,
They shall approach it." Compassing that path,
Circuitous we journey'd; and discourse,
Much more than I relate, between us pass'd:
Till at the point, whence the steps led below,
Arrived, there Plutus, the great foe, we found.

CANTO VII

ARGUMENT.—In the present Canto, Dante describes his descent into the fourth circle, at the beginning of which he sees Plutus stationed. Here one like doom awaits the prodigal and the avaricious; which is, to meet in direful conflict, rolling great weights against each other with mutual upbraidings. From hence Virgil takes occasion to show how vain the goods that are committed into the charge of Fortune; and this moves our author to inquire what being that Fortune is, of whom he speaks: which question being resolved, they go down into the fifth circle, where they find the wrathful and gloomy tormented in the Stygian lake. Having made a compass round great part of this lake, they come at last to the base of a lofty tower.

"AH me! O Satan! Satan!"[1] loud exclaim'd
Plutus, in accent hoarse of wild alarm:
And the kind sage, whom no event surprised,
To comfort me thus spake: "Let not thy fear
Harm thee, for power in him, be sure, is none

[1] "Pape Satan, Pape Satan, aleppe;" words without meaning.

To blood; and the wild party from the woods[4]
Will chase the other[5] with much injury forth.
Then it behooves that this must fall,[6] within
Three solar circles;[7] and the other rise
By borrow'd force of one, who under shore
Now rests.[8] It shall a long space hold aloof
Its forehead, keeping under heavy weight
The other opprest, indignant at the load,
And grieving sore. The just are two in number.[9]
But they neglected. Avarice, envy, pride,
Three fatal sparks, have set the hearts of all
On fire." Here ceased the lamentable sound;
And I continued thus: "Still would I learn
More from thee, further parley still entreat.
Of Farinata and Tegghiaio[10] say,
They who so well deserved; of Giacopo,[11]
Arrigo, Mosca,[12] and the rest, who bent
Their minds on working good. Oh! tell me where
They bide, and to their knowledge let me come.
For I am prest with keen desire to hear
If Heaven's sweet cup, or poisonous drug of Hell,
Be to their lip assign'd." He answer'd straight:
"These are yet blacker spirits. Various crimes
Have sunk them deeper in the dark abyss.
If thou so far descendest, thou mayst see them.
But to the pleasant world, when thou return'st,
Of me make mention, I entreat thee, there.
No more I tell thee, answer thee no more."

[4] "The wild party from the woods." So called, because it was headed by Veri de' Cerchi, whose family had lately come into the city from Acona, and the woody country of the Val di Nievole.

[5] "The other." The opposite party of the Neri, at the head of which was Corso Donati.

[6] "This must fall." The Bianchi.

[7] "Three solar circles." Three years.

[8] "Of one, who under shore now rests." Charles of Valois, by whose means the Neri were replaced.

[9] "The just are two in number." Who these two were, the commentators are not agreed. Some understand them to be Dante himself and his friend Guido Cavalcanti.

[10] "Of Farinata and Tegghiaio." See Canto x. and notes, and Canto xvi. and notes.

[11] "Giacopo." Giacopo Rusticucci. See Canto xvi. and notes.

[12] "Arrigo, Mosca." Of Arrigo, who is said by the commentators to have been of the noble family of the Fifanti, no mention afterward occurs. Mosca degli Uberti, or de' Lamberti, is introduced in Canto xxviii.

Decrees, from us conceal'd, as in the grass
The serpent train. Against her nought avails
Your utmost wisdom. She with foresight plans,
Judges, and carries on her reign, as theirs
The other powers divine. Her changes know
None intermission: by necessity
She is made swift, so frequent come who claim
Succession in her favors. This is she,
So execrated e'en by those whose debt
To her is rather praise: they wrongfully
With blame requite her, and with evil word;
But she is blessed, and for that recks not:
Amidst the other primal beings glad
Rolls on her sphere, and in her bliss exults.
Now on our way pass we, to heavier woe
Descending: for each star is falling now,
That mounted at our entrance, and forbids
Too long our tarrying." We the circle cross'd
To the next steep, arriving at a well,
That boiling pours itself down to a foss
Sluiced from its source. Far murkier was the wave
Than sablest grain: and we in company
Of the inky waters, journeying by their side,
Enter'd, though by a different track, beneath.
Into a lake, the Stygian named, expands
The dismal stream, when it hath reach'd the foot
Of the gray wither'd cliffs. Intent I stood
To gaze, and in the marish sunk descried
A miry tribe, all naked, and with looks
Betokening rage. They with their hands alone
Struck not, but with the head, the breast, the feet,
Cutting each other piecemeal with their fangs.
    The good instructor spake: "Now seest thou, son!
The souls of those, whom anger overcame.
This too for certain know, that underneath
The water dwells a multitude, whose sighs
Into these bubbles make the surface heave,
As thine eye tells thee wheresoe'er it turn.
Fix'd in the slime, they say: 'Sad once were we,
In the sweet air made gladsome by the sun,

Carrying a foul and lazy mist within:
Now in these murky settlings are we sad.'
Such dolorous strain they gurgle in their throats,
But word distinct can utter none." Our route
Thus compass'd we, a segment widely stretch'd
Between the dry embankment, and the core
Of the loath'd pool, turning meanwhile our eyes
Downward on those who gulp'd its muddy lees;
Nor stopp'd, till to a tower's low base we came.

CANTO VIII

ARGUMENT.—A signal having been made from the tower, Phlegyas, the ferryman
of the lake, speedily crosses it, and conveys Virgil and Dante to the other side.   On
their passage, they meet with Filippo Argenti, whose fury and torment are described.
They then arrive at the city of Dis, the entrance whereto is denied, and the portals
closed against them by many Demons.

MY theme pursuing, I relate, that ere
We reach'd the lofty turret's base, our eyes
Its height ascended, where we mark'd uphung
Two cressets, and another saw from far
Return the signal, so remote, that scarce
The eye could catch its beam. I, turning round
To the deep source of knowledge, thus inquired:
"Say what this means; and what, that other light
In answer set: what agency doth this?"
     "There on the filthy waters," he replied,
"E'en now what next awaits us mayst thou see,
If the marsh-gendered fog conceal it not."
     Never was arrow from the cord dismiss'd,
That ran its way so nimbly through the air,
As a small bark, that through the waves I spied
Toward us coming, under the sole sway
Of one that ferried it, who cried aloud:
"Art thou arrived, fell spirit?"—"Phlegyas, Phlegyas,[1]
This time thou criest in vain," my lord replied;
"No longer shalt thou have us, but while o'er
The slimy pool we pass." As one who hears
Of some great wrong he hath sustain'd, whereat

[1] Phlegyas, so incensed against Apollo   by whose vengeance he was cast into
for having violated his daughter Coronis,   Tartarus. See Virgil, Æneas, l. vi. 618.
that he set fire to the temple of that deity,

Inly he pines: so Phlegyas inly pined
In his fierce ire. My guide, descending, stepp'd
Into the skiff, and bade me enter next,
Close at his side; nor, till my entrance, seem'd
The vessel freighted. Soon as both embark'd,
Cutting the waves, goes on the ancient prow,
More deeply than with others it is wont.

While we our course o'er the dead channel held,
One drench'd in mire before me came, and said:
"Who art thou, that thus comest ere thine hour?"

I answer'd: "Though I come, I tarry not:
But who art thou, that art become so foul?"

"One, as thou seest, who mourn:" he straight
    replied.

To which I thus: "In mourning and in woe,
Curst spirit! tarry thou. I know thee well,
E'en thus in filth disguised." Then stretch'd he forth
Hands to the bark; whereof my teacher sage
Aware, thrusting him back: "Away! down there
To the other dogs!" then, with his arms my neck
Encircling, kiss'd my cheek, and spake: "O soul,
Justly disdainful! blest was she in whom
Thou wast conceived. He in the world was one
For arrogance noted: to his memory
No virtue lends its lustre; even so
Here is his shadow furious. There above,
How many now hold themselves mighty kings,
Who here like swine shall wallow in the mire,
Leaving behind them horrible dispraise."

I then: "Master! him fain would I behold
Whelm'd in these dregs, before we quit the lake."

He thus: "Or ever to thy view the shore
Be offer'd, satisfied shall be that wish,
Which well deserves completion." Scarce his words
Were ended, when I saw the miry tribes
Set on him with such violence, that yet
For that render I thanks to God, and praise.
"To Filippo Argenti!" [2] cried they all:

[2] Boccaccio tells us, "he was a man remarkable for the large proportions and extraordinary vigor of his bodily frame, and the extreme waywardness and irascibility of his temper."—"Decameron." G. ix. N. 8.

And on himself the moody Florentine
Turn'd his avenging fangs. Him here we left,
Nor speak I of him more. But on mine ear
Sudden a sound of lamentation smote,
Whereat mine eye unbarr'd I sent abroad.

And thus the good instructor: "Now, my son
Draws near the city, that of Dis is named,
With its grave denizens, a mighty throng."

I thus: "The minarets already, Sir!
There, certes, in the valley I descry,
Gleaming vermilion, as if they from fire
Had issued." He replied: "Eternal fire,
That inward burns, shows them with ruddy flame
Illumed; as in this nether Hell thou seest."

We came within the fosses deep, that moat
This region comfortless. The walls appear'd
As they were framed of iron. We had made
Wide circuit, ere a place we reach'd, where loud
The mariner cried vehement: "Go forth:
The entrance is here." Upon the gates I spied
More than a thousand, who of old from Heaven
Were shower'd. With ireful gestures, "Who is this,"
They cried, "that, without death first felt, goes through
The regions of the dead?" My sapient guide
Made sign that he for secret parley wish'd;
Whereat their angry scorn abating, thus
They spake: "Come thou alone; and let him go,
Who hath so hardily enter'd this realm.
Alone return he by his witless way;
If well he knew it, let him prove. For thee,
Here shalt thou tarry, who through clime so dark
Hast been his escort." Now bethink thee, reader!
What cheer was mine at sound of those curst words.
I did believe I never should return.

"O my loved guide! who more than seven times[3]

----

[3] "Seven times." The commentators, says Venturi, perplex themselves with the inquiry what seven perils these were from which Dante had been delivered by Virgil. Reckoning the beasts in the first Canto as one of them, and adding Charon, Minos, Cerberus, Plutus, Phlegyas, and Filippo Argenti, as so many others, we shall have the number; and if this be not satisfactory, we may suppose a determinate to have been put for an indeterminate number.

Security hast render'd me, and drawn
From peril deep, whereto I stood exposed,
Desert me not," I cried, "in this extreme.
And, if our onward going be denied,
Together trace we back our steps with speed."
  My liege, who thither had conducted me,
Replied: "Fear not: for of our passage none
Hath power to disappoint us, by such high
Authority permitted. But do thou
Expect me here; meanwhile, thy wearied spirit
Comfort, and feed with kindly hope, assured
I will not leave thee in this lower world."
This said, departs the sire benevolent,
And quits me. Hesitating I remain
At war, 'twixt will and will not, in my thoughts.
  I could not hear what terms he offer'd them,
But they conferr'd not long, for all at once
Pellmell rush'd back within. Closed were the gates,
By those our adversaries, on the breast
Of my liege lord: excluded, he return'd
To me with tardy steps. Upon the ground
His eyes were bent, and from his brow erased
All confidence, while thus in sighs he spake:
"Who hath denied me these abodes of woe?"
Then thus to me: "That I am anger'd, think
No ground of terror: in this trial I
Shall vanquish, use what arts they may within
For hindrance. This their insolence, not new,[4]
Erewhile at gate less secret they display'd,
Which still is without bolt; upon its arch
Thou saw'st the deadly scroll: and even now,
On this side of its entrance, down the steep,
Passing the circles, unescorted, comes
One whose strong might can open us this land."

[4] Virgil assures our poet that these evil spirits had formerly shown the same insolence when our Saviour descended into hell. They attempted to prevent him from entering at the gate, over which Dante had read the fatal inscription. "That gate which," says the Roman poet, "an angel had just passed, by whose aid we shall overcome this opposition, and gain admittance into the city."

CANTO IX

ARGUMENT.—After some hindrances, and having seen the hellish furies and other monsters, the Poet, by the help of an angel, enters the city of Dis, wherein he discovers that the heretics are punished in tombs burning with intense fire; and he, together with Virgil, passes onward between the sepulchres and the walls of the city.

THE hue,[1] which coward dread on my pale cheeks
Imprinted when I saw my guide turn back,
Chased that from his which newly they had worn,
And inwardly restrain'd it. He, as one
Who listens, stood attentive: for his eye
Not far could lead him through the sable air,
And the thick-gathering cloud. "It yet behoves
We win this fight;" thus he began: "if not,
Such aid to us is offer'd—Oh! how long
Me seems it, ere the promised help arrive."

I noted, how the sequel of his words
Cloked their beginning; for the last he spake
Agreed not with the first. But not the less
My fear was at his saying; sith I drew
To import worse, perchance, than that he held,
His mutilated speech. "Doth ever any
Into this rueful concave's extreme depth
Descend, out of the first degree, whose pain
Is deprivation merely of sweet hope?"

Thus I inquiring. "Rarely," he replied,
"It chances, that among us any makes
This journey, which I wend. Erewhile, 'tis true,
Once came I here beneath, conjured by fell
Erichtho,[2] sorceress, who compell'd the shades
Back to their bodies. No long space my flesh
Was naked of me, when within these walls
She made me enter, to draw forth a spirit
From out of Judas' circle. Lowest place
Is that of all, obscurest, and removed

---

[1] "The hue." Virgil, perceiving that Dante was pale with fear, restrained those outward tokens of displeasure which his own countenance had betrayed.

[2] Erichtho, a Thessalian sorceress (Lucan, "Pharsal." l. vi.), was employed by Sextus, son of Pompey the Great, to conjure up a spirit, who should inform him of the issue of the civil wars between his father and Cæsar.

Farthest from Heaven's all-circling orb. The road
Full well I know: thou therefore rest secure.
That lake, the noisome stench exhaling, round
The city of grief encompasses, which now
We may not enter without rage." Yet more
He added: but I hold it not in mind,
For that mine eye toward the lofty tower
Had drawn me wholly, to its burning top;
Where, in an instant, I beheld uprisen
At once three hellish furies stain'd with blood.
In limb and motion feminine they seem'd;
Around them greenest hydras twisting roll'd
Their volumes; adders and cerastes crept
Instead of hair, and their fierce temples bound.

He, knowing well the miserable hags
Who tend the queen of endless woe, thus spake:
"Mark thou each dire Erynnis. To the left,
This is Megæra; on the right hand, she
Who wails, Alecto; and Tisiphone
I' th' midst." This said, in silence he remain'd.
Their breast they each one clawing tore; themselves
Smote with their palms, and such thrill clamour raised,
That to the bard I clung, suspicion-bound.
"Hasten Medusa: so to adamant
Him shall we change;" all looking down exclaim'd:
"E'en when by Theseus' might assail'd, we took
No ill revenge." "Turn thyself round and keep
Thy countenance hid; for if the Gorgon dire
Be shown, and thou shouldst view it, thy return
Upwards would be forever lost." This said,
Himself, my gentle master, turn'd me round;
Nor trusted he my hands, but with his own
He also hid me. Ye of intellect
Sound and entire, mark well the lore[3] conceal'd

---

[3] The Poet probably intends to call the reader's attention to the allegorical and mystic sense of the present Canto, and not, as Venturi supposes, to that of the whole work. Landino supposes this hidden meaning to be that in the case of those vices which proceed from intem- perance, reason, figured under the person of Virgil, with the ordinary grace of God, may be a sufficient safeguard; but that in the instance of more heinous crimes, such as those we shall hereafter see punished, a special grace, represented by the angel, is requisite for our defence.

Under close texture of the mystic strain.

And now there came o'er the perturbed waves
Loud-crashing, terrible, a sound that made
Either shore tremble, as if of a wind
Impetuous, from conflicting vapors sprung,
That 'gainst some forest driving all his might,
Plucks off the branches, beats them down, and hurls
Afar; then, onward passing, proudly sweeps
His whirlwind rage, while beasts and shepherds fly.

Mine eyes he loosed, and spake: "And now direct
Thy visual nerve along that ancient foam,
There, thickest where the smoke ascends." As frogs
Before their foe the serpent, through the wave
Ply swiftly all, till at the ground each one
Lies on a heap; more than a thousand spirits
Destroy'd, so saw I fleeing before one
Who pass'd with unwet feet the Stygian sound.
He, from his face removing the gross air,
Oft his left hand forth stretch'd, and seem'd alone
By that annoyance wearied. I perceived
That he was sent from Heaven; and to my guide
Turn'd me, who signal made, that I should stand
Quiet, and bend to him. Ah me! how full
Of noble anger seem'd he. To the gate
He came, and with his wand touch'd it, whereat
Open without impediment it flew.

"Outcasts of heaven! O abject race, scorn'd!"
Began he, on the horrid grunsel standing,
"Whence doth this wild excess of insolence
Lodge in you? wherefore kick you 'gainst that will
Ne'er frustrate of its end, and which so oft
Hath laid on you enforcement of your pangs?
What profits at the Fates to butt the horn?
Your Cerberus,[4] if ye remember, hence
Bears still, peel'd of their hair, his throat and maw."

[4] "Your Cerberus." Cerberus is feigned to have been dragged by Hercules, bound with a threefold chain, of which, says the angel, he still bears the marks. Lombardi blames the other interpreters for having supposed that the angel attributes this exploit to Hercules, a fabulous hero, rather than to our Saviour. It would seem as if the good father had forgotten that Cerberus is himself no less a creature of the imagination than the hero who encountered him.

This said, he turn'd back o'er the filthy way,
And syllable to us spake none; but wore
The semblance of a man by other care
Beset, and keenly prest, than thought of him
Who in his presence stands. Then we our steps
Toward that territory moved, secure
After the hallow'd words. We, unopposed,
There enter'd; and, my mind eager to learn
What state a fortress like to that might hold,
I, soon as enter'd, throw mine eye around,
And see, on every part, wide-stretching space,
Replete with bitter pain and torment ill.

As where Rhone stagnates on the plains of Arles,[5]
Or as at Pola,[6] near Quarnaro's gulf,
That closes Italy and laves her bounds,
The place is all thick spread with sepulchres;
So was it here, save what in horror here
Excell'd: for 'midst the graves were scattered flames,
Wherewith intensely all throughout they burn'd,
That iron for no craft there hotter needs.

Their lids all hung suspended; and beneath,
From them forth issued lamentable moans,
Such as the sad and tortured well might raise.

I thus: "Master! say who are these, interr'd
Within these vaults, of whom distinct we hear
The dolorous sighs." He answer thus return'd:
"The arch-heretics are here, accompanied
By every sect their followers; and much more
Than thou believest, the tombs are freighted: like
With like is buried; and the monuments
Are different in degrees of heat." This said,
He to the right hand turning, on we pass'd
Betwixt the afflicted and the ramparts high.

---

[5] "The plains of Arles." In Provence. These sepulchres are mentioned in the Life of Charlemagne, which has been attributed to Archbishop Turpin, cap. 28, and 30, and by Fazio degli Uberti, Dittamondo, L. iv. cap. xxi.

[6] "At Pola." A city of Istria, situated near the gulf of Quarnaro, in the Adriatic Sea.

CANTO X

ARGUMENT.—Dante, having obtained permission from his guide, holds discourse with Farinata degli Uberti and Cavalcante Cavalcanti, who lie in their fiery tombs that are yet open, and not to be closed up till after the last judgment. Farinata predicts the Poet's exile from Florence; and shows him that the condemned have knowledge of future things, but are ignorant of what is at present passing, unless it be revealed by some newcomer from earth.

NOW by a secret pathway we proceed,
     Between the walls, that hem the region round,
     And the tormented souls: my master first,
I close behind his steps. "Virtue supreme!"
I thus began: "Who through these ample orbs
In circuit lead'st me, even as thou will'st;
Speak thou, and satisfy my wish. May those,
Who lie within these sepulchres, be seen?
Already all the lids are raised, and none
O'er them keeps watch." He thus in answer spake:
"They shall be closed all, what-time they here
From Josaphat[1] return'd shall come, and bring
Their bodies, which above they now have left.
The cemetery on this part obtain,
With Epicurus, all his followers,
Who with the body make the spirit die.
Here therefore satisfaction shall be soon,
Both to the question ask'd, and to the wish[2]
Which thou conceal'st in silence." I replied:
"I keep not, guide beloved! from thee my heart
Secreted, but to shun vain length of words;
A lesson erewhile taught me by thyself."

    "O Tuscan! thou, who through the city of fire
Alive art passing, so discreet of speech:
Here, please thee, stay awhile. Thy utterance
Declares the place of thy nativity
To be that noble land, with which perchance

---

[1] "Josaphat." It seems to have been a common opinion among the Jews, as well as among many Christians, that the general judgment will be held in the valley of Josaphat, or Jehoshaphat. "I will also gather all nations, and will bring them down into the valley of Jehoshaphat, and will plead with them there for my people, and for my heritage Israel, whom they have scattered among the nations, and parted my land."—Joel, iii. 2.

[2] "The wish." The wish that Dante had not expressed was to see and converse with the followers of Epicurus; among whom, we shall see, were Farinata degli Uberti and Cavalcante Cavalcanti.

I too severely dealt." Sudden that sound
Forth issued from a vault, whereat, in fear,
I somewhat closer to my leader's side
Approaching, he thus spake: "What dost thou? Turn:
Lo! Farinata[3] there, who hath himself
Uplifted: from his girdle upwards, all
Exposed, behold him." On his face was mine
Already fix'd: his breast and forehead there
Erecting, seem'd as in high scorn he held
E'en Hell. Between the sepulchres, to him
My guide thrust me, with fearless hands and prompt;
This warning added: "See thy words be clear."

He, soon as there I stood at the tomb's foot,
Eyed me a space; then in disdainful mood
Address'd me: "Say what ancestors were thine."

I, willing to obey him, straight reveal'd
The whole, nor kept back aught: whence he, his brow
Somewhat uplifting, cried: "Fiercely were they
Adverse to me, my party, and the blood
From whence I sprang: twice,[4] therefore, I abroad
Scatter'd them." "Though driven out, yet they each
time
From all parts," answer'd I, "return'd; an art
Which yours have shown they are not skill'd to learn."

Then, peering forth from the unclosed jaw,
Rose from his side a shade,[5] high as the chin,
Leaning, methought, upon its knees upraised.
It look'd around, as eager to explore
If there were other with me; but perceiving
That fond imagination quench'd, with tears
Thus spake: "If thou through this blind prison go'st,
Led by thy lofty genius and profound,

[3] "Farinata." Farinata degli Uberti, a noble Florentine, was the leader of the Ghibelline faction, when they obtained a signal victory over the Guelfi at Montaperto, near the river Arbia. Macchiavelli calls him "a man of exalted soul, and great military talents."—"Hist. of Flor." b. ii. His grandson, Bonifacio, commonly called Fazio degli Uberti, wrote a poem, entitled the "Dittamonodo," in imitation of Dante.

[4] "Twice." The first time in 1248, when they were driven out by Frederick the Second. See G. Villani, lib. vi. c. xxxiv.; and the second time in 1260. See note to v. 83.

[5] "A shade." The spirit of Cavalcante Cavalcanti, a noble Florentine, of the Guelf party.

Where is my son?[6] and wherefore not with thee?"
I straight replied: "Not of myself I come;
By him, who there expects me, through this clime
Conducted, whom perchance Guido thy son
Had in contempt."[7] Already had his words
And mode of punishment read me his name,
Whence I so fully answer'd. He at once
Exclaim'd, up starting, "How! said'st thou, he *had*?
No longer lives he? Strikes not on his eye
The blessed daylight?" Then, of some delay
I made ere my reply, aware, down fell
Supine, nor after forth appear'd he more.

    Meanwhile the other, great of soul, near whom
I yet was station'd, changed not countenance stern,
Nor moved the neck, nor bent his ribbed side.
"And if," continuing the first discourse,
"They in this art," he cried, "small skill have shown;
That doth torment me more e'en than this bed.
But not yet fifty times[8] shall be relumed
Her aspect, who reigns here queen of this realm,[9]
Ere thou shalt know the full weight of that art.
So to the pleasant world mayst thou return,
As thou shalt tell me why, in all their laws,
Against my kin this people is so fell."

    "The slaughter[10] and great havoc," I replied,
"That color'd Arbia's flood with crimson stain—

---

[6] "My son." Guido, the son of Cavalcante Cavalcanti; "he whom I call the first of my friends," says Dante in his "Vita Nuova" where the commencement of their friendship is related. From the character given of him by contemporary writers, his temper was well formed to assimilate with that of our Poet. "He was," according to G. Villani, lib. viii. c. xli., "of a philosophical and elegant mind, if he had not been too delicate and fastidious."

[7] "———— Guido they soon
      Had in contempt."
Guido Cavalcanti, being more given to philosophy than poetry, was perhaps no great admirer of Virgil.

[8] "Not yet fifty times." "Not fifty months shall be passed, before thou shalt learn, by woeful experience, the difficulty of returning from banishment to thy native city."

[9] "Queen of this realm." The moon, one of whose titles in heathen mythology was Proserpine, queen of the shades below.

[10] "The slaughter." "By means of Farinata degli Uberti, the Guelfi were conquered by the army of King Manfredi, near the river Arbia, with so great a slaughter, that those who escaped from that defeat took refuge, not in Florence, which city they considered as lost to them, but in Lucca."—Macchiavelli, "Hist. of Flor." b. ii. and G. Villani, lib. vi. c. lxxx. and lxxxi.

To these impute, that in our hallow'd dome
Such orisons[11] ascend." Sighing he shook
The head, then thus resumed: "In that affray
I stood not singly, nor, without just cause,
Assuredly, should with the rest have stirr'd;
But singly there I stood,[12] when, by consent
Of all, Florence had to the ground been razed,
The one who openly forbade the deed."

"So may thy lineage find at last repose,"
I thus adjured him, "as thou solve this knot,
Which now involves my mind. If right I hear,
Ye seem to view beforehand that which time
Leads with him, of the present uninform'd."

"We view, as one who hath an evil sight,"
He answer'd, "plainly, objects far remote;
So much of his large splendor yet imparts
The Almighty Ruler: but when they approach,
Or actually exist, our intellect
Then wholly fails; nor of your human state,
Except what others bring us, know we aught.
Hence therefore mayst thou understand, that all
Our knowledge in that instant shall expire,
When on futurity the portals close."

Then conscious of my fault,[13] and by remorse
Smitten, I added thus: "Now shalt thou say
To him there fallen, that his offspring still
Is to the living join'd; and bid him know,
That if from answer, silent, I abstain'd,

[11] "Such orisons." This appears to allude to certain prayers which were offered up in the churches of Florence, for deliverance from the hostile attempts of the Uberti; or, it may be that the public councils being held in churches, the speeches delivered in them against the Uberti are termed "orisons," or prayers.

[12] "Singly there I stood." Guido Novello assembled a council of the Ghibellini at Empoli; where it was agreed by all, that, in order to maintain the ascendancy of the Ghibelline party in Tuscany, it was necessary to destroy Florence, which could serve only (the people of that city being Guelfi) to enable the party attached to the church to recover its strength. This cruel sentence, passed upon so noble a city, met with no opposition from any of its citizens or friends, except Farinata degli Uberti, who openly and without reserve forbade the measure; affirming, that he had endured so many hardships, with no other view than that of being able to pass his days in his own country. Macchiavelli, Hist. of Flor. b. ii.

[13] "My fault." Dante felt remorse for not having returned an immediate answer to the inquiry of Cavalcante, from which delay he was led to believe that his son Guido was no longer living.

'Twas that my thought was occupied, intent
Upon that error, which thy help hath solved."
　　But now my master summoning me back
I heard, and with more eager haste besought
The spirit to inform me, who with him
Partook his lot.　He answer thus return'd:
"More than a thousand with me here are laid.
Within is Frederick,[14] second of that name,
And the Lord Cardinal,[15] and of the rest
I speak not."　He, this said, from sight withdrew.
But I my steps toward the ancient bard
Reverting, ruminated on the words
Betokening me such ill.　Onward he moved,
And thus, in going, question'd:　"Whence the amaze
That holds thy senses wrapt?"　I satisfied
The inquiry, and the sage enjoin'd me straight:
"Let thy safe memory store what thou hast heard,
To thee importing harm; and note thou this,"
With his raised finger bidding me take heed,
"When thou shalt stand before her gracious beam,[16]
Whose bright eye all surveys, she of thy life
The future tenor will to thee unfold."
　　Forthwith he to the left hand turn'd his feet:
We left the wall, and toward the middle space
Went by a path that to a valley strikes,
Which e'en thus high exhaled its noisome steam.

[14] "Frederick." The Emperor Frederick II., who died in 1250. See notes to Canto xiii.

[15] "The Lord Cardinal." Ottaviano Ubaldini, a Florentine, made cardinal in 1245, and deceased about 1273. On account of his great influence, he was generally known by the appellation of "the Cardinal." It is reported of him that he declared if there were any such thing as a human soul he had lost his for the Ghibellini.

[16] "Her gracious beam." Beatrice.

CANTO XI

ARGUMENT.—Dante arrives at the verge of a rocky precipice which encloses the
seventh circle, where he sees the sepulchre of Anastasius the Heretic; behind the lid
of which pausing a little, to make himself capable by degrees of enduring the fetid
smell that steamed upward from the abyss, he is instructed by Virgil concerning the
manner in which the three following circles are disposed, and what description of
sinners is punished in each. He then inquires the reason why the carnal, the
gluttonous, the avaricious and prodigal, the wrathful and gloomy, suffer not their
punishments within the city of Dis. He next asks how the crime of usury is an
offence against God; and at length the two Poets go toward the place from whence a
passage leads down to the seventh circle.

UPON the utmost verge of a high bank,
    By craggy rocks environ'd round, we came.
    Where woes beneath, more cruel yet, were
        stow'd:
And here, to shun the horrible excess
Of fetid exhalation upward cast
From the profound abyss, behind the lid
Of a great monument we stood retired,
Whereon this scroll I mark'd: "I have in charge
Pope Anastasius,[1] whom Photinus drew
From the right path." "Ere our descent, behoves
We make delay, that somewhat first the sense,
To the dire breath accustom'd, afterward
Regard it not." My master thus; to whom
Answering I spake: "Some compensation find,
That the time pass not wholly lost." He then:
"Lo! how my thoughts e'en to thy wishes tend.
My son! within these rocks," he thus began,
"Are three close circles in gradation placed,
As these which now thou leavest. Each one is full
Of spirits accurst; but that the sight alone
Hereafter may suffice thee, listen how
And for what cause in durance they abide.
    "Of all malicious act abhorr'd in Heaven,
The end is injury; and all such end
Either by force or fraud works other's woe.
But fraud, because of man's peculiar evil,

---

[1] By some supposed to have been Anastasius II.; by others, the fourth of that name;
while a third set, jealous of the integrity of the papal faith, contend that our poet
has confounded him with Anastasius I., Emperor of the East.

To God is more displeasing; and beneath,
The fraudulent are therefore doom'd to endure
Severer pang. The violent occupy
All the first circle; and because, to force,
Three persons are obnoxious, in three rounds,
Each within other separate, is it framed.
To God, his neighbor, and himself, by man
Force may be offer'd; to himself I say,
And his possessions, as thou soon shalt hear
At full. Death, violent death, and painful wounds
Upon his neighbor he inflicts; and wastes,
By devastation, pillage, and the flames,
His substance. Slayers, and each one that smites
In malice, plunderers, and all robbers, hence
The torment undergo of the first round,
In different herds. Man can do violence
To himself and his own blessings: and for this,
He, in the second round must aye deplore
With unavailing penitence his crime,
Whoe'er deprives himself of life and light,
In reckless lavishment his talent wastes,
And sorrows there where he should dwell in joy.
To God may force be offer'd, in the heart
Denying and blaspheming His high power,
And Nature with her kindly law contemning.
And thence the inmost round marks with its seal
Sodom, and Cahors, and all such as speak
Contemptuously of the Godhead in their hearts.
   "Fraud, that in every conscience leaves a sting,
May be by man employ'd on one, whose trust
He wins, or on another, who withholds
Strict confidence. Seems as the latter way
Broke but the bond of love which Nature makes.
Whence in the second circle have their nest,
Dissimulation, witchcraft, flatteries,
Theft, falsehood, simony, all who seduce
To lust, or set their honesty at pawn,
With such vile scum as these. The other way
Forgets both Nature's general love, and that
Which thereto added afterward gives birth
To special faith. Whence in the lesser circle,

Point of the universe, dread seat of Dis,
The traitor is eternally consumed."
    I thus: "Instructor, clearly thy discourse
Proceeds, distinguishing the hideous chasm
And its inhabitants with skill exact.
But tell me this: they of the dull, fat pool,
Whom the rain beats, or whom the tempest drives,
Or who with tongues so fierce conflicting meet,
Wherefore within the city fire-illumed
Are not these punish'd, if God's wrath be on them?
And if it be not, wherefore in such guise
Are they condemn'd?" He answer thus return'd:
"Wherefore in dotage wanders thus thy mind,
Not so accustom'd? or what other thoughts
Possess it? Dwell not in thy memory
The words, wherein thy ethic page² describes
Three dispositions adverse to Heaven's will,
Incontinence, malice, and mad brutishness,
And how incontinence the least offends
God, and least guilt incurs? If well thou note
This judgment, and remember who they are,
Without these walls to vain repentance doom'd,
Thou shalt discern why they apart are placed
From these fell spirits, and less wreakful pours
Justice divine on them its vengeance down."
    "O sun! who healest all imperfect sight,
Thou so content'st me, when thou solvest my doubt,
That ignorance not less than knowledge charms.
Yet somewhat turn thee back," I in these words
Continued, "where thou said'st, that usury
Offends celestial Goodness; and this knot
Perplex'd unravel." He thus made reply:
"Philosophy, to an attentive ear,
Clearly points out, not in one part alone,
How imitative Nature takes her course
From the celestial mind, and from its art:
And where her laws³ the Stagirite unfolds,

---

² "Thy ethic page." He refers to
Aristotle's Ethics, lib. vii. c. 1: "——let
it be defined that respecting morals there
are three sorts of things to be avoided.

malice, incontinence, and brutishness."
³ "Her laws." Aristotle's Physics, lib.
ii. c. 2: "Art imitates nature."

Not many leaves scann'd o'er, observing well
Thou shalt discover, that your art on her
Obsequious follows, as the learner treads
In his instructor's step; so that your art
Deserves the name of second in descent
From God. These two, if thou recall to mind
Creation's holy book,[4] from the beginning
Were the right source of life and excellence
To human-kind. But in another path
The usurer walks; and Nature in herself
And in her follower thus he sets at nought,
Placing elsewhere his hope.[5] But follow now
My steps on forward journey bent; for now
The Pisces play with undulating glance
Along the horizon, and the Wain[6] lies all
O'er the northwest; and onward there a space
Is our steep passage down the rocky height."

CANTO XII

ARGUMENT.—Descending by a very rugged way into the seventh circle, where the violent are punished, Dante and his leader find it guarded by the Minotaur; whose fury being pacified by Virgil, they step downward from crag to crag; till, drawing near the bottom, they descry a river of blood, wherein are tormented such as have committed violence against their neighbor. At these, when they strive to emerge from the blood, a troop of Centaurs, running along the side of the river, aim their arrows; and three of their band opposing our travellers at the foot of the steep, Virgil prevails so far that one consents to carry them both across the stream; and on their passage, Dante is informed by him of the course of the river, and of those that are punished therein.

THE place, where to descend the precipice
We came, was rough as Alp; and on its verge
Such object lay, as every eye would shun.
As is that ruin, which Adice's stream[1]

[4] "Creation's holy book." Genesis, c. ii. v. 15: "And the Lord God took the man, and put him into the Garden of Eden, to dress it, and to keep it." And, Genesis, c. iii. v. 19: "In the sweat of thy face shalt thou eat bread."

[5] "Placing elsewhere his hope." The usurer, trusting in the produce of his wealth lent out on usury, despises nature directly, because he does not avail himself of her means for maintaining or enriching himself; and indirectly, because he does not avail himself of the means which art, the follower and imitator of nature, would afford him for the same purposes.

[6] "The Wain." The constellation Boötes, or Charles's Wain.

[1] "Adice's stream." After a great deal having been said on the subject, it still appears very uncertain at what part of the river this fall of the mountain happened.

On this side Trento struck, shouldering the wave,
Or loosed by earthquake or for lack of prop;
For from the mountain's summit, whence it moved
To the low level, so the headlong rock
Is shiver'd, that some passage it might give
To him who from above would pass; e'en such
Into the chasm was that descent: and there
At point of the disparted ridge lay stretch'd
The infamy of Crete,[2] detested brood
Of the feign'd heifer:[3] and at sight of us
It gnaw'd itself, as one with rage distract.
To him my guide exclaim'd: "Perchance thou deem'st
The King of Athens[4] here, who, in the world
Above, thy death contrived. Monster! avaunt!
He comes not tutor'd by thy sister's art,[5]
But to behold your torments is he come."

  Like to a bull, that with impetuous spring
Darts, at the moment when the fatal blow
Hath struck him, but unable to proceed
Plunges on either side; so saw I plunge
The Minotaur; whereat the sage exclaim'd:
"Run to the passage! while he storms, 'tis well
That thou descend." Thus down our road we took
Through those dilapidated crags, that oft
Moved underneath my feet, to weight like theirs
Unused. I pondering went, and thus he spake:
"Perhaps thy thoughts are of this ruin'd steep,
Guarded by the brute violence, which I
Have vanquish'd now. Know then, that when I erst
Hither descended to the nether Hell,
This rock was not yet fallen. But past doubt,
(If well I mark) not long ere He arrived,[6]
Who carried off from Dis the mighty spoil
Of the highest circle, then through all its bounds

---

[2] "The infamy of Crete." The Minotaur.

[3] "The feign'd heifer." Pasiphaë.

[4] "The King of Athens." Theseus, who was enabled by the instruction of Ariadne, the sister of the Minotaur, to destroy that monster.

[5] "Thy sister's art." Ariadne.

[6] Our Saviour, who, according to Dante, when he ascended from Hell, carried with him the souls of the Patriarchs, and of other just men, out of the first circle. See Canto iv.

Such trembling seized the deep concave and foul,
I thought the universe was thrill'd with love,
Whereby, there are who deem, the world hath oft
Been into chaos turn'd: and in that point,
Here, and elsewhere, that old rock toppled down.
But fix thine eyes beneath: the river of blood
Approaches, in the which all those are steep'd,
Who have by violence injured." O blind lust!
O foolish wrath! who so dost goad us on
In the brief life, and in the eternal then
Thus miserably o'erwhelm us.   I beheld
An ample foss, that in a bow was bent,
As circling all the plain; for so my guide
Had told.   Between it and the rampart's base,
On trail ran Centaurs, with keen arrows arm'd,
As to the chase they on the earth were wont.
    At seeing us descend they each one stood;
And issuing from the troop, three sped with bows
And missile weapons chosen first; of whom
One cried from far: "Say, to what pain ye come
Condemn'd, who down this steep have journey'd. Speak
From whence ye stand, or else the bow I draw."
    To whom my guide: "Our answer shall be made
To Chiron, there, when nearer him we come.
Ill was thy mind, thus ever quick and rash."
Then me he touch'd and spake: "Nessus is this,
Who for the fair Deïanira died,
And wrought himself revenge[7] for his own fate.
He in the midst, that on his breast looks down,
Is the great Chiron who Achilles nursed;
That other, Pholus, prone to wrath."   Around
The foss these go by thousands, aiming shafts
At whatsoever spirit dares emerge
From out the blood, more than his guilt allows.
    We to those beasts, that rapid strode along,
Drew near; when Chiron took an arrow forth,

[7] Nessus, when dying by the hand of Hercules, charged Deïanira to preserve the gore from his wound; for that if the affections of Hercules should at any time be estranged from her, it would recall them. Deïanira had occasion to try the experiment; and the venom, as Nessus had intended, caused Hercules to expire in torments.

And with the notch push'd back his shaggy beard
To the cheek-bone, then, his great mouth to view
Exposing, to his fellows thus exclaim'd:
"Are ye aware, that he who comes behind
Moves what he touches?   The feet of the dead
Are not so wont."   My trusty guide, who now
Stood near his breast, where the two natures join,
Thus made reply: "He is indeed alive,
And solitary so must needs by me
Be shown the gloomy vale, thereto induced
By strict necessity, not by delight.
She left her joyful harpings in the sky,
Who this new office to my care consign'd.
He is no robber, no dark spirit I.
But by that virtue, which empowers my step
To tread so wild a path, grant us, I pray,
One of thy band, whom we may trust secure,
Who to the ford may lead us, and convey
Across, him mounted on his back; for he
Is not a spirit that may walk the air."

    Then on his right breast turning, Chiron thus
To Nessus spake: "Return, and be their guide.
And if ye chance to cross another troop,
Command them keep aloof."   Onward we moved,
The faithful escort by our side, along
The border of the crimson-seething flood,
Whence, from those steep'd within, loud shrieks arose.

    Some there I mark'd, as high as to their brow
Immersed, of whom the mighty Centaur thus:
"These are the souls of tyrants, who were given
To blood and rapine.   Here they wail aloud
Their merciless wrongs.   Here Alexander dwells,
And Dionysius fell, who many a year
Of woe wrought for fair Sicily.   That brow,
Whereon the hair so jetty clustering hangs,
Is Azzolino;[8] that with flaxen locks

---

[8] Azzolino, or Ezzolino di Romano, Lord of Padua, Vicenza, Verona, and Brescia, who died in 1260. His atrocities form the subject of a Latin tragedy, Eccerinis, by Albertino Mussato, of Padua, contemporary of Dante, and the most elegant writer of Latin verse of that age.

Obizzo[9] of Este, in the world destroy'd
By his foul step-son." To the bard revered
I turn'd me round, and thus he spake: "Let him
Be to thee now first leader, me but next
To him in rank." Then further on a space
The Centaur paused, near some, who at the throat
Were extant from the wave; and, showing us
A spirit by itself apart retired,
Exclaim'd: "He[10] in God's bosom smote the heart,
Which yet is honored on the bank of Thames."

A race I next espied who held the head,
And even all the bust, above the stream.
'Midst these I many a face remember'd well.
Thus shallow more and more the blood became,
So that at last it but imbrued the feet;
And there our passage lay athwart the foss.

"As ever on this side the boiling wave
Thou seest diminishing," the Centaur said,
"So on the other, be thou well assured,
It lower still and lower sinks its bed,
Till in that part it reuniting join,
Where 'tis the lot of tyranny to mourn.
There Heaven's stern justice lays chastising hand
On Attila, who was the scourge of earth,
On Sextus and on Pyrrhus,[11] and extracts
Tears ever by the seething flood unlock'd
From the Rinieri, of Corneto this,
Pazzo the other named,[12] who fill'd the ways

[9] "Obizzo of Este." Marquis of Ferrara and of the Marca d' Ancona, was murdered by his own son (whom, for that most unnatural act, Dante calls his step-son) for the sake of the treasures which his rapacity had amassed.

[10] "He." "Henrie, the brother of this Edmund, and son to the foresaid King of Almaine (Richard, brother of Henry III of England), as he returned from Affrike, where he had been with Prince Edward, was slain at Viterbo in Italy by the hand of Guy de Montfort, the son of Simon de Montfort, Earl of Leicester, in revenge of the same Simon's death. The murther was committed afore the high altar, as the same Henrie kneeled there to hear divine service." A. D. 1272. —Holinshed's Chron., p. 275. See also Giov. Villani, "Hist." lib. vii. c. xl., where it is said "that the heart of Henry was put into a golden cup, and placed on a pillar at London Bridge for a memorial to the English of the said outrage."

[11] Sextus, either the son of Tarquin the Proud or of Pompey the Great; and Pyrrhus, King of Epirus.

[12] Two noted marauders, by whose depredations the public ways were infested. The latter was of the noble family of Pazzi in Florence.

With violence and war." This said, he turn'd,
And quitting us, alone repass'd the ford.

CANTO XIII

ARGUMENT.—Still in the seventh circle, Dante enters its second compartment, which contains both those who have done violence on their own persons and those who have violently consumed their goods; the first changed into rough and knotted trees whereon the harpies build their nests, the latter chased and torn by black female mastiffs. Among the former, Piero delle Vigne is one who tells him the cause of his having committed suicide, and moreover in what manner the souls are transformed into those trunks. Of the latter crew, he recognizes Lano, a Siennese, and Giacomo, a Paduan; and lastly, a Florentine, who had hung himself from his own roof, speaks to him of the calamities of his countrymen.

ERE Nessus yet had reach'd the other bank,
    We enter'd on a forest, where no track
    Of steps had worn a way. Not verdant there
The foliage, but of dusky hue; not light
The boughs and tapering, but with knares deform'd
And matted thick: fruits there were none, but thorns
Instead, with venom fill'd. Less sharp than these,
Less intricate the brakes, wherein abide
Those animals, that hate the cultured fields,
Betwixt Corneto and Cecina's stream.[1]
    Here the brute harpies make their nest, the same
Who from the Strophades the Trojan band
Drove with dire boding of their future woe.
Broad are their pennons, of the human form
Their neck and countenance, arm'd with talons keen
The feet, and the huge belly fledged with wings.
These sit and wail on the drear mystic wood.
    The kind instructor in these words began:
"Ere further thou proceed, know thou art now
I' th' second round, and shalt be, till thou come
Upon the horrid sand: look therefore well
Around thee, and such things thou shalt behold,
As would my speech discredit." On all sides
I heard sad plainings breathe, and none could see
From whom they might have issued. In amaze
Fast bound I stood. He, as it seem'd, believed

[1] A wild and woody tract, abounding in deer, goats, and wild boars. Cecina is a river not far to the south of Leg-horn; Corneto, a small city on the same coast, in the patrimony of the Church.

That I had thought so many voices came
From some amid those thickets close conceal'd,
And thus his speech resum'd: "If thou lop off
A single twig from one of those ill plants,
The thought thou hast conceived shall vanish quite."
   Thereat a little stretching forth my hand,
From a great wilding gather'd I a branch,
And straight the trunk exclaim'd: "Why pluck'st thou
    me?"
Then, as the dark blood trickled down its side,
These words it added: "Wherefore tear'st me thus?
Is there no touch of mercy in thy breast?
Men once were we, that now are rooted here.
Thy hand might well have spared us, had we been
The souls of serpents." As a brand yet green,
That burning at one end from the other sends
A groaning sound, and hisses with the wind
That forces out its way, so burst at once
Forth from the broken splinter words and blood.
   I, letting fall the bough, remain'd as one
Assail'd by terror; and the sage replied:
"If he, O injured spirit! could have believed
What he hath seen but in my verse described,
He never against thee had stretch'd his hand.
But I, because the thing surpass'd belief,
Prompted him to this deed, which even now
Myself I rue. But tell me, who thou wast;
That, for this wrong to do thee some amends,
In the upper world (for thither to return
Is granted him) thy fame he may revive."
"That pleasant word of thine," the trunk replied,
"Hath so inveigled me, that I from speech
Cannot refrain, wherein if I indulge
A little longer, in the snare detain'd,
Count it not grievous. I it was,[2] who held

[2] "I it was." Piero delle Vigne, a native of Capua, who from a low condition raised himself, by his eloquence and legal knowledge, to the office of Chancellor to the Emperor Frederick II. The courtiers, envious of his exalted situation, forged letters to make Frederick believe that he held a secret and traitorous intercourse with the Pope, who was then at enmity with the Emperor. He was cruelly condemned to lose his eyes. Driven to despair by his unmerited calamity he dashed out his brains against the walls of a church, in the year 1245.

Both keys to Frederick's heart, and turn'd the wards,
Opening and shutting, with a skill so sweet,
That besides me, into his inmost breast
Scarce any other could admittance find.
The faith I bore to my high charge was such,
It cost me the life-blood that warm'd my veins.
The harlot, who ne'er turn'd her gloating eyes
From Cæsar's household, common vice and pest
Of courts, 'gainst me inflamed the minds of all;
And to Augustus they so spread the flame,
That my glad honours changed to bitter woes.
My soul, disdainful and disgusted, sought
Refuge in death from scorn, and I became,
Just as I was, unjust toward myself.
By the new roots, which fix this stem, I swear,
That never faith I broke to my liege lord,
Who merited such honour; and of you,
If any to the world indeed return,
Clear he from wrong my memory, that lies
Yet prostrate under envy's cruel blow."

   First somewhat pausing, till the mournful words
Were ended, then to me the bard began:
"Lose not the time; but speak, and of him ask,
If more thou wish to learn." Whence I replied:
"Question thou him again of whatsoe'er
Will, as thou think'st, content me; for no power
Have I to ask, such pity is at my heart."

   He thus resumed: "So may he do for thee
Freely what thou entreatest, as thou yet
Be pleased, imprison'd spirit! to declare,
How in these gnarled joints the soul is tied;
And whether any ever from such frame
Be loosen'd, if thou canst, that also tell."

   Thereat the trunk breathed hard, and the wind soon
Changed into sounds articulate like these:
"Briefly ye shall be answer'd. When departs
The fierce soul from the body, by itself
Thence torn asunder, to the seventh gulf
By Minos doom'd, into the wood it falls,
No place assign'd, but wheresoever chance

Hurls it; there sprouting, as a grain of spelt,
It rises to a sapling, growing thence
A savage plant. The harpies, on its leaves
Then feeding, cause both pain, and for the pain
A vent to grief. We, as the rest, shall come
For our own spoils, yet not so that with them
We may again be clad; for what a man
Takes from himself it is not just he have.
Here we perforce shall drag them; and throughout
The dismal glade our bodies shall be hung,
Each on the wild thorn of his wretched shade."
   Attentive yet to listen to the trunk
We stood, expecting further speech, when us
A noise surprised; as when a man perceives
The wild boar and the hunt approach his place
Of station'd watch, who of the beasts and boughs
Loud rustling round him hears. And lo! there came
Two naked, torn with briers, in headlong flight,
That they before them broke each fan o' th' wood.
"Haste now," the foremost cried, "now haste thee,
    death!"
The other, as seem'd, impatient of delay,
Exclaiming, "Lano![3] not so bent for speed
Thy sinews, in the lists of Toppo's field."
And then, for that perchance no longer breath
Sufficed him, of himself and of a bush
One group he made. Behind them was the wood
Full of black female mastiffs, gaunt and fleet,
As greyhounds that have newly slipt the leash.
On him, who squatted down, they stuck their fangs,
And having rent him piecemeal bore away
The tortured limbs. My guide then seized my hand,
And led me to the thicket, which in vain
Mourn'd through its bleeding wounds: "O Giacomo
Of Sant' Andrea![4] what avails it thee,"

[3] Lano, a Siennese, who being reduced by prodigality to a state of extreme want, found his existence no longer supportable; and having been sent by his countrymen on a military expedition to assist the Florentines against the Aretini, took that opportunity of exposing himself to certain death, in the engagement which took place at Toppo, near Arezzo. See G. Villani, Hist. lib. vii. c. cxix.

[4] Jacopo da Sant' Andrea, a Paduan, who, having wasted his property in the most wanton acts of profusion, killed himself in despair.

It cried, "that of me thou hast made thy screen?
For thy ill life, what blame on me recoils?"
    When o'er it he had paused, my master spake:
"Say who wast thou, that at so many points
Breathest out with blood thy lamentable speech?"
    He answer'd: "O ye spirits! arrived in time
To spy the shameful havoc that from me
My leaves hath sever'd thus, gather them up,
And at the foot of their sad parent-tree
Carefully lay them. In that city[5] I dwelt,
Who for the Baptist her first patron changed,
Whence he for this shall cease not with his art
To work her woe: and if there still remain'd not
On Arno's passage some faint glimpse of him,
Those citizens, who rear'd once more her walls
Upon the ashes left by Attila,
Had labor'd without profit of their toil.
I slung the fatal noose[6] from my own roof."

CANTO XIV

ARGUMENT.—They arrive at the beginning of the third of those compartments into which this seventh circle is divided. It is a plain of dry and hot
sand, where three kinds of violence are punished; namely, against God, against
Nature, and against Art; and those who have thus sinned, are tormented
by flakes of fire, which are eternally showering down upon them. Among
the violent against God is found Capaneus, whose blasphemies they hear.
Next, turning to the left along the forest of self-slayers, and having journeyed
a little onward, they meet with a streamlet of blood that issues from the
forest and traverses the sandy plain. Here Virgil speaks to our Poet of a huge
ancient statue that stands within Mount Ida in Crete, from a fissure in which
statue there is a dripping of tears, from which the said streamlet, together with
the three other infernal rivers, are formed.

SOON as the charity of native land
        Wrought in my bosom, I the scatter'd leaves
        Collected, and to him restored, who now
Was hoarse with utterance. To the limit thence
We came, which from the third the second round
Divides, and where of justice is display'd

---

[5] " ——— Florence, that city which
changed her first patron Mars for St. John
the Baptist."

[6] "I slung the fatal noose." We are
not informed who this suicide was; some
calling him Rocco de' Mozzi, and others
Lotto degli Agli.

Contrivance horrible. Things then first seen
Clearlier to manifest, I tell how next
A plain we reach'd, that from its sterile bed
Each plant repell'd. The mournful wood waves **round**
Its garland on all sides, as round the wood
Spreads the sad foss. There, on the very edge,
Our steps we stay'd. It was an area wide
Of arid sand and thick, resembling most
The soil that erst by Cato's foot was trod.
 Vengeance of heaven! Oh! how shouldst thou **be**
  fear'd
By all, who read what here mine eyes beheld.
 Of naked spirits many a flock I saw,
All weeping piteously, to different laws
Subjected; for on the earth some lay supine,
Some crouching close were seated, others paced
Incessantly around; the latter tribe
More numerous, those fewer who beneath
The torment lay, but louder in their grief.
 O'er all the sand fell slowly wafting down
Dilated flakes of fire, as flakes of snow
On Alpine summit, when the wind is hush'd.
As, in the torrid Indian clime, the son
Of Ammon saw, upon his warrior band
Descending, solid flames, that to the ground
Came down; whence he bethought him with his **troop**
To trample on the soil; for easier thus
The vapor was extinguish'd, while alone:
So fell the eternal fiery flood, wherewith
The marle glow'd underneath, as under stove
The viands, doubly to augment the pain.
Unceasing was the play of wretched hands,
Now this, now that way glancing, to shake **off**
The heat, still falling fresh. I thus began:
"Instructor! thou who all things overcomest,
Except the hardy demons that rush'd forth
To stop our entrance at the gate, say who
Is yon huge spirit, that, as seems, heeds not
The burning, but lies writhen in proud **scorn,**
As by the sultry tempest immatured?"

Straight he himself, who was aware I ask'd
My guide of him, exclaim'd: "Such as I was
When living, dead such now I am. If Jove
Weary his workman out, from whom in ire
He snatch'd the lightnings, that at my last day
Transfix'd me; if the rest he weary out,
At their black smithy laboring by turns,
In Mongibello, while he cries aloud,
'Help, help, good Mulciber!' as erst he cried
In the Phlegræan warfare; and the bolts
Launch he, full aim'd at me, with all his might;
He never should enjoy a sweet revenge."
    Then thus my guide, in accent higher raised
Than I before had heard him: "Capaneus!
Thou art more punish'd, in that this thy pride
Lives yet unquench'd: no torment, save thy rage,
Were to thy fury pain proportion'd full."
    Next turning round to me, with milder lip
He spake: "This of the seven kings was one,
Who girt the Theban walls with siege, and held,
As still he seems to hold, God in disdain,
And sets His high omnipotence at naught.
But, as I told him, his despiteful mood
Is ornament well suits the breast that wears it.
Follow me now; and look thou set not yet
Thy foot in the hot sand, but to the wood
Keep ever close." Silently on we pass'd
To where there gushes from the forest's bound
A little brook, whose crimson'd wave yet lifts
My hair with horror. As the rill, that runs
From Bulicame,[1] to be portion'd out
Among the sinful women, so ran this
Down through the sand; its bottom and each bank
Stone-built, and either margin at its side,
Whereon I straight perceived our passage lay.
    "Of all that I have shown thee, since that gate
We enter'd first, whose threshold is to none

[1] A warm medicinal spring near Viterbo; the waters of which, as Landino and Vellutelli affirm, passed by a place of ill-fame. Venturi conjectures that Dante would imply that it was the scene of licentious merriment among those who frequented its baths.

Denied, naught else so worthy of regard,
As is this river, has thine eye discern'd,
O'er which the flaming volley all is quench'd."
    So spake my guide; and I him thence besought,
That having given me appetite to know,
The food he too would give, that hunger craved.
    "In midst of ocean," forthwith he began,
"A desolate country lies, which Crete is named;
Under whose monarch, in old times, the world
Lived pure and chaste. A mountain rises there,
Call'd Ida, joyous once with leaves and streams,
Deserted now like a forbidden thing.
It was the spot which Rhea, Saturn's spouse,
Chose for the secret cradle of her son;
And better to conceal him, drown'd in shouts
His infant cries. Within the mount, upright
An ancient form there stands, and huge, that turns
His shoulders toward Damiata; and at Rome,
As in his mirror, looks. Of finest gold
His head is shaped, pure silver are the breast
And arms, thence to the middle is of brass,
And downward all beneath well-temper'd steel,
Save the right foot of potter's clay, on which
Than on the other more erect he stands.
Each part, except the gold, is rent throughout;
And from the fissure tears distil, which join'd
Penetrate to that cave. They in their course,
Thus far precipitated down the rock,
Form Acheron, and Styx, and Phlegethon;
Then by this straiten'd channel passing hence
Beneath e'en to the lowest depth of all,
Form there Cocytus, of whose lake (thyself
Shalt see it) I here give thee no account."
    Then I to him: "If from our world this sluice
Be thus derived; wherefore to us but now
Appears it at this edge?" He straight replied:
"The place, thou know'st, is round: and though great
    part
Thou have already past, still to the left
Descending to the nethermost, not yet

Hast thou the circuit made of the whole orb.
Wherefore, if aught of new to us appear,
It needs not bring up wonder in thy looks."
    Then I again inquired: "Where flow the streams
Of Phlegethon and Lethe? for of one
Thou tell'st not; and the other, of that shower,
Thou say'st, is form'd." He answer thus return'd:
"Doubtless thy questions all well pleased I hear.
Yet the red seething wave[2] might have resolved
One thou proposest. Lethe thou shalt see,
But not within this hollow, in the place
Whither,[3] to lave themselves, the spirits go,
Whose blame hath been by penitence removed."
He added: "Time is now we quit the wood.
Look thou my steps pursue: the margins give
Safe passage, unimpeded by the flames;
For over them all vapor is extinct."

CANTO XV

ARGUMENT.—Taking their way upon one of the mounds by which the streamlet, spoken of in the last Canto, was embanked, and having gone so far that they could no longer have discerned the forest if they had turned round to look for it, they meet a troop of spirits that come along the sand by the side of the pier. These are they who have done violence to Nature; and among them Dante distinguishes Brunetto Latini, who had been formerly his master; with whom, turning a little backward, he holds a discourse which occupies the remainder of this Canto.

ONE of the solid margins bears us now
        Envelop'd in the mist, that, from the stream
        Arising, hovers o'er, and saves from fire
Both piers and water. As the Flemings rear
Their mound, 'twixt Ghent and Bruges, to chase back
The ocean, fearing his tumultuous tide
That drives toward them; or the Paduans theirs
Along the Brenta, to defend their towns
And castles, ere the genial warmth be felt
On Chiarentana's[1] top; such were the mounds,
So framed, though not in height or bulk to these
Made equal, by the master, whosoe'er

[2] Phlegethon.   [3] The other side of Purgatory.
[1] A part of the Alps where the Brenta rises, swollen by melting snows.

He was, that raised them here. We from the wood
Were now so far removed, that turning round
I might not have discern'd it, when we met
A troop of spirits, who came beside the pier.

   They each one eyed us, as at eventide
One eyes another under a new moon;
And toward us sharpen'd their sight, as keen
As an old tailor at his needle's eye.

   Thus narrowly explored by all the tribe,
I was agnized of one, who by the skirt
Caught me, and cried, "What wonder have we here?"

   And I, when he to me outstretch'd his arm,
Intently fix'd my ken on his parch'd looks,
That, although smirch'd with fire, they hinder'd not
But I remember'd him; and toward his face
My hand inclining, answer'd: "Ser Brunetto!²
And are ye here?" He thus to me: "My son!
Oh let it not displease thee, if Brunetto
Latini but a little space with thee
Turn back, and leave his fellows to proceed."

   I thus to him replied: "Much as I can,
I thereto pray thee; and if thou be willing
That I here seat me with thee, I consent;
His leave, with whom I journey, first obtain'd."

   "O son!" said he, "whoever of this throng
One instant stops, lies then a hundred years,
No fan to ventilate him, when the fire
Smitest sorest. Pass thou therefore on. I close
Will at thy garments walk, and then rejoin
My troop, who go mourning their endless doom."

   I dared not from the path descend to tread
On equal ground with him, but held my head
Bent down, as one who walks in reverent guise.

   "What chance or destiny," thus he began,
"Ere the last day, conducts thee here below?
And who is this that shows to thee the way?"

---

² "Ser Brunetto, a Florentine, the secretary or chancellor of the city, and Dante's preceptor, hath left us a work so little read, that both the subject of it and the language of it have been mistaken. It is in the French spoken in the reign of St. Louis, under the title of 'Tresor'; and contains a species of philosophical lectures."

"There up aloft," I answer'd, "in the life
Serene, I wander'd in a valley lost,
Before mine age had to its fulness reach'd.
But yester-morn I left it: then once more
Into that vale returning, him I met;
And by this path homeward he leads me back."

   "If thou," he answer'd, "follow but thy star,
Thou canst not miss at last a glorious haven;
Unless in fairer days my judgment err'd.
And if my fate so early had not chanced,
Seeing the heavens thus bounteous to thee, I
Had gladly given thee comfort in thy work.
But that ungrateful and malignant race,
Who in old times came down from Fesole,
Ay and still smack of their rough mountain flint,
Will for thy good deeds show thee enmity.
Nor wonder; for amongst ill-savor'd crabs
It suits not the sweet fig-tree lay her fruit.
Old fame reports them in the world for blind,
Covetous, envious, proud. Look to it well:
Take heed thou cleanse thee of their ways. For thee,
Thy fortune hath such honor in reserve,
That thou by either party shalt be craved
With hunger keen: but be the fresh herb far
From the goat's tooth. The herd of Fesole
May of themselves make litter, not touch the plant,
If any such yet spring on their rank bed,
In which the holy seed revives, transmitted
From those true Romans, who still there remain'd,
When it was made the nest of so much ill."

   "Were all my wish fulfill'd," I straight replied,
"Thou from the confines of man's nature yet
Hadst not been driven forth; for in my mind
Is fix'd, and now strikes full upon my heart,
The dear, benign, paternal image, such
As thine was, when so lately thou didst teach me
The way for man to win eternity:
And how I prized the lesson, it behoves,
That, long as life endures, my tongue should speak.
What of my fate thou tell'st, that write I down;

And, with another text[3] to comment on,
For her I keep it, the celestial dame,
Who will know all, if I to her arrive.
This only would I have thee clearly note:
That, so my conscience have no plea against me,
Do Fortune as she list, I stand prepared.
Not new or strange such earnest to mine ear.
Speed Fortune then her wheel, as likes her best;
The clown his mattock; all things have their course."

    Thereat my sapient guide upon his right
Turn'd himself back, then looked at me, and spake:
"He listens to good purpose who takes note."
I not the less still on my way proceed,
Discoursing with Brunetto, and inquire
Who are most known and chief among his tribe.
    "To know of some is well;" he thus replied,
"But of the rest silence may best beseem.
Time would not serve us for report so long.
In brief I tell thee, that all these were clerks,
Men of great learning and no less renown,
By one same sin polluted in the world.
With them is Priscian; and Accorso's son,
Francesco,[4] herds among the wretched throng:
And, if the wish of so impure a blotch
Possess'd thee, him[5] thou also mightst have seen,
Who by the servants' servant was transferr'd
From Arno's seat to Bacchiglione, where
His ill-strain'd nerves he left. I more would add,
But must from further speech and onward way
Alike desist; for yonder I behold
A mist new-risen on the sandy plain.
A company, with whom I may not sort,

---

[3] "With another text." He refers to the predictions of Farinata, in Canto x.

[4] "Francesco." Accorso, a Florentine, interpreted the Roman law at Bologna, and died in 1229, at the age of 78. His authority was so great as to exceed that of all the other interpreters, so that Cino da Pistoia termed him the Idol of Advocates. His sepulchre, and that of his son Francesco here spoken of, is at Bologna, with this short epitaph: *"Sepulcrum Accursii Glossatoris et Francisci eus Filii."*

[5] "Him." Andrea de' Mozzi, who, that his scandalous life might be less exposed to observation, was translated either by Nicholas III or Boniface VIII from the see of Florence to that of Vicenza, through which passes the river Bacchiglione. He died at Vicenza.

Approaches. I commend my *Treasure* to thee,
Wherein I yet survive; my sole request."
    This said, he turn'd, and seem'd as one of those
Who o'er Verona's champaign try their speed
For the green mantle; and of them he seem'd,
Not he who loses but who gains the prize.

CANTO XVI

ARGUMENT.—Journeying along the pier, which crosses the sand, they are now so near the end of it as to hear the noise of the stream falling into the eighth circle, when they meet the spirits of three military men; who judging Dante, from his dress, to be a countryman of theirs, entreat him to stop. He complies and speaks with them. The two Poets then reach the place where the water descends, being the termination of this third compartment in the seventh circle; and here Virgil, having thrown down into the hollow a cord, wherewith Dante was girt, they behold at that signal a monstrous and horrible figure come swimming up to them.

NOW came I where the water's din was heard
    As down it fell into the other round,
    Resounding like the hum of swarming bees:
When forth together issued from a troop,
That pass'd beneath the fierce tormenting storm,
Three spirits, running swift. They toward us came,
And each one cried aloud, "Oh! do thou stay,
Whom, by the fashion of thy garb, we deem
To be some inmate of our evil land."
    Ah me! what wounds I mark'd upon their limbs,
Recent and old, inflicted by the flames.
E'en the remembrance of them grieves me yet.
    Attentive to their cry, my teacher paused,
And turned to me his visage, and then spake:
"Wait now: our courtesy these merit well:
And were't not for the nature of the place,
Whence glide the fiery darts, I should have said,
That haste had better suited thee than them."
    They, when we stopp'd, resumed their ancient wail,
And, soon as they had reach'd us, all the three
Whirl'd round together in one restless wheel.
As naked champions, smear'd with slippery oil
Are wont, intent, to watch their place of hold
And vantage, ere in closer strife they meet;

Thus each one, as he wheel'd, his countenance
At me directed, so that opposite
The neck moved ever to the twinkling feet.
  "If woe of this unsound and dreary waste,"
Thus one began, "added to our sad cheer
Thus peel'd with flame, do call forth scorn on us
And our entreaties, let our great renown
Incline thee to inform us who thou art,
That dost imprint, with living feet unharm'd,
The soil of Hell. He, in whose track thou seest
My steps pursuing, naked though he be
And reft of all, was of more high estate
Than thou believest; grandchild of the chaste
Gualdrada,[1] him they Guidoguerra call'd,
Who in his lifetime many a noble act
Achieved, both by his wisdom and his sword.
The other, next to me that beats the sand,
Is Aldobrandi,[2] name deserving well,
In the upper world, of honor; and myself,
Who in this torment do partake with them,
Am Rusticucci,[3] whom, past doubt, my wife,
Of savage temper, more than aught beside
Hath to this evil brought." If from the fire
I had been shelter'd, down amidst them straight

[1] "Gualdrada." Gualdrada was the daughter of Bellincione Berti, of whom mention is made in the Paradise, Cantos xv and xvi. He was of the family of Ravignani, a branch of the Adimari. The Emperor Otho IV being at a festival in Florence, where Gualdrada was present, was struck with her beauty; and inquiring who she was, was answered by Bellincione, that she was the daughter of one who, if it was his Majesty's pleasure, would make her admit the honor of his salute. On overhearing this, she arose from her seat, and blushing, desired her father that he would not be so liberal in his offers. The Emperor was delighted by her resolute modesty, and calling to him Guido, one of his barons, gave her to him in marriage; at the same time raising him to the rank of a count, and bestowing on her the whole of Casentino, and a part of the territory of Romagna, as her portion. Two sons were the offspring of this union, Guglielmo and Ruggieri; the latter was father of Guidoguerra, who, at the head of four hundred Florentines of the Guelf party, was signally instrumental to the victory of Charles of Anjou at Benevento, over Manfredi, King of Naples, in 1265. One consequence of this was the expulsion of the Ghibellini and the re-establishment of the Guelfi at Florence.

[2] Tegghiaio Aldobrandi endeavored to dissuade the Florentines from the attack which they meditated against the Siennese; the rejection of his counsel occasioned the defeat which the former sustained at Montaperto, and the consequent banishment of the Guelfi from Florence.

[3] Giacopo Rusticucci, a Florentine, remarkable for his opulence and generosity of spirit.

I then had cast me; nor my guide, I deem,
Would have restrain'd my going: but that fear
Of the dire burning vanquish'd the desire,
Which made me eager of their wish'd embrace.
  I then began: "Not scorn, but grief much more,
Such as long time alone can cure, your doom
Fix'd deep within me, soon as this my lord
Spake words, whose tenor taught me to expect
That such a race, as ye are, was at hand.
I am a countryman of yours, who still
Affectionate have utter'd, and have heard
Your deeds and names renown'd. Leaving the gall,
For the sweet fruit I go, that a sure guide
Hath promised to me. But behoves, that far
As to the centre first I downward tend."
  "So may long space thy spirit guide thy limbs,"
He answer straight return'd; "and so thy fame
Shine bright when thou art gone, as thou shalt tell,
If courtesy and valor, as they wont,
Dwell in our city, or have vanish'd clean:
For one amidst us late condemn'd to wail,
Borsiere,[4] yonder walking with his peers,
Grieves us no little by the news he brings."
  "An upstart multitude and sudden gains,
Pride and excess, O Florence! have in thee
Engender'd, so that now in tears thou mourn'st!"
  Thus cried I, with my face upraised, and they
All three, who for an answer took my words,
Look'd at each other, as men look when truth
Comes to their ear. "If at so little cost,"
They all at once rejoin'd, "thou satisfy
Others who question thee, O happy thou!
Gifted with words so apt to speak thy thought.
Wherefore, if thou escape this darksome clime,
Returning to behold the radiant stars,
When thou with pleasure shalt retrace the past,[5]
See that of us thou speak among mankind."

---

[4] Guglielmo Borsiere, a Florentine, whom Boccaccio terms "a man of courteous and elegant manners, and of great readiness in conversation."

[5] *"Quando ti gioverà dicere io fui."*
So Tasso, "G. L." c. xv. st. 38:
  "Quando mi gioverà narrar altrui
   Le novità vedute, e dire; io fui."

This said, they broke the circle, and so swift
Fled, that as pinions seem'd their nimble feet.
 Not in so short a time might one have said
"Amen," as they had vanish'd. Straight my guide
Pursued his track. I follow'd: and small space
Had we past onward, when the water's sound
Was now so near at hand, that we had scarce
Heard one another's speech for the loud din.
 E'en as the river,[6] that first holds its course
Unmingled from the Mount of Vesulo,
On the left side of Apennine, toward
The east, which Acquacheta higher up
They call, ere it descend into the vale,
At Forli,[7] by that name no longer known,
Rebellows o'er Saint Benedict, roll'd on
From the Alpine summit down a precipice,
Where space[8] enough to lodge a thousand spreads;
Thus downward from a craggy steep we found
That this dark wave resounded, roaring loud,
So that the ear its clamour soon had stunn'd.
 I had a cord[9] that braced my girdle round,
Wherewith I erst had thought fast bound to take
The painted leopard. This when I had all
Unloosen'd from me (so my master bade)
I gather'd up, and stretch'd it forth to him.
Then to the right he turn'd, and from the brink
Standing few paces distant, cast it down
Into the deep abyss. "And somewhat strange,"
Thus to myself I spake, "signal so strange
Betokens, which my guide with earnest eye
Thus follows." Ah! what caution must men use

[6] He compares the fall of Phlegethon to that of the Montone (a river in Romagna) from the Apennines above the Abbey of St. Benedict. All the other streams that rise between the sources of the Po and the Montone, and fall from the left side of the Apennines, join the Po and accompany it to the sea.

[7] There it loses the name of Acquacheta, and takes that of Montone.

[8] Either because the abbey was capable of containing more than those who oc-cupied it, or because (says Landino) the lords of that territory had intended to build a castle near the water-fall, and to collect within its walls the population of the neighboring villages.

[9] "A cord." It is believed that our poet in early life, had entered into the order of St. Francis. By observing the rules of that profession he had designed "to take the painted leopard" (that animal represented Pleasure) "with this cord."

With those who look not at the deed alone,
But spy into the thoughts with subtle skill.

"Quickly shall come," he said, "what I expect;
Thine eye discover quickly that, whereof
Thy thought is dreaming." Ever to that truth,
Which but the semblance of a falsehood wears,
A man, if possible, should bar his lip;
Since, although blameless, he incurs reproach.
But silence here were vain; and by these notes,
Which now I sing, reader, I swear to thee,
So may they favor find to latest times!
That through the gross and murky air I spied
A shape come swimming up, that might have quell'd
The stoutest heart with wonder; in such guise
As one returns, who hath been down to loose
An anchor grappled fast against some rock,
Or to aught else that in the salt wave lies,
Who, upward springing, close draws in his feet.

CANTO XVII

ARGUMENT.—The monster Geryon is described; to whom while Virgil is speaking
in order that he may carry them both down to the next circle, Dante, by permission,
goes further along the edge of the void, to descry the third species of sinners contained
in this compartment, namely, those who have done violence to Art; and then returning to his master, they both descend, seated on the back of Geryon.

"LO! the fell monster[1] with the deadly sting,
        Who passes mountains, breaks through fenced
            walls
And firm embattled spears, and with his filth
Taints all the world." Thus me my guide address'd,
And beckon'd him, that he should come to shore,
Near to the stony causeway's utmost edge.
    Forthwith that image vile of Fraud appear'd,
His head and upper part exposed on land,
But laid not on the shore his bestial train.
His face the semblance of a just man's wore,
So kind and gracious was its outward cheer;
The rest was serpent all: two shaggy claws

------

[1] "The fell monster." Fraud.

Reach'd to the arm-pits; and the back and breast,
And either side, were painted o'er with nodes
And orbits. Colours variegated more
Nor Turks nor Tartars e'er on cloth of state
With interchangeable embroidery wove,
Nor spread Arachne o'er her curious loom.
As oft-times a light skiff, moor'd to the shore,
Stands part in water, part upon the land;
Or, as where dwells the greedy German boor,
The beaver settles, watching for his prey;
So on the rim, that fenced the sand with rock,
Sat perch'd the fiend of evil. In the void
Glancing, his tail upturn'd its venomous fork,
With sting like scorpion's arm'd. Then thus my guide,
"Now need our way must turn few steps apart,
Far as to that ill beast, who couches there."
   Thereat, toward the right our downward course
We shaped, and, better to escape the flame
And burning marle, ten paces on the verge
Proceeded. Soon as we to him arrive,
A little farther on mine eye beholds
A tribe of spirits, seated on the sand
Near to the void. Forthwith my master spake:
"That to the full thy knowledge may extend
Of all this round contains, go now, and mark
The mien these wear: but hold not long discourse.
Till thou returnest, I with him meantime
Will parley, that to us he may vouchsafe
The aid of his strong shoulders." Thus alone,
Yet forward on the extremity I paced
Of that seventh circle, where the mournful tribe
Were seated. At the eyes forth gush'd their pangs,
Against the vapors and the torrid soil
Alternately their shifting hands they plied.
Thus use the dogs in summer still to ply
Their jaws and feet by turns, when bitten sore
By gnats, or flies, or gadflies swarming round.
   Noting the visages of some, who lay
Beneath the pelting of that dolorous fire,
One of them all I knew not; but perceived,

That pendent from his neck each bore a pouch[2]
With colours and with emblems various mark'd,
On which it seem'd as if their eye did feed.

And when, amongst them, looking round I came,
A yellow purse[3] I saw with azure wrought,
That wore a lion's countenance and port.
Then, still my sight pursuing its career,
Another[4] I beheld, than blood more red,
A goose display of whiter wing than curd.
And one, who bore a fat and azure swine[5]
Pictured on his white scrip, address'd me thus:
"What dost thou in this deep? Go now and know,
Since yet thou livest, that my neighbor here
Vitaliano[6] on my left shall sit.
A Paduan with these Florentines am I.
Oft-times they thunder in mine ears, exclaiming,
'Oh! haste that noble knight,[7] he who the pouch
With the three goats will bring.'" This said, he writhed
The mouth, and loll'd the tongue out, like an ox
That licks his nostrils. I, lest longer stay
He ill might brook, who bade me stay not long,
Backward my steps from those sad spirits turn'd.

My guide already seated on the haunch
Of the fierce animal I found; and thus
He me encouraged. "Be thou stout: be bold.
Down such a steep flight must we now descend.
Mount thou before: for, that no power the tail
May have to harm thee, I will be i' th' midst."
As one, who hath an ague fit so near,
His nails already are turn'd blue, and he
Quivers all o'er, if he but eye the shade;
Such was my cheer at hearing of his words.
But shame soon interposed her threat, who makes
The servant bold in presence of his lord.

[2] A purse, whereon the armorial bearings of each were emblazoned. According to Landino, our Poet implies that the usurer can pretend to no other honor than such as he derives from his purse and his family. The description of persons by their heraldic insignia is remarkable.

[3] "A yellow purse." The arms of the Gianfigliazzi of Florence.

[4] The arms of the Ubbriachi, another Florentine family of high distinction.

[5] The arms of the Scrovigni, a noble family of Padua.

[6] Vitaliano del Dente, a Paduan.

[7] Giovanni Bujamonti, the most infamous usurer of his time.

I settled me upon those shoulders huge,
And would have said, but that the words to aid
My purpose came not, "Look thou clasp me firm."
    But he whose succour then not first I proved,
Soon as I mounted, in his arms aloft,
Embracing, held me up; and thus he spake:
"Geryon! now move thee: be thy wheeling gyres
Of ample circuit, easy thy descent.
Think on the unusual burden thou sustain'st."
    As a small vessel, backening out from land,
Her station quits; so thence the monster loosed,
And, when he felt himself at large, turn'd round
There, where the breast had been, his forked tail.
Thus, like an eel, outstretch'd at length he steer'd,
Gathering the air up with retractile claws.
    Not greater was the dread, when Phaëton
The reins let drop at random, whence high heaven,
Whereof signs yet appear, was wrapt in flames;
Nor when ill-fated Icarus perceived,
By liquefaction of the scalded wax,
The trusted pennons loosen'd from his loins,
His sire exclaiming loud, "Ill way thou keep'st,"
Than was my dread, when round me on each part
The air I view'd, and other object none
Save the fell beast. He, slowly sailing, wheels
His downward motion, unobserved of me,
But that the wind, arising to my face,
Breathes on me from below. Now on our right
I heard the cataract beneath us leap
With hideous crash; whence bending down to explore,
New terror I conceived at the steep plunge;
For flames I saw, and wailings smote mine ear:
So that, all trembling, close I crouch'd my limbs,
And then distinguish'd, unperceived before,
By the dread torments that on every side
Drew nearer, how our downward course we wound.
    As falcon, that hath long been on the wing,
But lure nor bird hath seen, while in despair
The falconer cries, "Ah me! thou stoop'st to earth,"
Wearied descends, whence nimbly he arose

In many an airy wheel, and lighting sits
At distance from his lord in angry mood;
So Geryon lighting places us on foot
Low down at base of the deep-furrow'd rock,
And, of his burden there discharged, forthwith
Sprang forward, like an arrow from the string.

CANTO XVIII

ARGUMENT.—The Poet describes the situation and form of the eighth circle, divided
into ten gulfs, which contain as many different descriptions of fraudulent sinners;
but in the present Canto he treats only of two sorts: the first is of those who, either
for their own pleasure, or for that of another, have seduced any woman from her duty;
and these are scourged of demons in the first gulf: the other sort is of flatterers,
who in the second gulf are condemned to remain immersed in filth.

THERE is a place within the depths of Hell
Call'd Malebolge, all of rock dark-stain'd
With hue ferruginous, e'en as the steep
That round it circling winds. Right in the midst
Of that abominable region yawns
A spacious gulf profound, whereof the frame
Due time shall tell. The circle, that remains,
Throughout its round, between the gulf and base
Of the high craggy banks, successive forms
Ten bastions, in its hollow bottom raised.
    As where, to guard the walls, full many a foss
Begirds some stately castle, sure defence
Affording to the space within; so here
Were model'd these: and as like fortresses,
E'en from their threshold to the brink without,
Are flank'd with bridges; from the rock's low base
Thus flinty paths advanced, that 'cross the moles
And dykes struck onward far as to the gulf,
That in one bound collected cuts them off.
Such was the place, wherein we found ourselves
From Geryon's back dislodged. The bard to left
Held on his way, and I behind him moved.
    On our right hand new misery I saw,
New pains, new executioners of wrath,
That swarming peopled the first chasm. Below
Were naked sinners. Hitherward they came,

Meeting our faces, from the middle point;
With us beyond, but with a larger stride.
E'en thus the Romans,[1] when the year returns
Of Jubilee, with better speed to rid
The thronging multitudes, their means devise
For such as pass the bridge; that on one side
All front toward the castle, and approach
Saint Peter's fane, on the other toward the mount.

Each diverse way, along the grisly rock,
Horn'd demons I beheld, with lashes huge,
That on their back unmercifully smote.
Ah! how they made them bound at the first stripe!
None for the second waited, nor the third.

Meantime, as on I pass'd, one met my sight,
Whom soon as view'd, "Of him," cried I, "not yet
Mine eye hath had his fill." I therefore stay'd
My feet to scan him, and the teacher kind
Paused with me, and consented I should walk
Backward a space; and the tormented spirit,
Who thought to hide him, bent his visage down.
But it avail'd him naught; for I exclaim'd:
"Thou who dost cast thine eye upon the ground,
Unless thy features do belie thee much,
Venedico[2] art thou. But what brings thee
Into this bitter seasoning?" He replied:
"Unwillingly I answer to thy words.
But thy clear speech, that to my mind recalls
The world I once inhabited, constrains me.
Know then 't was I who led fair Ghisola
To do the Marquis' will, however fame
The shameful tale have bruited. Nor alone
Bologna hither sendeth me to mourn.
Rather with us the place is so o'erthrong'd,
That not so many tongues this day are taught,

---

[1] In the year 1300, Pope Boniface VIII, to remedy the inconvenience occasioned by the press over the bridge of St. Angelo during the time of the Jubilee, caused it to be divided lengthwise by a partition. G. Villani, who was present, describes the order that was preserved, lib. viii. c. xxxvi. It was at this time, and on this occasion, that he first conceived the design of "compiling his book."

[2] Venedico Caccianimico, a Bolognese, who prevailed on his sister Ghisola to prostitute herself to Obizzo da Este. (See Canto xii.)

Betwixt the Reno and Savena's stream,
To answer *Sipa*[3] in their country's phrase.
And if of that securer proof thou need,
Remember but our craving thirst for gold."

　　Him speaking thus, a demon with his throng
Struck and exclaim'd, "Away, corrupter! here
Women are none for sale." Forthwith I join'd
My escort, and few paces thence we came
To where a rock forth issued from the bank.
That easily ascended, to the right
Upon its splinter turning, we depart
From those eternal barriers. When arrived
Where, underneath, the gaping arch lets pass
The scourged souls: "Pause here," the teacher said,
"And let these others miserable now
Strike on thy ken; faces not yet beheld,
For that together they with us have walk'd."

　　From the old bridge we eyed the pack, who came
From the other side toward us, like the rest,
Excoriate from the lash. My gentle guide,
By me unquestion'd, thus his speech resumed:
"Behold that lofty shade, who this way tends,
And seems too woe-begone to drop a tear.
How yet the regal aspect he retains!
Jason is he, whose skill and prowess won
The ram from Colchis. To the Lemnian isle
His passage thither led him, when those bold
And pitiless women had slain all their males.
There he with tokens and fair witching words
Hypsipyle[4] beguiled, a virgin young,
Who first had all the rest herself beguiled.
Impregnated, he left her there forlorn.
Such is the guilt condemns him to this pain.
Here too Medea's injuries are avenged.
All bear him company, who like deceit
To his have practised. And thus much to know

---

[3] "To answer Sipa." He denotes
Bologna by its situation between the rivers
Savena to the east and Reno to the west,
and by a peculiarity of dialect, the use
of the affirmative "sipa" instead either of
"si" or of "sia."
[4] She deceived the other women, by
concealing her father Thoas, when they
slew their males.

Of the first vale suffice thee, and of those
Whom its keen torments urge." Now had we come
Where, crossing the next pier, the straiten'd path
Bestrides its shoulders to another arch.

    Hence, in the second chasm we heard the ghosts,
Who gibber in low melancholy sounds,
With wide-stretch'd nostrils snort, and on themselves
Smite with their palms. Upon the banks a scurf,
From the foul steam condensed, encrusting hung,
That held sharp combat with the sight and smell.

    So hollow is the depth, that from no part,
Save on the summit of the rocky span,
Could I distinguish aught. Thus far we came;
And thence I saw, within the foss below,
A crowd immersed in ordure, that appear'd
Draff of the human body. There beneath
Searching with eye inquisitive, I mark'd
One with his head so grimed, 't were hard to deem
If he were clerk or layman. Loud he cried:
"Why greedily thus bendest more on me,
Than on these other filthy ones, thy ken?"

    "Because, if true my memory," I replied,
"I heretofore have seen thee with dry locks;
And thou Alessio⁵ art, of Lucca sprung.
Therefore than all the rest I scan thee more."

    Then beating on his brain, these words he spake:
"Me thus low down my flatteries have sunk,
Wherewith I ne'er enough could glut my tongue."

    My leader thus: "A little further stretch
Thy face, that thou the visage well mayst note
Of that besotted, sluttish courtesan,
Who there doth rend her with defiled nails,
Now crouching down, now risen on her feet.
Thaïs⁶ is this, the harlot, whose false lip
Answer'd her doting paramour that ask'd,
'Thankest me much!'—'Say rather, wondrously,'
And, seeing this, here satiate be our view."

---

⁵ Of the old Interminei family.

⁶ "Thaïs." In the Eunuchus of Terence, Thraso asks if Thaïs was obliged to him for his present and Gnatho replies, that she had expressed her obligation in the most forcible terms.

CANTO XIX

ARGUMENT.—They come to the third gulf, wherein are punished those who have been guilty of simony. These are fixed with the head downward in certain apertures, so that no more of them than the legs appears without, and on the soles of their feet are seen burning flames. Dante is taken down by his guide into the bottom of the gulf; and there finds Pope Nicholas V, whose evil deeds, together with those of other pontiffs, are bitterly reprehended. Virgil then carries him up again to the arch, which affords them a passage over the following gulf.

WOE to thee, Simon Magus! woe to you,
    His wretched followers! who the things of God,
    Which should be wedded unto goodness, them,
Rapacious as ye are, do prostitute
For gold and silver in adultery.
Now must the trumpet sound for you, since yours
Is the third chasm. Upon the following vault
We now had mounted, where the rock impends
Directly o'er the centre of the foss.
    Wisdom Supreme! how wonderful the art,
Which Thou dost manifest in Heaven, in earth,
And in the evil world, how just a meed
Allotting by Thy virtue unto all.
    I saw the livid stone, throughout the sides
And in its bottom full of apertures,
All equal in their width, and circular each.
Nor ample less nor larger they appear'd
Than, in Saint John's fair dome[1] of me beloved,
Those framed to hold the pure baptismal streams,
One of the which I brake, some few years past,
To save a whelming infant: and be this
A seal to undeceive whoever doubts
The motive of my deed. From out the mouth
Of every one emerged a sinner's feet,
And of the legs high upward as the calf.
The rest beneath was hid. On either foot
The soles were burning; whence the flexile joints
Glanced with such violent motion, as had snapt

---

[1] The apertures in the rock were of the same dimensions as the fonts of St. John the Baptist at Florence, one of which Dante had broken to rescue a child that was playing near and fell in. He intimates that his motive for breaking the font had been maliciously represented by his enemies.

Asunder cords or twisted withes. As flame,
Feeding on unctuous matter, glides along
The surface, scarcely touching where it moves;
So here, from heel to point, glided the flames.

"Master! say who is he, than all the rest
Glancing in fiercer agony, on whom
A ruddier flame doth prey?" I thus inquired.

"If thou be willing," he replied, "that I
Carry thee down, where least the slope bank falls,
He of himself shall tell thee, and his wrongs."

I then: "As pleases thee, to me is best.
Thou art my lord; and know'st that ne'er I quit
Thy will: what silence hides, that knowest thou."

Thereat on the fourth pier we came, we turn'd
And on our left descended to the depth,
A narrow strait, and perforated close.

Nor from his side my leader set me down,
Till to his orifice he brought, whose limb
Quivering express'd his pang. "Whoe'er thou art,
Sad spirit! thus reversed, and as a stake
Driven in the soil,"—I in these words began;
"If thou be able, utter forth thy voice."

There stood I like the friar, that doth shrive
A wretch for murder doom'd, who, e'en when fix'd,
Calleth him back, whence death awhile delays.

He shouted: "Ha! already standest there?
Already standest there, O Boniface![2]
By many a year the writing play'd me false.
So early dost thou surfeit with the wealth,
For which thou fearedst not in guile to take
The lovely lady, and then mangle her?"

I felt as those who, piercing not the drift
Of answer made them, stand as if exposed
In mockery, nor know what to reply;
When Virgil thus admonish'd: "Tell him quick,
'I am not he, not he whom thou believest.'"

And I, as was enjoin'd me, straight replied.

[2] The spirit mistakes Dante for Boniface VIII (who was then alive, and not expected to arrive so soon, a prophecy predicting the death of that pope at a later period. Boniface died in 1303.

That heard, the spirit all did wrench his feet,
And, sighing, next in woeful accent spake:
"What then of me requirest? If to know
So much imports thee, who I am, that thou
Hast therefore down the bank descended, learn
That in the mighty mantle I was robed,[3]
And of a she-bear was indeed the son,
So eager to advance my whelps, that there
My having in my purse above I stow'd,
And here myself. Under my head are dragg'd
The rest, my predecessors in the guilt
Of simony. Stretch'd at their length, they lie
Along an opening in the rock. 'Midst them
I also low shall fall, soon as he comes,
For whom I took thee, when so hastily
I question'd. But already longer time
Hath past, since my soles kindled, and I thus
Upturn'd have stood, than is his doom to stand
Planted with fiery feet. For after him,
One yet of deeds more ugly shall arrive,
From forth the west, a shepherd without law,[4]
Fated to cover both his form and mine.
He a new Jason[5] shall be call'd, of whom
In Maccabees we read; and favor such
As to that priest his King indulgent show'd,
Shall be of France's monarch[6] shown to him."
    I know not if I here too far presumed,
But in this strain I answer'd: "Tell me now
What treasures from Saint Peter at the first
Our Lord demanded, when he put the keys
Into his charge? Surely he ask'd no more
But 'Follow me!' Nor Peter,[7] nor the rest,

---

[3] Nicholas III of the Orsini family, whom the Poet therefore calls "figliuol dell' orsa," "son of the she-bear." He died in 1281.

[4] Bertrand de Got, Archbishop of Bordeaux, who succeeded to the pontificate in 1305, as Clement V. He transferred the Holy See to Avignon in 1308 (where it remained till 1376), and died in 1314.

[5] "But after the death of Seleucus, when Antiochus, called Epiphanes, took the kingdom, Jason, the brother of Onias, labored to be high-priest, promising unto the king, by intercession, three hundred and threescore talents of silver, and of another revenue eighty talents."—Maccab. b. ii. ch. iv, 7, 8.

[6] Philip IV. See G. Villani, lib. viii. c. lxxx.

[7] Acts of the Apostles, ch. i. 26.

Or gold or silver of Matthias took,
When lots were cast upon the forfeit place
Of the condemned soul.[8] Abide thou then;
Thy punishment of right is merited:
And look thou well to that ill-gotten coin,
Which against Charles[9] thy hardihood inspired.
If reverence of the keys restrain'd me not,
Which thou in happier time didst hold, I yet
Severer speech might use. Your avarice
O'ercasts the world with mourning, under foot
Treading the good, and raising bad men up.
Of shepherds like to you, the Evangelist
Was ware, when her, who sits upon the waves,
With kings in filthy whoredom he beheld;
She who with seven heads tower'd at her birth,
And from ten horns her proof of glory drew,
Long as her spouse in virtue took delight.
Of gold and silver ye have made your god,
Differing wherein from the idolater,
But that he worships one, a hundred ye?
Ah, Constantine![10] to how much ill gave birth,
Not thy conversion, but that plenteous dower,
Which the first wealthy Father gain'd from thee."

　　Meanwhile, as thus I sung, he, whether wrath
Or conscience smote him, violent upsprang
Spinning on either sole. I do believe
My teacher well was pleased, with so composed
A lip he listen'd ever to the sound
Of the true words I utter'd. In both arms
He caught, and, to his bosom lifting me,
Upward retraced the way of his descent.

　　Nor weary of his weight, he press'd me close,
Till to the summit of the rock we came,
Our passage from the fourth to the fifth pier.
His cherish'd burden there gently he placed

---

[8] "The condemned soul." Judas.

[9] Nicholas III was enraged against Charles I, King of Sicily, because he rejected with scorn his proposition for an alliance between their families. See G. Villani, Hist., lib. iii.

[10] He alludes to the pretended gift of the Lateran by Constantine to Sylvester, of which Dante himself seems to imply a doubt, in his treatise "De Monarchiâ."

Upon the rugged rock and steep, a path
Not easy for the clambering goat to mount.
Thence to my view another vale appear'd.

CANTO XX

ARGUMENT.—The Poet relates the punishment of such as presumed, while living,
to predict future events. It is to have their faces reversed and set the contrary
way on their limbs, so that, being deprived of the power to see before them, they are
constrained ever to walk backward. Among these Virgil points out to him Amphiaraüs, Tiresias, Aruns, and Manto (from the mention of whom he takes occasion
to speak of the origin of Mantua), together with several others, who had practised
the arts of divination and astrology.

AND now the verse proceeds to torments new,
    Fit argument of this the twentieth strain
    Of the first song, whose awful theme records
The spirits whelm'd in woe. Earnest I look'd
Into the depth, that open'd to my view,
Moisten'd with tears of anguish, and beheld
A tribe, that came along the hollow vale,
In silence weeping: such their step as walk
Quires, chanting solemn litanies, on earth.
    As on them more direct mine eye descends,
Each wonderously seem'd to be reversed
At the neck-bone, so that the countenance
Was from the reins averted; and because
None might before him look, they were compell'd
To advance with backward gait. Thus one perhaps
Hath been by force of palsy clean transposed,
But I ne'er saw it nor believe it so.
    Now, reader! think within thyself, so God
Fruit of thy reading give thee! how I long
Could keep my visage dry, when I beheld
Near me our form distorted in such guise,
That on the hinder parts fallen from the face
The tears down-streaming roll'd. Against a rock
I leant and wept, so that my guide exclaim'd:
"What, and art thou, too, witless as the rest?
Here pity most doth show herself alive,
When she is dead. What guilt exceedeth his,
Who with Heaven's judgment in his passion strives?

Raise up thy head, raise up, and see the man
Before whose eyes[1] earth gaped in Thebes, when all
Cried out 'Amphiaraüs, whither rushest?
Why leavest thou the war?' He not the less
Fell ruining far as to Minos down,
Whose grapple none eludes. Lo! how he makes
The breast his shoulders; and who once too far
Before him wish'd to see, now backward looks,
And treads reverse his path. Tiresias note,
Who semblance changed, when woman he became
Of male, through every limb transform'd; and then
Once more behoved him with his rod to strike
The two entwining serpents, ere the plumes,
That mark'd the better sex, might shoot again.
"Aruns,[2] with rere his belly facing, comes.
On Luni's mountains 'midst the marbles white,
Where delves Carrara's hind, who wons beneath,
A cavern was his dwelling, whence the stars
And main-sea wide in boundless view he held.
"The next, whose loosen'd tresses overspread
Her bosom, which thou seest not (for each hair
On that side grows) was Manto, she who search'd
Through many regions, and at length her seat
Fix'd in my native land: whence a short space
My words detain thy audience. When her sire
From life departed, and in servitude
The city dedicate to Bacchus mourn'd,
Long time she went a wanderer through the world.
Aloft in Italy's delightful land
A lake there lies, at foot of that proud Alp
That o'er the Tyrol locks Germania in,
Its name Benacus, from whose ample breast
A thousand springs, methinks, and more, between
Camonica and Garda, issuing forth,
Water the Apennine. There is a spot[3]

---

[1] Amphiaraüs, one of the seven kings
who besieged Thebes. He is said to have
been swallowed up by an opening of the
earth.
[2] Said to have dwelt in the mountains
of Luni (whence that territory is still
called Lunigiana), above Carrara, celebrated for its marble.
[3] "There is a spot." Prato di Fame,
where the dioceses of Trento, Verona,
and Brescia meet.

At midway of that lake, where he who bears
Of Trento's flock the pastoral staff, with him
Of Brescia, and the Veronese, might each
Passing that way his benediction give.
A garrison of goodly site and strong
Peschiera[4] stands, to awe with front opposed
The Bergamese and Brescian, whence the shore
More slope each way descends. There, whatsoe'er
Benacus' bosom holds not, tumbling o'er
Down falls, and winds a river flood beneath
Through the green pastures. Soon as in his course
The stream makes head, Benacus then no more
They call the name, but Mincius, till at last
Reaching Governo, into Po he falls.
Not far his course hath run, when a wide flat
It finds, which overstretching as a marsh
It covers, pestilent in summer oft.
Hence journeying, the savage maiden saw
Midst of the fen a territory waste
And naked of inhabitants. To shun
All human converse, here she with her slaves,
Plying her arts, remain'd, and liv'd, and left
Her body tenantless. Thenceforth the tribes,
Who round were scatter'd, gathering to that place,
Assembled; for its strength was great, enclosed
On all parts by the fen. On those dead bones
They rear'd themselves a city, for her sake
Calling it Mantua, who first chose the spot,
Nor ask'd another omen for the name;
Wherein more numerous the people dwelt,
Ere Casalodi's madness[5] by deceit
Was wronged of Pinamonte. If thou hear
Henceforth another origin assign'd
Of that my country, I forewarn thee now,
That falsehood none beguile thee of the truth."

---

[4] "Peschiera." A garrison situated to the south of the lake, where it empties and forms the Mincius.

[5] Alberto da Casalodi, in possession of Mantua, was persuaded by Pinamonte Buonacossi to ingratiate himself with the people by banishing to their own castles the nobles, who were obnoxious to them. Pinamonte then put himself at the head of the populace, drove out Casalodi and his adherents, and obtained the sovereignty for himself.

I answer'd, "Teacher, I conclude thy words
So certain, that all else shall be to me
As embers lacking life. But now of these,
Who here proceed, instruct me, if thou see
Any that merit more especial note.
For thereon is my mind alone intent."

He straight replied: "That spirit, from whose cheek
The beard sweeps o'er his shoulders brown, what time
Græcia was emptied of her males, that scarce
The cradles were supplied, the seer was he
In Aulis, who with Calchas gave the sign
When first to cut the cable. Him they named
Eurypilus: so sings my tragic strain,
In which majestic measure well thou know'st,
Who know'st it all. That other, round the loins
So slender of his shape, was Michael Scot,[6]
Practised in every slight of magic wile.

"Guido Bonatti[7] see: Asdente mark,[8]
Who now were willing he had tended still
The thread and cordwain, and too late repents.

"See next the wretches, who the needle left,
The shuttle and the spindle, and became
Diviners: baneful witcheries they wrought
With images and herbs. But onward now:
For now doth Cain with fork of thorns[9] confine
On either hemisphere, touching the wave
Beneath the towers of Seville. Yesternight
The moon was round. Thou mayst remember well:
For she good service did thee in the gloom
Of the deep wood." This said, both onward moved.

---

[6] "It is not long since there was in this city (Florence) a great master in necromancy, called Michele Scotto, because he was from Scotland." Boccaccio, Decameron G. viii. N. 9.

[7] An astrologer of Forli, on whose skill Guido da Montefeltro, lord of that place, so relied, that he is reported never to have gone into battle, except in the hour recommended to him by Bonatti. Landino and Vellutello speak of his book on astrology. Macchiavelli mentions him in the History of Florence, l. i. p. 24. ed.

1550. "He flourished about 1230 and 1260. Though a learned astronomer he was seduced by astrology, through which he was greatly in favor with many princes."

[8] A shoemaker at Parma, who deserted his business to practice the arts of divination.

[9] By Cain and the thorns ("The Man in the Moon") the Poet denotes that luminary. The same superstition is alluded to in the Paradise, Canto ii. 52.

CANTO XXI

ARGUMENT.—Still in the eighth circle, which bears the name of Malebolge, they look down from the bridge that passes over its fifth gulf, upon the barterers or public peculators. These are plunged in a lake of boiling pitch, and guarded by Demons, to whom Virgil, leaving Dante apart, presents himself; and license being obtained to pass onward, both pursue their way.

THUS we from bridge to bridge, with other talk,
    The which my drama cares not to rehearse,
    Pass'd on; and to the summit reaching, stood
To view another gap, within the round
Of Malebolge, other bootless pangs.
    Marvellous darkness shadow'd o'er the place.
    In the Venetians' arsenal as boils
Through wintry months tenacious pitch, to smear
Their unsound vessels; for the inclement time
Seafaring men restrains, and in that while
His bark one builds anew, another stops
The ribs of his that hath made many a voyage,
One hammers at the prow, one at the poop,
This shapeth oars, that other cables twirls,
The mizzen one repairs, and main-sail rent;
So, not by force of fire but art divine,
Boil'd here a glutinous thick mass, that round
Limed all the shore beneath. I that beheld,
But therein naught distinguish'd, save the bubbles
Raised by the boiling, and one mighty swell
Heave, and by turns subsiding fall. While there
I fix'd my ken below, "Mark! mark!" my guide
Exclaiming, drew me toward him from the place
Wherein I stood. I turn'd myself, as one
Impatient to behold that which beheld
He needs must shun, whom sudden fear unmans,
That he his flight delays not for the view.
Behind me I discern'd a devil black,
That running up advanced along the rock.
Ah! what fierce cruelty his look bespake.
In act how bitter did he seem, with wings
Buoyant outstretch'd and feet of nimblest tread.
His shoulder, proudly eminent and sharp,

Was with a sinner charged; by either haunch
He held him, the foot's sinew griping fast.
　　"Ye of our bridge!" he cried, "keen-talon'd fiends!
Lo! one of Santa Zita's elders. Him
Whelm ye beneath, while I return for more.
That land hath store of such. All men are there,
Except Bonturo, barterers: of 'no'
For lucre there an 'ay' is quickly made."
　　Him dashing down, o'er the rough rock he turn'd;
Nor ever after thief a mastiff loosed
Sped with like eager haste. That other sank,
And forthwith writhing to the surface rose.
But those dark demons, shrouded by the bridge,
Cried, "Here the hallow'd visage saves not: here
Is other swimming than in Serchio's wave,
Wherefore, if thou desire we rend thee not,
Take heed thou mount not o'er the pitch." This said,
They grappled him with more than hundred hooks,
And shouted: "Cover'd thou must sport thee here;
So, if thou canst, in secret mayst thou filch."
E'en thus the cook bestirs him, with his grooms,
To thrust the flesh into the caldron down
With flesh-hooks, that it float not on the top.
　　Me then my guide bespake: "Lest they descry
That thou art here, behind a craggy rock
Bend low and screen thee: and whate'er of force
Be offer'd me, or insult, fear thou not;
For I am well advised, who have been erst
In the like fray." Beyond the bridge's head
Therewith he pass'd; and reaching the sixth pier,
Behoved him then a forehead terror-proof.
　　With storm and fury, as when dogs rush forth
Upon the poor man's back, who suddenly
From whence he standeth makes his suit; so rush'd
Those from beneath the arch, and against him
Their weapons all they pointed. He, aloud:
"Be none of you outrageous: ere your tine
Dare seize me, come forth from amongst you one,
Who having heard my words, decide he then

If he shall tear these limbs." They shouted loud,
"Go, Malacoda!" Whereat one advanced,
The others standing firm, and as he came,
"What may this turn avail him?" he exclaim'd.

"Believest thou, Malacoda! I had come
Thus far from all your skirmishing secure,"
My teacher answer'd, "without will divine
And destiny propitious? Pass we then;
For so Heaven's pleasure is, that I should lead
Another through this savage wilderness."

Forthwith so fell his pride, that he let drop
The instrument of torture at his feet,
And to the rest exclaim'd: "We have no power
To strike him." Then to me my guide: "O thou!
Who on the bridge among the crags dost sit
Low crouching, safely now to me return."

I rose, and toward him moved with speed; the fiends
Meantime all forward drew: me terror seized,
Lest they should break the compact they had made.
Thus issuing from Caprona,[1] once I saw
Th' infantry, dreading lest his covenant
The foe should break; so close he hemm'd them round.

I to my leader's side adhered, mine eyes
With fixt and motionless observance bent
On their unkindly visage. They their hooks
Protruding, one the other thus bespake:
"Wilt thou I touch him on the hip?" To whom
Was answer'd: "Even so; nor miss thy aim."

But he, who was in conference with my guide,
Turn'd rapid round; and thus the demon spake:
"Stay, stay thee, Scarmiglione!" Then to us
He added: "Further footing to your step
This rock affords not, shiver'd to the base
Of the sixth arch. But would ye still proceed,
Up by this cavern go: not distant far,
Another rock will yield you passage safe.

[1] "From Caprona." The surrender of the castle of Caprona to the combined forces of Florence and Lucca, on condition that the garrison should march out in safety, to which event Dante was a witness, took place in 1290. See G. Villani, Hist. lib. vii. c. cxxxvi.

Yesterday,[2] later by five hours than now,
Twelve hundred threescore years and six had fill'd
The circuit of their course, since here the way
Was broken. Thitherward I straight despatch
Certain of these my scouts, who shall espy
If any on the surface bask. With them
Go ye: for ye shall find them nothing fell.
Come, Alichino, forth," with that he cried,
"And Calcabrina, and Cagnazzo thou!
The troop of ten let Barbariccia lead.
With Libicocco, Draghinazzo haste,
Fang'd Ciriatta, Graffiacane fierce,
And Farfarello, and mad Rubicant.
Search ye around the bubbling tar. For these,
In safety lead them, where the other crag
Uninterrupted traverses the dens."

    I then: "O master! what a sight is there.
Ah! without escort, journey we alone,
Which, if thou know the way, I covet not.
Unless thy prudence fail thee, dost not mark
How they do gnarl upon us, and their scowl
Threatens us present tortures?" He replied:
"I charge thee, fear not: let them, as they will,
Gnarl on: 'tis but in token of their spite
Against the souls who mourn in torment steep'd."

    To leftward o'er the pier they turn'd; but each
Had first between his teeth prest close the tongue,
Toward their leader for a signal looking,
Which he with sound obscene triumphant gave.

---

[2] "Yesterday." This passage fixes the era of Dante's descent at Good Friday, in the year 1300 (thirty-four years from our blessed Lord's incarnation being added to 1266), and at the thirty-fifth year of our Poet's age. See Canto i. v.

1. The awful event alluded to, the Evangelists inform us, happened "at the ninth hour," that is, our sixth, when "the rocks were rent," and the convulsion, according to Dante, was felt even in the depths of Hell. See Canto xii. v. 38.

CANTO XXII

ARGUMENT.—Virgil and Dante proceed, accompanied by the Demons, and see other sinners of the same description in the same gulf. The device of Ciampolo, one of these, to escape from the Demons, who had laid hold on him.

IT hath been heretofore my chance to see
    Horsemen with martial order shifting camp,
    To onset sallying, or in muster ranged,
Or in retreat sometimes outstretch'd for flight:
Light-armed squadrons and fleet foragers
Scouring thy plains, Arezzo! have I seen,
And clashing tournaments, and tilting jousts,
Now with the sound of trumpets, now of bells,
Tabors,[1] or signals made from castled heights,
And with inventions multiform, our own,
Or introduced from foreign land; but ne'er
To such a strange recorder I beheld,
In evolution moving, horse nor foot,
Nor ship, that tack'd by sign from land or star.

    With the ten Demons on our way we went;
Ah, fearful company! but in the church
With saints, with gluttons at the tavern's mess.

    Still earnest on the pitch I gazed, to mark
All things whate'er the chasm contain'd, and those
Who burn'd within. As dolphins that, in sign
To mariners, heave high their arched backs,
That thence forewarn'd they may advise to save
Their threaten'd vessel; so, at intervals,
To ease the pain, his back some sinner show'd,
Then hid more nimbly than the lightning-glance.

    E'en as the frogs, that of a watery moat
Stand at the brink, with the jaws only out,
Their feet and of the trunk all else conceal'd,
Thus on each part the sinners stood; but soon
As Barbariccia was at hand, so they
Drew back under the wave. I saw, and yet

---

[1] "Tabour, a drum, a common accompaniment of war, is mentioned as one of the instruments of martial music in this battle (in Richard Cœur-de-Lion) with characteristical propriety. It was imported into the European armies from the Saracens in the holy war." Warton's Hist. of English Poetry, v. i. § 4. p. 167.

My heart doth stagger, one, that waited thus,
As it befalls that oft one frog remains,
While the next springs away: and Graffiacan,
Who of the fiends was nearest, grappling seized
His clotted locks, and dragg'd him sprawling up,
That he appear'd to me an otter. Each
Already by their names I knew, so well
When they were chosen I observed, and mark'd
How one the other call'd. "O Rubicant!
See that his hide thou with thy talons flay,"
Shouted together all the cursed crew.

Then I: "Inform thee, Master! if thou may,
What wretched soul is this, on whom their hands
His foes have laid." My leader to his side
Approach'd, and whence he came inquired; to whom
Was answer'd thus: "Born in Navarre's domain,[2]
My mother placed me in a lord's retinue;
For she had borne me to a losel vile,
A spendthrift of his substance and himself.
The good King Thibault[3] after that I served:
To peculating here my thoughts were turn'd,
Whereof I give account in this dire heat."

Straight Ciriatto, from whose mouth a tusk
Issued on either side, as from a boar,
Ripp'd him with one of these. 'Twixt evil claws
The mouse had fallen: but Barbariccia cried,
Seizing him with both arms: "Stand thou apart
While I do fix him on my prong transpierced."
Then added, turning to my guide his face,
"Inquire of him, if more thou wish to learn,
Ere he again be rent." My leader thus:
"Then tell us of the partners in thy guilt;
Knowest thou any sprung of Latin land

---

[2] His name is said to be Ciampolo.
[3] "Thibault I, King of Navarre, died on June 8, 1233, as much to be commended for the desire he showed of aiding the war in the Holy Land, as reprehensible and faulty for his design of oppressing the rights and privileges of the Church. Thibault undoubtedly merits praise, as for his other endowments, so especially for his cultivation of the liberal arts, his exercise and knowledge of music and poetry, in which he so much excelled that he was accustomed to compose verses and sing them to the viol, and to exhibit his poetical compositions publicly in his palace. that they might be criticised by all."

Under the tar?" "I parted," he replied,
"But now from one, who sojourn'd not far thence;
So were I under shelter now with him,
Nor hook nor talon then should scare me more."

   "Too long we suffer," Libicocco cried;
Then, darting forth a prong, seized on his arm,
And mangled bore away the sinewy part.
Him Draghinazzo by his thighs beneath
Would next have caught; whence angrily their chief,
Turning on all sides round, with threatening brow
Restrain'd them. When their strife a little ceased,
Of him, who yet was gazing on his wound,
My teacher thus without delay inquired:
"Who was the spirit, from whom by evil hap
Parting, as thou hast told, thou camest to shore?"

   "It was the friar Gomita," [4] he rejoin'd,
"He of Gallura, vessel of all guile,
Who had his master's enemies in hand,
And used them so that they commend him well.
Money he took, and them at large dismiss'd;
So he reports; and in each other charge
Committed to his keeping play'd the part
Of barterer to the height. With him doth herd
The chief of Logodoro, Michel Zanche.[5]
Sardinia is a theme whereof their tongue
Is never weary. Out! alas! behold
That other, how he grins. More would I say,
But tremble lest he mean to maul me sore."

   Their captain then to Farfarello turning,
Who roll'd his moony eyes in act to strike,
Rebuked him thus: "Off, cursed bird! avaunt!"

   "If ye desire to see or hear," he thus
Quaking with dread resumed, "or Tuscan spirits
Or Lombard, I will cause them to appear.
Meantime let these ill talons bate their fury,
So that no vengeance they may fear from them,

---

[4] He was intrusted by Nino de' Visconti
with the government of Gallura, one of
the four jurisdictions of Sardinia. He
took a bribe from his master's enemies
and allowed them to escape. See also
Canto xxxiii and Purgatory, Canto viii.

[5] President of Logodoro, of the four
Sardinian jurisdictions. See Canto xxxiii.
Note to v. 136.

And I, remaining in this self-same place,
Will, for myself but one, make seven appear,
When my shrill whistle shall be heard; for so
Our custom is to call each other up."
    Cagnazzo at that word deriding grinn'd,
Then wagg'd the head and spake: "Hear his device,
Mischievous as he is, to plunge him down."
    Whereto he thus, who fail'd not in rich store
Of nice-wove toils: "Mischief, forsooth, extreme!
Meant only to procure myself more woe."
    No longer Alichino then refrain'd,
But thus, the rest gainsaying, him bespake:
"If thou do cast thee down, I not on foot
Will chase thee, but above the pitch will beat
My plumes. Quit we the vantage ground, and let
The bank be as a shield; that we may see,
If singly thou prevail against us all."
    Now, reader, of new sport expect to hear.
    They each one turn'd his eyes to the other shore,
He first, who was the hardest to persuade.
The spirit of Navarre chose well his time,
Planted his feet on land, and at one leap
Escaping, disappointed their resolve.
    Them quick resentment stung, but him the most
Who was the cause of failure: in pursuit
He therefore sped, exclaiming, "Thou art caught."
    But little it avail'd; terror outstripp'd
His following flight; the other plunged beneath,
And he with upward pinion raised his breast:
E'en thus the water-fowl, when she perceives
The falcon near, dives instant down, while he
Enraged and spent retires. That mockery
In Calcabrina fury stirr'd, who flew
After him, with desire of strife inflamed;
And, for the barterer had 'scaped, so turn'd
His talons on his comrade. O'er the dyke
In grapple close they join'd; but the other proved
A goshawk able to rend well his foe;
And in the boiling lake both fell. The heat
Was umpire soon between them; but in vain

To lift themselves they strove, so fast were glued
Their pennons. Barbariccia, as the rest,
That chance lamenting, four in flight despatch'd
From the other coast, with all their weapons arm'd.
They, to their post on each side speedily
Descending, stretch'd their hooks toward the fiends,
Who flounder'd, inly burning from their scars:
And we departing left them to that broil.

CANTO XXIII

ARGUMENT.—The enraged Demons pursue Dante, but he is preserved from them
by Virgil. On reaching the sixth gulf, he beholds the punishment of the hypocrites;
which is, to pace continually round the gulf under the pressure of caps and hoods,
that are gilt on the outside, but leaden within. He is addressed by two of these,
Catalano and Loderingo, Knights of St. Mary, otherwise called Joyous Friars of
Bologna. Caïaphas is seen fixed to a cross on the ground, and lies so stretched along
the way, that all tread on him in passing.

IN silence and in solitude we went,
    One first, the other following his steps,
    As minor friars journeying on their road.
The present fray had turn'd my thoughts to muse
Upon old Æsop's fable,[1] where he told
What fate unto the mouse and frog befell;
For language hath not sounds more like in sense,
Than are these chances, if the origin
And end of each be heedfully compared.
And as one thought bursts from another forth,
So afterward from that another sprang,
Which added doubly to my former fear.
For thus I reason'd: "These through us have been
So foil'd, with loss and mockery so complete,
As needs must sting them sore. If anger then
Be to their evil will conjoin'd, more fell
They shall pursue us, than the savage hound
Snatches the leveret panting 'twixt his jaws."
    Already I perceived my hair stand all
On end with terror, and look'd eager back.

[1] "Æsop's fable." The fable of the
frog, who offered to carry the mouse
across a ditch, with the intention of
drowning him, when both were carried
off by a kite. It is not among those
Greek fables which go under the name
of Æsop.

"Teacher," I thus began, "if speedily
Thyself and me thou hide not, much I dread
Those evil talons. Even now behind
They urge us: quick imagination works
So forcibly, that I already feel them."
    He answer'd: "Were I form'd of leaded glass,
I should not sooner draw unto myself
Thy outward image, than I now imprint
That from within. This moment came thy thoughts
Presented before mine, with similar act
And countenance similar, so that from both
I one design have framed. If the right coast
Incline so much, that we may thence descend
Into the other chasm, we shall escape
Secure from this imagined pursuit."
    He had not spoke his purpose to the end,
When I from far beheld them with spread wings
Approach to take us. Suddenly my guide
Caught me, even as a mother that from sleep
Is by the noise aroused, and near her sees
The climbing fires, who snatches up her babe
And flies ne'er pausing, careful more of him
Than of herself, that but a single vest
Clings round her limbs. Down from the jutting beach
Supine he cast him to that pendent rock,
Which closes on one part the other chasm.
    Never ran water with such hurrying pace
Adown the tube to turn a land-mill's wheel,
When nearest it approaches to the spokes,
As then along that edge my master ran,
Carrying me in his bosom, as a child,
Not a companion. Scarcely had his feet
Reach'd to the lowest of the bed beneath,
When over us the steep they reach'd: but fear
In him was none; for that high Providence,
Which placed them ministers of the fifth foss,
Power of departing thence took from them all.
    There in the depth we saw a painted tribe,
Who paced with tardy steps around, and wept,
Faint in appearance and o'ercome with toil.

Caps had they on, with hoods, that fell low down
Before their eyes, in fashion like to those
Worn by the monks in Cologne.[2] Their outside
Was overlaid with gold, dazzling to view,
But leaden all within, and of such weight,
That Frederick's[3] compared to these were straw.
Oh, everlasting wearisome attire!

We yet once more with them together turn'd
To leftward, on their dismal moan intent.
But by the weight opprest, so slowly came
The fainting people, that our company
Was changed, at every movement of the step.

Whence I my guide address'd: "See that thou find
Some spirit, whose name may by his deeds be known;
And to that end look round thee as thou go'st."

Then one, who understood the Tuscan voice,
Cried after us aloud: "Hold in your feet,
Ye who so swiftly speed through the dusk air.
Perchance from me thou shalt obtain thy wish."

Whereat my leader, turning, me bespake:
"Pause, and then onward at their pace proceed."

I staid, and saw two spirits in whose look
Impatient eagerness of mind was mark'd
To overtake me; but the load they bare
And narrow path retarded their approach.

Soon as arrived, they with an eye askance
Perused me, but spake not: then turning, each
To other thus conferring said: "This one
Seems, by the action of his throat, alive;
And, be they dead, what privilege allows
They walk unmantled by the cumbrous stole?"

Then thus to me: "Tuscan, who visitest
The college of the mourning hypocrites,
Disdain not to instruct us who thou art."

"By Arno's pleasant stream," I thus replied,
"In the great city I was bred and grew,
And wear the body I have ever worn.

[2] They wore unusually large cowls.
[3] The Emperor Frederick II is said to have punished those who were guilty of high treason by wrapping them up in lead and casting them into a furnace.

But who are ye, from whom such mighty grief,
As now I witness, courseth down your cheeks?
What torment breaks forth in this bitter woe?"

"Our bonnets gleaming bright with orange hue,"
One of them answer'd, "are so leaden gross,
That with their weight they make the balances
To crack beneath them. Joyous friars[4] we were,
Bologna's natives; Catalano I,
He Loderingo named; and by thy land
Together taken, as men used to take
A single and indifferent arbiter,
To reconcile their strifes. How there we sped,
Gardingo's vicinage[5] can best declare."

"O friars!" I began, "your miseries—"
But there brake off, for one had caught mine eye,
Fix'd to a cross with three stakes on the ground:
He, when he saw me, writhed himself, throughout
Distorted, ruffling with deep sighs his beard.
And Catalano, who thereof was 'ware,
Thus spake: "That pierced spirit,[6] whom intent
Thou view'st, was he who gave the Pharisees
Counsel, that it were fitting for one man

---

[4] "Joyous friars." "Those who ruled the city of Florence on the part of the Ghibellines perceiving this discontent and murmuring, which they were fearful might produce a rebellion against themselves, in order to satisfy the people, made choice of two knights, Frati Gaudenti (joyous friars) of Bologna, on whom they conferred the chief power in Florence; one named M. Catalano de' Malavolti, the other M. Loderingo di Liandolo; one an adherent of the Guelf, the other of the Ghibelline party. It is to be remarked, that the Joyous Friars were called Knights of St. Mary, and became knights on taking that habit: their robes were white, the mantle sable, and the arms a white field and red cross with two stars: their office was to defend widows and orphans, they were to act as mediators; they had internal regulations, like other religious bodies. The above-mentioned M. Loderingo was the founder of that order. But it was not long before they too well de-served the appellation given them, and were found to be more bent on enjoying themselves than on any other object. These two friars were called in by the Florentines, and had a residence assigned them in the palace belonging to the people, over against the Abbey. Such was the dependence placed on the character of their order, it was expected they would be impartial, and would save the commonwealth any unnecessary expense; instead of which, though inclined to opposite parties, they secretly and hypocritically concurred in promoting their own advantage rather than the public good."—G. Villani, b. vii. c. xiii. This happened in 1266.

[5] The name of that part of the city which was inhabited by the powerful Ghibelline family of the Uberti, and destroyed under the partial and iniquitous administration of Catalano and Loderingo.

[6] "That pierced spirit." Caïaphas.

To suffer for the people. He doth lie
Transverse; nor any passes, but him first
Behoves make feeling trial how each weighs.
In straits like this along the foss are placed
The father of his consort,[7] and the rest
Partakers in that council, seed of ill
And sorrow to the Jews." I noted then,
How Virgil gazed with wonder upon him,
Thus abjectly extended on the cross
In banishment eternal. To the friar
He next his words address'd: "We pray ye tell,
If so be lawful, whether on our right
Lies any opening in the rock, whereby
We both may issue hence, without constraint
On the dark angels, that compell'd they come
To lead us from this depth." He thus replied:
"Nearer than thou dost hope, there is a rock
From the great circle moving, which o'ersteps
Each vale of horror, save that here his cope
Is shatter'd. By the ruin ye may mount:
For on the side it slants, and most the height
Rises below." With head bent down awhile
My leader stood; then spake: "He warn'd us ill,
Who yonder hangs the sinners on his hook."
   To whom the friar: "At Bologna erst
I many vices of the Devil heard;
Among the rest was said, 'He is a liar,
And the father of lies!' " When he had spoke,
My leader with large strides proceeded on,
Somewhat disturb'd with anger in his look.
   I therefore left the spirits heavy laden,
And, following, his beloved footsteps mark'd.

[7] Annas, father-in-law to Caïaphas.

CANTO XXIV

ARGUMENT.—Under the escort of his faithful master, Dante not without difficulty makes his way out of the sixth gulf; and in the seventh, sees the robbers tormented by venomous and pestilent serpents. The soul of Vanni Fucci, who had pillaged the sacristy of St. James in Pistoia, predicts some calamities that impended over that city, and over the Florentines.

IN the year's early nonage,[1] when the sun
  Tempers his tresses in Aquarius' urn,
  And now toward equal day the nights recede;
Whenas the rime upon the earth puts on
Her dazzling sister's image, but not long
Her milder sway endures; then riseth up
The village hind, whom fails his wintry store,
And looking out beholds the plain around
All whiten'd; whence impatiently he smites
His thighs, and to his hut returning in,
There paces to and fro, wailing his lot,
As a discomfited and helpless man;
Then comes he forth again, and feels new hope
Spring in his bosom, finding e'en thus soon
The world hath changed its countenance, grasps his crook,
And forth to pasture drives his little flock:
So me my guide dishearten'd, when I saw
His troubled forehead; and so speedily
That ill was cured; for at the fallen bridge
Arriving, toward me with a look as sweet,
He turn'd him back, as that I first beheld
At the steep mountain's foot. Regarding well
The ruin, and some counsel first maintain'd
With his own thought, he open'd wide his arm
And took me up. As one, who, while he works,
Computes his labor's issue, that he seems
Still to foresee the effect; so lifting me
Up to the summit of one peak, he fix'd
His eye upon another. "Grapple that,"
Said he, "but first make proof, if it be such
As will sustain thee." For one capt with lead

1 "At the latter part of January, when the sun enters Aquarius, and the equinox draws near, when the hoar-frosts in the morning often wear the appearance of snow, but are melted by the rising sun."

This were no journey. Scarcely he, though light,
And I, though onward push'd from crag to crag,
Could mount. And if the precinct of this coast
Were not less ample than the last, for him
I know not, but my strength had surely fail'd.
But Malebolge all toward the mouth
Inclining of the nethermost abyss,
The site of every valley hence requires,
That one side upward slope, the other fall.
     At length the point from whence the utmost stone
Juts down, we reach'd; soon as to that arrived,
So was the breath exhausted from my lungs
I could no further, but did seat me there.
     "Now needs thy best of man;" so spake my guide:
"For not on downy plumes, nor under shade
Of canopy reposing, fame is won;
Without which whosoe'r consumes his days,
Leaveth such vestige of himself on earth,
As smoke in air or foam upon the wave.
Thou therefore rise: vanquish thy weariness
By the mind's effort, in each struggle form'd
To vanquish, if she suffer not the weight
Of her corporeal frame to crush her down.
A longer ladder yet remains to scale.
From these to have escaped sufficeth not,
If well thou note me, profit by my words."
     I straightway rose, and show'd myself less spent
Than I in truth did feel me. "On," I cried,
"For I am stout and fearless." Up the rock
Our way we held, more rugged than before,
Narrower, and steeper far to climb. From talk
I ceased not, as we journey'd, so to seem
Least faint; whereat a voice from the other foss
Did issue forth, for utterance suited ill.
Though on the arch that crosses there I stood,
What were the words I knew not, but who spake
Seem'd moved in anger. Down I stoop'd to look;
But my quick eye might reach not to the depth
For shrouding darkness; wherefore thus I spake:
"To the next circle, teacher, bend thy steps,

And from the wall dismount we; for as hence
I hear and understand not, so I see
Beneath, and naught discern." "I answer not,"
Said he, "but by the deed. To fair request
Silent performance maketh best return."

We from the bridge's head descended, where
To the eighth mound it joins; and then, the chasm
Opening to view, I saw a crowd within
Of serpents terrible, so strange of shape
And hideous, that remembrance in my veins
Yet shrinks the vital current. Of her sands
Let Libya vaunt no more: if Jaculus,
Pareas and Chelyder be her brood,
Cenchris and Amphisbæna, plagues so dire
Or in such numbers swarming ne'er she show'd,
Not with all Ethiopia, and whate'er
Above the Erythræan sea is spawn'd.

Amid this dread exuberance of woe
Ran naked spirits wing'd with horrid fear,
Nor hope had they of crevice where to hide,
Or heliotrope to charm them out of view.
With serpents were their hands behind them bound,
Which through their reins infix'd the tail and head,
Twisted in folds before. And lo! on one
Near to our side, darted an adder up,
And, where the neck is on the shoulders tied,
Transpierced him. Far more quickly than e'er pen
Wrote O or I, he kindled, burn'd, and changed
To ashes all, pour'd out upon the earth.
When there dissolved he lay, the dust again
Uproll'd spontaneous, and the self-same form
Instant resumed. So mighty sages tell,
The Arabian Phœnix, when five hundred years
Have well-nigh circled, dies, and springs forthwith
Renascent: blade nor herb throughout his life
He tastes, but tears of frankincense alone
And odorous amomum: swaths of nard
And myrrh his funeral shroud. As one that falls,
He knows not how, by force demoniac dragg'd

To earth, or through obstruction fettering up
In chains invisible the powers of man,
Who, risen from his trance, gazeth around,
Bewilder'd with the monstrous agony
He hath endured, and wildly staring sighs;
So stood aghast the sinner when he rose.

Oh! how severe God's judgment, that deals out
Such blows in stormy vengeance. Who he was,
My teacher next inquired; and thus in few
He answer'd: "Vanni Fucci[2] am I call'd,
Not long since rained down from Tuscany
To this dire gullet. Me the bestial life
And not the human pleased, mule that I was,
Who in Pistoia found my worthy den."

I then to Virgil: "Bid him stir not hence;
And ask what crime did thrust him thither: once
A man I knew him, choleric and bloody."

The sinner heard and feign'd not, but toward me
His mind directing and his face, wherein
Was dismal shame depictured, thus he spake:
"It grieves me more to have been caught by thee
In this sad plight, which thou beholdest, than
When I was taken from the other life.
I have no power permitted to deny
What thou inquirest. I am doom'd thus low
To dwell, for that the sacristy by me
Was rifled of its goodly ornaments,
And with the guilt another falsely charged.
But that thou mayst not joy to see me thus,
So as thou e'er shalt 'scape this darksome realm,
Open thine ears and hear what I forebode.
Reft of the Neri first Pistoia[3] pines;
Then Florence[4] changeth citizens and laws;

[2] Said to have been an illegitimate off-spring of the family of Lazari in Pistoia, to have robbed the sacristy of the church of St. James in that city, and to have charged Vanni della Nona with the sacrilege; in consequence of which the latter suffered death.

[3] "In May, 1301, the Bianchi party of Pistoia, with the help of the Bianchi who ruled Florence, drove out the party of the Neri from the former place, destroying their houses, palaces, and farms."

[4] "Then Florence." "Soon after the Bianchi will be expelled from Florence, the Neri will prevail, and the laws and people will be changed."

From Valdimagra,[5] drawn by wrathful Mars,
A vapor rises, wrapt in turbid mists,
And sharp and eager driveth on the storm
With arrowy hurtling o'er Piceno's field,
Whence suddenly the cloud shall burst, and strike
Each helpless Bianco prostrate to the ground.
This have I told, that grief may rend thy heart."

CANTO XXV

ARGUMENT.—The sacrilegious Fucci vents his fury in blasphemy, is seized by
serpents, and flying is pursued by Cacus in the form of a Centaur, who is described
with a swarm of serpents on his haunch, and a dragon on his shoulders breathing
forth fire. Our Poet then meets with the spirits of three of his countrymen, two of
whom undergo a marvelous transformation in his presence.

WHEN he had spoke, the sinner raised his hands[1]
        Pointed in mockery and cried: "Take them,
                God!
I level them at thee." From that day forth
The serpents were my friends; for round his neck
One of them rolling twisted, as it said,
"Be silent, tongue!" Another, to his arms
Upgliding, tied them, riveting itself
So close, it took from them the power to move.
    Pistoia! ah, Pistoia! why dost doubt
To turn thee into ashes, cumbering earth
No longer, since in evil act so far
Thou hast outdone thy seed? I did not mark,
Through all the gloomy circles of the abyss,
Spirit, that swell'd so proudly 'gainst his God;

[5] Alluding to the victory obtained by
the Marquis Morello Malaspina of Valdimagra, who put himself at the head of
the Neri, and defeated their opponents the
Bianchi, in the Campo Piceno near Pistoia,
soon after the occurrence related in the
preceding note on v. 142. Currado Malaspina is introduced in the eighth Canto
of the Purgatory; where it appears, that
although on the present occasion they
espoused contrary sides, most important
favors were nevertheless conferred by that

family on our Poet, at a subsequent period
of his exile, in 1307.
[1] "The practice of thrusting out the
thumb between the first and second
fingers, to express the feelings of insult
and contempt, has prevailed very generally among the nations of Europe, and
for many ages had been denominated
'making the fig,' or described at least by
some equivalent expression."—Douce's
"Illustrations of Shakespeare," vol. i. p.
492, ed. 1807.

Not him,[2] who headlong fell from Thebes. He fled,
Nor utter'd more; and after him there came
A Centaur full of fury, shouting, "Where,
Where is the caitiff?" On Maremma's marsh[3]
Swarm not the serpent tribe, as on his haunch
They swarm'd, to where the human face begins.
Behind his head, upon the shoulders, lay
With open wings a dragon, breathing fire
On whomsoe'er he met. To me my guide:
"Cacus is this, who underneath the rock
Of Aventine spread oft a lake of blood.
He, from his brethren parted, here must tread
A different journey, for his fraudful theft
Of the great herd that near him stall'd; whence found
His felon deeds their end, beneath the mace
Of stout Alcides, that perchance laid on
A hundred blows, and not the tenth was felt."

While yet he spake, the Centaur sped away:
And under us three spirits came, of whom
Nor I nor he was ware, till they exclaim'd,
"Say who are ye!" We then brake off discourse,
Intent on these alone. I knew them not:
But, as it chanceth oft, befell that one
Had need to name another. "Where," said he,
"Doth Cianfa[4] lurk?" I, for a sign my guide
Should stand attentive, placed against my lips
The finger lifted. If, O reader! now
Thou be not apt to credit what I tell,
No marvel; for myself do scarce allow
The witness of mine eyes. But as I look'd
Toward them, lo! a serpent with six feet
Springs forth on one, and fastens full upon him:
His midmost grasp'd the belly, a forefoot
Seized on each arm (while deep in either cheek
He flesh'd his fangs); the hinder on the thighs
Were spread, 'twixt which the tail inserted curl'd
Upon the reins behind. Ivy ne'er clasp'd
A dodder'd oak, as round the other's limbs

[2] Capaneus. Canto xiv.
[3] Near the Tuscan shore.
[4] Said to have been of the family of Donati at Florence.

The hideous monster intertwined his own.
Then, as they both had been of burning wax,
Each melted into other, mingling hues,
That which was either now was seen no more.
Thus up the shrinking paper, ere it burns,
A brown tint glides, not turning yet to black,
And the clean white expires. The other two
Look'd on exclaiming, "Ah! how dost thou change,
Agnello![5] See! Thou art nor double now,
Nor only one." The two heads now became
One, and two figures blended in one form
Appear'd, where both were lost. Of the four lengths
Two arms were made: the belly and the chest,
The thighs and legs, into such members changed
As never eye hath seen. Of former shape
All trace was vanish'd. Two, yet neither, seem'd
That image miscreate, and so pass'd on
With tardy steps. As underneath the scourge
Of the fierce dog-star that lays bare the fields,
Shifting from brake to brake the lizard seems
A flash of lightning, if he thwart the road;
So toward the entrails of the other two
Approaching seem'd an adder all on fire,
As the dark pepper-grain livid and swart.
In that part, whence our life is nourish'd first,
Once he transpierced; then down before him fell
Stretch'd out. The pierced spirit look'd on him,
But spake not; yea, stood motionless and yawn'd,
As if by sleep or feverous fit assail'd.
He eyed the serpent, and the serpent him.
One from the wound, the other from the mouth
Breathed a thick smoke, whose vapory columns join'd.

Lucan in mute attention now may hear,
Nor thy disastrous fate, Sabellus, tell,
Nor thine, Nasidius. Ovid now be mute.
What if in warbling fiction he record
Cadmus and Arethusa, to a snake
Him changed, and her into a fountain clear,
I envy not; for never face to face

---

[5] "Agnello." Agnello Brunelleschi.

Two natures thus transmuted did he sing,
Wherein both shapes were ready to assume
The other's substance. They in mutual guise
So answer'd that the serpent split his train
Divided to a fork, and the pierced spirit
Drew close his steps together, legs and thighs
Compacted, that no sign of juncture soon
Was visible: the tail, disparted, took
The figure which the spirit lost; its skin
Softening, his indurated to a rind.
The shoulders next I mark'd, that entering join'd
The monster's arm-pits, whose two shorter feet
So lengthen'd, as the others dwindling shrunk.
The feet behind then twisting up became
That part that man conceals, which in the wretch
Was cleft in twain. While both the shadowy smoke
With a new color veils, and generates
The excrescent pile on one, peeling it off
From the other body, lo! upon his feet
One upright rose, and prone the other fell.
Nor yet their glaring and malignant lamps
Were shifted, though each feature changed beneath.
Of him who stood erect, the mounting face
Retreated toward the temples, and what there
Superfluous matter came, shot out in ears
From the smooth cheeks; the rest, not backward dragg'd,
Of its excess did shape the nose; and swell'd
Into due size protuberant the lips.
He, on the earth who lay, meanwhile extends
His sharpen'd visage, and draws down the ears
Into the head, as doth the slug his horns.
His tongue, continuous before and apt
For utterance, severs; and the other's fork
Closing unites. That done, the smoke was laid.
The soul, transform'd into the brute, glides off,
Hissing along the vale, and after him
The other talking sputters; but soon turn'd
His new-grown shoulders on him, and in few
Thus to another spake: "Along this path
Crawling, as I have done, speed Buoso now!"

So saw I fluctuate in successive change
The unsteady ballast of the seventh hold:
And here if aught my pen have swerved, events
So strange may be its warrant. O'er mine eyes
Confusion hung, and on my thoughts amaze.

Yet 'scaped they not so covertly, but well
I mark'd Sciancato: he alone it was
Of the three first that came, who changed not: tho'
The other's fate, Gaville! still dost rue.

CANTO XXVI

ARGUMENT.—Remounting by the steps, down which they have descended to the
seventh gulf, they go forward to the arch that stretches over the eighth, and from
thence behold numberless flames wherein are punished the evil counsellors, each flame
containing a sinner, save one, in which were Diomede and Ulysses, the latter of whom
relates the manner of his death.

FLORENCE, exult! for thou so mightily
Hast thriven, that o'er land and sea thy wings
Thou beatest, and thy name spreads over hell.
Among the plunderers, such the three I found
Thy citizens; whence shame to me thy son,
And no proud honour to thyself redounds.

But if our minds, when dreaming near the dawn,
Are of the truth presageful, thou ere long
Shalt feel what Prato[1] (not to say the rest)
Would fain might come upon thee; and that chance
Were in good time, if it befell thee now.
Would so it were, since it must needs befall!
For as time wears me, I shall grieve the more.

We from the depth departed; and my guide
Remounting scaled the flinty steps, which late
We downward traced, and drew me up the steep.
Pursuing thus our solitary way

[1] "Shalt feel what Prato." The Poet
prognosticates the calamities which were
soon to befall his native city, and which,
he says, even her nearest neighbor, Prato,
would wish her. The calamities more
particularly pointed at are said to be the
fall of a wooden bridge over the Arno,
in May, 1304, where a large multitude
were assembled to witness a representa-
tion of hell and the infernal torments, in
consequence of which accident many lives
were lost; and a conflagration, that in the
following month destroyed more than
1,700 houses. See G. Villani, Hist. lib.
viii. c. lxx. and lxxi.

Among the crags and splinters of the rock,
Sped not our feet without the help of hands.

    Then sorrow seized me, which e'en now revives,
As my thought turns again to what I saw,
And, more than I am wont, I rein and curb
The powers of nature in me, lest they run
Where Virtue guides not; that, if aught of good
My gentle star or something better gave me,
I envy not myself the precious boon.

    As in that season, when the sun least veils
His face that lightens all, what time the fly
Gives way to the shrill gnat, the peasant then,
Upon some cliff reclined, beneath him sees
Fire-flies innumerous spangling o'er the vale,
Vineyard or tilth, where his day-labor lies;
With flames so numberless throughout its space
Shone the eighth chasm, apparent, when the depth
Was to my view exposed. As he, whose wrongs
The bears avenged, as its departure saw
Elijah's chariot, when the steeds erect
Raised their steep flight for heaven; his eyes meanwhile,
Straining pursued them, till the flame alone,
Upsoaring like a misty speck, he kenn'd:
E'en thus along the gulf moves every flame,
A sinner so enfolded close in each,
That none exhibits token of the theft.

    Upon the bridge I forward bent to look
And grasp'd a flinty mass, or else had fallen,
Though push'd not from the height. The guide, who mark'd
How I did gaze attentive, thus began:
"Within these ardours are the spirits; each
Swathed in confining fire." "Master! thy word,"
I answer'd, "hath assured me; yet I deem'd
Already of the truth, already wish'd
To ask thee who is in yon fire, that comes
So parted at the summit, as it seem'd
Ascending from that funeral pile[2] where lay
The Theban brothers." He replied: "Within,

[2] The flame is said to have divided the bodies of Eteocles and Polynices, as if conscious of the enmity that actuated them while living.

Ulysses there and Diomede endure
Their penal tortures, thus to vengeance now
Together hasting, as erewhile to wrath
These in the flame with ceaseless groans deplore
The ambush of the horse,[3] that open'd wide
A portal for the goodly seed to pass,
Which sow'd imperial Rome; nor less the guile
Lament they, whence, of her Achilles 'reft,
Deïdamia yet in death complains.
And there is rued the stratagem that Troy
Of her Palladium spoil'd."—"If they have power
Of utterance from within these sparks," said I,
"O master! think my prayer a thousand-fold
In repetition urged, that thou vouchsafe
To pause till here the horned flame arrive.
See, how toward it with desires I bend."

He thus: "Thy prayer is worthy of much praise,
And I accept it therefore; but do thou
Thy tongue refrain: to question them be mine;
For I divine thy wish; and they perchance,
For they were Greeks,[4] might shun discourse with thee."

When there the flame had come, where time and place
Seem'd fitting to my guide, he thus began:
"O ye, who dwell two spirits in one fire!
If, living, I of you did merit aught,
Whate'er the measure were of that desert,
When in the world my lofty strain I pour'd,
Move ye not on, till one of you unfold
In what clime death o'ertook him self-destroy'd."

Of the old flame forthwith the greater horn
Began to roll, murmuring, as a fire
That labors with the wind, then to and fro
Wagging the top, as a tongue uttering sounds,
Threw out its voice, and spake: "When I escaped
From Circe, who beyond a circling year
Had held me near Caieta by her charms,
Ere thus Æneas yet had named the shore;
Nor fondness for my son, nor reverence

---

[3] The wooden horse that caused Æneas to quit Troy and seek his fortune in Italy, where his descendants founded Rome.
[4] Perhaps implying arrogance.

Of my old father, nor return of love,
That should have crown'd Penelope with joy,
Could overcome in me the zeal I had
To explore the world, and search the ways of life,
Man's evil and his virtue. Forth I sail'd
Into the deep illimitable main,
With but one bark, and the small faithful band
That yet cleaved to me. As Iberia far,
Far as Marocco, either shore I saw,
And the Sardinian and each isle beside
Which round that ocean bathes. Tardy with age
Were I and my companions, when we came
To the strait pass,[5] where Hercules ordain'd
The boundaries not to be o'erstepp'd by man.
The walls of Seville to my right I left,
On the other hand already Ceuta past.
'O brothers!' I began, 'who to the west
Through perils without number now have reach'd;
To this the short remaining watch, that yet
Our senses have to wake, refuse not proof
Of the unpeopled world, following the track
Of Phœbus. Call to mind from whence ye sprang:
Ye were not form'd to live the life of brutes,
But virtue to pursue and knowledge high.'
With these few words I sharpen'd for the voyage
The mind of my associates, that I then
Could scarcely have withheld them. To the dawn
Our poop we turn'd, and for the witless flight
Made our oars wings, still gaining on the left.
Each star of the other pole night now beheld,
And ours so low, that from the ocean floor
It rose not. Five times reillumed, as oft
Vanish'd the light from underneath the moon,
Since the deep way we enter'd, when from far
Appear'd a mountain dim,[6] loftiest methought

[5] The Strait of Gibraltar.
[6] The mountain of Purgatory.—Among
various opinions respecting the situation
of the terrestrial paradise, Pietro Lombardo relates, that "it was separated by
a long space, either of sea or land, from
the regions inhabited by men, and placed
in the ocean, reaching as far as to the
lunar circle, so that the waters of the
deluge did not reach it."—Sent. lib. ii.
dist. 17.

Of all I e'er beheld. Joy seized us straight;
But soon to mourning changed. From the new land
A whirlwind sprung, and at her foremost side
Did strike the vessel. Thrice it whirl'd her round
With all the waves; the fourth time lifted up
The poop, and sank the prow: so fate decreed:
And over us the booming billow closed." [7]

CANTO XXVII

ARGUMENT.—The Poet, treating of the same punishment as in the last Canto,
relates that he turned toward a flame in which was the Count Guido da Montefeltro,
whose inquiries respecting the state of Romagna he answers; and Guido is thereby
induced to declare who he is, and why condemned to that torment.

NOW upward rose the flame, and still'd its light
To speak no more, and now pass'd on with leave
From the mild poet gain'd; when following came
Another, from whose top a sound confused,
Forth issuing, drew our eyes that way to look.
    As the Sicilian bull,[1] that rightfully
His cries first echoed who had shaped its mould,
Did so rebellow, with the voice of him
Tormented, that the brazen monster seem'd
Pierced through with pain; thus, while no way they found,
Nor avenue immediate through the flame,
Into its language turn'd the dismal words:
But soon as they had won their passage forth,
Up from the point, which vibrating obey'd
Their motion at the tongue, these sounds were heard:
"O thou! to whom I now direct my voice,
That lately didst exclaim in Lombard phrase,
'Depart thou; I solicit thee no more;'
Though somewhat tardy I perchance arrive,
Let it not irk thee here to pause awhile,

---

[7] "Closed." Venturi refers to Pliny and
Solinus for the opinion that Ulysses was
the founder of Lisbon, from whence he
thinks it was easy for the fancy of a poet
to send him on yet further enterprises.
The story (which it is not unlikely that
our author borrowed from some legend
of the Middle Ages) may have taken its
rise partly from the obscure oracle returned by the ghost of Tiresias to Ulysses
(eleventh book of the Odyssey), and
partly from the fate which there was
reason to suppose had befallen some ad-
venturous explorers of the Atlantic Ocean.
[1] The engine of torture invented by
Perillus, for the tyrant Phalaris.

And with me parley: lo! it irks not me,
And yet I burn. If but e'en now thou fall
Into this blind world, from that pleasant land
Of Latium, whence I draw my sum of guilt,
Tell me if those who in Romagna dwell
Have peace or war. For of the mountains there[2]
Was I, betwixt Urbino and the height
Whence Tiber first unlocks his mighty flood."

Leaning I listen'd yet with heedful ear,
When, as he touch'd my side, the leader thus:
"Speak thou: he is a Latian." My reply
Was ready, and I spake without delay:
"O spirit! who art hidden here below,
Never was thy Romagna without war
In her proud tyrants' bosoms, nor is now:
But open war there left I none. The state,
Ravenna hath maintain'd this many a year,
Is stedfast. There Polenta's eagle[3] broods;
And in his broad circumference of plume
O'ershadows Cervia. The green talons grasp
The land,[4] that stood erewhile the proof so long
And piled in bloody heap the host of France.

"The old mastiff of Verrucchio and the young,[5]
That tore Montagna[6] in their wrath, still make,
Where they are wont, an augre of their fangs.

"Lamone's city, and Santerno's,[7] range

[2] Montefeltro.

[3] "Polenta's eagle." Guido Novello da Polenta, who bore an eagle for his coat-of-arms. The name of Polenta was derived from a castle so called in the neighborhood of Brittonoro. Cervia is a small maritime city, about fifteen miles to the south of Ravenna. Guido was the son of Ostasio da Polenta, and made himself master of Ravenna in 1265. In 1322 he was deprived of his sovereignty, and died at Bologna in 1323. This last and most munificent patron of Dante is enumerated among the poets of his time.

[4] The territory of Forli, the inhabitants of which, in 1282, were enabled, by the stratagem of Guido da Montefeltro, the governor, to defeat the French army by which it had been besieged. See G. Villani, lib. vii. c. lxxxi. The Poet informs Guido, its former ruler, that it is now in the possession of Sinibaldo Ordolaffi, whom he designates by his coat-of-arms, a lion vert.

[5] Malatesta and Malatestino his son, lords of Rimini, called from their ferocity, the mastiffs of Verrucchio, which was the name of their castle. Malatestino was, perhaps, the husband of Francesca, daughter of Guido da Polenta. See notes to Canto v. 113.

[6] Montagna de' Parcitati, a noble and leader of the Ghibelline party at Rimini, murdered by Malatestino.

[7] Lamone is the river at Faenza, and Santerno at Imola.

Under the lion of the snowy lair,[8]
Inconstant partisan, that changeth sides,
Or ever summer yields to winter's frost.
And she, whose flank is wash'd of Savio's wave,[9]
As 'twixt the level and the steep she lies,
Lives so 'twixt tyrant power and liberty.

"Now tell us, I entreat thee, who art thou:
Be not more hard than others. In the world,
So may thy name still rear its forehead high."

Then roar'd awhile the fire, its sharpen'd point
On either side waved, and thus breathed at last:
"If I did think my answer were to one
Who ever could return unto the world,
This flame should rest unshaken. But since ne'er,
If true be told me, any from this depth
Has found his upward way, I answer thee,
Nor fear lest infamy record the words.

"A man of arms[10] at first, I clothed me then
In good Saint Francis' girdle, hoping so
To have made amends. And certainly my hope
Had fail'd not, but that he, whom curses light on,
The high priest,[11] again seduced me into sin.
And how, and wherefore, listen while I tell.
Long as this spirit moved the bones and pulp
My mother gave me, less my deeds bespake
The nature of the lion than the fox.
All ways of winding subtlety I knew,
And with such art conducted, that the sound
Reach'd the world's limit. Soon as to that part
Of life I found me come, and when each behoves
To lower sails and gather in the lines;
That, which before had pleased me, then I rued,
And to repentance and confession turn'd,
Wretch that I was; and well it had bested me.

---

[8] Machinardo Pagano, whose arms were a lion azure on a field argent. See also Purgatory, Canto xiv. 122.
[9] Cesena, situated at the foot of a mountain, and washed by the river Savio, that often descends with a swollen and rapid stream from the Apennines.
[10] Guido da Montefeltro.
[11] Boniface VIII.

The chief of the new Pharisees[12] meantime,
Waging his warfare near the Lateran,
Not with the Saracens or Jews (his foes
All Christians were, nor against Acre one
Had fought,[13] nor traffick'd in the Soldan's land),
He, his great charge nor sacred ministry,
In himself reverenced, nor in me that cord
Which used to mark with leanness whom it girded.
As in Soracte, Constantine besought,
To cure his leprosy, Sylvester's aid;
So me, to cure the fever of his pride,
This man besought: my counsel to that end
He ask'd; and I was silent; for his words
Seem'd drunken: but forthwith he thus resumed:
'From thy heart banish fear: of all offence
I hitherto absolve thee. In return,
Teach me my purpose so to execute,
That Penestrino cumber earth no more.
Heaven, as thou knowest, I have power to shut
And open: and the keys are therefore twain,
The which my predecessor[14] meanly prized.'
   "Then, yielding to the forceful arguments,
Of silence, as more perilous I deem'd,
And answer'd: 'Father! since thou washest me
Clear of that guilt wherein I now must fall,
Large promise with performance scant, be sure,
Shall make thee triumph in thy lofty seat.'
   "When I was number'd with the dead, then came
Saint Francis for me; but a cherub dark
He met, who cried, 'Wrong me not; he is mine,
And must below to join the wretched crew,

---

[12] Boniface VIII, whose enmity to the family of Colonna prompted him to destroy their houses near the Lateran. Wishing to obtain possession of their other seat, Penestrino, he consulted with Guido da Montefeltro, offering him absolution for his past sins, as well as for that which he was then tempting him to commit. Guido's advice was that kind words and fair promises would put his enemies into his power; and they accordingly soon afterward fell into the snare laid for them, 1298.

[13] Alluding to the renegade Christians, by whom the Saracens, in April, 1291, were assisted to recover St. John d'Acre, the last possession of the Christians in the Holy Land.

[14] Celestine V. See notes to Canto iii.

For the deceitful counsel which he gave.
E'er since I watch'd him, hovering at his hair.
No power can the impenitent absolve;
Nor to repent, and will, at once consist,
By contradiction absolute forbid.'
Oh misery! how I shook myself, when he
Seized me, and cried, 'Thou haply thought'st me not
A disputant in logic so exact!'
To Minos down he bore me; and the judge
Twined eight times round his callous back the tail,
Which biting with excess of rage, he spake:
'This is a guilty soul, that in the fire
Must vanish.' Hence, perdition-doom'd, I rove
A prey to rankling sorrow, in this garb."
  When he had thus fulfill'd his words, the flame
In dolour parted, beating to and fro,
And writhing its sharp horn. We onward went,
I and my leader, up along the rock,
Far as another arch, that overhangs
The foss, wherein the penalty is paid
Of those who load them with committed sin.

CANTO XXVIII

ARGUMENT.—They arrive in the ninth gulf, where the sowers of scandal, schismatics, and heretics, are seen with their limbs maimed or divided in different ways. Among these the Poet finds Mohammed, Piero da Medicina, Curio, Mosca, and Bertrand de Born.

WHO, e'en in words unfetter'd, might at full
        Tell of the wounds and blood that now I saw,
        Though he repeated oft the tale? No tongue
So vast a theme could equal, speech and thought
Both impotent alike. If in one band
Collected, stood the people all, who e'er
Pour'd on Apulia's happy soil their blood,
Slain by the Trojans, and in that long war,[1]
When of the rings the measured booty made
A pile so high, as Rome's historian writes
Who errs not; with the multitude, that felt
The griding force of Guiscard's Norman steel,[2]

[1] The war of Hannibal in Italy.
[2] Robert Guiscard, conqueror of Naples, died 1110. See Paradise, Canto xviii.

And those the rest,[3] whose bones are gather'd yet
At Ceperano, there where treachery
Branded the Apulian name, or where beyond
Thy walls, O Tagliacozzo,[4] without arms
The old Alardo conquer'd; and his limbs
One were to show transpierced, another his
Clean lopt away; a spectacle like this
Were but a thing of naught, to the hideous sight
Of the ninth chasm. A rundlet, that hath lost
Its middle or side stave, gapes not so wide
As one I mark'd, torn from the chin throughout
Down to the hinder passage: 'twixt the legs
Dangling his entrails hung, the midriff lay
Open to view, and wretched ventricle,
That turns the englutted aliment to dross.

   Whilst eagerly I fix on him my gaze,
He eyed me, with his hands laid his breast bare,
And cried, "Now mark how I do rip me: lo!
How is Mohammed mangled: before me
Walks Ali[5] weeping, from the chin his face
Cleft to the forelock; and the others all,
Whom here thou seest, while they lived, did sow
Scandal and schism, and therefore thus are rent.
A fiend is here behind, who with his sword
Hacks us thus cruelly, slivering again
Each of this ream, when we have compast round
The dismal way; for first our gashes close
Ere we repass before him. But, say who
Art thou, that standest musing on the rock,
Haply so lingering to delay the pain
Sentenced upon thy crimes." "Him death not yet,"
My guide rejoin'd, "hath overta'en, nor sin
Conducts to torment; but, that he may make
Full trial of your state, I who am dead
Must through the depths of Hell, from orb to orb,
Conduct him. Trust my words; for they are true."

[3] The army of Manfredi, which, through the treachery of the Apulian troops, was overcome by Charles of Anjou in 1265. See the Purgatory, Canto iii.

[4] "O Tagliacozzo." He alludes to the victory which Charles gained over Conradino, by the sage advice of the Sieur de Valeri, in 1268.

[5] The disciple of Mohammed.

More than a hundred spirits, when that they heard,
Stood in the foss to mark me through amaze
Forgetful of their pangs. "Thou, who perchance
Shalt shortly view the sun, this warning thou
Bear to Dolcino:[6] bid him, if he wish not
Here soon to follow me, that with good store
Of food he arm him, lest imprisoning snows
Yield him a victim to Novara's power;
No easy conquest else": with foot upraised
For stepping, spake Mohammed, on the ground
Then fix'd it to depart. Another shade,
Pierced in the throat, his nostrils mutilate
E'en from beneath the eyebrows, and one ear
Lopt off, who, with the rest, through wonder stood
Gazing, before the rest advanced, and bared
His wind-pipe, that without was all o'ersmear'd
With crimson stain. "O thou!" said he, "whom sin
Condemns not, and whom erst (unless too near
Resemblance do deceive me) I aloft
Have seen on Latian ground, call thou to mind
Piero of Medicina,[7] if again
Returning, thou behold'st the pleasant land[8]
That from Vercelli slopes to Marcabò;
And there instruct the twain,[9] whom Fano boasts
Her worthiest sons, Guido and Angelo,

[6] "Dolcino." In 1305, a friar, called Dolcino, who belonged to no regular order, contrived to raise in Novara, in Lombardy, a large company of the meaner sort of people, declaring himself to be a true apostle of Christ and promulgating a community of property and of wives, with many other such heretical doctrines. He blamed the Pope, cardinals, and other prelates of the holy Church, for not observing their duty, nor leading the angelic life, and affirmed that he ought to be pope. He was followed by more than three thousand men and women, who lived promiscuously on the mountains together, like beasts, and, when they wanted provisions, supplied themselves by depredation and rapine. After two years, many were struck with compunction at the dissolute life they led, and his sect was much diminished; and, through fail-ure of food and the severity of the snows, he was taken by the people of Novara, and burnt, with Margarita, his companion, and many others, whom he had seduced.

[7] "Medicina." A place in the territory of Bologna. Piero fomented dissensions among the inhabitants of that city, and among the leaders of the neighboring states.

[8] Lombardy.

[9] "The twain." Guido del Cassero and Angiolello da Cagnano, two of the worthiest and most distinguished citizens of Fano, were invited by Malatestino da Rimini to an entertainment, on pretence that he had some important business to transact with them; and, according to instructions given by him, they were drowned in their passage near Cattolica, between Rimini and Fano.

That if 'tis given us here to scan aright
The future, they out of life's tenement
Shall be cast forth, and whelm'd under the waves
Near to Cattolica, through perfidy
Of a fell tyrant. 'Twixt the Cyprian isle
And Balearic, ne'er hath Neptune seen
An injury so foul, by pirates done,
Or Argive crew of old. That one-eyed traitor
(Whose realm there is a spirit here were fain
His eye had still lack'd sight of) them shall bring
To conference with him, then so shape his end,
That they shall need not 'gainst Focara's wind[10]
Offer up vow nor prayer." I answering thus:
"Declare, as thou dost wish that I above
May carry tidings of thee, who is he,
In whom that sight doth wake such sad remembrance."

   Forthwith he laid his hand on the cheek-bone
Of one, his fellow-spirit, and his jaws
Expanding, cried: "Lo! this is he I wot of:
He speaks not for himself: the outcast this,
Who overwhelm'd the doubt in Cæsar's mind,[11]
Affirming that delay to men prepared
Was ever harmful." Oh! how terrified
Methought was Curio, from whose throat was cut
The tongue, which spake that hardy word. Then one,
Maim'd of each hand, uplifted in the gloom
The bleeding stumps, that they with gory spots
Sullied his face, and cried: "Remember thee
Of Mosca[12] too; I who, alas! exclaim'd,

[10] "Focara's wind." Focara is a mountain, from which a wind blows that is peculiarly dangerous to the navigators of that coast.

[11] "The doubt in Cæsar's mind." Curio, whose speech (according to Lucan) determined Julius Cæsar to proceed when he had arrived at Rimini (the ancient Ariminum), and doubted whether he should prosecute the civil war.

[12] "Mosca." Buondelmonte was engaged to marry a lady of the Amidei family, but broke his promise, and united himself to one of the Donati. This was so much resented by the former, that a meeting of themselves and their kinsmen was held, to consider of the best means of revenging the insult. Mosca degli Uberti, or de' Lamberti, persuaded them to resolve on the assassination of Buondelmonte, exclaiming to them, "the thing once done, there is an end." This counsel and its effects were the source of many terrible calamities to the State of Florence. "This murder," says G. Villani, lib. v. cap. xxxviii, "was the cause and beginning of the accursed Guelf and Ghibelline parties in Florence." It happened in 1215. See the Paradise, Canto xvi. 139.

'The deed once done, there is an end,' that proved
A seed of sorrow to the Tuscan race."
   I added: "Ay, and death to thine own tribe."
   Whence, heaping woe on woe, he hurried off,
As one grief-stung to madness. But I there
Still linger'd to behold the troop, and saw
Thing, such as I may fear without more proof
To tell of, but that conscience makes me firm,
The boon companion, who her strong breastplate
Buckles on him, that feels no guilt within,
And bids him on and fear not. Without doubt
I saw, and yet it seems to pass before me,
A headless trunk, that even as the rest
Of the sad flock paced onward. By the hair
It bore the sever'd member, lantern-wise
Pendent in hand, which look'd at us, and said,
"Woe's me!" The spirit lighted thus himself;
And two there were in one, and one in two.
How that may be, he knows who ordereth so.
   When at the bridge's foot direct he stood,
His arm aloft he rear'd, thrusting the head
Full in our view, that nearer we might hear
The words, which thus it utter'd: "Now behold
This grievous torment, thou, who breathing go'st
To spy the dead: behold, if any else
Be terrible as this. And, that on earth
Thou mayst bear tidings of me, know that I
Am Bertrand,[13] he of Born, who gave King John
The counsel mischievous. Father and son
I set at mutual war. For Absalom
And David more did not Ahitophel,
Spurring them on maliciously to strife.
For parting those so closely knit, my brain
Parted, alas! I carry from its source,
That in this trunk inhabits. Thus the law
Of retribution fiercely works in me."

[13] "Bertrand." Bertrand de Born, Vicomte de Hautefort, near Perigueux in Guienne, who incited John to rebel against his father, Henry II of England. Bertrand holds a distinguished place among the Provencal poets.

CANTO XXIX

ARGUMENT.—Dante, at the desire of Virgil, proceeds onward to the bridge that crosses the tenth gulf, from whence he hears the cries of the alchemists and forgers, who are tormented therein; but not being able to discern anything on account of the darkness, they descend the rock, that bounds this, the last of the compartments in which the eighth circle is divided, and then behold the spirits who are afflicted by divers plagues and diseases. Two of them, namely, Grifolino of Arezzo, and Capocchio of Siena, are introduced speaking.

SO were mine eyes inebriate with the view
    Of the vast multitude, whom various wounds
    Disfigured, that they long'd to stay and weep.
But Virgil roused me: "What yet gazest on?
Wherefore doth fasten yet thy sight below
Among the maim'd and miserable shades?
Thou hast not shown in any chasm beside
This weakness. Know, if thou wouldst number them,
That two and twenty miles the valley winds
Its circuit, and already is the moon
Beneath our feet: the time permitted now
Is short; and more, not seen, remains to see."
    "If thou," I straight replied, "hadst weigh'd the cause,
For which I look'd, thou hadst perchance excused
The tarrying still." My leader part pursued
His way, the while I follow'd, answering him,
And adding thus: "Within that cave I deem,
Whereon so fixedly I held my ken,
There is a spirit dwells, one of my blood,
Wailing the crime that costs him now so dear."
    Then spake my master: "Let thy soul no more
Afflict itself for him. Direct elsewhere
Its thought, and leave him. At the bridge's foot
I mark'd how he did point with menacing look
At thee, and heard him by the others named
Geri of Bello.[1] Thou so wholly then
Wert busied with his spirit, who once ruled
The towers of Hautefort, that thou lookedst not
That way, ere he was gone." "O guide beloved!

[1] "Geri of Bello." A kinsman of the Poet's, who was murdered by one of the Sacchetti family. His being placed here, may be considered as a proof that Dante was more impartial in the allotment of his punishments than has generally been supposed.

His violent death yet unavenged," said I,
"By any, who are partners in his shame,
Made him contemptuous; therefore, as I think,
He pass'd me speechless by; and, doing so,
Hath made me more compassionate his fate."

So we discoursed to where the rock first show'd
The other valley, had more light been there,
E'en to the lowest depth. Soon as we came
O'er the last cloister in the dismal rounds
Of Malebolge, and the brotherhood
Were to our view exposed, then many a dart
Of sore lament assail'd me, headed all
With points of thrilling pity, that I closed
Both ears against the volley with mine hands.

As were the torment, if each lazar-house
Of Valdichiana,[2] in the sultry time
'Twixt July and September, with the isle
Sardinia and Maremma's pestilent fen,[3]
Had heap'd their maladies all in one foss
Together; such was here the torment: dire
The stench, as issuing streams from fester'd limbs.

We on the utmost shore of the long rock
Descended still to leftward. Then my sight
Was livelier to explore the depth, wherein
The minister of the most mighty Lord,
All-searching Justice, dooms to punishment
The forgers noted on her dread record.

More rueful was it not methinks to see
The nation in Ægina[4] droop, what time
Each living thing, e'en to the little worm,
All fell, so full of malice was the air
(And afterward, as bards of yore have told,
The ancient people were restored anew
From seed of emmets), than was here to see

[2] The valley through which passes the river Chiana, bounded by Arezzo, Cortona, Montepulciano, and Chiusi. In the autumn it was formerly rendered unwholesome by the stagnation of the water, but has since been drained by the Emperor Leopold II. The Chiana is mentioned as a remarkably sluggish stream, in the Paradise, Canto xiii. 21.

[3] See note to Canto xxv, v. 18.

[4] "In Ægina." He alludes to the fable of the ants changed into Myrmidons.—Ovid, Met. lib. vii.

The spirits, that languish'd through the murky vale,
Up-piled on many a stack. Confused they lay,
One o'er the belly, o'er the shoulders one
Roll'd of another; sideling crawl'd a third
Along the dismal pathway. Step by step
We journey'd on, in silence looking round,
And listening those diseased, who strove in vain
To lift their forms. Then two I mark'd, that sat
Propt 'gainst each other, as two brazen pans
Set to retain the heat. From head to foot,
A tetter bark'd them round. Nor saw I e'er
Groom currying so fast, for whom his lord
Impatient waited, or himself perchance
Tired with long watching, as of these each one
Plied quickly his keen nails, through furiousness
Of ne'er abated pruriency. The crust
Came drawn from underneath, in flakes, like scales
Scraped from the bream, or fish of broader mail.

"O thou! who with thy fingers rendest off
Thy coat of proof," thus spake my guide to one,
"And sometimes makest tearing pincers of them,
Tell me if any born of Latian land
Be among these within: so may thy nails
Serve thee for everlasting to this toil."

"Both are of Latium," weeping he replied,
"Whom tortured thus thou seest: but who art thou
That hast inquired of us?" To whom my guide:
"One that descend with this man, who yet lives,
From rock to rock, and show him Hell's abyss."

Then started they asunder, and each turn'd
Trembling toward us, with the rest, whose ear
Those words redounding struck. To me my liege
Address'd him: "Speak to them whate'er thou list."

And I therewith began: "So may no time
Filch your remembrance from the thoughts of men
In the upper world, but after many suns
Survive it, as ye tell me, who ye are,
And of what race ye come. Your punishment,
Unseemly and disgustful in its kind,
Deter you not from opening thus much to me."

"Arezzo was my dwelling," [5] answer'd one,
"And me Albero of Siena brought
To die by fire: but that, for which I died,
Leads me not here. True is, in sport I told him,
That I had learn'd to wing my flight in air;
And he, admiring much, as he was void
Of wisdom, will'd me to declare to him
The secret of mine art: and only hence,
Because I made him not a Dædalus,
Prevail'd on one supposed his sire to burn me.
But Minos to this chasm, last of the ten,
For that I practised alchemy on earth,
Has doom'd me. Him no subterfuge eludes."

Then to the bard I spake: "Was ever race
Light as Siena's?[6] Sure not France herself
Can show a tribe so frivolous and vain."

The other leprous spirit heard my words,
And thus return'd: "Be Stricca[7] from this charge
Exempted, he who knew so temperately
To lay out fortune's gifts; and Niccolo,
Who first the spice's costly luxury
Discover'd in that garden,[8] where such seed
Roots deepest in the soil; and be that troop
Exempted, with whom Caccia of Asciano
Lavish'd his vineyards and wide-spreading woods,
And his rare wisdom Abbagliato show'd
A spectacle for all. That thou mayst know
Who seconds thee against the Sienese
Thus gladly, bend this way thy sharpen'd sight,
That well my face may answer to thy ken;
So shalt thou see I am Capocchio's ghost,[9]
Who forged transmuted metals by the power

[5] Grifolino of Arezzo, who promised Albero, son of the Bishop of Siena, that he would teach him the art of flying; and, because he did not keep his promise, Albero prevailed on his father to have him burnt for a necromancer.

[6] The same imputation is again cast on the Sienese, Purgatory, Canto xiii, 141.

[7] This is said ironically. Stricca, Niccolo Salimbeni, Caccia of Asciano, and Abbagliato, or Meo de' Folcacchieri, belonged to a company of prodigal and luxurious youth in Siena, called the "brigata godereccia." Niccolo was the inventor of a new manner of using cloves in cookery, and which was termed the "costuma ricca."

[8] "In that garden." Siena.

[9] Capocchio of Siena who is said to have been a fellow-student of Dante's, in natural philosophy.

Of alchemy; and if I scan thee right,
Thou needs must well remember how I aped
Creative nature by my subtle art."

CANTO XXX

ARGUMENT.—In the same gulf, other kinds of impostors, as those who have counterfeited the persons of others, or debased the current coin, or deceived by speech under
false pretences, are described as suffering various diseases. Sinon of Troy and Adamo
of Brescia mutually reproach each other with their several impostures.

WHAT time resentment burn'd in Juno's breast
From Semele against the Theban blood,
As more than once in dire mischance was rued;
Such fatal frenzy seized on Athamas,
That he his spouse beholding with a babe
Laden on either arm, "Spread out," he cried,
"The meshes, that I take the lioness
And the young lions at the pass:" then forth
Stretch'd he his merciless talons, grasping one,
One helpless innocent, Learchus named,
Whom swinging down he dash'd upon a rock;
And with her other burden, self-destroy'd,
The hapless mother plunged. And when the pride
Of all presuming Troy fell from its height,
By fortune overwhelm'd, and the old king
With his realm perish'd; then did Hecuba,
A wretch forlorn and captive, when she saw
Polyxena first slaughter'd, and her son,
Her Polydorus, on the wild sea-beach
Next met the mourner's view, then reft of sense
Did she run barking even as a dog;
Such mighty power had grief to wrench her soul.
But ne'er the Furies, or of Thebes, or Troy,
With such fell cruelty were seen, their goads
Infixing in the limbs of man or beast,
As now two pale and naked ghosts I saw,
That gnarling wildly scamper'd, like the swine
Excluded from his stye. One reach'd Capocchio,
And in the neck-joint sticking deep his fangs,

Dragg'd him, that, o'er the solid pavement rubb'd
His belly stretch'd out prone. The other shape,
He of Arezzo, there left trembling, spake:
"That sprite of air is Schicchi;[1] in like mood
Of random mischief vents he still his spite."
　　To whom I answering: "Oh! as thou dost hope
The other may not flesh its jaws on thee,
Be patient to inform us, who it is,
Ere it speed hence."—"That is the ancient soul
Of wretched Myrrha," he replied, "who burn'd
With most unholy flame for her own sire,
And a false shape assuming, so perform'd
The deed of sin; e'en as the other there,
That onward passes, dared to counterfeit
Donati's features, to feign'd testament
The seal affixing, that himself might gain,
For his own share, the lady of the herd."
　　When vanish'd the two furious shades, on whom
Mine eye was held, I turn'd it back to view
The other cursed spirits. One I saw
In fashion like a lute, had but the groin
Been sever'd where it meets the forked part.
Swoln dropsy, disproportioning the limbs
With ill-converted moisture, that the paunch
Suits not the visage, open'd wide his lips,
Gasping as in the hectic man for drought,
One toward the chin, the other upward curl'd.
　　"O ye! who in this world of misery,
Wherefore I know not, are exempt from pain,"
Thus he began, "attentively regard
Adamo's woe.[2] When living, full supply
Ne'er lack'd me of what most I coveted;
One drop of water now, alas! I crave.
The rills, that glitter down the grassy slopes

[1] Gianni Schicchi, of the family of Cavalcanti, possessed such a faculty of molding his features to the resemblance of others, that he was employed by Simon Donati to personate Buoso Donati, then recently deceased, and to make a will, leaving Simon his heir; for which service he was remunerated with a mare of ex-traordinary value, here called "the lady of the herd."

[2] Adamo of Brescia, at the instigation of Guido, Alessandro, and their brother Aghiunlfo, lords of Romena, counterfeited the coin of Florence; for which crime he was burnt.

Of Casentino,[3] making fresh and soft
The banks whereby they glide to Arno's stream,
Stand ever in my view; and not in vain;
For more the pictured semblance dries me up,
Much more than the disease, which makes the flesh
Desert these shrivel'd cheeks. So from the place,
Where I transgress'd, stern justice urging me,
Takes means to quicken more my laboring sighs.
There is Romena, where I falsified
The metal with the Baptist's form imprest,
For which on earth I left my body burnt.
But if I here might see the sorrowing soul
Of Guido, Alessandro, or their brother,
For Branda's limpid spring[4] I would not change
The welcome sight. One is e'en now within,
If truly the mad spirits tell, that round
Are wandering. But wherein besteads me that?
My limbs are fetter'd. Were I but so light,
That I each hundred years might move one inch,
I had set forth already on this path,
Seeking him out amidst the shapeless crew,
Although eleven miles it wind, not less
Than half of one across. They brought me down
Among this tribe; induced by them, I stamp'd
The florens with three carats of alloy." [5]

    "Who are that abject pair," I next inquired,
"That closely bounding thee upon thy right
Lie smoking, like a hand in winter steep'd
In the chill stream?"—"When to this gulf I dropp'd,"
He answer'd, "here I found them; since that hour
They have not turn'd, nor ever shall, I ween,
Till time hath run his course. One is that dame,
The false accuser[6] of the Hebrew youth;
Sinon the other, that false Greek from Troy.
Sharp fever drains the reeky moistness out,
In such a cloud upsteam'd." When that he heard,

---

[3] Romena, a part of Casentino.
[4] A fountain at Siena.
[5] The floren was a coin that ought to
have had twenty-four carats of pure gold.
Villani relates that it was first used at
Florence in 1252, an era of great prosperity for the republic; before which time
their most valuable coinage was of silver.
[6] Potiphar's wife.

One, gall'd perchance to be so darkly named,
With clench'd hand smote him on the braced paunch,
That like a drum resounded: but forthwith
Adamo smote him on the face, the blow
Returning with his arm, that seem'd as hard.

   "Though my o'erweighty limbs have ta'en from me
The power to move," said he, "I have an arm
At liberty for such employ." To whom
Was answer'd: "When thou wentest to the fire,
Thou hadst it not so ready at command;
Then readier when it coin'd the impostor gold."

   And thus the dropsied: "Ay, now speak'st thou true:
But there thou gavest not such true testimony,
When thou wast question'd of the truth, at Troy."

   "If I spake false, thou falsely stamp'dst the coin,"
Said Sinon; "I am here for but one fault,
And thou for more than any imp beside."

   "Remember," he replied, "O perjured one!
The horse remember, that did teem with death;
And all the world be witness to thy guilt."

   "To thine," return'd the Greek, "witness the thirst
Whence thy tongue cracks, witness the fluid mound
Rear'd by thy belly up before thine eyes,
A mass corrupt." To whom the coiner thus:
"Thy mouth gapes wide as ever to let pass
Its evil saying. Me if thirst assails,
Yet I am stuft with moisture. Thou art parch'd:
Pains rack thy head: no urging wouldst thou need
To make thee lap Narcissus' mirror up."

   I was all fix'd to listen, when my guide
Admonish'd: "Now beware. A little more,
And I do quarrel with thee." I perceived
How angrily he spake, and toward him turn'd
With shame so poignant, as remember'd yet
Confounds me. As a man that dreams of harm
Befallen him, dreaming wishes it a dream,
And that which is, desires as if it were not;
Such then was I, who, wanting power to speak,
Wish'd to excuse myself, and all the while
Excused me, though unweeting that I did.

"More grievous fault than thine has been, less shame,"
My master cried, "might expiate. Therefore cast
All sorrow from thy soul; and if again
Chance bring thee, where like conference is held,
Think I am ever at thy side. To hear
Such wrangling is a joy for vulgar minds."

CANTO XXXI

ARGUMENT.—The Poets, following the sound of a loud horn, are led by it to the
ninth circle, in which there are four rounds, one enclosed within the other, and
containing as many sorts of traitors; but the present Canto shows only that the circle
is encompassed with Giants, one of whom. Antæus, takes them both in his arms and
places them at the bottom of the circle.

THE very tongue, whose keen reproof before
    Had wounded me, that either cheek was stain'd,
    Now minister'd my cure. So have I heard,
Achilles' and his father's javelin caused
Pain first, and then the boon of health restored.
    Turning our back upon the vale of woe,
We cross'd the encircled mound in silence. There
Was less than day and less than night, that far
Mine eye advanced not: but I heard a horn
Sounded so loud, the peal it rang had made
The thunder feeble. Following its course
The adverse way, my strained eyes were bent
On that one spot. So terrible a blast
Orlando[1] blew not, when that dismal rout
O'erthrew the host of Charlemain, and quench'd
His saintly warfare. Thitherward not long
My head was raised, when many a lofty tower
Methought I spied. "Master," said I, "what land
Is this?" He answer'd straight: "Too long a space
Of intervening darkness has thine eye
To traverse: thou hast therefore widely err'd
In thy imagining. Thither arrived

[1] "When Charlemain with all his peer-
    age fell at Fontarabia."
Milton, Paradise Lost, b. i. 586. See
Warton's Hist. of Eng. Poetry, vol. i. sect.
iii. p. 132. "This is the horn which
Orlando won from the giant Jatmund,
and which, as Turpin and the Islandic
bards report, was endued with magical
power, and might be heard at the distance of twenty miles." See the Paradise,
Canto xviii.

Thou well shalt see, how distance can delude
The sense. A little therefore urge thee on."
 Then tenderly he caught me by the hand;
"Yet know," said he, "ere farther we advance,
That it less strange may seem, these are not towers,
But giants. In the pit they stand immersed,
Each from his navel downward, round the bank."
 As when a fog disperseth gradually,
Our vision traces what the mist involves
Condensed in air; so piercing through the gross
And gloomy atmosphere, as more and more
We near'd toward the brink, mine error fled
And fear came o'er me. As with circling round
Of turrets, Montereggion[2] crowns his walls;
E'en thus the shore, encompassing the abyss,
Was turreted with giants, half their length
Uprearing, horrible, whom Jove from Heaven
Yet threatens, when his muttering thunder rolls.
 Of one already I descried the face,
Shoulders and breast, and of the belly huge
Great part, and both arms down along his ribs.
 All-teeming Nature, when her plastic hand
Left framing of these monsters, did display
Past doubt her wisdom, taking from mad War
Such slaves to do his bidding; and if she
Repent her not of the elephant and whale,
Who ponders well confesses her therein
Wiser and more discreet; for when brute force
And evil will are back'd with subtlety,
Resistance none avails. His visage seem'd
In length and bulk, as doth the pine[3] that tops
Saint Peter's Roman fane; and the other bones
Of like proportion, so that from above
The bank, which girdled him below, such height
Arose his stature, that three Friezelanders

[2] A castle near Siena.
[3] "The pine." "The large pine of bronze, which once ornamented the top of the mole of Adrian, afterwards decorated the top of the belfry of St. Peter; and having (according to Buti) been thrown down by lightning, it was transferred to the place where it now is, in the Pope's garden, by the side of the great corridor of Belvedere. In the time of our Poet, the pine was then either on the belfry or on the steps of St. Peter's."

Had striven in vain to reach but to his hair.
Full thirty ample palms was he exposed
Downward from whence a man his garment loops.
"Raphel[4] baï ameth, sabì almì:"
So shouted his fierce lips, which sweeter hymns
Became not; and my guide address'd him thus:
"O senseless spirit! let thy horn for thee
Interpret: therewith vent thy rage, if rage
Or other passion wring thee. Search thy neck,
There shalt thou find the belt that binds it on.
Spirit confused! lo, on thy mighty breast
Where hangs the baldrick!" Then to me he spake:
"He doth accuse himself. Nimrod is this,
Through whose ill counsel in the world no more
One tongue prevails. But pass we on, nor waste
Our words; for so each language is to him,
As his to others, understood by none."

 Then to the leftward turning sped we forth,
And at a sling's throw found another shade
Far fiercer and more huge. I cannot say
What master hand had girt him; but he held
Behind the right arm fetter'd, and before,
The other, with a chain, that fasten'd him
From the neck down; and five times round his form
Apparent met the wreathed links. "This proud one
Would of his strength against almighty Jove
Make trial," said my guide: "whence he is thus
Requited: Ephialtes him they call.
Great was his prowess, when the giants brought
Fear on the gods: those arms, which then he plied,
Now moves he never." Forthwith I return'd:
"Fain would I, if 't were possible, mine eyes,
Of Briareus immeasurable, gain'd
Experience next." He answered: "Thou shalt see
Not far from hence Antæus, who both speaks
And is unfetter'd, who shall place us there
Where guilt is at its depth. Far onward stands
Whom thou wouldst fain behold, in chains, and made

---

[4] Unmeaning sounds, meant, it is supposed, to express the confusion at the building
of Babel.

Like to this spirit, save that in his looks
More fell he seems." By violent earthquake rock'd
Ne'er shook a tower, so reeling to its base,
As Ephialtes. More than ever then
I dreaded death; nor than the terror more
Had needed, if I had not seen the cords
That held him fast. We, straightway journeying on,
Came to Antæus, who, five ells complete
Without the head, forth issued from the cave.

"O thou, who in the fortunate vale,[5] that made
Great Scipio heir of glory, when his sword
Drove back the troop of Hannibal in flight,
Who thence of old didst carry for thy spoil
An hundred lions; and if thou hadst fought
In the high conflict on thy brethren's side,
Seems as men yet believed, that through thine arm
The sons of earth had conquer'd; now vouchsafe
To place us down beneath, where numbing cold
Locks up Cocytus. Force not that we crave
Or Tityus' help or Typhon's. Here is one
Can give what in this realm ye covet. Stoop
Therefore, nor scornfully distort thy lip.
He in the upper world can yet bestow
Renown on thee; for he doth live, and looks
For life yet longer, if before the time
Grace call him not unto herself." Thus spake
The teacher. He in haste forth stretch'd his hands,
And caught my guide. Alcides[6] whilom felt
That grapple, straiten'd sore. Soon as my guide
Had felt it, he bespake me thus: "This way,
That I may clasp thee;" then so caught me up,
That we were both one burden. As appears
The tower of Carisenda,[7] from beneath
Where it doth lean, if chance a passing cloud
So sail across, that opposite it hangs;
Such then Antæus seem'd, as at mine ease
I mark'd him stooping. I were fain at times

[5] The country near Carthage.
[6] The combat between Hercules (Alcides) and Antæus is adduced by the poet in his treatise "De Monarchiâ," lib. ii., as proof of God's judgment displayed in the duel, according to the singular superstition of those times.
[7] The leaning tower at Bologna.

To have past another way. Yet in the abyss,
That Lucifer with Judas low ingulfs,
Lightly he placed us; nor, there leaning, stay'd;
But rose, as in a bark the stately mast.

CANTO XXXII

ARGUMENT.—This Canto treats of the first, and, in part, of the second of those
rounds, into which the ninth and last, or frozen circle, is divided. In the former,
called Caïna, Dante finds Camiccione de' Pazzi, who gives him an account of other
sinners who are there punished; and in the next, named Antenora, he hears in like
manner from Bocca degli Abbati who his fellow-sufferers are.

COULD I command rough rhymes and hoarse, to
                suit
              That hole of sorrow o'er which every rock
His firm abutment rears, then might the vein
Of fancy rise full springing: but not mine
Such measures, and with faltering awe I touch
The mighty theme; for to describe the depth
Of all the universe, is no emprise
To jest with, and demands a tongue not used
To infant babbling. But let them assist
My song, the tuneful maidens, by whose aid
Amphion wall'd in Thebes; so with the truth
My speech shall best accord. Oh ill-starr'd folk,
Beyond all others wretched! who abide
In such a mansion, as scarce thought finds words
To speak of, better had ye here on earth
Been flocks, or mountain goats. As down we stood
In the dark pit beneath the giants' feet,
But lower far than they, and I did gaze
Still on the lofty battlement, a voice
Bespake me thus: "Look how thou walkest. Take
Good heed, thy soles do tread not on the heads
Of thy poor brethren." Thereupon I turn'd,
And saw before and underneath my feet
A lake, whose frozen surface liker seem'd
To glass than water. Not so thick a veil
In winter e'er hath Austrian Danube spread
O'er his still course, nor Tanais far remote
Under the chilling sky. Roll'd o'er that mass

Had Tabernich or Pietrapana[1] fallen,
Not e'en its rim had creak'd. As peeps the frog
Croaking above the wave, what time in dreams
The village gleaner oft pursues her toil,
So, to where modest shame appears, thus low
Blue pinch'd and shrined in ice the spirits stood,
Moving their teeth in shrill note like the stork.
His face each downward held; their mouth the cold,
Their eyes express'd the dolour of their heart.

A space I look'd around, then at my feet
Saw two so strictly join'd, that of their head
The very hairs were mingled. "Tell me ye,
Whose bosoms thus together press," said I,
"Who are ye?" At that sound their necks they bent;
And when their looks were lifted up to me,
Straightway their eyes, before all moist within,
Distill'd upon their lips, and the frost bound
The tears betwixt those orbs, and held them there.
Plank unto plank hath never cramp closed up
So stoutly. Whence, like two enraged goats,
They clash'd together: them such fury seized.

And one, from whom the cold both ears had reft,
Exclaim'd, still looking downward: "Why on us
Dost speculate so long? If thou wouldst know
Who are these two,[2] the valley, whence his wave
Bisenzio slopes, did for its master own
Their sire Alberto, and next him themselves.
They from one body issued: and throughout
Caïna thou mayst search, nor find a shade
More worthy in congealment to be fix'd;
Not him,[3] whose breast and shadow Arthur's hand
At that one blow dissever'd; not Focaccia,[4]

---

[1] "Tabernich or Pietrapana." The one a mountain in Sclavonia, the other in that tract of country called the Garfagnana, not far from Lucca.

[2] Alessandro and Napoleone, sons of Alberto Alberti, who murdered each other. They were proprietors of the valley of Falterona, where the Bisenzio rises, falling into the Arno six miles from Florence.

[3] Mordred, son of King Arthur. In the romance of Lancelot of the Lake, Arthur, having discovered the traitorous intentions of his son, pierces him through with his lance, so that the sunbeam passes through the body.

[4] Focaccia of Cancellieri (the Pistoian family), whose atrocious act of revenge against his uncle is said to have given rise to the parties, Bianchi and Neri, in the year 1300.

No, not this spirit, whose o'erjutting head
Obstructs my onward view; he bore the name
Of Mascheroni:[5] Tuscan if thou be,
Well knowest who he was. And to cut short
All further question, in my form behold
What once was Camiccione.[6] I await
Carlino[7] here my kinsman, whose deep guilt
Shall wash out mine." A thousand visages
Then mark'd I, which the keen and eager cold
Had shaped into a doggish grin; whence creeps
A shivering horror o'er me, at the thought
Of those frore shallows. While we journey'd on
Toward the middle, at whose point unites
All heavy substance, and I trembling went
Through that eternal chilness, I know not
If will it were, or destiny, or chance,
But, passing 'midst the heads, my foot did strike
With violent blow against the face of one.

    "Wherefore dost bruise me?" weeping he exclaim'd;
"Unless thy errand be some fresh revenge
For Montaperto,[8] wherefore troublest me?"

    I thus: "Instructor, now await me here,
That I through him may rid me of my doubt:
Thenceforth what haste thou wilt." The teacher paused
And to that shade I spake, who bitterly
Still cursed me in his wrath. "What art thou, speak,
That railest thus on others?" He replied:
"Now who art thou, that smiting others' cheeks,
Through Antenora[9] roamest, with such force
As were past sufferance, wert thou living still?"

    "And I am living, to thy joy perchance,"
Was my reply, "if fame be dear to thee,

[5] Sassol Mascheroni, a Florentine, who murdered his uncle.

[6] Camiccione de' Pazzi of Valdarno, by whom his kinsman Ubertino was treacherously put to death.

[7] "Carlino." One of the same family. He betrayed the Castel di Piano Travigne, in Valdarno, to the Florentines, after the refugees of the Bianca and Ghibelline party had defended it against a siege for twenty-nine days, in the summer of 1302.

[8] The defeat of the Guelfi at Montaperto through the treachery of Bocca degli Abbati, who, during the engagement, cut off the hand of Giacopo del Vacca de' Pazzi, the Florentine standard-bearer.

[9] "So called from Antenor, who, according to Dictys Cretensis (de Bello Troj. lib. v.) and Dares Phrygius (De Excidio Trojæ) betrayed Troy his country." Lombardi.

That with the rest I may thy name enrol."

"The contrary of what I covet most,"
Said he, "thou tender'st: hence! nor vex me more.
Ill knowest thou to flatter in this vale."

Then seizing on his hinder scalp I cried:
"Name thee, or not a hair shall tarry here."

"Rend all away," he answer'd, "yet for that
I will not tell, nor show thee, who I am,
Though at my head thou pluck a thousand times."

Now I had grasp'd his tresses, and stript off
More than one tuft, he barking, with his eyes
Drawn in and downward, when another cried,
"What ails thee, Bocca?   Sound not loud enough
Thy chattering teeth, but thou must bark outright?
What devil wrings thee?"—"Now," said I, "be dumb,
Accursed traitor!   To thy shame, of thee
True tidings will I bear."—"Off!" he replied;
"Tell what thou list: but, as thou 'scape from hence,
To speak of him whose tongue hath been so glib,
Forget not: here he wails the Frenchman's gold.
'Him of Duera,'[10] thou canst say, 'I mark'd,
Where the starved sinners pine.'   If thou be ask'd
What other shade was with them, at thy side
Is Beccaria,[11] whose red gorge distain'd
The biting axe of Florence.   Further on,
If I misdeem not, Soldanieri[12] bides,
With Ganellon,[13] and Tribaldello,[14] him
Who oped Faenza when the people slept."

We now had left him, passing on our way,
When I beheld two spirits by the ice
Pent in one hollow, that the head of one

[10] Buoso of Cremona, of the family of Duera, bribed by Guy de Montfort to leave a pass between Piedmont and Parma, with the defence of which he had been intrusted by the Ghibellines, open to the army of Charles of Anjou, A. D. 1265, at which the people of Cremona were so enraged that they extirpated the whole family. G. Villani.

[11] Abbot of Vallombrosa, Pope's legate at Florence, beheaded for his intrigues with the Ghibellines.

[12] "Gianni Soldanieri," says Villani, Hist. lib. vii. c. xiv., "put himself at the head of the people, in the hopes of rising into power, not aware that the result would be mischief to the Ghibelline party, and his own ruin."—A. D. 1266.

[13] The betrayer of Charlemain, mentioned by Archbishop Turpin. He is a type of treachery with the poets of the Middle Ages.

[14] Tribaldello de' Manfredi, bribed to betray the city of Faenza, 1282.

Was cowl unto the other; and as bread
Is raven'd up through hunger, the uppermost
Did so apply his fangs to the other's brain,
Where the spine joins it. Not more furiously
On Menalippus' temples Tydeus gnaw'd,
Than on that skull and on its garbage he.

    "O thou! who show'st so beastly sign of hate
'Gainst him thou prey'st on, let me hear," said I,
"The cause, on such condition, that if right
Warrant thy grievance, knowing who ye are,
And what the color of his sinning was,
I may repay thee in the world above,
If that, wherewith I speak, be moist so long."

CANTO XXXIII

ARGUMENT.—The Poet is told by Count Ugolino de' Gherardeschi of the cruel
manner in which he and his children were famished in the tower at Pisa, by command
of the Archbishop Ruggieri. He next discourses of the third round, called Ptolomea,
wherein those are punished who have betrayed others under the semblance of kindness;
and among these he finds the Friar Alberigo de' Manfredi, who tells him of one
whose soul was already tormented in that place, though his body appeared still to
be alive upon the earth, being yielded up to the governance of a fiend.

HIS jaws uplifting from their fell repast,
    That sinner wiped them on the hairs o' the head,
    Which he behind had mangled, then began:
"Thy will obeying, I call up afresh
Sorrow past cure; which, but to think of, wrings
My heart, or ere I tell on 't. But if words,
That I may utter, shall prove seed to bear
Fruit of eternal infamy to him,
The traitor whom I gnaw at, thou at once
Shalt see me speak and weep. Who thou mayst be
I know not, nor how here below art come:
But Florentine thou seemest of a truth,
When I do hear thee. Know, I was on earth
Count Ugolino,[1] and the Archbishop he

[1] "Count Ugolino." — "In the year
1288, in the month of July, Pisa was
much divided by competitors for the
sovereignty; one party, composed of certain of the Guelfi, being headed by the
Judge Nino di Gallura de' Visconti; another, consisting of others of the same
faction, by the Count Ugolino de' Gherardeschi; and a third by the Archbishop
Ruggieri degli Ubaldini, with the Lan-

Ruggieri. Why I neighbor him so close,
Now list. That through effect of his ill thoughts
In him my trust reposing, I was ta'en
And after murder'd, need is not I tell.
What therefore thou canst not have heard, that is,
How cruel was the murder, shalt thou hear,
And know if he have wrong'd me. A small grate
Within that mew, which for my sake the name
Of Famine bears, where others yet must pine,
Already through its opening several moons
Had shown me, when I slept the evil sleep
That from the future tore the curtain off.
This one, methought, as master of the sport,
Rode forth to chase the gaunt wolf, and his
          whelps,
Unto the mountain[2] which forbids the sight
Of Lucca to the Pisan. With lean brachs
Inquisitive and keen, before him ranged

franchi, Sismondi, Gualandi, and other Ghibelline houses. The Count Ugolino, to effect his purpose, united with the archbishop and his party, and having betrayed Nino, his sister's son, they contrived that he and his followers should either be driven out of Pisa, or their persons seized. Nino hearing this, and not seeing any means of defending himself, retired to Calci, his castle, and formed an alliance with the Florentines and the people of Lucca, against the Pisans. The count, before Nino was gone, in order to cover his treachery, when everything was settled for his expulsion, quitted Pisa, and repaired to a manor of his called Settimo; whence, as soon as he was informed of Nino's departure, he returned to Pisa with great rejoicing and festivity, and was elevated to the supreme power with every demonstration of triumph and honor. But his greatness was not of long continuance. It pleased the Almighty that a total reverse of fortune should ensue, as a punishment for his acts of treachery and guilt; for he was said to have poisoned the Count Anselmo da Capraia, his sister's son, on account of the envy and fear excited in his mind by the high esteem in which the gracious manners of Anselmo were held by the Pisans. The power of the Guelfi being so much diminished, the archbishop devised means to betray the Count Ugolino, and caused him to be suddenly attacked in his palace by the fury of the people, whom he had exasperated, by telling them that Ugolino had betrayed Pisa, and given up their castles to the citizens of Florence and of Lucca. He was immediately compelled to surrender; his bastard son and his grandson fell in the assault; and two of his sons, with their two sons also, were conveyed to prison. . . . In the following March, the Pisans, who had imprisoned the Count Ugolino, with two of his sons and two of his grandchildren, the offspring of his son the Count Guelfo, in a tower on the Piazza of the Anziani, caused the tower to be locked, the key thrown into the Arno, and all food to be withheld from them. In a few days they died of hunger; but the Count first with loud cries declared his penitence, and yet neither priest nor friar was allowed to shrive him. All the five, when dead, were dragged out of the prison, and meanly interred; and from thenceforward the tower was called the Tower of Famine, and so shall ever be." G. Villani, lib. vii.

[2] The mountain S. Giuliano between Pisa and Lucca.

Lanfranchi with Sismondi and Gualandi.
After short course the father and the sons
Seem'd tired and lagging, and methought I saw
The sharp tusks gore their sides. When I awoke,
Before the dawn, amid their sleep I heard
My sons (for they were with me) weep and ask
For bread. Right cruel art thou, if no pang
Thou feel at thinking what my heart foretold;
And if not now, why use thy tears to flow?
Now had they waken'd; and the hour drew near
When they were wont to bring us food; the mind
Of each misgave him through his dream, and I
Heard, at its outlet underneath, lock'd up
The horrible tower: whence, uttering not a word,
I look'd upon the visage of my sons.
I wept not: so all stone I felt within.
They wept: and one, my little Anselm, cried,
'Thou lookest so! Father, what ails thee?' Yet
I shed no tear, nor answer'd all that day
Nor the next night, until another sun
Came out upon the world. When a faint beam
Had to our doleful prison made its way,
And in four countenances I descried
The image of my own, on either hand
Through agony I bit; and they, who thought
I did it through desire of feeding, rose
O' the sudden, and cried, 'Father, we should grieve
Far less if thou wouldst eat of us: thou gavest
These weeds of miserable flesh we wear;
And do thou strip them off from us again.'
Then, not to make them sadder, I kept down
My spirit in stillness. That day and the next
We all were silent. Ah, obdurate earth!
Why open'dst not upon us? When we came
To the fourth day, then Gaddo at my feet
Outstretch'd did fling him, crying, 'Hast no help
For me, my father!' There he died; and e'en
Plainly as thou seest me, saw I the three
Fall one by one 'twixt the fifth day and sixth:
Whence I betook me, now grown blind, to grope
Over them all, and for three days aloud

Call'd on them who were dead. Then, fasting got
The mastery of grief." Thus having spoke,
Once more upon the wretched skull his teeth
He fasten'd like a mastiff's 'gainst the bone,
Firm and unyielding. O thou Pisa! shame
Of all the people, who their dwelling make
In that fair region, where the Italian voice
Is heard; since that thy neighbors are so slack
To punish, from their deep foundations rise
Capraia and Gorgona,[3] and dam up
The mouth of Arno; that each soul in thee
May perish in the waters. What if fame
Reported that thy castles were betray'd
By Ugolino, yet no right hadst thou
To stretch his children on the rack. For them,
Brigata, Uguccione, and the pair
Of gentle ones, of whom my song hath told,
Their tender years, thou modern Thebes, did make
Uncapable of guilt. Onward we pass'd,
Where others, skarf'd in rugged folds of ice,
Not on their feet were turn'd, but each reversed.

There, very weeping suffers not to weep;
For, at their eyes, grief, seeking passage, finds
Impediment, and rolling inward turns
For increase of sharp anguish: the first tears
Hang cluster'd, and like crystal vizors show,
Under the socket brimming all the cup.

Now though the cold had from my face dislodged
Each feeling, as 't were callous, yet me seem'd
Some breath of wind I felt. "Whence cometh this,"
Said I, "my Master? Is not here below
All vapor quench'd?"—"Thou shalt be speedily,"
He answer'd, "where thine eyes shall tell thee whence,
The cause descrying of this airy shower."

Then cried out one, in the chill crust who mourn'd:
"O souls! so cruel, that the farthest post
Hath been assign'd you, from this face remove
The harden'd veil; that I may vent the grief
Impregnate at my heart, some little space,

[3] Small islands near the mouth of the Arno.

Ere it congeal again." I thus replied:
"Say who thou wast, if thou wouldst have mine
      aid;
And if I extricate thee not, far down
As to the lowest ice may I descend."
   "The friar Alberigo," [4] answer'd he,
"Am I, who from the evil garden pluck'd
Its fruitage, and am here repaid, the date
More luscious for my fig."—"Hah!" I exclaim'd,
"Art thou, too, dead?" "How in the world aloft
It fareth with my body," answer'd he,
"I am right ignorant. Such privilege
Hath Ptolomea,[5] that oft-times the soul
Drops hither, ere by Atropos divorced.
And that thou mayst wipe out more willingly
The glazed tear-drops that o'erlay mine eyes,
Know that the soul, that moment she betrays,
As I did, yields her body to a fiend
Who after moves and governs it at will,
Till all its time be rounded: headlong she
Falls to this cistern. And perchance above
Doth yet appear the body of a ghost,
Who here behind me winters. Him thou know'st,
If thou but newly art arrived below.
The years are many that have passed away,
Since to this fastness Branca Doria[6] came."
   "Now," answer'd I, "methinks thou mockest me;
For Branca Doria never yet hath died,
But doth all natural functions of a man,
Eats, drinks, and sleeps, and putteth raiment on."

---

[4] "The friar Alberigo." Alberigo de'
Manfredi, of Faenza, one of the Frati
Godenti (Joyous Friars), who having
quarrelled with some of his brotherhood,
under pretence of wishing to be recon-
ciled, invited them to a banquet, at the
conclusion of which he called for the
fruit, a signal for the assassins to rush in
and despatch those whom he had marked
for destruction. Hence, adds Landino, it
is said proverbially of one who has been
stabbed, that he had had some of the
friar Alberigo's fruit.

[5] "Ptolomea." This circle is named
Ptolomea from Ptolemy the son of Abu-
bus, by whom Simon and his sons were
murdered, at a great banquet he had
made for them. See I Maccabees, ch.
xvi. Or from Ptolemy, King of Egypt,
the betrayer of Pompey the Great.
[6] "Branca Doria." The family of Doria
was possessed of great influence in Genoa.
Branca is said to have murdered his
father-in-law, Michel Zanche. See Canto
xxii.

He thus: "Not yet unto that upper foss
By th' evil talons guarded, where the pitch
Tenacious boils, had Michel Zanche reach'd,
When this one left a demon in his stead
In his own body, and of one his kin,
Who with him treachery wrought. But now put forth
Thy hand, and ope mine eyes." I oped them not.
Ill manners were best courtesy to him.

Ah Genoese! men perverse in every way
With every foulness stain'd why from the earth
Are ye not cancel'd? Such an one of yours
I with Romagna's darkest spirit[7] found,
As, for his doings, even now in soul
Is in Cocytus plunged, and yet doth seem
In body still alive upon the earth.

CANTO XXXIV

ARGUMENT.—In the fourth and last round of the ninth circle, those who have
betrayed their benefactors are wholly covered with ice. And in the midst is Lucifer,
at whose back Dante and Virgil ascend, till by a secret path they reach the surface of
the other hemisphere of the earth, and once more obtain sight of the stars.

"THE banners of Hell's Monarch do come forth
Toward us; therefore look," so spake my guide,
"If thou discern him." As, when breathes a cloud
Heavy and dense, or when the shades of night
Fall on our hemisphere, seems view'd from far
A windmill, which the blast stirs briskly round;
Such was the fabric then methought I saw.

To shield me from the wind, forthwith I drew
Behind my guide: no covert else was there.

Now came I (and with fear I bid my strain
Record the marvel) where the souls were all
Whelm'd underneath, transparent, as through glass
Pellucid the frail stem. Some prone were laid;
Others stood upright, this upon the soles,
That on his head, a third with face to feet
Arch'd like a bow. When to the point we came,
Whereat my guide was pleased that I should see

[7] The friar Alberigo.

The creature eminent in beauty once,
He from before me stepp'd and made me pause.
    "Lo!" he exclaim'd, "lo! Dis; and lo! the place,
Where thou hast need to arm thy heart with strength."
    How frozen and how faint I then became,
Ask me not, reader! for I write it not;
Since words would fail to tell thee of my state.
I was not dead nor living. Think thyself,
If quick conception work in thee at all,
How I did feel. That emperor, who sways
The realm of sorrow, at mid breast from the ice
Stood forth; and I in stature am more like
A giant, than the giants are his arms.
Mark now how great that whole must be, which suits
With such a part. If he were beautiful
As he is hideous now, and yet did dare
To scowl upon his Maker, well from him
May all our misery flow. Oh what a sight!
How passing strange it seem'd, when I did spy
Upon his head three faces: one in front
Of hue vermilion, the other two with this
Midway each shoulder join'd and at the crest;
The right 'twixt wan and yellow seem'd; the left
To look on, such as come from whence old Nile
Stoops to the lowlands. Under each shot forth
Two mighty wings, enormous as became
A bird so vast. Sails never such I saw
Outstretch'd on the wide sea. No plumes had they,
But were in texture like a bat; and these
He flapp'd i' th' air, that from him issued still
Three winds, wherewith Cocytus to its depth
Was frozen. At six eyes he wept: the tears
Adown three chins distill'd with bloody foam.
At every mouth his teeth a sinner champ'd,
Bruised as with ponderous engine; so that three
Were in this guise tormented. But far more
Than from that gnawing, was the foremost pang'd
By the fierce rending, whence oft-times the back
Was stript of all its skin. "That upper spirit,
Who hath worst punishment," so spake my guide,

"Is Judas, he that hath his head within
And plies the feet without. Of th' other two,
Whose heads are under, from the murky jaw
Who hangs, is Brutus:[1] lo! how he doth writhe
And speaks not. The other, Cassius, that appears
So large of limb. But night now reascends;
And it is time for parting. All is seen."

I clipp'd him round the neck; for so he bade:
And noting time and place, he, when the wings
Enough were oped, caught fast the shaggy sides,
And down from pile to pile descending stepp'd
Between the thick fell and the jagged ice.

Soon as he reach'd the point, whereat the thigh
Upon the swelling of the haunches turns,
My leader there, with pain and struggling hard,
Turn'd round his head where his feet stood before,
And grappled at the fell as one who mounts;
That into Hell methought we turn'd again.

"Expect that by such stairs as these," thus spake
The teacher, panting like a man forespent,
"We must depart from evil so extreme:"
Then at a rocky opening issued forth,
And placed me on the brink to sit, next join'd
With wary step my side. I raised mine eyes,
Believing that I Lucifer should see
Where he was lately left, but saw him now
With legs held upward. Let the grosser sort,
Who see not what the point was I had past,
Bethink them if sore toil oppress'd me then.

"Arise," my master cried, "upon thy feet.
The way is long, and much uncouth the road;
And now within one hour and a half of noon[2]
The sun returns." It was no palace-hall

---

[1] "Brutus." Landino struggles to extricate Brutus from the unworthy lot which
is here assigned him. He maintains that
by Brutus and Cassius are not meant the
individuals known by those names, but
any who put a lawful monarch to death.
Yet if Cæsar was such, the conspirators
might be regarded as deserving of their
doom. If Dante, however, believed Brutus to have been actuated by evil motives
in putting Cæsar to death, the excellence
of the patriot's character in other respects
would only have aggravated his guilt in
that particular.

[2] The Poet uses the Hebrew manner of
computing the day, according to which
the third hour answers to our twelve
o'clock at noon.

Lofty and luminous wherein we stood,
But natural dungeon where ill-footing was
And scant supply of light. "Ere from the abyss
I separate," thus when risen I began:
"My guide! vouchsafe few words to set me free
From error's thraldom. Where is now the ice?
How standeth he in posture thus reversed?
And how from eve to morn in space so brief
Hath the sun made his transit?" He in few
Thus answering spake: "Thou deemest thou art still
On the other side the centre, where I grasp'd
The abhorred worm that boreth through the world.
Thou wast on the other side, so long as I
Descended; when I turn'd, thou didst o'erpass
That point, to which from every part is dragg'd
All heavy substance. Thou art now arrived
Under the hemisphere opposed to that,
Which the great continent doth overspread,
And underneath whose canopy expired
The Man, that was born sinless and so lived.
Thy feet are planted on the smallest sphere,
Whose other aspect is Judecca. Morn
Here rises, when there evening sets: and he,
Whose shaggy pile we scaled, yet standeth fix'd,
As at the first. On this part he fell down
From Heaven; and th' earth here prominent before,
Through fear of him did veil her with the sea,
And to our hemisphere retired. Perchance,
To shun him, was the vacant space left here,
By what of firm land on this side appears,[3]
That sprang aloof." There is a place beneath,
From Belzebub as distant, as extends
The vaulted tomb;[4] discover'd not by sight,
But by the sound of brooklet, that descends
This way along the hollow of a rock,
Which, as it winds with no precipitous course,
The wave hath eaten. By that hidden way
My guide and I did enter, to return

[3] The mountain of Purgatory.
[4] "The vaulted tomb" ("La tomba"). This word is used to express the whole depth of the infernal region.

To the fair world: and heedless of repose
We climb'd, he first, I following his steps,
Till on our view the beautiful lights of Heaven
Dawn'd through a circular opening in the cave:
Thence issuing we again beheld the stars.

PURGATORY

CANTO I

ARGUMENT.—The Poet describes the delight he experienced at issuing a little before dawn from the infernal regions, into the pure air that surrounds the isle of Purgatory; and then relates how, turning to the right, he beheld four stars never seen before, but by our first parents, and met on his left the shade of Cato of Utica, who, having warned him and Virgil what is needful to be done before they proceed on their way through Purgatory, disappears; and the two poets go toward the shore, where Virgil cleanses Dante's face with the dew, and girds him with a reed, as Cato had commanded.

O'ER better waves to speed her rapid course
    The light bark of my genius lifts the sail,
    Well pleased to leave so cruel sea behind;
And of that second region will I sing,
In which the human spirit from sinful blot
Is purged, and for ascent to Heaven prepares.
    Here, O ye hallow'd Nine! for in your train
I follow, here the deaden'd strain revive;
Nor let Calliope refuse to sound
A somewhat higher song, of that loud tone
Which when the wretched birds of chattering note[1]
Had heard, they of forgiveness lost all hope.
    Sweet hue of eastern sapphire, that was spread
O'er the serene aspect of the pure air,
High up as the first circle,[2] to mine eyes
Unwonted joy renew'd, soon as I 'scaped
Forth from the atmosphere of deadly gloom,
That had mine eyes and bosom fill'd with grief.
    The radiant planet,[3] that to love invites,
Made all the orient laugh, and veil'd beneath
The Pisces' light,[4] that in his [her] escort came.

[1] "Birds of chattering note." For the fable of the daughters of Pierus who challenged the muses to sing, and were by them changed into magpies, see Ovid, Met. lib. v. fab. 5.

[2] "The first circle." Either, as some suppose, the moon; or, as Lombardi (who likes to be as far off the rest of the commentators as possible) will have it, the highest circle of the stars.

[3] "Planet." Venus.

[4] The constellation of the Fish veiled by the more luminous body of Venus, then a morning star.

To the right hand I turn'd, and fix'd my mind
On the other pole attentive, where I saw
Four stars[5] ne'er seen before save by the ken
Of our first parents.[6] Heaven of their rays
Seem'd joyous. O thou northern site! bereft
Indeed, and widow'd, since of these deprived.

As from this view I had desisted, straight
Turning a little toward the other pole,
There from whence now the wain[7] had disappear'd,
I saw an old man[8] standing by my side
Alone, so worthy of reverence in his look,
That ne'er from son to father more was owed.
Low down his beard, and mix'd with hoary white,
Descended, like his locks, which, parting, fell
Upon his breast in double fold. The beams
Of those four luminaries on his face
So brightly shone, and with such radiance clear
Deck'd it, that I beheld him as the sun.

"Say who are ye, that stemming the blind stream,
Forth from the eternal prison-house have fled?"
He spoke and moved those venerable plumes.
"Who hath conducted, or with lantern sure
Lights you emerging from the depth of night,
That makes the infernal valley ever black?
Are the firm statutes of the dread abyss
Broken, or in high Heaven new laws ordain'd,
That thus, condemn'd, ye to my caves approach?"

My guide, then laying hold on me, by words
And intimations given with hand and head,
Made my bent knees and eye submissive pay
Due reverence; then thus to him replied:

"Not of myself I come; a Dame from heaven[9]
Descending, him besought me in my charge
To bring. But since thy will implies, that more
Our true condition I unfold at large,
Mine is not to deny thee thy request.

---

[5] Symbolical of the four cardinal virtues, Prudence, Justice, Fortitude, and Temperance.
[6] "Our first parents." In the terrestrial paradise, placed on the summit of Purgatory.
[7] Charles's Wain, or Boötes.
[8] "An old man." Cato.
[9] Beatrice. See Hell, ii. 54.

This mortal ne'er hath seen the farthest gloom;
But erring by his folly had approach'd
So near, that little space was left to turn.
Then, as before I told, I was despatch'd
To work his rescue; and no way remain'd
Save this which I have ta'en. I have display'd
Before him all the regions of the bad;
And purpose now those spirits to display,
That under thy command are purged from sin.
How I have brought him would be long to say.
From high descends the virtue, by whose aid
I to thy sight and hearing him have led.
Now may our coming please thee. In the search
Of liberty he journeys: that how dear,
They know who for her sake have life refused.
Thou knowest, to whom death for her was sweet
In Utica, where thou didst leave those weeds,
That in the last great day will shine so bright.
For us the eternal edicts are unmoved;
He breathes, and I of Minos am not bound,
Abiding in that circle, where the eyes
Of thy chaste Marcia beam, who still in look
Prays thee, O hallow'd spirit! to own her thine.
Then by her love we implore thee, let us pass
Through thy seven regions;[10] for which, best thanks
I for thy favour will to her return,
If mention there below thou not disdain."

    "Marcia so pleasing in my sight was found,"
He then to him rejoin'd, "while I was there,
That all she ask'd me I was fain to grant.
Now that beyond the accursed stream she dwells,
She may no longer move me, by that law,[11]
Which was ordain'd me, when I issued thence.
Not so, if Dame from Heaven, as thou sayst,
Moves and directs thee; then no flattery needs.
Enough for me that in her name thou ask.

[10] "Through thy seven regions." The seven rounds of Purgatory, in which the seven capital sins are punished.

[11] "By that law." When he was delivered by Christ from Limbo, a change of affections accompanied his change of place.

Go therefore now: and with a slender reed[12]
See that thou duly gird him, and his face
Lave, till all sordid stain thou wipe from thence.
For not with eye, by any cloud obscured,
Would it be seemly before him to come,
Who stands the foremost minister in Heaven.
This islet all around, there far beneath,
Where the wave beats it, on the oozy bed
Produces store of reeds. No other plant,
Cover'd with leaves, or harden'd in its stalk,
There lives, not bending to the water's sway.
After, this way return not; but the sun
Will show you, that now rises, where to take
The mountain in its easiest ascent."

He disappear'd; and I myself upraised
Speechless, and to my guide retiring close,
Toward him turn'd mine eyes. He thus began:
"My son! observant thou my steps pursue.
We must retreat to rereward; for that way
The champain to its low extreme declines."

The dawn had chased the matin hour of prime,
Which fled before it, so that from afar
I spied the trembling of the ocean stream.

We traversed the deserted plain, as one
Who, wander'd from his track, thinks every step
Trodden in vain till he regain the path.

When we had come, where yet the tender dew
Strove with the sun, and in a place where fresh
The wind breathed o'er it, while it slowly dried;
Both hands extended on the watery grass
My master placed, in graceful act and kind.
Whence I of his intent before apprised,
Stretch'd out to him my cheeks suffused with tears.
There to my visage he anew restored
That hue which the dun shades of Hell conceal'd.

Then on the solitary shore arrived,
That never sailing on its waters saw
Man that could after measure back his course,
He girt me in such manner as had pleased

[12] A type of simplicity and patience.

Him who instructed; and, oh strange to tell!
As he selected every humble plant,
Wherever one was pluck'd another there
Resembling, straightway in its place arose.

CANTO II

ARGUMENT.—They behold a vessel under conduct of an angel, coming over the waves with spirits to Purgatory, among whom, when the passengers have landed, Dante recognizes his friend Casella; but, while they are entertained by him with a song, they hear Cato exclaiming against their negligent loitering, and at that rebuke hasten forward to the mountain.

NOW had the sun[1] to that horizon reach'd,
That covers, with the most exalted point
Of its meridian circle, Salem's walls;
And night, that opposite to him her orb
Rounds, from the stream of Ganges issued forth,
Holding the scales,[2] that from her hands are dropt
When she reigns highest:[3] so that where I was,
Aurora's white and vermeil-tinctured cheek
To orange turn'd as she in age increased.
    Meanwhile we linger'd by the water's brink,
Like men, who, musing on their road, in thought
Journey, while motionless the body rests.
When lo! as, near upon the hour of dawn,
Through the thick vapors Mars with fiery beam
Glares down in west, over the ocean floor;
So seem'd, what once again I hope to view,
A light, so swiftly coming through the sea,
No winged course might equal its career.
From which when for a space I had withdrawn
Mine eyes, to make inquiry of my guide,
Again I look'd, and saw it grown in size
And brightness: then on either side appear'd
Something, but what I knew not, of bright hue,

[1] "Now had the sun." Dante was now antipodal to Jerusalem; so that while the sun was setting with respect to that place, which he supposes to be the middle of the inhabited earth, to him it was rising.

[2] The constellation Libra.

[3] "When she reigns highest" is (according to Venturi, whom I have followed) "when the autumnal equinox is passed." Lombardi supposes it to mean "when the nights begin to increase, that is, after the summer solstice."

And by degrees from underneath it came
Another. My preceptor silent yet
Stood, while the brightness, that we first discern'd,
Open'd the form of wings: then when he knew
The pilot, cried aloud, "Down, down; bend low
Thy knees; behold God's angel: fold thy hands:
Now shalt thou see true ministers indeed.
Lo! how all human means he sets at naught;
So that nor oar he needs, nor other sail
Except his wings, between such distant shores.
Lo! how straight up to Heaven he holds them rear'd,
Winnowing the air with those eternal plumes,
That not like mortal hairs fall off or change."

As more and more toward us came, more bright
Appear'd the bird of God, nor could the eye
Endure his splendor near: I mine bent down.
He drove ashore in a small bark so swift
And light, that in its course no wave it drank.
The heavenly steersman at the prow was seen,
Visibly written Blessed in his looks.
Within a hundred spirits and more there sat.
   "In Exitu[4] Israel de Egypto,"
All with one voice together sang, with what
In the remainder of that hymn is writ.
Then soon as with the sign of holy cross
He bless'd them, they at once leap'd out on land:
He, swiftly as he came, return'd. The crew,
There left, appear'd astounded with the place,
Gazing around, as one who sees new sights.

From every side the sun darted his beams,
And with his arrowy radiance from mid heaven
Had chased the Capricorn, when that strange tribe,
Lifting their eyes toward us: "If ye know,
Declare what path will lead us to the mount."

Them Virgil answer'd: "Ye suppose, perchance,
Us well acquainted with this place: but here,
We, as yourselves, are strangers. Not long erst
We came, before you but a little space,
By other road so rough and hard, that now

4 "In Exitu." "When Israel came out of Egypt." Ps. cxiv.

The ascent will seem to us as play." The spirits,
Who from my breathing had perceived I lived,
Grew pale with wonder. As the multitude
Flock round a herald sent with olive branch,
To hear what news he brings, and in their haste
Tread one another down; e'en so at sight
Of me those happy spirits were fix'd, each one
Forgetful of its errand to depart
Where, cleansed from sin, it might be made all fair.
    Then one I saw darting before the rest
With such fond ardour to embrace me, I
To do the like was moved. O shadows vain!
Except in outward semblance: thrice my hands
I clasp'd behind it, they as oft return'd
Empty into my breast again. Surprise
I need must think was painted in my looks,
For that the shadow smiled and backward drew.
To follow it I hasten'd, but with voice
Of sweetness it enjoin'd me to desist.
Then who it was I knew, and pray'd of it,
To talk with me it would a little pause.
It answer'd: "Thee as in my mortal frame
I loved, so loosed from it I love thee still,
And therefore pause: but why walkest thou here?"
    "Not without purpose once more to return,
Thou find'st me, my Casella,[5] where I am,
Journeying this way;" I said: "but how of thee
Hath so much time been lost?" He answer'd straight:
    "No outrage hath been done to me, if he,[6]
Who when and whom he chooses takes, hath oft
Denied me passage here; since of just will
His will he makes. These three months past[7] indeed,
He, who so chose to enter, with free leave

[5] "My Casella." A Florentine, celebrated for his skill in music, "in whose
company, says Landino, "Dante often re-
created his spirits, wearied by severer
studies." See Dr. Burney's History of
Music, vol. ii. cap. iv., p. 322. See also
Milton's sonnet to Henry Lawes:
"Dante shall give fame leave to set thee
    higher

Than his Casella, whom he wooed to
    sing,
Met in the milder shades of Purgatory."
[6] "He." The conducting angel.
[7] "These three months past." Since the
time of the Jubilee, during which all
spirits not condemned to eternal punishment were supposed to pass over to
Purgatory as soon as they pleased.

Hath taken; whence I wandering by the shore[8]
Where Tiber's wave grows salt, of him gain'd kind
Admittance, at that river's mouth, toward which
His wings are pointed; for there always throng
All such as not to Acheron descend."
    Then I: "If new law taketh not from thee
Memory or custom of love-tuned song,
That whilom all my cares had power to 'swage;
Please thee therewith a little to console
My spirit, that encumber'd with its frame,
Travelling so far, of pain is overcome."
    "Love, that discourses in my thoughts," he then
Began in such soft accents, that within
The sweetness thrills me yet. My gentle guide,
And all who came with him, so well were pleased,
That seem'd naught else might in their thoughts have
        room.
    Fast fix'd in mute attention to his notes
We stood, when lo! that old man venerable
Exclaiming, "How is this, ye tardy spirits?
What negligence detains you loitering here?
Run to the mountain to cast off those scales,
That from your eyes the sight of God conceal."
    As a wild flock of pigeons, to their food
Collected, blade or tares, without their pride
Accustom'd, and in still and quiet sort,
If aught alarm them, suddenly desert
Their meal, assail'd by more important care;
So I that new-come troop beheld, the song
Deserting, hasten to the mountain's side,
As one who goes, yet, where he tends, knows not.
    Nor with less hurried step did we depart.

8 "The shore." Ostia.

CANTO III

ARGUMENT.—Our Poet, perceiving no shadow except that cast by his own body, is fearful that Virgil has deserted him; but he is freed from that error, and both arrive together at the foot of the mountain; on finding it too steep to climb, they inquire the way from a troop of spirits that are coming toward them, and are by them shown which is the easiest ascent. Manfredi, King of Naples, who is one of these spirits, bids Dante inform his daughter Costanza, Queen of Arragon, of the manner in which he had died.

THEM sudden flight had scatter'd o'er the plain,
  Turn'd toward the mountain, whither reason's
    voice
Drives us: I, to my faithful company
Adhering, left it not. For how, of him
Deprived, might I have sped? or who, beside,
Would o'er the mountainous tract have led my steps?
He, with the bitter pang of self-remorse,
Seem'd smitten. O clear conscience, and upright!
How doth a little failing wound thee sore.
  Soon as his feet desisted (slackening pace)
From haste, that mars all decency of act,
My mind, that in itself before was wrapt,
Its thought expanded, as with joy restored;
And full against the steep ascent I set
My face, where highest to Heaven its top o'erflows.
  The sun, that flared behind, with ruddy beam
Before my form was broken; for in me
His rays resistance met. I turn'd aside
With fear of being left, when I beheld
Only before myself the ground obscured.
When thus my solace, turning him around,
Bespake me kindly: "Why distrustest thou?
Believest not I am with thee, thy sure guide?
It now is evening there, where buried lies
The body in which I cast a shade, removed
To Naples[1] from Brundusium's wall. Nor thou
Marvel, if before me no shadow fall,
More than that in the skyey element
One ray obstructs not other. To endure
Torments of heat and cold extreme, like frames

---

[1] "To Naples." Virgil died at Brundusium, from whence his body is said to have been removed to Naples.

That virtue hath disposed, which, how it works,
Wills not to us should be reveal'd. Insane,
Who hopes our reason may that space explore,
Which holds three persons in one substance knit.
Seek not the wherefore, race of human kind;
  Could ye have seen the whole, no need had been
For Mary to bring forth. Moreover, ye
Have seen such men desiring fruitlessly;
To whose desires, repose would have been given,
That now but serve them for eternal grief.
I speak of Plato, and the Stagirite,
And others many more." And then he bent
Downward his forehead, and in troubled mood
Broke off his speech. Meanwhile we had arrived
Far as the mountain's foot, and there the rock
Found of so steep ascent, that nimblest steps
To climb it had been vain. The most remote,
Most wild, untrodden path, in all the tract
'Twixt Lerice and Turbia,[2] were to this
A ladder easy and open of access.
  "Who knows on which hand now the steep declines?"
My master said, and paused; "so that he may
Ascend, who journeys without aid of wing?"
And while, with looks directed to the ground,
The meaning of the pathway he explored,
And I gazed upward round the stony height;
On the left hand appear'd to us a troop
Of spirits, that toward us moved their steps;
Yet moving seem'd not, they so slow approach'd.
  I thus my guide address'd: "Upraise thine eyes:
Lo! that way some, of whom thou mayst obtain
Counsel, if of thyself thou find'st it not."
  Straightway he look'd, and with free speech replied:
"Let us tend thither: they but softly come.
And thou be firm in hope, my son beloved."
  Now was that crowd from us distant as far,
(When we some thousand steps, I say, had past,)
As at a throw the nervous arm could fling;

_____

[2] "Twixt Lerice and Turbia." At that time the two extremities of the Genoese republic; the former on the east, the latter on the west.

When all drew backward on the massy crags
Of the steep bank, and firmly stood unmoved,
As one, who walks in doubt, might stand to look.
   "O spirits perfect! O already chosen!"
Virgil to them began: "by that blest peace,
Which, as I deem, is for you all prepared,
Instruct us where the mountain low declines,
So that attempt to mount it be not vain.
For who knows most, him loss of time most grieves."
   As sheep, that step from forth their fold, by one,
Or pairs, or three at once; meanwhile the rest
Stand fearfully, bending the eye and nose
To ground, and what the foremost does, that do
The others, gathering round her if she stops,
Simple and quiet, nor the cause discern;
So saw I moving to advance the first,
Who of that fortunate crew were at the head,
Of modest mien, and graceful in their gait.
When they before me had beheld the light
From my right side fall broken on the ground,
So that the shadow reach'd the cave; they stopp'd,
And somewhat back retired: the same did all
Who follow'd, though unweeting of the cause.
   "Unask'd of you, yet freely I confess,
This is a human body which ye see.
That the sun's light is broken on the ground,
Marvel not: but believe, that not without
Virtue derived from Heaven, we to climb
Over this wall aspire." So them bespake
My master; and that virtuous tribe rejoin'd:
"Turn, and before you there the entrance lies;"
Making a signal to us with bent hands.
   Then of them one began. "Whoe'er thou art,
Who journey'st thus this way, thy visage turn;
Think if me elsewhere thou hast ever seen."
   I toward him turn'd, and with fix'd eye beheld.
Comely and fair, and gentle of aspect
He seem'd, but on one brow a gash was mark'd.
   When humbly I disclaim'd to have beheld
Him ever: "Now behold!" he said, and show'd

High on his breast a wound: then smiling spake.
  "I am Manfredi,[3] grandson to the Queen
Costanza:[4] whence I pray thee, when return'd,
To my fair daughter[5] go, the parent glad
Of Aragonia and Sicilia's pride;
And of the truth inform her, if of me
Aught else be told. When by two mortal blows
My frame was shatter'd, I betook myself
Weeping to Him, who of free will forgives.
My sins were horrible: but so wide arms
Hath goodness infinite, that it receives
All who turn to it. Had this text divine
Been of Cosenza's shepherd better scann'd,
Who then by Clement[6] on my hunt was set,
Yet at the bridge's head my bones had lain,
Near Benevento, by the heavy mole
Protected; but the rain now drenches them,
And the wind drives, out of the kingdom's bounds,
Far as the stream of Verde,[7] where, with lights
Extinguish'd, he removed them from their bed.
Yet by their curse we are not so destroy'd,
But that the eternal love may turn, while hope
Retains her verdant blossom. True it is,
That such one as in contumacy dies

---

[3] "Manfredi." King of Naples and Sicily, and the natural son of Frederick II. He was lively and agreeable in his manners, delighted in poetry, music, and dancing. But he was luxurious and ambitious, void of religion, and in his philosophy an Epicurean. He fell in the battle with Charles of Anjou in 1265, alluded to in Canto xxviii of Hell, ver. 13, or rather in that of Benevento. The successes of Charles were so rapidly followed up, that our author, exact as he generally is, might not have thought it necessary to distinguish them in point of time. "Dying excommunicated, King Charles did not allow of his being buried in sacred ground, but he was interred near the bridge of Benevento; and on his grave there was cast a stone by every one of the army, whence there was formed a great mound of stones. But some have

said, that afterward, by command of the Pope, the Bishop of Cosenza took up his body and sent it out of the kingdom, because it was the land of the Church; and that it was buried by the river Verde, on the borders of the kingdom and of Campagna."

[4] See Paradise, Canto iii. 121.

[5] Costanza, the daughter of Manfredi, and wife of Peter III, King of Arragon, by whom she was mother to Frederick, King of Sicily, and James, King of Arragon. With the latter of these she was at Rome, 1296.

[6] "Clement." Pope Clement IV.

[7] "The stream of Verde." A river near Ascoli, that falls into the Tronto. The "extinguished lights" formed part of the ceremony at the interment of one excommunicated.

Against the holy Church, though he repent,
Must wander thirty-fold for all the time
In his presumption past: if such decree
Be not by prayers of good men shorter made.
Look therefore if thou canst advance my bliss;
Revealing to my good Costanza, how
Thou hast beheld me, and beside, the terms
Laid on me of that interdict; for here
By means of those below much profit comes."

CANTO IV

ARGUMENT.—Dante and Virgil ascend the mountain of Purgatory, by a steep and narrow path pent in on each side by rock, till they reach a part of it that opens into a ledge or cornice. There seating themselves, and turning to the east, Dante wonders at seeing the sun on their left, the cause of which is explained to him by Virgil; and while they continue their discourse, a voice addresses them, at which they turn, and find several spirits behind the rock, and among the rest one named Belacqua, who had been known to our Poet on earth, and who tells that he is doomed to linger there on account of his having delayed his repentance to the last.

WHEN by sensations of delight or pain,
    That any of our faculties hath seized,
    Entire the soul collects herself, it seems
She is intent upon that power alone;
And thus the error is disproved, which holds
The soul not singly lighted in the breast.
And therefore whenas aught is heard or seen,
That firmly keeps the soul toward it turn'd,
Time passes, and a man perceives it not.
For that, whereby we hearken, is one power;
Another that, which the whole spirit hath:
This is as it were bound, while that is free.
    This found I true by proof, hearing that spirit
And wondering; for full fifty steps[1] aloft
The sun had measured, unobserved of me,
When we arrived where all with one accord
The spirits shouted, "Here is what ye ask."
    A larger aperture oft-times is stopt,
With forked stake of thorn by villager,
When the ripe grape imbrowns, than was the path,

[1] Three hours twenty minutes; fifteen degrees being reckoned to an hour.

By which my guide, and I behind him close,
Ascended solitary, when that troop
Departing left us. On Sanleo's[2] road
Who journeys, or to Noli[3] low descends,
Or mounts Bismantua's[4] height, must use his feet;
But here a man had need to fly, I mean
With the swift wing and plumes of high desire,
Conducted by his aid, who gave me hope,
And with light furnish'd to direct my way.

We through the broken rock ascended, close
Pent on each side, while underneath the ground
Ask'd help of hands and feet. When we arrived
Near on the highest ridge of the steep bank,
Where the plain level open'd, I exclaim'd,
"O Master! say, which way can we proceed."

He answer'd, "Let no step of thine recede.
Behind me gain the mountain, till to us
Some practised guide appear." That eminence
Was lofty, that no eye might reach its point;
And the side proudly rising, more than line
From the mid quadrant to the centre drawn.
I, wearied, thus began: "Parent beloved!
Turn and behold how I remain alone,
If thou stay not."—"My son!" he straight replied,
"Thus far put forth thy strength;" and to a track
Pointed, that, on this side projecting, round
Circles the hill. His words so spurr'd me on,
That I, behind him, clambering, forced myself,
Till my feet press'd the circuit plain beneath.
There both together seated, turn'd we round
To eastward, whence was our ascent: and oft
Many beside have with delight look'd back.

First on the nether shores I turn'd mine eyes,
Then raised them to the sun, and wondering mark'd
That from the left it smote us. Soon perceived
That poet sage, how at the car of light

---

[2] "Sanleo." A fortress on the summit of Montefeltro. The situation is described by Troya, Veltro Allegorico, p. 11. It is a conspicuous object to travellers along the cornice on the Riviera di Genoa.

[3] "Noli." In the Genoese territory, between Finale and Savona.

[4] "Bismantua." A steep mountain in the territory of Reggio.

Amazed[5] I stood, where 'twixt us and the north
Its course it enter'd.   Whence he thus to me:
"Were Leda's offspring[6] now in company
Of that broad mirror, that high up and low
Imparts his light beneath, thou mightst behold
The ruddy Zodiac nearer to the Bears
Wheel, if its ancient course it not forsook.
How that may be, if thou wouldst think; within
Pondering, imagine Sion with this mount
Placed on the earth, so that to both be one
Horizon, and two hemispheres apart,
Where lies the path[7] that Phaëton ill knew
To guide his erring chariot: thou wilt see[8]
How of necessity by this, on one,
He passes, while by that on the other side;
If with clear view thine intellect attend."

   "Of truth, kind teacher!" I exclaim'd, "so clear
Aught saw I never, as I now discern,
Where seem'd my ken to fail, that the mid orb[9]
Of the supernal motion (which in terms
Of art is call'd the Equator, and remains
Still 'twixt the sun and winter) for the cause
Thou hast assign'd, from hence toward the north
Departs, when those, who in the Hebrew land
Were dwellers, saw it towards the warmer part.
But if it please thee, I would gladly know,

---

[5] "Amazed." He wonders that being turned to the east he should see the sun on his left, since in all the regions on this side of the tropic of Cancer it is seen on the right of one who turns his face toward the east; not recollecting that he was now antipodal to Europe, from whence he had seen the sun taking an opposite course.

[6] "As the constellation of the Gemini is nearer the Bears than Aries is, it is certain that if the sun, instead of being in Aries, had been in Gemini, both the sun and that portion of the Zodiac made 'ruddy' by the sun, would have been seen to 'wheel nearer to the Bears.' By the 'ruddy Zodiac' must necessarily be understood that portion of the Zodiac affected or made red by the sun; for the whole of

the Zodiac never changes, nor appears to change, with respect to the remainder of the heavens."—Lombardi.

[7] "The path." The ecliptic.

[8] "Thou wilt see." "If you consider that this mountain of Purgatory, and that of Sion, are antipodal to each other, you will perceive that the sun must rise on opposite sides of the respective eminences."

[9] "That the mid orb." "That the equator (which is always situated between that part where, when the sun is, he causes summer, and the other where his absence produces winter) recedes from this mountain toward the north, at the time when the Jews inhabiting Mount Sion saw it depart toward the south."—Lombardi.

How far we have to journey: for the hill
Mounts higher, than this sight of mine can mount."
　　He thus to me: "Such is this steep ascent,
That it is ever difficult at first,
But more a man proceeds, less evil grows.[10]
When pleasant it shall seem to thee, so much
That upward going shall be easy to thee
As in a vessel to go down the tide,
Then of this path thou wilt have reach'd the end.
There hope to rest thee from thy toil. No more
I answer, and thus far from certain know."
As he his words had spoken, near to us
A voice there sounded: "Yet ye first perchance
May to repose you by constraint be led."
At sound thereof each turn'd; and on the left
A huge stone we beheld, of which nor I
Nor he before was ware.　Thither we drew;
And there were some, who in the shady place
Behind the rock were standing, as a man
Through idleness might stand.　Among them one,
Who seem'd to be much wearied, sat him down,
And with his arms did fold his knees about,
Holding his face between them downward bent.
　　"Sweet Sir!" I cried, "behold that man who shows
Himself more idle than if laziness
Were sister to him."　Straight he turn'd to us,
And, o'er the thigh lifting his face, observed,
Then in these accents spake: "Up then, proceed,
Thou valiant one."　Straight who it was I knew;
Nor could the pain I felt (for want of breath
Still somewhat urged me) hinder my approach.
And when I came to him, he scarce his head
Uplifted, saying, "Well hast thou discern'd,
How from the left the sun his chariot leads?"
　　His lazy acts and broken words my lips
To laughter somewhat moved; when I began:
"Belacqua,[11] now for thee I grieve no more.

[10] Because in ascending he gets rid of the weight of his sins.

[11] In the margin of the Monte Casino MS. there is found this brief notice: "This Belacqua was an excellent master of the harp and lute, but very negligent in his affairs both spiritual and temporal."

But tell, why thou art seated upright there.
Waitest thou escort to conduct thee hence?
Or blame I only thine accustom'd ways?"
Then he: "My brother! of what use to mount,
When, to my suffering, would not let me pass
The bird of God, who at the portal sits?
Behoves so long that Heaven first bear me round
Without its limits, as in life it bore;
Because I, to the end, repentant sighs
Delay'd; if prayer do not aid me first,
That riseth up from heart which lives in grace.
What other kind avails, not heard in Heaven?"

    Before me now the poet, up the mount
Ascending, cried: "Haste thee: for see the sun
Has touch'd the point meridian; and the night
Now covers with her foot Marocco's shore."

CANTO V

ARGUMENT.—They meet with others, who had deferred their repentance till overtaken by a violent death, when sufficient space being allowed them, they were then
saved; and among these, Giacopo del Cassero, Buonconte da Montefeltro, and Pia,
a lady of Siena.

NOW had I left those spirits, and pursued
    The steps of my conductor; when behind,
    Pointing the finger at me, one exclaim'd:
"See, how it seems as if the light not shone
From the left hand[1] of him beneath,[2] and he,
As living, seems to be led on." Mine eyes,
I at that sound reverting, saw them gaze,
Through wonder, first at me; and then at me
And the light broken underneath, by turns.
"Why are thy thoughts thus riveted," my guide
Exclaim'd, "that thou hast slack'd thy pace? or how
Imports it thee, what thing is whisper'd here?
Come after me, and to their babblings leave

---

[1] The sun was, therefore, on the right
of our travellers. For, as before, when
seated and looking to the east whence
they had ascended, the sun was on their
left; so now that they are again going
forward, it must be on the opposite side
of them.

[2] Of Dante, following Virgil.

The crowd. Be as a tower, that, firmly set,
Shakes not its top for any blast that blows.
He, in whose bosom thought on thought shoots out,
Still of his aim is wide, in that the one
Sicklies and wastes to naught the other's strength."
    What other could I answer, save "I come"?
I said it, somewhat with that color tinged,
Which oft-times pardon meriteth for man.
    Meanwhile traverse along the hill there came,
A little way before us, some who sang
The "Miserere" in responsive strains.
When they perceived that through my body I
Gave way not for the rays to pass, their song
Straight to a long and hoarse exclaim they changed;
And two of them, in guise of messengers,
Ran on to meet us, and inquiring ask'd:
"Of your condition we would gladly learn."
    To them my guide: "Ye may return, and bear
Tidings to them who sent you, that his frame
Is real flesh. If, as I deem, to view
His shade they paused, enough is answer'd them:
Him let them honor: they may prize him well."
    Ne'er saw I fiery vapors with such speed
Cut through the serene air at fall of night,
Nor August's clouds athwart the setting sun,
That upward these did not in shorter space
Return; and, there arriving, with the rest
Wheel back on us, as with loose rein a troop.
    "Many," exclaim'd the bard, "are these, who throng
Around us: to petition thee, they come.
Go therefore on, and listen as thou go'st."
    "O spirit! who go'st on to blessedness,
With the same limbs that clad thee at thy birth,"
Shouting they came: "a little rest thy step.
Look if thou any one amongst our tribe
Hast e'er beheld, that tidings of him there[3]
Thou mayst report. Ah, wherefore go'st thou on?
Ah, wherefore tarriest thou not? We all
By violence died, and to our latest hour

---

[3] "There." Upon the earth.

Were sinners, but then warn'd by light from Heaven;
So that, repenting and forgiving, we
Did issue out of life at peace with God,
Who, with desire to see Him, fills our heart."
  Then I: "The visages of all I scan,
Yet none of ye remember. But if aught
That I can do may please you, gentle spirits!
Speak, and I will perform it; by that peace,
Which, on the steps of guide so excellent
Following, from world to world, intent I seek."
  In answer he began: "None here distrusts
Thy kindness, though not promised with an oath;
So as the will fail not for want of power.
Whence I, who sole before the other speak,
Entreat thee, if thou ever see that land[4]
Which lies between Romagna and the realm
Of Charles, that of thy courtesy thou pray
Those who inhabit Fano, that for me
Their adorations duly be put up,
By which I may purge off my grievous sins.
From thence I came.[5] But the deep passages,
Whence issued out the blood[6] wherein I dwelt,
Upon my bosom in Antenor's land[7]
Were made, where to be more secure I thought.
The author of the deed was Este's prince,
Who, more than right could warrant, with his wrath
Pursued me. Had I toward Mira fled,
When overta'en at Oriaco, still
Might I have breathed. But to the marsh I sped;
And in the mire and rushes tangled there
Fell, and beheld my life-blood float the plain."
  Then said another: "Ah! so may the wish,
That takes thee o'er the mountain, be fulfill'd,
As thou shalt graciously give aid to mine.

[4] The Marca d' Ancona, between Romagna and Apulia, the kingdom of Charles of Anjou.

[5] Giacopo del Cassero, a citizen of Fano, who having spoken ill of Azzo da Este, Marquis of Ferrara, was by his orders put to death. Giacopo was overtaken by the assassins at Oriaco, near the Brenta, whence, if he had fled toward Mira, higher up on that river, instead of making for the marsh on the sea-shore, he might have escaped.

[6] Supposed to be the seat of life.

[7] Padua, said to be founded by Antenor. This implies a reflection on the Paduans. See Hell, xxxii. 89.

Of Montefeltro I;[8] Buonconte I:
Giovanna[9] nor none else have care for me;
Sorrowing with these I therefore go." I thus:
"From Campaldino's field what force or chance
Drew thee, that ne'er thy sepulture was known?"

    "Oh!" answer'd he, "at Casentino's foot
A stream there courseth, named Archiano, sprung
In Apennine above the hermit's seat.[10]
E'en where its name is cancel'd,[11] there came I,
Pierced in the throat, fleeing away on foot,
And bloodying the plain. Here sight and speech
Fail'd me; and, finishing with Mary's name,
I fell, and tenantless my flesh remain'd.
I will report the truth; which thou again
Tell to the living. Me God's angel took,
Whilst he of Hell exclaim'd: 'O thou from Heaven!
Say wherefore hast thou robb'd me? Thou of him
The eternal portion bear'st with thee away,
For one poor tear that he deprives me of.
But of the other, other rule I make.'

    "Thou know'st how in the atmosphere collects
That vapour dank, returning into water
Soon as it mounts where cold condenses it.
That evil will,[12] which in his intellect
Still follows evil, came; and raised the wind
And smoky mist, by virtue of the power
Given by his nature. Thence the valley, soon
As day was spent, he cover'd o'er with cloud,
From Pratomagno to the mountain range;[13]
And stretch'd the sky above; so that the air
Impregnate changed to water. Fell the rain;
And to the fosses came all that the land

---

[8] Buonconte, son of Guido da Montefeltro (see also the twenty-seventh canto
of Hell), fell in the battle of Campaldino
(1289), fighting on the side of the
Aretini. In this engagement our Poet took
a distinguished part.

[9] Wife or kinswoman of Buonconte.

[10] The hermitage of Camaldoli.

[11] Between Bibbiena and Poppi, where
the Archiano joins the Arno.

[12] The Devil. This notion of the Evil
Spirit having power over the elements,
appears to have arisen from his being
termed the "prince of the air," in the
New Testament.

[13] From Pratomagno, now called Prato
Vecchio (which divides the Valdarno
from Casentino), as far as to the Apennines.

Contain'd not; and, as mightiest streams are wont,
To the great river, with such headlong sweep,
Rush'd, that naught stay'd its course. My stiffen'd frame
Laid at his mouth, the fell Archiano found,
And dashed it into Arno; from my breast
Loosening the cross, that of myself I made
When overcome with pain. He hurl'd me on,
Along the banks and bottom of his course;
Then in his muddy spoils encircling wrapt."

"Ah! when thou to the world shalt be return'd,
And rested after thy long road," so spake
Next the third spirit; "then remember me.
I once was Pia.[14] Sienna gave me life;
Maremma took it from me. That he knows,
Who me with jewel'd ring had first espoused."

CANTO VI

ARGUMENT.—Many besides, who are in like case with those spoken of in the last
Canto, beseech our Poet to obtain for them the prayers of their friends, when he shall
be returned to this world. This moves him to express a doubt to his guide, how the
dead can be profited by the prayers of the living; for the solution of which doubt
he is referred to Beatrice. Afterward he meets with Sordello the Mantuan, whose
affection, shown to Virgil his countryman, leads Dante to break forth into an invective
against the unnatural divisions with which Italy, and more especially Florence, was
distracted.

WHEN from their game of dice men separate,
He who hath lost remains in sadness fix'd,
Revolving in his mind what luckless throws
He cast: but, meanwhile, all the company
Go with the other; one before him runs,
And one behind his mantle twitches, one
Fast by his side bids him remember him.
He stops not; and each one, to whom his hand
Is stretch'd, well knows he bids him stand aside;
And thus[1] he from the press defends himself.
E'en such was I in that close-crowding throng;

---

[14] "Pia." She is said to have been a
Siennese lady, of the family of Tolommei,
secretly made away with by her husband,
Nello della Pietra, of the same city, in
Maremma, where he had some posses-
sions.

[1] "And thus." It was usual for money
to be given to bystanders at play by
winners.

And turning so my face around to all,
And promising, I 'scaped from it with pains.
  Here of Arezzo him[2] I saw, who fell
By Ghino's cruel arm; and him beside,[3]
Who in his chase was swallow'd by the stream.
Here Frederic Novello,[4] with his hand
Stretch'd forth, entreated; and of Pisa he,[5]
Who put the good Marzucco to such proof
Of constancy. Count Orso[6] I beheld;
And from its frame a soul dismiss'd for spite
And envy, as it said, but for no crime;
I speak of Peter de la Brosse:[7] and here,
While she yet lives, that Lady of Brabant,
Let her beware; lest for so false a deed
She herd with worse than these. When I was freed
From all those spirits, who pray'd for others' prayers
To hasten on their state of blessedness;
Straight I began: "O thou, my luminary!
It seems expressly in thy text denied,
That Heaven's supreme decree can ever bend
To supplication; yet with this design
Do these entreat. Can then their hope be vain?

[2] Benincasa of Arezzo, eminent for his skill in jurisprudence, who having condemned to death Turrino da Turrita, brother of Ghino di Tacco, for his robberies in Maremma, was murdered by Ghino, in an apartment of his own house, in the presence of many witnesses. Ghino was not only suffered to escape in safety, but obtained so high a reputation by the liberality with which he dispensed the fruits of his plunder, and treated those who fell into his hands with so much courtesy, that he was afterward invited to Rome, and knighted by Boniface VIII.

[3] Cione, or Ciacco de' Tarlatti of Arezzo, carried by his horse into the Arno, and there drowned, while in pursuit of enemies.

[4] "Frederic Novello." Son of the Conte Guido da Battifolle, and slain by one of the family of Bostoli.

[5] Farinata de' Scornigiani, of Pisa. His father, Marzucco, who had entered the order of the Frati Minori, so entirely overcame his resentment, that he even kissed the hands of the slayer of his son, and as he was following the funeral, exhorted his kinsmen to reconciliation.

[6] "Count Orso." Son of Napoleone da Cerbaia, slain by Alberto da Mangona, his uncle.

[7] Secretary of Philip III of France. The courtiers envying the high place which he held in the King's favor, prevailed on Mary of Brabant to charge him falsely with an attempt upon her person; for which supposed crime he suffered death. So say the Italian commentators. Henault represents the matter very differently: "Pierre de la Brosse, formerly barber to St. Louis, afterward the favorite of Philip, fearing the too great attachment of the King for his wife Mary, accuses this princess of having poisoned Louis, eldest son of Philip, by his first marriage. This calumny is discovered by a nun of Nivelle, in Flanders. La Brosse is hanged."

Or is thy saying not to me reveal'd?"
    He thus to me: "Both what I write is plain,
And these deceived not in their hope; if well
Thy mind consider, that the sacred height
Of judgment doth not stoop, because love's flame
In a short moment all fulfills, which he,
Who sojourns here, in right should satisfy.
Besides, when I this point concluded thus,
By praying no defect could be supplied;
Because the prayer had none access to God.
Yet in this deep suspicion rest thou not
Contented, unless she assure thee so,
Who betwixt truth and mind infuses light:
I know not if thou take me right; I mean
Beatrice. Her thou shalt behold above,
Upon this mountain's crown, fair seat of joy."
    Then I: "Sir! let us mend our speed; for now
I tire not as before: and lo! the hill[8]
Stretches its shadow far." He answer'd thus:
"Our progress with this day shall be as much
As we may now despatch; but otherwise
Than thou supposest is the truth. For there
Thou canst not be, ere thou once more behold
Him back returning, who behind the steep
Is now so hidden, that, as erst, his beam
Thou dost not break. But lo! a spirit there
Stands solitary, and toward us looks:
It will instruct us in the speediest way."
    We soon approach'd it. O thou Lombard spirit!
How didst thou stand, in high abstracted mood,
Scarce moving with slow dignity thine eyes.
It spoke not aught, but let us onward pass,
Eying us as a lion on his watch.
But Virgil, with entreaty mild, advanced,
Requesting it to show the best ascent.
It answer to his question none return'd;
But of our country and our kind of life
Demanded. When my courteous guide began,
"Mantua," the shadow, in itself absorb'd,

    [8] "The hill." It was now past the moon.

Rose toward us from the place in which it stood,
And cried, "Mantuan! I am thy countryman,
Sordello." [9] Each the other then embraced.
    Ah, slavish Italy! thou inn of grief!
Vessel without a pilot in loud storm!
Lady no longer of fair provinces,
But brothel-house impure! this gentle spirit,
Even from the pleasant sound of his dear land
Was prompt to greet a fellow citizen
With such glad cheer: while now thy living ones
In thee abide not without war; and one
Malicious gnaws another; ay, of those
Whom the same wall and the same moat contains.
Seek, wretched one! around the sea-coasts wide;
Then homeward to thy bosom turn; and mark,
If any part of thee sweet peace enjoy.
What boots it, that thy reins Justinian's hand
Refitted, if thy saddle be unprest?
Naught doth he now but aggravate thy shame.
Ah, people! thou obedient still should'st live,
And in the saddle let thy Cæsar sit,
If well thou marked'st that which God commands.
    Look how that beast to fellness hath relapsed,
From having lost correction of the spur,
Since to the bridle thou hast set thine hand,
O German Albert! [10] who abandon'st her
That is grown savage and unmanageable,
When thou shouldst clasp her flanks with forked heels.
Just judgment from the stars fall on thy blood;
And be it strange and manifest to all;
Such as may strike thy successor [11] with dread;
For that thy sire [12] and thou have suffer'd thus,

---

[9] Sordello's life is wrapt in obscurity. He distinguished himself by his skill in Provençal poetry and many feats of military prowess have been attributed to him. It is probable that he was born at the end of the twelfth, and died about the middle of the succeeding, century.

[10] The Emperor Albert I succeeded Adolphus in 1298, and was murdered in 1308. See Paradise. Canto xix. 114.

[11] Henry of Luxemburg, by whose interposition in the affairs of Italy our Poet hoped to have been reinstated in his native city.

[12] The Emperor Rodolph, too intent on increasing his power in Germany to give much of his thoughts to Italy, "the garden of the empire."

Through greediness of yonder realms detain'd,
The garden of the empire to run waste.
Come, see the Capulets and Montagues,[13]
The Filippeschi and Monaldi,[14] man
Who carest for naught! those sunk in grief, and these
With dire suspicion rack'd. Come, cruel one!
Come, and behold the oppression of the nobles,
And mark their injuries; and thou mayst see
What safety Santafiore can supply.[15]
Come and behold thy Rome, who calls on thee,
Desolate widow, day and night with moans,
"My Cæsar, why dost thou desert my side?"
Come, and behold what love among thy people:
And if no pity touches thee for us,
Come, and blush for thine own report. For me,
If it be lawful, O Almighty Power!
Who wast on earth for our sakes crucified,
Are thy just eyes turn'd elsewhere? or is this
A preparation, in the wondrous depth
Of thy sage counsel made, for some good end,
Entirely from our reach of thought cut off?
So are the Italian cities all o'erthrong'd
With tyrants, and a great Marcellus made
Of every petty factious villager.

My Florence! thou mayst well remain unmoved
At this digression, which affects not thee:
Thanks to thy people, who so wisely speed.
Many have justice in their heart, that long
Waiteth for counsel to direct the bow,
Or ere it dart unto its aim: but thine
Have it on their lips' edge. Many refuse
To bear the common burdens: readier thine
Answer uncall'd, and cry, "Behold I stoop!"

Make thyself glad, for thou hast reason now,
Thou wealthy! thou at peace! thou wisdom-fraught!
Facts best will witness if I speak the truth.
Athens and Lacedæmon, who of old
Enacted laws, for civil arts renown'd,

---

[13] Two powerful Ghibelline families of Verona.

[14] Two rival families in Orvieto.

[15] A place between Pisa and Siena.

Made little progress in improving life
Toward thee, who usest such nice subtlety,
That to the middle of November scarce
Reaches the thread thou in October weavest.
How many times within thy memory,
Customs, and laws, and coins, and offices
Have been by thee renew'd, and people changed.
    If thou remember'st well and canst see clear,
Thou wilt perceive thyself like a sick wretch,
Who finds no rest upon her down, but oft
Shifting her side, short respite seeks from pain.

CANTO VII

ARGUMENT.—The approach of night hindering further ascent, Sordello conducts
our Poet apart to an eminence, from whence they behold a pleasant recess, in form
of a flowery valley, scooped out of the mountain; where are many famous spirits, and
among them the Emperor Rodolph, Ottocar, King of Bohemia, Philip III of France,
Henry of Navarre, Peter III of Arragon, Charles I of Naples, Henry III of England,
and William, Marquis of Montferrat.

AFTER their courteous greetings joyfully
    Seven times exchanged, Sordello backward drew
    Exclaiming, "Who are ye?"—"Before this mount
By spirits worthy of ascent to God
Was sought, my bones had by Octavius' care
Been buried. I am Virgil; for no sin
Deprived of Heaven, except for lack of faith."
So answer'd him in few my gentle guide.
    As one, who aught before him suddenly
Beholding, whence his wonder riseth, cries,
"It is, yet is not," wavering in belief;
Such he appear'd; then downward bent his eyes,
And, drawing near with reverential step,
Caught him, where one of mean estate might clasp
His lord. "Glory of Latium!" he exclaim'd,
"In whom our tongue its utmost power display'd;
Boast of my honor'd birth-place! what desert
Of mine, what favour, rather, undeserved,
Shows thee to me? If I to hear that voice
Am worthy, say if from below thou comest,

And from what cloister's pale."—"Through every
   orb
Of that sad region," he replied, "thus far
Am I arrived, by heavenly influence led:
And with such aid I come. Not for my doing,
But for not doing, have I lost the sight
Of that high Sun, whom thou desirest, and who
By me too late was known. There is a place[1]
There underneath, not made by torments sad,
But by dun shades alone; where mourning's voice
Sounds not of anguish sharp, but breathes in sighs.
There I with little innocents abide,
Who by death's fangs were bitten, ere exempt
From human taint. There I with those abide,
Who the three holy virtues[2] put not on,
But understood the rest,[3] and without blame
Follow'd them all. But, if thou know'st, and canst,
Direct us how we soonest may arrive,
Where Purgatory its true beginning takes."

He answer'd thus: "We have no certain place
Assign'd us: upward I may go, or round.
Far as I can, I join thee for thy guide.
But thou beholdest now how day declines;
And upward to proceed by night, our power
Excels: therefore it may be well to choose
A place of pleasant sojourn. To the right
Some spirits sit apart retired. If thou
Consentest, I to these will lead thy steps:
And thou wilt know them, not without delight."

"How chances this?" was answer'd: "whoso wish'd
To ascend by night, would he be thence debarr'd
By other, or through his own weakness fail?"

The good Sordello then, along the ground
Trailing his finger, spoke: "Only this line
Thou shalt not overpass, soon as the sun
Hath disappear'd; not that aught else impedes
Thy going upward, save the shades of night.
These, with the want of power, perplex the will.

---

[1] Limbo. See Hell, Canto iv. 24.   [3] "The rest." Prudence, Justice, Forti-
[2] Faith, Hope, and Charity.   tude, and Temperance.

With them thou haply mightst return beneath,
Or to and fro around the mountain's side
Wander, while day is in the horizon shut."

My master straight, as wondering at his speech,
Exclaim'd: "Then lead us quickly, where thou sayst
That, while we stay, we may enjoy delight."

A little space we were removed from thence,
When I perceived the mountain hollow'd out,
Even as large valleys hollow'd out on earth.

"That way," the escorting spirit cried, "we go,
Where in a bosom the high bank recedes:
And thou await renewal of the day."

Betwixt the steep and plain, a crooked path
Led us traverse into the ridge's side,
Where more than half the sloping edge expires.

Refulgent gold, and silver thrice refined,
And scarlet grain and ceruse, Indian wood
Of lucid dye serene, fresh emeralds

But newly broken, by the herbs and flowers
Placed in that fair recess, in color all
Had been surpass'd, as great surpasses less.

Nor nature only there lavish'd her hues,
But of the sweetness of a thousand smells
A rare and undistinguish'd fragrance made.

"Salve Regina," [4] on the grass and flowers,
Here chanting, I beheld those spirits sit,
Who not beyond the valley could be seen.

"Before the westering sun sink to his bed,"
Began the Mantuan, who our steps had turn'd,
" 'Mid those, desire not that I lead ye on.

For from this eminence ye shall discern
Better the acts and visages of all,
Than, in the nether vale, among them mix'd.

He, who sits high above the rest, and seems
To have neglected that he should have done,
And to the others' song moves not his lip,

The Emperor Rodolph call, who might have heal'd
The wounds whereof fair Italy hath died,

---

[4] "Salve Regina." The beginning of a prayer to the Virgin.

So that by others she revives but slowly.

He, who with kindly visage comforts him,
Sway'd in that country,[5] where the water springs,
That Moldaw's river to the Elbe, and Elbe
Rolls to the ocean: Ottocar[6] his name:
Who in his swaddling-clothes was of more worth
Than Wenceslaus his son, a bearded man,
Pamper'd with rank luxuriousness and ease.

And that one with the nose deprest,[7] who close
In counsel seems with him of gentle look,[8]
Flying expired, withering the lily's flower.
Look there, how he doth knock against his breast.
The other ye behold, who for his cheek
Makes of one hand a couch, with frequent sighs.
They are the father and the father-in-law
Of Gallia's bane:[9] his vicious life they know
And foul; thence comes the grief that rends them thus.

    "He, so robust of limb,[10] who measure keeps
In song with him of feature prominent,[11]
With every virtue bore his girdle braced.

[5] "That country." Bohemia.

[6] "Ottocar." King of Bohemia, who was killed in the battle of Marchfield, fought with Rodolph, August 26, 1278. Wenceslaus II, his son, who succeeded him in the Kingdom of Bohemia, died in 1305. The latter is again taxed with luxury in the Paradise, xix. 123.

[7] "That one with the nose deprest." Philip III, of France, father of Philip IV. He died in 1285, at Perpignan, in his retreat from Arragon.

[8] "Him of gentle look." Henry of Navarre, father of Jane, married to Philip IV, of France, whom Dante calls "mal di Francia."—"Gallia's bane."

[9] "Gallia's bane." G. Villani, lib. vii. cap. cxlvi, speaks with equal resentment of Philip IV. "In 1291, on the night of the calends of May, Philip le Bel, King of France, by advice of Biccio and Musciatto Franzesi, ordered all the Italians, who were in his country and realm, to be seized, under pretence of seizing the money-lenders, but thus he caused the good merchants also to be seized and ransomed; for which he was much blamed and held in great abhorrence. And from thenceforth the realm of France fell evermore into degradation and decline. And it is observable that between the taking of Acre and this seizure in France, the merchants of Florence received great damage and ruin of their property."

[10] "He, so robust of limb." Peter III, called the Great, King of Arragon, who died in 1285, leaving four sons, Alonzo, James, Frederick, and Peter. The two former succeeded him in the Kingdom of Arragon, and Frederick in that of Sicily.

[11] "Him of feature prominent." "Dal maschio naso"—"with the masculine nose." Charles I, King of Naples, Count of Anjou, and brother of St. Louis. He died in 1284. The annalist of Florence remarks that "there had been no sovereign of the house of France, since the time of Charlemagne, by whom Charles was surpassed either in military renown and prowess, or in the loftiness of his understanding."

And if that stripling,[12] who behind him sits,
King after him had lived, his virtue then
From vessel to like vessel had been pour'd;
Which may not of the other heirs be said.
By James and Frederick his realms are held;
Neither the better heritage obtains.
Rarely into the branches of the tree
Doth human worth mount up: and so ordains
He who bestows it, that as His free gift
It may be call'd. To Charles[13] my words apply
No less than to his brother in song;
Which Pouille and Provence now with grief confess.
So much that plant degenerates from its seed,
As, more than Beatrix and Margaret,
Costanza[14] still boasts of her valorous spouse.

"Behold the King of simple life and plain,
Harry of England,[15] sitting there alone:
He through his branches better issue[16] spreads.

"That one, who, on the ground, beneath the rest,
Sits lowest, yet his gaze directs aloft,
Is William, that brave Marquis,[17] for whose cause,
The deed of Alexandria and his war
Makes Montferrat and Canavese weep."

[12] "That stripling." Either (as the old commentators suppose) Alonzo III, King of Arragon, the eldest son of Peter III, who died in 1291, at the age of 27; or, according to Venturi, Peter, the youngest son. The former was a young prince of virtue sufficient to have justified the eulogium and the hopes of Dante.

[13] "To Charles." "Al Nausto"—Charles II, King of Naples, is no less inferior to his father, Charles I, than James and Frederick to theirs, Peter III.

[14] "Costanza." Widow of Peter III. She has been already mentioned in the third Canto, v. 112. By Beatrix and Margaret are probably meant two of the daughters of Raymond Berenger, Count of Provence; the latter married to St. Louis of France, the former to his brother Charles of Anjou, King of Naples. See Paradise, Canto vi. 135. Dante therefore considers Peter as the most illustrious of the three monarchs.

[15] "Harry of England." Henry III. The contemporary annalist speaks of this king in similar terms. G. Villani, lib. v. cap. iv. "From Richard was born Henry, who reigned after him, who was a plain man of good faith, but of little courage."

[16] "Better issue." Edward I, of whose glory our Poet was perhaps a witness, in his visit to England. "From the said Henry was born the good King Edward, who reigns in our times, who has done great things, whereof we shall make mention in due place."—G. Villani, ibid.

[17] "William, that brave Marquis." William, Marquis of Montferrat, was treacherously seized by his own subjects, at Alessandria in Lombardy, A. D. 1290, and ended his life in prison. A war ensued between the people of Alessandria and those of Montferrat and the Canavese, now part of Piedmont.

CANTO VIII

ARGUMENT.—Two Angels, with flaming swords broken at the points, descend to keep watch over the valley, into which Virgil and Dante entering by desire of Sordello, our Poet meets with joy the spirit of Nino, the judge of Gallura, one who was well known to him. Meantime three exceedingly bright stars appear near the pole, and a serpent creeps subtly into the valley, but flees at hearing the approach of those angelic guards. Lastly, Conrad Malaspina predicts to our Poet his future banishment.

NOW was the hour that wakens fond desire
In men at sea, and melts their thoughtful heart
Who in the morn have bid sweet friends farewell,
And pilgrim newly on his road with love
Thrills, if he hear the vesper bell from far,
That seems to mourn for the expiring day:
When I, no longer taking heed to hear,
Began, with wonder, from those spirits to mark
One risen from its seat, which with its hand
Audience implored. Both palms it join'd and raised,
Fixing its stedfast gaze toward the east,
As telling God, "I care for naught beside."
    "Te Lucis Ante," [1] so devoutly then
Came from its lip, and in so soft a strain,
That all my sense in ravishment was lost.
And the rest after, softly and devout,
Follow'd through all the hymn, with upward gaze
Directed to the bright supernal wheels.
    Here, reader! for the truth make thine eyes keen:
For of so subtle texture is this veil,
That thou with ease mayst pass it through unmark'd.
    I saw that gentle band silently next
Look up, as if in expectation held,
Pale and in lowly guise; and, from on high,
I saw, forth issuing descend beneath,
Two Angels, with two flame-illumined swords,
Broken and mutilated of their points.
Green as the tender leaves but newly born,
Their vesture was, the which, by wings as green
Beaten, they drew behind them, fann'd in air.
A little over us one took his stand;

[1] "Te lucis ante terminum," the first verse of the hymn in the last part of the sacred office, termed "complin."

The other lighted on the opposing hill;
So that the troop were in the midst contain'd.

   Well I descried the whiteness on their heads;
But in their visages the dazzled eye
Was lost, as faculty that by too much
Is overpower'd. "From Mary's bosom both
Are come," exclaim'd Sordello, "as a guard
Over the vale, 'gainst him, who hither tends,
The serpent." Whence, not knowing by which path
He came, I turn'd me round; and closely press'd,
All frozen, to my leader's trusted side.

   Sordello paused not: "To the valley now
(For it is time) let us descend; and hold
Converse with those great shadows: haply much
Their sight may please ye." Only three steps down
Methinks I measured, ere I was beneath,
And noted one who look'd as with desire
To know me. Time was now that air grew dim;
Yet not so dim, that, 'twixt his eyes and mine,
It clear'd not up what was conceal'd before.
Mutually toward each other we advanced.
Nino, thou courteous judge![2] what joy I felt,
When I perceived thou wert not with the bad.

   No salutation kind on either part
Was left unsaid. He then inquired: "How long,
Since thou arrived'st at the mountain's foot,
Over the distant waves?"—"Oh!" answer'd I,
"Through the sad seats of woe this morn I came;
And still in my first life, thus journeying on,
The other strive to gain." Soon as they heard
My words, he and Sordello backward drew,
As suddenly amazed. To Virgil one,
The other to a spirit turn'd, who near
Was seated, crying: "Conrad![3] up with speed:
Come, see what of His grace high God hath will'd."
Then turning round to me: "By that rare mark
Of honour, which thou owest to Him, who hides
So deeply His first cause it hath no ford;

[2] Nino di Gallura de' Visconti, nephew to Count Ugolino de' Gherardeschi, and betrayed by him.

[3] Father to Marcello Malaspina.

When thou shalt be beyond the vast of waves,
Tell my Giovanna,[4] that for me she call
There, where reply to innocence is made.
Her mother,[5] I believe, loves me no more;
Since she has changed the white and wimpled folds,[6]
Which she is doom'd once more with grief to wish.
By her it easily may be perceived,
How long in woman lasts the flame of love,
If sight and touch do not relume it oft.
For her so fair a burial will not make
The viper,[7] which calls Milan to the field,
As had been made by shrill Gallura's bird." [8]

He spoke, and in his visage took the stamp
Of that right zeal, which with due temperature
Glows in the bosom. My insatiate eyes
Meanwhile to Heaven had travel'd, even there
Where the bright stars are slowest, as a wheel
Nearest the axle; when my guide inquired:
"What there aloft, my son, has caught thy gaze?"

I answer'd: "The three torches,[9] with which here
The pole is all on fire." He then to me:
"The four resplendent stars, thou saw'st this morn,
Are there beneath; and these, risen in their stead."

While yet he spoke, Sordello to himself
Drew him, and cried: "Lo there our enemy!"
And with his hand pointed that way to look.

Along the side, where barrier none arose
Around the little vale, a serpent lay,
Such haply as gave Eve the bitter food.
Between the grass and flowers, the evil snake
Came on, reverting oft his lifted head;

[4] The daughter of Nino, and wife of Riccardo da Camino, of Trevigi.

[5] "Her mother." Beatrice, Marchioness of Este, wife of Nino, and after his death married to Galeazzo de' Visconti of Milan.

[6] The weeds of widowhood.

[7] The arms of Galeazzo and the ensign of the Milanese.

[8] The cock was the ensign of Gallura, Nino's province in Sardinia. It is not known whether Beatrice had any further cause to regret her nuptials with Galeazzo, than a certain shame which appears, however unreasonably, to have attached to a second marriage.

[9] The three evangelical virtues, Faith, Hope, and Charity, are supposed to rise in the evening, to denote their belonging to the contemplative; as the four others are made to rise in the morning to signify their belonging to the active life: or perhaps it may mark the succession, in order of time, of the Gospel to the heathen system of morality.

And, as a beast that smooths its polish'd coat,
Licking his back. I saw not, nor can tell,
How those celestial falcons from their seat
Moved, but in motion each one well descried.
Hearing the air cut by their verdant plumes,
The serpent fled; and, to their stations, back
The Angels up return'd with equal flight.

   The spirit, (who to Nino, when he call'd,
Had come), from viewing me with fixed ken,
Through all that conflict, loosen'd not his sight.

   "So may the lamp, which leads thee up on high,
Find, in thy free resolve, of wax so much,
As may suffice thee to the enamel'd height."
It thus began: "If any certain news
Of Valdimagra and the neighbour part
Thou know'st, tell me, who once was mighty there.
They call'd me Conrad Malaspina; not
That old one, but from him I sprang. The love
I bore my people is now here refined."

   "In your domains," I answer'd, "ne'er was I.
But, through all Europe, where do those men dwell,
To whom their glory is not manifest?
The fame, that honours your illustrious house,
Proclaims the nobles, and proclaims the land;
So that he knows it, who was never there.
I swear to you, so may my upward route
Prosper, your honoured nation not impairs
The value of her coffer and her sword.
Nature and use give her such privilege,
That while the world is twisted from his course
By a bad head, she only walks aright,
And has the evil way in scorn." He then:
"Now pass thee on: seven times the tired sun[10]
Revisits not the couch, which with four feet
The forked Aries covers, ere that kind
Opinion shall be nail'd into thy brain

[10] "The sun shall not enter into the constellation of Aries seven times more, before thou shalt have still better cause for the good opinion thou expressest of Valdimagra, in the kind reception thou shalt there meet with." Dante was hospitably received by the Marchese Marcello, or Morello Malaspina, during his banishment, A. D. 1307.

With stronger nails than other's speech can drive;
If the sure course of judgment be not stay'd."

CANTO IX

ARGUMENT.—Dante is carried up the mountain, asleep and dreaming, by Lucia; and,
on awakening, finds himself, two hours after sunrise, with Virgil, near the gate of
Purgatory, through which they are admitted by the Angel deputed by St. Peter to
keep it.

NOW the fair consort of Tithonus old,
    Arisen from her mate's beloved arms,
    Look'd palely o'er the eastern cliff; her brow,
Lucent with jewels, glitter'd, set in sign
Of that chill animal,[1] who with his train
Smites fearful nations: and where then we were,
Two steps of her ascent the night had past;
And now the third was closing up its wing,[2]
When I, who had so much of Adam with me,
Sank down upon the grass, o'ercome with sleep,
There where all five[3] were seated. In that hour,
When near the dawn the swallow her sad lay,
Remembering haply ancient grief,[4] renews;
And when our minds, more wanderers from the flesh,
And less by thought restrain'd, are, as 't were, full
Of holy divination in their dreams;
Then, in a vision, did I seem to view
A golden-feather'd eagle in the sky,
With open wings, and hovering for descent;
And I was in that place, methought, from whence
Young Ganymede, from his associates 'reft,
Was snatch'd aloft to the high consistory.
"Perhaps," thought I within me, "here alone
He strikes his quarry, and elsewhere disdains

[1] "Of that chill animal." The scorpion.
[2] "The third was closing up its wing."
The night being divided into four watches,
I think he may mean that the third was
past, and the fourth and last was begun,
so that there might be some faint glimmering of morning twilight; and not
merely, as Lombardi supposes, that the
third watch was drawing toward its close,
which would still leave an insurmountable
difficulty in the first verse.
[3] "All five." Virgil, Dante, Sordello,
Nino, and Corrado Malaspina.
[4] "Remembering haply ancient grief."
Progne having been changed into a
swallow after the outrage done her by
Tereus.

To pounce upon the prey." Therewith, it seem'd,
A little wheeling in his aëry tour,
Terrible as the lightning, rush'd he down,
And snatch'd me upward even to the fire.
There both, I thought, the eagle and myself
Did burn; and so intense the imagined flames,
That needs my sleep was broken off. As erst
Achilles shook himself, and round him roll'd
His waken'd eyeballs, wondering where he was,
Whenas his mother had from Chiron fled
To Scyros, with him sleeping in her arms;
There whence the Greeks did after sunder him;
E'en thus I shook me, soon as from my face
The slumber parted, turning deadly pale,
Like one ice-struck with dread. Sole at my side
My comfort stood: and the bright sun was now
More than two hours aloft: and to the sea
My looks were turn'd. "Fear not," my master cried,
"Assured we are at happy point. Thy strength
Shrink not, but rise dilated. Thou art come
To Purgatory now. Lo! there the cliff
That circling bounds it. Lo! the entrance there,
Where it doth seem disparted. Ere the dawn
Usher'd the day-light, when thy wearied soul
Slept in thee, o'er the flowery vale beneath
A lady came, and thus bespake me: 'I
Am Lucia.[5] Suffer me to take this man,
Who slumbers. Easier so his way shall speed.'
Sordello and the other gentle shapes
Tarrying, she bare thee up: and, as day shone,
This summit reach'd: and I pursued her steps.
Here did she place thee. First, her lovely eyes
That open entrance show'd me; then at once
She vanish'd with thy sleep." Like one, whose doubts
Are chased by certainty, and terror turn'd
To comfort on discovery of the truth,
Such was the change in me: and as my guide
Beheld me fearless, up along the cliff
He moved, and I behind him, toward the height.

[5] "Lucia." See Hell, c. ii 97 and Paradise, c. xxxii. 123.

Reader! thou markest how my theme doth rise;
Nor wonder therefore, if more artfully
I prop the structure. Nearer now we drew,
Arrived whence, in that part, where first a breach
As of a wall appear'd, I could descry
A portal, and three steps beneath, that led
For inlet there, of different colour each;
And one who watch'd, but spake not yet a word.
As more and more mine eye did stretch its view,
I mark'd him seated on the highest step,
In visage such, as past my power to bear.
Grasp'd in his hand, a naked sword glanced back
The rays so toward me, that I oft in vain
My sight directed. "Speak, from whence ye stand;"
He cried: "What would ye? Where is your escort?
Take heed your coming upward harm ye not."

"A heavenly dame, not skill-less of these things,"
Replied the instructor, "told us, even now,
'Pass that way: here the gate is.'"—"And may she,
Befriending, prosper your ascent," resumed
The courteous keeper of the gate: "Come then
Before our steps." We straightway thither came.

The lowest stair[6] was marble white, so smooth
And polish'd, that therein my mirror'd form
Distinct I saw. The next of hue more dark
Than sablest grain, a rough and singed block,
Crack'd lengthwise and across. The third, that lay
Massy above, seem'd porphyry, that flamed
Red as the life-blood spouting from a vein.
On this God's angel either foot sustain'd,
Upon the threshold seated, which appear'd
A rock of diamond. Up the trinal steps
My leader cheerly drew me. "Ask," said he,
"With humble heart, that he unbar the bolt."

Piously at his holy feet devolved
I cast me, praying him for pity's sake
That he would open to me; but first fell

---

[6] The white step suggests the conscience of the penitent reflecting his offences; the burnt and cracked one, his contrition on their account; the porphyry, the fervor with which he resolves on the future pursuit of piety and virtue.

Thrice on my bosom prostrate. Seven times[7]
The letter, that denotes the inward stain,
He, on my forehead, with the blunted point
Of his drawn sword, inscribed. And "Look," he cried,
"When enter'd, that thou wash these scars away."

   Ashes, or earth ta'en dry out of the ground,
Were of one colour with the robe he wore.
From underneath that vestment forth he drew
Two keys,[8] of metal twain: the one was gold,
Its fellow silver. With the pallid first,
And next the burnish'd, he so ply'd the gate,
As to content me well. "Whenever one
Faileth of these, that in the key-hole straight
It turn not, to this alley then expect
Access in vain." Such were the words he spake.
"One is more precious:[9] but the other needs
Skill and sagacity, large share of each,
Ere its good task to disengage the knot
Be worthily perform'd. From Peter these
I hold, of him instructed that I err
Rather in opening, than in keeping fast;
So but the suppliant at my feet implore."

   Then of that hallow'd gate he thrust the door,
Exclaiming, "Enter, but this warning hear:
He forth again departs who looks behind."

   As in the hinges of that sacred ward
The swivels turn'd, sonorous metal strong,
Harsh was the grating; nor so surlily
Roar'd the Tarpeian, when by force bereft
Of good Metellus, thenceforth from his loss
To leanness doom'd. Attentively I turn'd,
Listening the thunder that first issued forth;
And "We praise thee, O God," methought I heard,

---

[7] "Seven times." Seven P's, to denote the seven sins (Peccata) of which he was to be cleansed in his passage through Purgatory.

[8] "Two keys." Lombardi remarks that painters have usually drawn St. Peter with two keys, the one of gold and the other of silver; but that Niccolo Alemanni, in his Dissertation de Parietinis Lateranensibus, produces instances of his being represented with one key, and with three. We have here, however, not St. Peter, but an angel deputed by him.

[9] The golden key denotes the divine authority by which the priest absolves the sinners; the silver, the learning and judgment requisite for the due discharge of that office.

In accents blended with sweet melody.
The strains came o'er mine ear, e'en as the sound
Of choral voices, that in solemn chant
With organ[10] mingle, and now high and clear
Come swelling, now float indistinct away.

CANTO X

ARGUMENT.—Being admitted at the gate of Purgatory, our Poets ascend a winding path up the rock, till they reach an open and level space that extends each way round the mountain. On the side that rises, and which is of white marble, are seen artfully engraven many stories of humility, which whilst they are contemplating, there approach the souls of those who expiate the sin of pride, and who are bent down beneath the weight of heavy stones.

WHEN we had passed the threshold of the gate,
(Which the soul's ill affection doth disuse,
Making the crooked seem the straighter path,)
I heard its closing sound. Had mine eyes turn'd,
For that offence what plea might have avail'd?
    We mounted up the riven rock, that wound
On either side alternate, as the wave
Flies and advances. "Here some little art
Behoves us," said my leader, "that our steps
Observe the varying flexure of the path."
    Thus we so slowly sped, that with cleft orb
The moon once more o'erhangs her watery couch,
Ere we that strait have threaded. But when free,
We came, and open, where the mount above
One solid mass retires; I spent with toil,
And both uncertain of the way, we stood,
Upon a plain more lonesome than the roads
That traverse desert wilds. From whence the brink
Borders upon vacuity, to foot
Of the steep bank that rises still, the space
Had measured thrice the stature of a man:
And, distant as mine eye could wing its flight,
To leftward now and now to right despatch'd,
That cornice equal in extent appear'd.

---

[10] "Organ." Organs were used in Italy as early as in the sixth century. If I remember rightly there is a passage in the Emperor Julian's writings, which shows that the organ was not unknown in his time.

Not yet our feet had on that summit moved,
When I discover'd that the bank, around,
Whose proud uprising all ascent denied,
Was marble white; and so exactly wrought
With quaintest sculpture, that not there alone
Had Polycletus, but e'en nature's self
Been shamed. The Angel (who came down to earth
With tidings of the peace so many years
Wept for in vain, that oped the heavenly gates
From their long interdict) before us seem'd,
In a sweet act, so sculptured to the life,
He look'd no silent image. One had sworn
He had said "Hail!" for she was imaged there,
By whom the key did open to God's love;
And in her act as sensibly imprest
That word, "Behold the handmaid of the Lord,"
As figure seal'd on wax. "Fix not thy mind
On one place only," said the guide beloved,
Who had me near him on that part where lies
The heart of man. My sight forthwith I turn'd,
And mark'd, behind the Virgin Mother's form,
Upon that side where he that moved me stood.
Another story graven on the rock.

I past athwart the bard, and drew me near,
That it might stand more aptly for my view.
There, in the self-same marble, were engraved
The cart and kine, drawing the sacred ark,
That from unbidden office awes mankind.
Before it came much people; and the whole
Parted in seven quires. One sense cried "Nay,"
Another, "Yes, they sing." Like doubt arose
Betwixt the eye and smell, from the curl'd fume
Of incense breathing up the well-wrought toil.
Preceding the blest vessel, onward came
With light dance leaping, girt in humble guise,
Israel's sweet harper: in that hap he seem'd
Less, and yet more, than kingly. Opposite
At a great palace, from the lattice forth
Look'd Michol, like a lady full of scorn
And sorrow. To behold the tablet next,

Which, at the back of Michol, whitely shone,
I moved me. There, was storied on the rock
The exalted glory of the Roman prince,
Whose mighty worth moved Gregory[1] to earn
His mighty conquest, Trajan the Emperor.
A widow at his bridle stood, attired
In tears and mourning. Round about them troop'd
Full throng of knights; and overhead in gold
The eagles floated, struggling with the wind.
The wretch appear'd amid all these to say:
"Grant vengeance, Sire! for, woe beshrew this heart,
My son is murder'd." He replying seem'd:
"Wait now till I return." And she, as one
Made hasty by her grief: "O Sire! if thou
Dost not return?"—"Where I am, who then is,
May right thee."—"What to thee is other's good,
If thou neglect thy own?"—"Now comfort thee;"
At length he answers. "It beseemeth well
My duty be perform'd, ere I move hence:
So justice wills; and pity bids me stay."

He, whose ken nothing new surveys, produced
That visible speaking, new to us and strange,
The like not found on earth. Fondly I gazed
Upon those patterns of meek humbleness,
Shapes yet more precious for their artist's sake;
When "Lo!" the poet whisper'd, "where this way
(But slack their pace) a multitude advance,
These to the lofty steps shall guide us on."

Mine eyes, though bent on view of novel sights,
Their loved allurement, were not slow to turn.

Reader! I would not that amazed thou miss
Of thy good purpose, hearing how just God
Decrees our debts be cancel'd. Ponder not
The form of suffering. Think on what succeeds:
Think that, at worst, beyond the mighty doom
It cannot pass. "Instructor!" I began,
"What I see hither tending, bears no trace
Of human semblance, nor of aught beside

---

[1] "Gregory." St. Gregory's prayers are said to have delivered Trajan from hell.
See Paradise, Canto xx. 40.

That my foil'd sight can guess." He answering thus:
"So curb'd to earth, beneath their heavy terms
Of torment stoop they, that mine eye at first
Struggled as thine. But look intently thither;
And disentangle with thy laboring view,
What, underneath those stones, approacheth: now,
E'en now, mayst thou discern the pangs of each."

    Christians and proud! O poor and wretched ones!
That, feeble in the mind's eye, lean your trust
Upon unstaid perverseness: know ye not
That we are worms, yet made at last to form
The winged insect,[2] imp'd with angel plumes,
That to Heaven's justice unobstructed soars?
Why buoy ye up aloft your unfledged souls?
Abortive then and shapeless ye remain,
Like the untimely embryon of a worm.

    As, to support incumbent floor or roof,
For corbel, is a figure sometimes seen,
That crumples up its knees unto its breast;
With the feign'd posture, stirring ruth unfeign'd
In the beholder's fancy; so I saw
These fashion'd, when I noted well their guise.

    Each, as his back was laden, came indeed
Or more or less contracted; and it seem'd
As he, who show'd most patience in his look,
Wailing exclaim'd: "I can endure no more."

CANTO XI

ARGUMENT.—After a prayer uttered by the spirits, who were spoken of in the last
Canto, Virgil inquires the way upward, and is answered by one, who declares himself
to have been Omberto, son of the Count of Santafiore. Next our Poet distinguishes
Oderigi, the illuminator, who discourses on the vanity of worldly fame, and points out
to him the soul of Provenzano Salvani.

O THOU Almighty Father! who dost make
    The heavens Thy dwelling, not in bounds con-
        fined,
But that, with love intenser, there Thou view'st
Thy primal effluence; hallow'd be Thy name:
Join, each created being, to extol

2 "The winged insect." The butterfly was an ancient and well-known symbol of the
human soul.

Thy might; for worthy humblest thanks and praise
Is Thy blest Spirit. May Thy kingdom's peace
Come unto us; for we, unless it come,
With all our striving, thither tend in vain.
As, of their will, the Angels unto Thee
Tender meet sacrifice, circling Thy throne
With loud hosannas; so of theirs be done
By saintly men on earth. Grant us, this day,
Our daily manna, without which he roams
Through this rough desert retrograde, who most
Toils to advance his steps. As we to each
Pardon the evil done us, pardon Thou
Benign, and of our merit take no count.
'Gainst the old adversary, prove Thou not
Our virtue, easily subdued; but free
From his incitements, and defeat his wiles.
This last petition, dearest Lord! is made
Not for ourselves; since that were needless now;
But for their sakes who after us remain."
     Thus for themselves and us good speed imploring,
Those spirits went beneath a weight like that
We sometimes feel in dreams; all, sore beset,
But with unequal anguish; wearied all;
Round the first circuit; purging as they go
The world's gross darkness off. In our behoof
If their vows still be offer'd, what can here
For them be vow'd and done by such, whose wills
Have root of goodness in them? Well beseems
That we should help them wash away the stains
They carried hence; that so, made pure and light,
They may spring upward to the starry spheres.
     "Ah! so may mercy-temper'd justice rid
Your burdens speedily; that ye have power
To stretch your wing, which e'en to your desire
Shall lift you; as ye show us on which hand
Toward the ladder leads the shortest way.
And if there be more passages than one,
Instruct us of that easiest to ascend:
For this man, who comes with me, and bears yet
The charge of fleshly raiment Adam left him,

Despite his better will, but slowly mounts."
From whom the answer came unto these words,
Which my guide spake, appear'd not; but 'twas said:
"Along the bank to rightward come with us;
And ye shall find a pass that mocks not toil
Of living man to climb: and were it not
That I am hinder'd by the rock, wherewith
This arrogant neck is tamed, whence needs I stoop
My visage to the ground; him, who yet lives,
Whose name thou speak'st not, him I fain would view;
To mark if e'er I knew him, and to crave
His pity for the fardel that I bear.
I was of Latium;[1] of a Tuscan born,
A mighty one: Aldobrandesco's name
My sire's, I know not if ye e'er have heard.
My old blood and forefathers' gallant deeds
Made me so haughty, that I clean forgot
The common mother; and to such excess
Wax'd in my scorn of all men, that I fell,
Fell therefore; by what fate, Siena's sons.
Each child in Campagnatico, can tell.
I am Omberto: not me, only, pride
Hath injured, but my kindred all involved
In mischief with her. Here my lot ordains
Under this weight to groan, till I appease
God's angry justice, since I did it not
Amongst the living, here amongst the dead."
    Listening I bent my visage down: and one
(Not he who spake) twisted beneath the weight
That urged him, saw me, knew me straight, and call'd;
Holding his eyes with difficulty fix'd
Intent upon me, stooping as I went
Companion of their way. "O!" I exclaim'd,
"Art thou not Oderigi?[2] art not thou
Agobbio's glory, glory of that art
Which they of Paris call the limner's skill?"
    "Brother!" said he, "with tints, that gayer smile,

[1] "I was of Latium." Omberto, the son of Guglielmo Aldobrandesco, Count of Santafiore, in the territory of Siena. His arrogance provoked his countrymen to such a pitch of fury against him that he was murdered by them at Campagnatico.

[2] The illuminator, or miniature painter, a friend of Giotto and Dante.

Bolognian Franco's[3] pencil lines the leaves.
His all the honour now; my light obscured.
In truth, I had not been thus courteous to him
The whilst I lived, through eagerness of zeal
For that pre-eminence my heart was bent on.
Here, of such pride, the forfeiture is paid.
Nor were I even here, if, able still
To sin, I had not turn'd me unto God.
O powers of man! how vain your glory, nipt
E'en in its height of verdure, if an age
Less bright succeed not. Cimabue thought
To lord it over painting's field; and now
The cry is Giotto's,[4] and his name eclipsed.
Thus hath one Guido from the other[5] snatch'd
The letter'd prize: and he, perhaps, is born,
Who shall drive either from their nest. The noise
Of worldly fame is but a blast of wind,
That blows from diverse points, and shifts its name,
Shifting the point it blows from. Shalt thou more
Live in the mouths of mankind, if thy flesh
Part shrivel'd from thee, than if thou hadst died
Before the coral and the pap were left;
Or e'er some thousand years have past? and that
Is, to eternity compared, a space
Briefer than is the twinkling of an eye
To the heaven's slowest orb. He there, who treads
So leisurely before me, far and wide
Through Tuscany resounded once; and now
Is in Siena scarce with whispers named:
There was he sovereign, when destruction caught
The maddening rage of Florence, in that day
Proud as she now is loathsome. Your renown
Is as the herb, whose hue doth come and go;

[3] Franco of Bologna, who is said to have been a pupil of Oderigi's.

[4] "The cry is Giotto's." In Giotto we have a proof at how early a period the fine arts were encouraged in Italy. His talents were discovered by Cimabue, while he was tending sheep for his father in the neighborhood of Florence, and he was afterward patronized by Pope Benedict XI and Robert, King of Naples; and enjoyed the society and friendship of Dante, whose likeness he has transmitted to posterity.

[5] Guido Cavalcanti, the friend of our Poet, had eclipsed the literary fame of Guido Guinicelli. See also the twenty-sixth Canto.

And his might withers it, by whom it sprang
Crude from the lap of earth." I thus to him:
"True are thy sayings: to my heart they breathe
The kindly spirit of meekness, and allay
What tumours rankle there. But who is he,
Of whom thou spakest but now?"—"This," he replied,
"Is Provenzano. He is here, because
He reach'd with grasp presumptuous, at the sway
Of all Siena. Thus he still hath gone,
Thus goeth never-resting, since he died.
Such is the acquittance render'd back of him,
Who, in the mortal life, too much hath dared."
I then: "If soul, that to life's verge delays
Repentance, linger in that lower space,
Nor hither mount, (unless good prayers befriend),
Or ever time, long as it lived, be past;
How chanced admittance was vouchsafed to him?"

"When at his glory's topmost height," said he,
"Respect of dignity all cast aside,
Freely he fix'd him on Siena's plain,
A suitor[6] to redeem his suffering friend,
Who languish'd in the prison-house of Charles;
Nor, for his sake, refused through every vein
To tremble. More I will not say; and dark,
I know, my words are; but thy neighbours soon
Shall help thee to a comment on the text.
This is the work, that from these limits freed him."

[6] Provenzano Salvani, for the sake of one of his friends who was detained in captivity by Charles I of Sicily, personally supplicated the people of Siena to contribute the ransom required by the King; and this act of self-abasement atoned for his general ambition. He fell at Vald' Elsa, where the Florentines discomfited the Sienese in June, 1269.

CANTO XII

ARGUMENT.—Dante, being desired by Virgil to look down on the ground which they are treading, observes that it is wrought over with imagery exhibiting various instances of pride recorded in history and fable. They leave the first cornice, and are ushered to the next by an angel who points out the way.

WITH equal pace, as oxen in the yoke,
I, with that laden spirit, journey'd on,
Long as the mild instructor suffer'd me;
But, when he bade me quit him, and proceed,
(For "Here," said he, "behoves with sail and oars
Each man, as best he may, push on his bark,")
Upright, as one disposed for speed, I raised
My body, still in thought submissive bow'd.
  I now my leader's track not loth pursued;
And each had shown how light we fared along,
When thus he warned me: "Bend thine eyesight down,
For thou, to ease the way, shalt find it good
To ruminate the bed beneath thy feet."
  As, in memorial of the buried, drawn
Upon earth-level tombs, the sculptured form
Of what was once, appears, (at sight whereof
Tears often stream forth, by remembrance waked,
Whose sacred stings the piteous often feel),
So saw I there, but with more curious skill
Of portraiture o'erwrought, whate'er of space
From forth the mountain stretches. On one part
Him I beheld, above all creatures erst
Created noblest, lightening fall from Heaven:
On the other side, with bolt celestial pierced,
Briareus; cumbering earth he lay, through dint
Of mortal ice-stroke. The Thymbræan god,[1]
With Mars, I saw, and Pallas, round their sire,
Arm'd still, and gazing on the giants' limbs
Strewn o'er the ethereal field. Nimrod I saw:
At foot of the stupendous work he stood,
As if bewilder'd, looking on the crowd
Leagued in his proud attempt on Sennaar's plain.
  O Niobe! in what a trance of woe

---

[1] "The Thymbræan god." Apollo.

Thee I beheld, upon that highway drawn,
Seven sons on either side thee slain. O Saul!
How ghastly didst thou look, on thine own sword
Expiring, in Gilboa, from that hour
Ne'er visited with rain from heaven, or dew.

O fond Arachne! thee I also saw,
Half spider now, in anguish, crawling up
The unfinish'd web thou weaved'st to thy bane.

O Rehoboam! here thy shape doth seem
Louring no more defiance; but fear-smote,
With none to chase him, in his chariot whirl'd.

Was shown beside upon the solid floor,
How dear Alcmæon forced his mother rate
That ornament, in evil hour received:
How, in the temple, on Sennacherib fell
His sons, and how a corpse they left him there.
Was shown the scath, and cruel mangling made
By Tomyris on Cyrus, when she cried,
"Blood thou didst thirst for: take thy fill of blood."
Was shown how routed in the battle fled
The Assyrians, Holofernes slain, and e'en
The relics of the carnage. Troy I mark'd,
In ashes and in caverns. Oh! how fallen,
How abject, Ilion, was thy semblance there.

What master of the pencil or the style
Had traced the shades and lines, that might have made
The subtlest workman wonder? Dead, the dead;
The living seem'd alive: with clearer view,
His eye beheld not, who beheld the truth,
Than mine what I did tread on, while I went
Low bending. Now swell out, and with stiff necks
Pass on, ye sons of Eve! vale not your looks,
Lest they descry the evil of your path.

I noted not (so busied was my thought)
How much we now had circled of the mount;
And of his course yet more the sun had spent;
When he, who with still wakeful caution went,
Admonish'd: "Raise thou up thy head: for know
Time is not now for slow suspense. Behold,
That way, an Angel hasting toward us. Lo,

When duly the sixth handmaid doth return
From service on the day. Wear thou, in look
And gesture, seemly grace of reverent awe;
That gladly he may forward us aloft.
Consider that this day ne'er dawns again."

   Time's loss he had so often warn'd me 'gainst,
I could not miss the scope at which he aim'd.

   The goodly shape approach'd us, snowy white
In vesture, and with visage casting streams
Of tremulous lustre like the matin star.
His arms he open'd, then his wings; and spake:
"Onward! the steps, behold, are near; and now
The ascent is without difficulty gain'd."

   A scanty few are they, who, when they hear
Such tidings, hasten. O, ye race of men!
Though born to soar, why suffer ye a wind
So slight to baffle ye? He led us on
Where the rock parted; here, against my front,
Did beat his wings; then promised I should fare
In safety on my way. As to ascend
That steep, upon whose brow the chapel stands,[2]
(O'er Rubaconte, looking lordly down
On the well-guided city[3]), up the right
The impetuous rise is broken by the steps
Carved in that old and simple age, when still
The registry[4] and label rested safe;
Thus is the acclivity relieved, which here,
Precipitous, from the other circuit falls:
But, on each hand, the tall cliff presses close.

   As, entering, there we turn'd, voices, in strain
Ineffable, sang: "Blessed[5] are the poor
In spirit." Ah! how far unlike to these

---

[2] "The chapel stands." The church of San Miniato in Florence, situated on a height that overlooks the Arno, where it is crossed by the bridge Rubaconte, so called from Messer Rubaconte da Mandella, of Milan, chief magistrate of Florence, by whom the bridge was founded in 1237. [The bridge is now generally known as the Ponte alle Grazie. —Ed.]

[3] "The well-guided city." This is said ironically of Florence.

[4] "The registry." In allusion to certain instances of fraud committed in Dante's time with respect to the public accounts and measures.

[5] "Blessed." "Blessed are the poor in spirit, for theirs is the kingdom of heaven." Matt. v. 3.

The straits of Hell: here songs to usher us,
There shrieks of woe. We climb the holy stairs:
And lighter to myself by far I seem'd
Than on the plain before; whence thus I spake:
"Say, master, of what heavy thing have I
Been lighten'd; that scarce aught the sense of toil
Affects me journeying?" He in few replied:
"When sin's broad characters,[6] that yet remain
Upon thy temples, though well nigh effaced,
Shall be, as one is, all clean razed out;
Then shall thy feet by heartiness of will
Be so o'ercome, they not alone shall feel
No sense of labor, but delight much more
Shall wait them, urged along their upward way."

    Then like to one, upon whose head is placed
Somewhat he deems not of, but from the becks
Of others, as they pass him by; his hand
Lends therefore help to assure him, searches, finds,
And well performs such office as the eye
Wants power to execute; so stretching forth
The fingers of my right hand, did I find
Six only of the letters, which his sword,
Who bare the keys, had traced upon my brow.
The leader, as he mark'd mine action, smiled.

CANTO XIII

ARGUMENT.—They gain the second cornice, where the sin of envy is purged; and having proceeded a little to the right, they hear voices uttered by invisible spirits recounting famous examples of charity, and next behold the shades, or souls, of the envious clad in sackcloth, and having their eyes sewed up with an iron thread. Amongst these Dante finds Sapia, a Siennese lady, from whom he learns the cause of her being there.

WE reach'd the summit of the scale, and stood
Upon the second buttress of that mount
Which healeth him who climbs. A cornice there,
Like to the former, girdles round the hill;
Save that its arch, with sweep less ample, bends.

[6] "Sin's broad characters." Of the seven P's, that denoted the same number of sins (Peccata) whereof he was to be cleansed (see Canto ix. 100), the first had now vanished in consequence of his having passed the place where the sin of pride, the chief of them, was expiated.

Shadow, nor image there, is seen: all smooth
The rampart and the path, reflecting naught
But the rock's sullen hue. "If here we wait,
For some to question," said the bard, "I fear
Our choice may haply meet too long delay."
    Then fixedly upon the sun his eyes
He fasten'd; made his right the central point
From whence to move; and turn'd the left aside.
"O pleasant light, my confidence and hope!
Conduct us thou," he cried, "on this new way,
Where now I venture; leading to the bourn
We seek. The universal world to thee
Owes warmth and lustre. If no other cause
Forbid, thy beams should ever be our guide."
    Far, as is measured for a mile on earth,
In brief space had we journey'd; such prompt will
Impell'd; and toward us flying, now were heard
Spirits invisible, who courteously
Unto love's table bade the welcome guest.
The voice, that first flew by, call'd forth aloud,
"They have no wine," so on behind us past,
Those sounds reiterating, nor yet lost
In the faint distance, when another came
Crying, "I am Orestes," [1] and alike
Wing'd its fleet way. "O father!" I exclaim'd,
"What tongues are these?" and as I question'd, lo!
A third exclaiming, "Love ye those have wrong'd you."
    "This circuit," said my teacher, "knots the scourge
For envy; and the cords are therefore drawn
By charity's correcting hand. The curb
Is of a harsher sound; as thou shalt hear
(If I deem rightly) ere thou reach the pass,
Where pardon sets them free. But fix thine eyes
Intently through the air; and thou shalt see
A multitude before thee seated, each
Along the shelving grot." Then more than erst
I oped mine eyes; before me view'd; and saw
Shadows with garments dark as was the rock;
And when we pass'd a little forth, I heard

[1] "Orestes." Alluding to his friendship with Pylades.

A crying, "Blessed Mary! pray for us,
Michael and Peter! all ye saintly host!"
   I do not think there walks on earth this day
Man so remorseless, that he had not yearn'd
With pity at the sight that next I saw.
Mine eyes a load of sorrow teem'd, when now
I stood so near them, that their semblances
Came clearly to my view. Of sackcloth vile
Their covering seem'd; and, on his shoulder, one
Did stay another, leaning; and all lean'd
Against the cliff. E'en thus the blind and poor,
Near the confessionals, to crave an alms,
Stand, each his head upon his fellow's sunk;
So most to stir compassion, not by sound
Of words alone, but that which moves not less,
The sight of misery. And as never beam
Of noon-day visiteth the eyeless man,
E'en so was heaven a niggard unto these
Of his fair light: for, through the orbs of all,
A thread of wire, impiercing, knits them up,
As for the taming of a haggard hawk.
It were a wrong, methought, to pass and look
On others, yet myself the while unseen.
To my sage counsel therefore did I turn.
He knew the meaning of the mute appeal,
Nor waited for my questioning, but said:
"Speak; and be brief, be subtile in thy words."
   On that part of the cornice, whence no rim
Engarlands its steep fall, did Virgil come;
On the other side me were the spirits, their cheeks
Bathing devout with penitential tears,
That through the dread impalement forced a way.
   I turn'd me to them, and "O shades!" said I,
"Assured that to your eyes unveil'd shall shine
The lofty light, sole object of your wish,
So may Heaven's grace clear whatsoe'er of foam
Floats turbid on the conscience, that thenceforth
The stream of mind roll limpid from its source;
As ye declare (for so shall ye impart
A boon I dearly prize) if any soul

Of Latium dwell among ye: and perchance
That soul may profit, if I learn so much."
    "My brother! we are, each one, citizens
Of one true city.[2] Any, thou wouldst say,
Who lived a stranger in Italia's land."
    So heard I answering, as appear'd, a voice
That onward came some space from whence I stood.
    A spirit I noted, in whose look was mark'd
Expectance. Ask ye how? The chin was raised
As in one reft of sight. "Spirit," said I,
"Who for thy rise art tutoring, (if thou be
That which didst answer to me), or by place,
Or name, disclose thyself, that I may know thee."
    "I was," it answer'd, "of Sienna: here
I cleanse away with these the evil life,
Soliciting with tears that He, who is,
Vouchsafe Him to us. Though Sapia[3] named,
In sapience I excell'd not; gladder far
Of other's hurt, than of the good befell me.
That thou mayst own I now deceive thee not,
Hear, if my folly were not as I speak it.
When now my tears sloped waning down the arch,
It so bechanced, my fellow-citizens
Near Colle met their enemies in the field;
And I pray'd God to grant what He had will'd.[4]
There were they vanquish'd, and betook themselves
Unto the bitter passages of flight.
I mark'd the hunt; and waxing out of bounds
In gladness, lifted up my shameless brow,
And, like the merlin[5] cheated by a gleam,
Cried: 'It is over. Heaven! I fear thee not.'
Upon my verge of life I wish'd for peace
With God; nor yet repentance had supplied
What I did lack of duty, were it not

2 " —— Citizens of one true city!"
"For here we have no continuing city,
but we seek one to come."—Heb. xiii. 14.
3 "Sapia." A lady of Sienna, living in
exile at Colle, so overjoyed at a defeat
which her countrymen sustained near
that place, that she declared nothing more
was wanting to make her die contented.

4 " —— What He had will'd." That
her countrymen should be defeated in
battle.
5 Induced by a gleam of fine weather
in the winter to escape from his master,
the merlin was soon oppressed by the
rigor of the season.

The hermit Piero,[6] touch'd with charity,
In his devout orisons thought on me.
But who art thou that question'st of our state,
Who go'st, as I believe, with lids unclosed,
And breathest in thy talk?"—"Mine eyes," said I,
"May yet be here ta'en from me; but not long;
For they have not offended grievously
With envious glances. But the woe beneath[7]
Urges my soul with more exceeding dread.
That nether load already weighs me down."

    She thus: "Who then, amongst us here aloft,
Hath brought thee, if thou weenest to return?"

    "He," answered I, "who standeth mute beside me.
I live: of me ask therefore, chosen spirit!
If thou desire I yonder yet should move
For thee my mortal feet."—"Oh!" she replied,
"This is so strange a thing, it is great sign
That God doth love thee. Therefore with thy prayer
Sometime assist me: and, by that I crave,
Which most thou covetest, that if thy feet
E'er tread on Tuscan soil, thou save my fame
Amongst my kindred. Them shalt thou behold
With that vain multitude,[8] who set their hope
On Telamone's haven; there to fail
Confounded, more than when the fancied stream
They sought, of Dian call'd: but they, who lead
Their navies, more than ruin'd hopes shall mourn."

---

[6] "The hermit Piero." Piero Petti-
nagno, a holy hermit of Florence.
[7] Dante felt that he was much more
subject to the sin of pride, than to that
of envy.
[8] The Sienese.

CANTO XIV

ARGUMENT.—Our Poet on this second cornice finds also the souls of Guido del Duca of Brettinoro, and Rinieri da Calboli of Romagna; the latter of whom, hearing that he comes from the banks of the Arno, inveighs against the degeneracy of all those who dwell in the cities visited by that stream; and the former, in like manner, against the inhabitants of Romagna. On leaving these, our Poets hear voices recording noted instances of envy.

" SAY,[1] who is he around our mountain winds,
      Or ever death has pruned his wing for flight;
      That opes his eyes, and covers them at will?"
   "I know not who he is, but know thus much;
He comes not singly. Do thou ask of him,
For thou art nearer to him; and take heed,
Accost him gently, so that he may speak."
   Thus on the right two spirits, bending each
Toward the other, talk'd of me; then both
Addressing me, their faces backward lean'd,
And thus the one[2] began: "O soul, who yet
Pent in the body, tendest towards the sky!
For charity, we pray thee, comfort us;
Recounting whence thou comest, and who thou art:
For thou dost make us, at the favor shown thee,
Marvel, as at a thing that ne'er hath been."
   "There stretches through the midst of Tuscany,"
I straight began, "a brooklet,[3] whose well-head
Springs up in Falterona; with his race
Not satisfied, when he some hundred miles
Hath measured. From his banks bring I this frame.
To tell you who I am were words mis-spent:
For yet my name scarce sounds on rumour's lip."
   "If well I do incorporate with my thought
The meaning of thy speech," said he, who first
Address'd me, "thou dost speak of Arno's wave."
   To whom the other:[4] "Why hath he conceal'd
The title of that river, as a man
Doth of some horrible thing?" The spirit, who

---

[1] "Say." The two spirits who thus speak to each other are Guido del Duca, of Brettinoro, and Rinieri da Calboli, of Romagna.

[2] "The one." Guido del Duca.

[3] The Arno, that rises in Falterona, a mountain in the Apennines. Its course is 120 miles.

[4] Rinieri da Calboli.

Thereof was question'd, did acquit him thus:
"I know not: but 'tis fitting well the name
Should perish of that vale; for from the source,[5]
Where teems so plenteously the Alpine steep
Maim'd of Pelorus, (that doth scarcely pass
Beyond that limit), even to the point
Where unto ocean is restored what heaven
Drains from the exhaustless store for all earth's streams,
Throughout the space is virtue worried down,
As 't were a snake, by all, for mortal foe;
Or through disastrous influence on the place,
Or else distortion of misguided wills
That custom goads to evil: whence in those,
The dwellers in that miserable vale,
Nature is so transform'd, it seems as they
Had shared of Circe's feeding. 'Midst brute swine,[6]
Worthier of acorns than of other food
Created for man's use, he shapeth first
His obscure way; then, sloping onward, finds
Curs,[7] snarlers more in spite than power, from whom
He turns with scorn aside: still journeying down,
By how much more the curst and luckless foss[8]
Swells out to largeness, e'en so much it finds
Dogs turning into wolves.[9] Descending still
Through yet more hollow eddies, next he meets
A race of foxes,[10] so replete with craft,
They do not fear that skill can master it.
Nor will I cease because my words are heard[11]
By other ears than thine. It shall be well
For this man,[12] if he keep in memory
What from no erring spirit I reveal.
Lo! I behold thy grandson,[13] that becomes

[5] From the rise of the Arno in the Apennines, whence Pelorus in Sicily was torn by a convulsion of the earth, even to the point where the same river unites with the ocean, Virtue is persecuted by all.

[6] The people of Casentino.

[7] "Curs." The Arno leaves Arezzo about four miles to the left.

[8] "Foss." So in his anger he terms the Arno.

[9] "Wolves." The Florentines.

[10] "Foxes." The Pisans.

[11] Guido still addresses Rinieri.

[12] For Dante, who has told us that he comes from the banks of Arno.

[13] "Thy grandson." Fulcieri da Calboli, grandson of Rinieri da Calboli, who is here spoken to. The atrocities predicted came to pass in 1302.

A hunter of those wolves, upon the shore
Of the fierce stream; and cows them all with dread.
Their flesh, yet living, sets he up to sale,
Then, like an aged beast, to slaughter dooms.
Many of life he reaves, himself of worth
And goodly estimation. Smear'd with gore,
Mark how he issues from the rueful wood;
Leaving such havoc, that in thousand years
It spreads not to prime lustihood again."

As one, who tidings hears of woe to come,
Changes his looks perturb'd, from whate'er part
The peril grasp him; so beheld I change
That spirit, who had turn'd to listen; struck
With sadness, soon as he had caught the word.

His visage, and the other's speech, did raise
Desire in me to know the names of both;
Whereof, with meek entreaty, I inquired.

The shade, who late address'd me, thus resumed:
"Thy wish imports, that I vouchsafe to do
For thy sake what thou wilt not do for mine.
But, since God's will is that so largely shine
His grace in thee, I will be liberal too.
Guido of Duca know then that I am.
Envy so parch'd my blood, that had I seen
A fellow man made joyous, thou had'st mark'd
A livid paleness overspread my cheek.
Such harvest reap I of the seed I sow'd.
O man! why place thy heart where there doth need
Exclusion of participants in good?
This is Rinieri's spirit; this, the boast
And honour of the house of Calboli;
Where of his worth no heritage remains.
Nor his the only blood, that hath been stript
('Twixt Po, the mount, the Reno, and the shore[14])
Of all that truth or fancy asks for bliss:
But, in those limits, such a growth has sprung
Of rank and venom'd roots, as long would mock
Slow culture's toil. Where is good Lizio?[15] where

[14] The boundaries of Romagna.
[15] "Lizio." Lizio da Valbona intro-   duced into Boccaccio's Decameron, G. v.
N. 4.

Mainardi, Traversaro, and Carpigna?[16]
O bastard slips of old Romagna's line!
When in Bologna the low artisan,[17]
And in Faenza yon Bernardin[18] sprouts,
A gentle cyon from ignoble stem.
Wonder not, Tuscan, if thou see me weep,
When I recall to mind those once loved names,
Guido of Prata,[19] and of Azzo him[20]
That dwelt with us; Tignoso[21] and his troop,
With Traversaro's house and Anastagio's,[22]
(Each race disherited); and beside these,
The ladies and the knights, the toils and ease,
That witch'd us into love and courtesy;
Where now such malice reigns in recreant hearts
O Brettinoro![23] wherefore tarriest still,
Since forth of thee thy family hath gone,
And many, hating evil, join'd their steps?
Well doeth he, that bids his lineage cease,
Bagnacavallo;[24] Castrocaro ill,
And Conio worse,[25] who care to propagate
A race of Counties[26] from such blood as theirs.
Well shall ye also do, Pagani,[27] then
When from amongst you hies your demon child;
Not so, howe'er, that thenceforth there remain

[16] Arrigo Manardi, of Faenza, or, as some say, of Brettinoro; Pier Traversaro, Lord of Ravenna; and Guido di Carpigna, of Montefeltro.

[17] One who had been a mechanic, named Lambertaccio, arrived at almost supreme power in Bologna.

[18] Benardin di Fosco, a man of low origin, but great talents, who governed at Faenza.

[19] "Prata." A place between Faenza and Ravenna.

[20] "Of Azzo him." Ugolino, of the Ubaldini family in Tuscany.

[21] Federigo Tignoso of Rimini.

[22] Two noble families of Ravenna.

[23] "O Brettinoro." A beautifully situated castle in Romagna, the hospitable residence of Guido del Duca, who is here speaking. Landino relates that there were several of this family who, when a stranger arrived among them, contended with one another by whom he should be entertained; and that in order to end this dispute, they set up a pillar with as many rings as there were fathers of families among them, a ring being assigned to each, and that accordingly as a stranger on his arrival hung his horse's bridle on one or other of these, he became his guest to whom the ring belonged.

[24] "Bagnacavallo." A castle between Imola and Ravenna.

[25] "—— Castrocaro ill, and Conio worse." Both in Romagna.

[26] "Counties." I have used this word here for "counts," as it is in Shakespeare.

[27] "Pagani." The Pagani were lords of Faenza and Imola. One of them, Machinardo, was named "the Demon," from his treachery. See Hell, Canto xxvii. 47 and note.

True proof of what ye were. O Hugolin,[28]
Thou sprung of Fantolini's line! thy name
Is safe; since none is look'd for after thee
To cloud its lustre, warping from thy stock.
But, Tuscan! go thy ways; for now I take
Far more delight in weeping, than in words.
Such pity for your sakes hath wrung my heart."

We knew those gentle spirits, at parting, heard
Our steps. Their silence therefore, of our way,
Assured us. Soon as we had quitted them,
Advancing onward, lo! a voice, that seem'd
Like volley'd lightning, when it rives the air,
Met us, and shouted, "Whosoever finds
Will slay me"; then fled from us, as the bolt
Lanced sudden from a downward-rushing cloud.
When it had given short truce unto our hearing,
Behold the other with a crash as loud
As the quick-following thunder: "Mark in me
Aglauros, turn'd to rock." I, at the sound
Retreating, drew more closely to my guide.

Now in mute stilness rested all the air;
And thus he spake: "There was the galling bit,
Which should keep man within his boundary.
But your old enemy so baits the hook,
He drags you eager to him. Hence nor curb
Avails you, nor reclaiming call. Heaven calls,
And, round about you wheeling, courts your gaze
With everlasting beauties. Yet your eye
Turns with fond doting still upon the earth.
Therefore He smites you who discerneth all."

[28] "Hugolin." Ugolino Ubaldini, a noble and virtuous person in Faenza, who, on account of his age probably, was not likely to leave any offspring behind him.

CANTO XV

ARGUMENT.—An Angel invites them to ascend the next steep. On their way Dante suggests certain doubts, which are resolved by Virgil; and, when they reach the third cornice, where the sin of anger is purged, our Poet, in a kind of waking dream, beholds remarkable instances of patience; and soon after they are enveloped in a dense fog.

AS much as 'twixt the third hour's close and dawn,
    Appeareth of Heaven's sphere, that ever whirls
    As restless as an infant in his play;
So much appear'd remaining to the sun
Of his slope journey towards the western goal.
    Evening was there, and here the noon of night;
And full upon our forehead smote the beams.
For round the mountain, circling, so our path
Had led us, that toward the sunset now
Direct we journey'd; when I felt a weight
Of more exceeding splendour, than before,
Press on my front. The cause unknown, amaze
Possess'd me! and both hands against my brows
Lifting, I interposed them, as a screen,
That of its gorgeous superflux of light
Clips the diminish'd orb. As when the ray,
Striking on water or the surface clear
Of mirror, leaps unto the opposite part,
Ascending at a glance, e'en as it fell,
And as much differs from the stone, that falls
Through equal space, (so practic skill hath shown);
Thus, with refracted light, before me seem'd
The ground there smitten; whence, in sudden haste,
My sight recoil'd. "What is this, sire beloved!
'Gainst which I strive to shield the sight in vain?"
Cried I, "and which toward us moving seems?"
    "Marvel not, if the family of Heaven,"
He answer'd, "yet with dazzling radiance dim
Thy sense. It is a messenger who comes,
Inviting man's ascent. Such sights ere long,
Not grievous, shall impart to thee delight,
As thy perception is by nature wrought
Up to their pitch." The blessed Angel, soon

As we had reach'd him, hail'd us with glad voice:
"Here enter on a ladder far less steep
Than ye have yet encounter'd." We forthwith
Ascending, heard behind us chanted sweet,
"Blessed the merciful," [1] and "Happy thou,
That conquer'st." Lonely each, my guide and I,
Pursued our upward way; and as we went,
Some profit from his words I hoped to win,
And thus of him inquiring, framed my speech:
"What meant Romagna's spirit, [2] when he spake
Of bliss exclusive, with no partner shared?"

He straight replied: "No wonder, since he knows
What sorrow waits on his own worst defect,
If he chide others, that they less may mourn.
Because ye point your wishes at a mark,
Where, by communion of possessors, part
Is lessen'd, envy bloweth up men's sighs.
No fear of that might touch ye, if the love
Of higher sphere exalted your desire.
For there, by how much more they call it *ours,*
So much propriety of each in good
Encreases more, and heighten'd chárity
Wraps that fair cloister in a brighter flame."

"Now lack I satisfaction more," said I,
"Than if thou hadst been silent at the first;
And doubt more gathers on my labouring thought.
How can it chance, that good distributed,
The many, that possess it, makes more rich,
Than if 't were shared by few?" He answering thus:
"Thy mind, reverting still to things of earth,
Strikes darkness from true light. The highest Good
Unlimited, ineffable, doth so speed
To love, as beam to lucid body darts,
Giving as much of ardour as it finds.
The sempiternal effluence streams abroad,
Spreading, wherever charity extends;
So that the more aspirants to that bliss
Are multiplied, more good is there to love,
And more is loved; as mirrors, that reflect,

[1] "Blessed the merciful." Matt. v. 7.   [2] Guido del Duca, of Brettinoro.

Each unto other, propagated light.
If these my words avail not to allay
Thy thirsting, Beatrice thou shalt see,
Who of this want, and of all else thou hast,
Shall rid thee to the full. Provide but thou,
That from thy temples may be soon erased,
E'en as the two already, those five scars,
That, when they pain thee worst, then kindliest heal."
   "Thou," I had said, "content'st me"; when I saw
The other round was gain'd, and wondering eyes
Did keep me mute. There suddenly I seem'd
By an ecstatic vision wrapt away;
And in a temple saw, methought, a crowd
Of many persons; and at the entrance stood
A dame, whose sweet demeanour did express
A mother's love, who said, "Child! why hast thou
Dealt with us thus? Behold thy sire and I
Sorrowing have sought thee"; and so held her peace;
And straight the vision fled. A female next
Appear'd before me, down whose visage coursed
Those waters, that grief forces out from one
By deep resentment stung, who seem'd to say:
'If thou, Pisistratus, be lord indeed
Over this city,[3] named with such debate
Of adverse gods, and whence each science sparkles,
Avenge thee of those arms, whose bold embrace
Hath clasp'd our daughter"; and to her, meseem'd,
Benign and meek, with visage undisturb'd,
Her sovran spake: "How shall we those requite[4]
Who wish us evil, if we thus condemn
The man that loves us?" After that I saw
A multitude, in fury burning, slay
With stones a stripling youth,[5] and shout amain
"Destroy, destroy"; and him I saw, who bow'd

---

[3] "Over this city." Athens, named after Minerva (Αθήνη), in consequence of her having produced a more valuable gift for it in the olive than Neptune had done in the horse.
[4] "How shall we those requite?" The answer of Pisistratus the tyrant to his wife, when she urged him to inflict the punishment of death on a young man, who, inflamed with love for his daughter, had snatched a kiss from her in public.
[5] "A stripling youth." The Proto-martyr Stephen.

Heavy with death unto the ground, yet made
His eyes, unfolded upward, gates to Heaven,
Praying forgiveness of the Almighty Sire,
Amidst that cruel conflict, on his foes,
With looks that win compassion to their aim.

Soon as my spirit, from her airy flight
Returning, sought again the things whose truth
Depends not on her shaping, I observed
She had not roved to falsehood in her dreams.

Meanwhile the leader, who might see I moved
As one who struggles to shake off his sleep,
Exclaim'd: "What ails thee, that thou canst not hold
Thy footing firm; but more than half a league
Hast travel'd with closed eyes and tottering gait,
Like to a man by wine or sleep o'ercharged?"

"Beloved father! so thou deign," said I,
"To listen, I will tell thee what appear'd
Before me, when so fail'd my sinking steps."

He thus: "Not if thy countenance were mask'd
With hundred vizards, could a thought of thine,
How small soe'er, elude me. What thou saw'st
Was shown, that freely thou mightst ope thy heart
To the waters of peace, that flow diffused
From their eternal fountain. I not ask'd,
What ails thee? for such cause as he doth, who
Looks only with that eye, which sees no more,
When spiritless the body lies; but ask'd,
To give fresh vigour to thy foot. Such goads,
The slow and loitering need; that they be found
Not wanting, when their hour of watch returns."

So on we journey'd, through the evening sky
Gazing intent, far onward as our eyes,
With level view, could stretch against the bright
Vespertine ray: and lo! by slow degrees
Gathering, a fog made towards us, dark as night.
There was no room for 'scaping; and that mist
Bereft us, both of sight and the pure air.

CANTO XVI

ARGUMENT.—As they proceed through the mist, they hear the voices of spirits praying. Marco Lombardo, one of these, points out to Dante the error of such as impute our actions to necessity; explains to him that man is endued with free will; and shows that much of human depravity results from the undue mixture of spiritual and temporal authority in rulers.

HELL'S dunnest gloom, or night unlustrous, dark,
Of every planet 'reft, and pall'd in clouds,
Did never spread before the sight a veil
In thickness like that fog, nor to the sense
So palpable and gross. Entering its shade,
Mine eye endured not with unclosed lids;
Which marking, near me drew the faithful guide,
Offering me his shoulder for a stay.

As the blind man behind his leader walks,
Lest he should err, or stumble unawares
On what might harm him or perhaps destroy;
I journey'd through that bitter air and foul,
Still listening to my escort's warning voice,
"Look that from me thou part not." Straight I heard
Voices, and each one seem'd to pray for peace,
And for compassion, to the Lamb of God
That taketh sins away. Their prelude still
Was "Agnus Dei"; and through all the choir,
One voice, one measure ran, that perfect seem'd
The concord of their song. "Are these I hear
Spirits, O master?" I exclaim'd; and he,
"Thou aim'st aright: these loose the bonds of wrath."

"Now who art thou, that through our smoke dost cleave,
And speak'st of us, as thou thyself e'en yet
Dividedst time by calends?" So one voice
Bespake me; whence my master said, "Reply;
And ask, if upward hence the passage lead."

"O being! who dost make thee pure, to stand
Beautiful once more in thy Maker's sight;
Along with me: and thou shalt hear and wonder."
Thus I, whereto the spirit answering spake:
"Long as 'tis lawful for me, shall my steps
Follow on thine; and since the cloudy smoke

Forbids the seeing, hearing in its stead
Shall keep us join'd." I then forthwith began:
"Yet in my mortal swathing, I ascend
To higher regions; and am hither come
Thorough the fearful agony of Hell.
And, if so largely God hath doled His grace,
That, clean beside all modern precedent,
He wills me to behold His kingly state;
From me conceal not who thou wast, ere death
Had loosed thee; but instruct me: and instruct
If rightly to the pass I tend; thy words
The way directing, as a safe escort."

"I was of Lombardy, and Marco call'd:[1]
Not inexperienced of the world, that worth
I still affected, from which all have turn'd
The nerveless bow aside. Thy course tends right
Unto the summit:" and, replying thus,
He added, "I beseech thee pray for me,
When thou shalt come aloft." And I to him:
"Accept my faith for pledge I will perform
What thou requirest. Yet one doubt remains,
That wrings me sorely, if I solve it not.
Singly before it urged me, doubled now
By thine opinion, when I couple that
With one elsewhere declared; each strengthening other.
The world indeed is even so forlorn
Of all good, as thou speak'st it, and so swarms
With every evil. Yet, beseech thee, point
The cause out to me, that myself may see,
And unto others show it: for in Heaven
One places it, and one on earth below."

Then heaving forth a deep and audible sigh,
"Brother!" he thus began, "the world is blind;
And thou in truth comest from it. Ye, who live,

[1] A Venetian gentleman. "Lombardo" both was his surname and denoted the country to which he belonged. G. Villani, lib. vii. cap. cxx., terms him "a wise and worthy courtier." Benvenuto da Imola, says Landino, relates of him, that being imprisoned and not able to pay his ransom, he wrote to his friend Riccardo da Camino, lord of Trevigi, who raised a contribution among the nobles of Lombardy; of which when Marco was informed, he wrote back with much indignation to Riccardo, that he had rather die than remain under obligations to so many benefactors. Riccardo then paid the whole out of his own purse.

Do so each cause refer to Heaven above,
E'en as its motion, of necessity,
Drew with it all that moves. If this were so,
Free choice in you were none; nor justice would
There should be joy for virtue, woe for ill.
Your movements have their primal bent from Heaven;
Not all: yet said I all; what then ensues?
Light have ye still to follow evil or good,
And of the will free power, which, if it stand
Firm and unwearied in Heaven's first assay,
Conquers at last, so it be cherish'd well,
Triumphant over all. To mightier force,
To better nature subject, ye abide
Free, not constrain'd by that which forms in you
The reasoning mind uninfluenced of the stars.
If then the present race of mankind err,
Seek in yourselves the cause, and find it there;
Herein thou shalt confess me no false spy.

    "Forth from His plastic hand, who charm'd beholds
Her image ere she yet exist, the soul
Comes like a babe, that wantons sportively,
Weeping and laughing in its wayward moods;
As artless, and as ignorant of aught,
Save that her Maker being one who dwells
With gladness ever, willingly she turns
To whate'er yields her joy. Of some slight good
The flavour soon she tastes; and, snared by that,
With fondness she pursues it; if no guide
Recall, no rein direct her wandering course.
Hence it behoved, the law should be a curb;
A sovereign hence behoved, whose piercing view
Might mark at least the fortress[2] and main tower
Of the true city. Laws indeed there are:
But who is he observes them? None; not he,
Who goes before, the shepherd of the flock,

---

[2] Justice, the most necessary virtue in the chief magistrate, as the commentators for the most part explain it. See also Dante's De Monarchiâ, book I. Yet Lombardi understands the law here spoken of to be the law of God; "the sovereign," a spiritual ruler, and "the true city," the society of true believers; so that "the fortress," according to him, denotes the principal parts of Christian duty.

Who[3] chews the cud but doth not cleave the hoof.
Therefore the multitude, who see their guide
Strike at the very good they covet most,
Feed there and look no further. Thus the cause
Is not corrupted nature in yourselves,
But ill-conducting, that hath turn'd the world
To evil. Rome, that turn'd it unto good,
Was wont to boast two suns,[4] whose several beams
Cast light on either way, the world's and God's.
One since hath quench'd the other; and the sword
Is grafted on the crook; and, so conjoin'd,
Each must perforce decline to worse, unawed
By fear of other. If thou doubt me, mark
The blade: each herb is judged of by its seed.
That land,[5] through which Adice and the Po
Their waters roll, was once the residence
Of courtesy and valour, ere the day[6]
That frown'd on Frederick; now secure may pass
Those limits, whosoe'er hath left, for shame,
To talk with good men, or come near their haunts.
Three aged ones are still found there, in whom
The old time chides the new: these deem it long
Ere God restore them to a better world:
The good Gherardo,[7] of Palazzo he,
Conrad;[8] and Guido of Castello,[9] named
In Gallic phrase more fitly the plain Lombard.
On this at last conclude. The Church of Rome,
Mixing two governments that ill assort,
Hath miss'd her footing, fallen into the mire,
And there herself and burden much defiled."

[3] "Who." He compares the Pope, on account of the union of the temporal with the spiritual power in his person, to an unclean beast in the Levitical law. "The camel, because he cheweth the cud, but divideth not the hoof." Levit. vi. 4.

[4] The Emperor and Bishop of Rome.

[5] "That land." Lombardy.

[6] Before the Emperor Frederick II was defeated at Parma, in 1248.

[7] Gherardo da Camino, of Trevigi. He is honorably mentioned in our Poet's Con- vito, p. 173. "Let us suppose that Ghe- rardo da Camino had been the grandson of the meanest hind that ever drank of the Sile or the Cagnano, and that his grandfather was not yet forgotten; who will dare to say that Gherardo da Camino was a mean man, and who will not agree with me in calling him noble?"

[8] Currado da Palazzo of Brescia.

[9] Of Reggio. All the Italians were called Lombards by the French.

"O Marco!" I replied, "thine arguments
Convince me: and the cause I now discern,
Why of the heritage no portion came
To Levi's offspring. But resolve me this:
Who that Gherardo is, that as thou say'st
Is left a sample of the perish'd race,
And for rebuke to this untoward age?"

    "Either thy words," said he, "deceive, or else
Are meant to try me; that thou, speaking Tuscan,
Appear'st not to have heard of good Gherardo;
The sole addition that, by which I know him;
Unless I borrow'd from his daughter Gaïa[10]
Another name to grace him. God be with you.
I bear you company no more. Behold
The dawn with white ray glimmering through the mist.
I must away—the angel comes—ere he
Appear." He said, and would not hear me more.

CANTO XVII

ARGUMENT.—The Poet issues from that thick vapour; and soon after his fancy represents to him in lively portraiture some noted examples of anger. This imagination is dissipated by the appearance of an angel, who marshals them onward to the fourth cornice, on which the sin of gloominess or indifference is purged; and here Virgil shows him that this vice proceeds from a defect of love, and that all love can be only of two sorts, either natural, or of the soul; of which sorts the former is always right, but the latter may err either in respect of object or of degree.

CALL to remembrance, reader, if thou e'er
    Hast on an Alpine height been ta'en by cloud,
    Through which thou saw'st no better than the mole
Doth through opacous membrane; then, whene'er
The watery vapours dense began to melt
Into thin air, how faintly the sun's sphere
Seem'd wading through them: so thy nimble thought
May image, how at first I rebeheld
The sun, that bedward now his couch o'erhung.

    Thus, with my leader's feet still equaling pace,
From forth that cloud I came, when now expired

---

[10] "His daughter Gaïa." A lady equally admired for her modesty, the beauty of her person, and the excellency of her talents. Gaïa may perhaps lay claim to the praise of having been the first among the Italian ladies, by whom the vernacular poetry was cultivated.

The parting beams from off the nether shores.

　　O quick and forgetive power! that sometimes dost
So rob us of ourselves, we take no mark
Though round about us thousand trumpets clang;
What moves thee, if the senses stir not? Light
Moves thee from Heaven, spontaneous, self-inform'd;
Or, likelier, gliding down with swift illapse
By will divine. Portray'd before me came
The traces of her dire impiety,
Whose form was changed into the bird, that most
Delights itself in song:[1] and here my mind
Was inwardly so wrapt, it gave no place
To aught that ask'd admittance from without.
Next shower'd into my fantasy a shape
As of one crucified, whose visage spake
Fell rancour, malice deep, wherein he died;
And round him Ahasuerus the great king;
Esther his bride; and Mordecai the just,
Blameless in word and deed. As of itself
That unsubstantial coinage of the brain
Burst, like a bubble, when the water fails
That fed it; in my vision straight uprose
A damsel[2] weeping loud, and cried, "O queen!
O mother! wherefore has intemperate ire
Driven thee to loathe thy being? Not to lose
Lavinia, desperate thou hast slain thyself.
Now hast thou lost me. I am she, whose tears
Mourn, ere I fall, a mother's timeless end."

　　E'en as a sleep breaks off, if suddenly
New radiance strikes upon the closed lids,
The broken slumber quivering ere it dies;
Thus, from before me, sunk that imagery,
Vanishing, soon as on my face there struck
The light, outshining far our earthly beam.

[1] I cannot think, with Vellutello, that the swallow is here meant. Dante probably alludes to the story of Philomela, as it is found in Homer's "Odyssey," b. xix. 518. Philomela intended to slay the son of her husband's brother Amphion, incited to it by the envy of his wife, who had six children, while herself had only two, but through mistake slew her own son Itylus, and for her punishment was transformed by Jupiter into a nightingale.

[2] Lavinia, mourning for her mother Amata, who, impelled by grief and indignation for the supposed death of Turnus, destroyed herself.

As round I turn'd me to survey what place
I had arrived at, "Here ye mount": exclaim'd
A voice, that other purpose left me none
Save will so eager to behold who spake,
I could not chuse but gaze. As 'fore the sun,
That weighs our vision down, and veils his form
In light transcendent, thus my virtue fail'd
Unequal. "This is Spirit from above,
Who marshals us our upward way, unsought;
And in his own light shrouds him. As a man
Doth for himself, so now is done for us.
For whoso waits imploring, yet sees need
Of his prompt aidance, sets himself prepared
For blunt denial, ere the suit be made.
Refuse we not to lend a ready foot
At such inviting: haste we to ascend,
Before it darken: for we may not then,
Till morn again return." So spake my guide;
And to one ladder both address'd our steps;
And the first stair approaching, I perceived
Near me as 't were the waving of a wing,
That fann'd my face, and whisper'd: "Blessed they,
The peace-makers: they know not evil wrath."

    Now to such height above our heads were raised
The last beams, follow'd close by hooded night,
That many a star on all sides through the gloom
Shone out. "Why partest from me, O my strength?"
So with myself I commun'd; for I felt
My o'ertoil'd sinews slacken. We had reach'd
The summit, and were fix'd like to a bark
Arrived at land. And waiting a short space,
If aught should meet mine ear in that new round,
Then to my guide I turn'd, and said: "Loved sire!
Declare what guilt is on this circle purged.
If our feet rest, no need thy speech should pause."

    He thus to me: "The love of good, whate'er
Wanted of just proportion, here fulfils.
Here plies afresh the oar, that loiter'd ill.
But that thou mayst yet clearlier understand,
Give ear unto my words; and thou shalt cull

Some fruit may please thee well, from this delay.
   "Creator, nor created being, e'er,
My son," he thus began, "was without love,
Or natural, or the free spirit's growth,
Thou hast not that to learn. The natural still
Is without error: but the other swerves,
If on ill object bent, or through excess
Of vigour, or defect. While e'er it seeks
The primal blessings,[3] or with measure due
The inferior,[4] no delight, that flows from it,
Partakes of ill. But let it warp to evil,
Or with more ardour than behoves, or less,
Pursue the good; the thing created then
Works 'gainst its Maker. Hence thou must infer
That love is germin of each virtue in ye,
And of each act no less, that merits pain.
Now[5] since it may not be, but love intend
The welfare mainly of the thing it loves,
All from self-hatred are secure; and since
No being can be thought to exist apart,
And independent of the first, a bar
Of equal force restrains from hating that.
   "Grant the distinction just; and it remains
The evil must be another's, which is loved.
Three ways such love is gender'd in your clay.
There is[6] who hopes (his neighbour's worth deprest)
Pre-eminence himself; and covets hence,
For his own greatness, that another fall.
There is[7] who so much fears the loss of power,
Fame, favour, glory, (should his fellow mount
Above him), and so sickens at the thought,
He loves their opposite: and there is he,[8]
Whom wrong or insult seems to gall and shame,
That he doth thirst for vengeance; and such needs
Must dote on other's evil. Here beneath,

---

[3] "The primal blessings." Spiritual good.

[4] "The inferior." Temporal good.

[5] "Now." "It is impossible for any being, either to hate itself, or to hate the First Cause of all, by which it exists. We can therefore rejoice only in the evil which befalls others."

[6] "There is." The proud.

[7] "There is." The envious.

[8] "There is he." The resentful.

This threefold love is mourn'd. Of the other sort
Be now instructed; that which follows good,
But with disorder'd and irregular course.

"All indistinctly apprehend a bliss,
On which the soul may rest; the hearts of all
Yearn after it; and to that wished bourn
All therefore strive to tend. If ye behold,
Or seek it, with a love remiss and lax;
This cornice, after just repenting, lays
Its penal torment on ye. Other good
There is, where man finds not his happiness:
It is not true fruition; not that blest
Essence, of every good the branch and root.
The love too lavishly bestow'd on this,
Along three circles over us, is mourn'd.
Account of that division tripartite
Expect not, fitter for thine own research."

CANTO XVIII

ARGUMENT.—Virgil discourses further concerning the nature of love. Then a multitude of spirits rush by; two of whom, in van of the rest, record instances of zeal
and fervent affection, and another, who was Abbot of San Zeno in Verona, declares
himself to Virgil and Dante; and lastly follow other spirits, shouting forth memorable
examples of the sin for which they suffer. The Poet, pursuing his meditations, falls
into a dreamy slumber.

THE teacher ended, and his high discourse
Concluding, earnest in my looks inquired
If I appear'd content; and I, whom still
Unsated thirst to hear him urged, was mute,
Mute outwardly, yet inwardly I said:
"Perchance my too much questioning offends."
But he, true father, mark'd the secret wish
By diffidence restrain'd; and, speaking, gave
Me boldness thus to speak: "Master! my sight
Gathers so lively virtue from thy beams,
That all, thy words convey, distinct is seen.
Wherefore I pray thee, father, whom this heart
Holds dearest, thou wouldst deign by proof t' unfold
That love, from which, as from their source, thou bring'st
All good deeds and their opposite." He then:

"To what I now disclose be thy clear ken
Directed; and thou plainly shalt behold
How much those blind have err'd, who make themselves
The guides of men. The soul, created apt
To love, moves versatile which way soe'er
Aught pleasing prompts her, soon as she is waked
By pleasure into act. Of substance true
Your apprehension forms its counterfeit;
And, in you the ideal shape presenting,
Attracts the soul's regard. If she, thus drawn,
Incline toward it; love is that inclining,
And a new nature knit by pleasure in ye.
Then, as the fire points up, and mounting seeks
His birth-place and his lasting seat, e'en thus
Enters the captive soul into desire,
Which is a spiritual motion, that ne'er rests
Before enjoyment of the thing it loves.
Enough to show thee, how the truth from those
Is hidden, who aver all love a thing
Praiseworthy in itself; although perhaps
Its matter seem still good. Yet if the wax
Be good, it follows not the impression must."
     "What love is," I return'd, "thy words, O guide!
And my own docile mind, reveal. Yet thence
New doubts have sprung. For, from without, if love
Be offered to us, and the spirit knows
No other footing; tend she right or wrong,
Is no desert of hers." He answering thus:
"What reason here discovers, I have power
To show thee: that which lies beyond, expect
From Beatrice, faith not reason's task.
Spirit, substantial form, with matter join'd,
Not in confusion mix'd, hath in itself
Specific virtue of that union born,
Which is not felt except it work, nor proved
But through effect, as vegetable life
By the green leaf. From whence his intellect
Deduced its primal notices of things,
Man therefore knows not, or his appetites
Their first affections; such in you, as zeal

In bees to gather honey; at the first,
Volition, meriting nor blame nor praise.
But o'er each lower faculty supreme,
That, as she list, are summon'd to her bar,
Ye have that virtue[1] in you, whose just voice
Uttereth counsel, and whose word should keep
The threshold of assent. Here is the source,
Whence cause of merit in you is derived;
E'en as the affections, good or ill, she takes,
Or severs, winnow'd as the chaff. Those men,[2]
Who, reasoning, went to depth profoundest, mark'd
That innate freedom; and were thence induced
To leave their moral teaching to the world.
Grant then, that from necessity arise
All love that glows within you; to dismiss
Or harbour it, the power is in yourselves.
Remember, Beatrice, in her style,
Denominates free choice by eminence
The noble virtue; if in talk with thee
She touch upon that theme." The moon, well nigh
To midnight hour belated, made the stars
Appear to wink and fade; and her broad disk
Seem'd like a crag on fire, as up the vault[3]
That course she journey'd, which the sun then warms
When they of Rome behold him at his set
Betwixt Sardinia and the Corsic isle.
And now the weight, that hung upon my thought,
Was lighten'd by the aid of that clear spirit,
Who raiseth Andes[4] above Mantua's name.
I therefore, when my questions had obtain'd
Solution plain and ample, stood as one
Musing in dreamy slumber; but not long
Slumber'd; for suddenly a multitude,
The steep already turning from behind,

---

[1] "That virtue." Reason.
[2] "Those men." The great moral philosophers among the heathen.
[3] "Up the vault." The moon passed with a motion opposite to that of the heavens, through the constellation of the Scorpion, in which the sun is, when to those who are in Rome he appears to set between the isles of Corsica and Sardinia.
[4] "Andes." Andes, now Pietola, made more famous than Mantua, near which it is situated, by having been the birthplace of Virgil.

Rush'd on. With fury and like random rout,
As echoing on their shores at midnight heard
Ismenus and Asopus,[5] for his Thebes
If Bacchus' help were needed; so came these
Tumultuous, curving each his rapid step,
By eagerness impell'd of holy love.

  Soon they o'ertook us; with such swiftness moved
The mighty crowd. Two spirits at their head
Cried, weeping, "Blessed Mary[6] sought with haste
The hilly region. Cæsar,[7] to subdue
Ilerda, darted in Marseilles his sting,
And flew to Spain."—"Oh, tarry not: away!"
The others shouted; "let not time be lost
Through slackness of affection. Hearty zeal
To serve reanimates celestial grace."

  "O ye! in whom intenser fervency
Haply supplies, where lukewarm erst ye fail'd,
Slow or neglectful, to absolve your part
Of good and virtuous; this man, who yet lives,
(Credit my tale, though strange,) desires to ascend,
So morning rise to light us. Therefore say
Which hand leads nearest to the rifted rock."

  So spake my guide; to whom a shade return'd:
"Come after us, and thou shalt find the cleft.
We may not linger: such resistless will
Speeds our unwearied course. Vouchsafe us then
Thy pardon, if our duty seem to thee
Discourteous rudeness. In Verona I
Was Abbot[8] of San Zeno, when the hand
Of Barbarossa grasp'd imperial sway,
That name ne'er utter'd without tears in Milan.
And there is he,[9] hath one foot in his grave,

---

[5] "Ismenus and Asopus." Rivers near Thebes.

[6] "And Mary arose in those days, and went into the hill country with haste, into a city of Judah; and entered into the house of Zacharias and saluted Elisabeth."—Luke i. 39.

[7] Cæsar left Brutus to complete the siege of Marseilles, and hastened on to the attack of Afranius and Petreius, the generals of Pompey, at Ilerda (Lerida) in Spain.

[8] Alberto, Abbot of San Zeno in Verona, when Frederick I was Emperor, by whom Milan was besieged and reduced to ashes, in 1162.

[9] "There is he." Alberto della Scala, Lord of Verona, who had made his natural son Abbot of San Zeno.

Who for that monastery ere long shall weep,
Ruing his power misused: for that his son,
Of body ill compact, and worse in mind,
And born in evil, he hath set in place
Of its true pastor." Whether more he spake,
Or here was mute, I know not: he had sped
E'en now so far beyond us. Yet thus much
I heard, and in remembrance treasured it.

   He then, who never fail'd me at my need,
Cried, "Hither turn. Lo! two with sharp remorse
Chiding their sin." In rear of all the troop
These shouted: "First they died,[10] to whom the sea
Open'd, or ever Jordan saw his heirs:
And they,[11] who with Æneas to the end
Endured not suffering, for their portion chose
Life without glory." Soon as they had fled
Past reach of sight, new thought within me rose
By others follow'd fast, and each unlike
Its fellow: till led on from thought to thought,
And pleasured with the fleeting train, mine eye
Was closed, and meditation changed to dream.

CANTO XIX

ARGUMENT.—The Poet, after describing his dream, relates how, at the summoning
of an Angel, he ascends with Virgil to the fifth cornice, where the sin of avarice is
cleansed, and where he finds Pope Adrian the fifth.

IT was the hour,[1] when of diurnal heat
   No reliques chafe the cold beams of the moon,
   O'erpower'd by earth, or planetary sway
Of Saturn; and the geomancer[2] sees
His Greater Fortune up the east ascend,
Where gray dawn checkers first the shadowy cone,

---

[10] "First they died." The Israelites,
who on account of their disobedience died
before reaching the promised land.

[11] "And they." Those Trojans, who,
wearied with their voyage, chose rather
to remain in Sicily with Acestes than accompany Æneas to Italy.

[1] "The hour." Near the dawn.

[2] "The geomancer." The geomancers,
when they divined, drew a figure consisting of sixteen marks, named from so
many stars which constitute the end of
Aquarius and the beginning of Pisces.
One of these they called "the greater fortune."

When, 'fore me in my dream, a woman's shape[3]
There came, with lips that stammer'd, eyes aslant,
Distorted feet, hands maim'd, and colour pale.
I look'd upon her: and, as sunshine cheers
Limbs numb'd by nightly cold, e'en thus my look
Unloosed her tongue; next, in brief space, her form
Decrepit raised erect, and faded face
With love's own hue illumed. Recovering speech,
She forthwith, warbling, such a strain began,
That I, how loth soe'er, could scarce have held
Attention from the song. "I," thus she sang,
"I am the Syren, she, whom mariners
On the wide sea are wilder'd when they hear;
Such fulness of delight the listener feels.
I, from his course, Ulysses[4] by my lay
Enchanted drew. Whoe'er frequents me once,
Parts seldom: so I charm him, and his heart
Contented knows no void." Or ere her mouth
Was closed, to shame her, at my side appear'd
A dame[5] of semblance holy. With stern voice
She utter'd: "Say, O Virgil! who is this?"
Which hearing, he approach'd, with eyes still bent
Toward that goodly presence: the other seized her,
And, her robes tearing, open'd her before,
And show'd the belly to me, whence a smell,
Exhaling loathsome, waked me. Round I turn'd
Mine eyes: and thus the teacher: "At the least
Three times my voice hath call'd thee. Rise, begone.
Let us the opening find where thou mayst pass."
  I straightway rose. Now day, pour'd down from high,
Fill'd all the circuits of the sacred mount;
And, as we journey'd, on our shoulder smote
The early ray. I follow'd, stooping low
My forehead, as a man, o'ercharged with thought,

[3] "A woman's shape." Worldly happiness. This allegory reminds us of the "Choice of Hercules."

[4] "Ulysses." It is not easy to determine why Ulysses, contrary to the authority of Homer, is said to have been drawn aside from his course by the song of the Siren. No improbable way of accounting for the contradiction is, to suppose that she is here represented as purposely deviating from the truth. Or Dante may have followed some legend of the Middle Ages.

[5] "A dame." Philosophy, or perhaps Truth.

Who bends him to the likeness of an arch
That midway spans the flood; when thus I heard,
"Come, enter here," in tone so soft and mild,
As never met the ear on mortal strand.

   With swan-like wings dispred and pointing up,
Who thus had spoken marshal'd us along,
Where, each side of the solid masonry,
The sloping walls retired; then moved his plumes,
And fanning us, affirm'd that those, who mourn,[6]
Are blessed, for that comfort shall be theirs.

   "What aileth thee, that still thou look'st to earth?"
Began my leader; while the angelic shape
A little over us his station took.

   "New vision," I replied, "hath raised in me
Surmisings strange and anxious doubts, whereon
My soul intent allows no other thought
Or room, or entrance."—"Hast thou seen," said he
"That old enchantress, her, whose wiles alone
The spirits o'er us weep for? Hast thou seen
How man may free him of her bonds? Enough.
Let thy heels spurn the earth; and thy raised ken
Fix on the lure, which Heaven's eternal King
Whirls in the rolling spheres." As on his feet
The falcon first looks down, then to the sky
Turns, and forth stretches eager for the food,
That woos him thither; so the call I heard:
So onward, far as the dividing rock
Gave way, I journey'd, till the plain was reach'd.

   On the fifth circle when I stood at large,
A race appear'd before me, on the ground
All downward lying prone and weeping sore.
"My soul hath cleaved to the dust," I heard
With sighs so deep, they well nigh choked the words.

   "O ye elect of God! whose penal woes
Both hope and justice mitigate, direct
Towards the steep rising our uncertain way."

   "If ye approach secure from this our doom,
Prostration, and would urge your course with speed,

---

[6]"Who mourn." "Blessed are they that mourn; for they shall be comforted."—
Matt. v. 4

See that ye still to rightward keep the brink."
    So them the bard besought; and such the words,
Beyond us some short space, in answer came.
    I noted what remain'd yet hidden from them:[7]
Thence to my liege's eyes mine eyes I bent,
And he, forthwith interpreting their suit,
Beckon'd his glad assent. Free then to act
As pleased me, I drew near, and took my stand
Over that shade whose words I late had mark'd.
And, "Spirit!" I said, "in whom repentant tears
Mature that blessed hour when thou with God
Shalt find acceptance, for a while suspend
For me that mightier care. Say who thou wast;
Why thus ye grovel on your bellies prone;
And if, in aught, ye wish my service there,
Whence living I am come." He answering spake:
"The cause why Heaven our back towards his cope
Reverses, shalt thou know: but me know first,
The successor of Peter,[8] and the name
And title of my lineage, from that stream[9]
That 'twixt Chiaveri and Siestri draws
His limpid waters through the lowly glen.
A month and little more by proof I learnt,
With what a weight that robe of sovereignty
Upon his shoulder rests, who from the mire
Would guard it; that each other fardel seems
But feathers in the balance. Late, alas!
Was my conversion: but, when I became
Rome's pastor, I discerned at once the dream
And cozenage of life; saw that the heart
Rested not there, and yet no prouder height
Lured on the climber: whereof, of that life
No more enamor'd, in my bosom love
Of purer being kindled. For till then

---

[7] "I noted what remain'd yet hidden from them." They were ignorant, it appeared, whether Dante was come there to be purged of his sins.

[8] "The successor of Peter." Ottobuono, of the family of Fieschi, Counts of Lavagno, died thirty-nine days after he be-came Pope, with the title of Adrian V, in 1276.

[9] "That stream." The river Lavagno, in the Genoese territory; to the east of which territory are situated Siestri and Chiaveri.

I was a soul in misery, alienate
From God, and covetous of all earthly things;
Now, as thou seest, here punish'd for my doting.
Such cleansing from the taint of avarice,
Do spirits, converted, need. This mount inflicts
No direr penalty. E'en as our eyes
Fasten'd below, nor e'er to loftier clime
Were lifted; thus hath justice level'd us,
Here on the earth. As avarice quench'd our love
Of good, without which is no working; thus
Here justice holds us prison'd, hand and foot
Chain'd down and bound, while Heaven's just Lord shall
      please,
So long to tarry, motionless, outstretch'd.''

   My knees I stoop'd, and would have spoke; but he,
Ere my beginning, by his ear perceived
I did him reverence; and "What cause,'' said he,
"Hath bow'd thee thus?''—"Compunction,'' I rejoin'd,
"And inward awe of your high dignity.''

   "Up,'' he exclaim'd, "brother! upon thy feet
Arise; err not: thy fellow-servant I,
(Thine and all others') of one Sovran Power.
If thou hast ever mark'd those holy sounds
Of gospel truth, 'nor shall be given in marriage,'
Thou mayst discern the reasons of my speech.
Go thy ways now; and linger here no more.
Thy tarrying is a let unto the tears,
With which I hasten that whereof thou spakest.
I have on earth a kinswoman;[10] her name
Alagia, worthy in herself, so ill
Example of our house corrupt her not:
And she is all remaineth of me there.''

[10] "A kinswoman.'' Alagia is said to have been the wife of the Marchese Marcello Malaspina, one of the Poet's protectors during his exile. See Canto viii. 133.

CANTO XX

ARGUMENT.—Among those of the fifth cornice, Hugh Capet records illustrious examples of voluntary poverty and of bounty; then tells who himself is, and speaks of
his descendants on the French throne; and, lastly, adds some noted instances of
avarice. When he has ended, the mountain shakes, and all the spirits sing "Glory to
God."

ILL strives the will, 'gainst will more wise that strives:
His pleasure therefore to mine own preferr'd,
I drew the sponge yet thirsty from the wave.
Onward I moved: he also onward moved,
Who led me, coasting still, wherever place
Along the rock was vacant; as a man
Walks near the battlements on narrow wall.
For those on the other part, who drop by drop
Wring out their all-infecting malady,
Too closely press the verge. Accurst be thou,
Inveterate wolf![1] whose gorge ingluts more prey,
Than every beast beside, yet is not fill'd;
So bottomless thy maw. Ye spheres of Heaven!
To whom there are, as seems, who attribute
All change in mortal state, when is the day
Of his appearing,[2] for whom fate reserves
To chase her hence? With wary steps and slow
We pass'd; and I attentive to the shades,
Whom piteously I heard lament and wail;
And, 'midst the wailing, one before us heard
Cry out "O blessed Virgin!" as a dame
In the sharp pangs of childbed; and "How poor
Thou wast," it added, "witness that low roof
Where thou didst lay thy sacred burden down.
O good Fabricius! thou didst virtue choose
With poverty, before great wealth with vice."
    The words so pleased me, that desire to know
The spirit, from whose lip they seem'd to come,
Did draw me onward. Yet it spake the gift
Of Nicholas,[3] which on the maidens he

[1] "Wolf." Avarice.
[2] He is thought to allude to Can
Grande della Scala. See Hell, Canto i. 98.
[3] An angel having revealed to him that
the father of a family was so impoverished
as to resolve on exposing the chastity of
his three daughters to sale, Nicholas threw
in at the window of their house three
bags of money, containing a sufficient portion for each of them.

Bounteous bestow'd, to save their youthful prime
Unblemish'd. "Spirit! who dost speak of deeds
So worthy, tell me who thou wast," I said,
"And why thou dost with single voice renew
Memorial of such praise. That boon vouchsafed
Haply shall meet reward; if I return
To finish the short pilgrimage of life,
Still speeding to its close on restless wing."

  "I," answer'd he, "will tell thee; not for help,
Which thence I look for; but that in thyself
Grace so exceeding shines, before thy time
Of mortal dissolution. I was root[4]
Of that ill plant, whose shade such poison sheds
O'er all the Christian land, that seldom thence
Good fruit is gather'd. Vengeance soon should come,
Had Ghent and Douay, Lille and Bruges power;[5]
And vengeance I of Heaven's great Judge implore.
Hugh Capet was I hight: from me descend
The Philips and the Louis, of whom France
Newly is govern'd: born of one, who plied
The slaughterer's trade[6] at Paris. When the race
Of ancient kings had vanish'd (all save one[7]
Wrapt up in sable weeds) within my gripe
I found the reins of empire, and such powers
Of new acquirement, with full store of friends,
That soon the widow'd circlet of the crown
Was girt upon the temples of my son,[8]
He, from whose bones the anointed race begins.

[4] "Root." Hugh Capet, ancestor of Philip IV.

[5] These cities had lately been seized by Philip IV. The spirit intimates the approaching defeat of the French army by the Flemings, in the battle of Courtrai, which happened in 1302.

[6] "The slaughterer's trade." This reflection on the birth of his ancestor induced Francis I to forbid the reading of Dante in his dominions. Hugh Capet, who came to the throne of France in 987, was, however, the grandson of Robert, who was the brother of Eudes, King of France in 888; and it may, therefore, well be questioned whether by Beccaio di Parigi is meant literally one who carried on the trade of a butcher, at Paris, and whether the sanguinary disposition of Hugh Capet's father is not stigmatized by this opprobrious appellation.

[7] The posterity of Charlemain, the second race of French monarchs, had failed, with the exception of Charles of Lorraine, who is said, on account of the melancholy temper of his mind, to have always clothed himself in black. Venturi suggests that Dante may have confounded him with Childeric III, the last of the Merovingian, or first, race, who was deposed and made a monk in 751.

[8] Hugh Capet caused his son Robert to be crowned at Orleans.

Till the great dower of Provence[9] had removed
The stains, that yet obscured our lowly blood,
Its sway indeed was narrow; but howe'er
It wrought no evil: there, with force and lies,
Began its rapine: after, for amends,
Poitou it seized, Navarre and Gascony.
To Italy came Charles; and for amends,
Young Conradine,[10] an innocent victim, slew;
And sent the angelic teacher[11] back to Heaven,
Still for amends. I see the time at hand,
That forth from France invites another Charles[12]
To make himself and kindred better known.
Unarm'd he issues, saving with that lance,
Which the arch-traitor tilted with,[13] and that
He carries with so home a thrust, as rives
The bowels of poor Florence. No increase
Of territory hence, but sin and shame
Shall be his guerdon; and so much the more
As he more lightly deems of such foul wrong.
I see the other[14] (who a prisoner late

---

[9] "The great dower of Provence." Louis IX and his brother Charles of Anjou married two of the four daughters of Raymond Berenger, Count of Provence. See Paradise, c. vi. 135.

[10] "Young Conradine." Charles of Anjou put Conradino to death in 1268, and became King of Naples.

[11] "The angelic teacher." Thomas Aquinas. He was reported to have been poisoned by a physician, who wished to ingratiate himself with Charles of Anjou. "In the year 1323, at the end of July, by the said Pope John and by his cardinals, was canonized at Avignon, Thomas Aquinas, of the order of Saint Dominic, a master in divinity and philosophy. A man most excellent in all science, and who expounded the sense of Scripture better than anyone since the time of Augustin. He lived in the time of Charles I, King of Sicily; and going to the council at Lyons, it is said that he was killed by a physician of the said king, who put poison for him into some sweetmeats, thinking to ingratiate himself with King Charles, because he was of the

lineage of the Lords of Aquino, who had rebelled against the king, and doubting lest he should be made cardinal; whence the Church of God received great damage. He died at the abbey of Fossanova, in Campagna." G. Villani, lib. ix.

[12] "Another Charles." Charles of Valois, brother of Philip IV, was sent by Pope Boniface VIII to settle the disturbed state of Florence. In consequence of the measures he adopted for that purpose, our Poet and his friends were condemned to exile and death.

[13] "———— with that lance." If I remember right, in one of the old romances, Judas is represented tilting with our Saviour.

[14] "The other." Charles, King of Naples, the eldest son of Charles of Anjou, having, contrary to the directions of his father, engaged with Ruggieri de Lauria, the admiral of Peter of Arragon, was made prisoner, and carried into Sicily, June, 1284. He afterward, in consideration of a large sum of money, married his daughter to Azzo VIII, Marquis of Ferrara.

Had stept on shore) exposing to the mart
His daughter, whom he bargains for, as do
The Corsairs for their slaves. O avarice!
What canst thou more, who hast subdued our blood
So wholly to thyself, they feel no care
Of their own flesh? To hide with direr guilt
Past ill and future, lo! the flower-de-luce[15]
Enters Alagna; in his Vicar Christ
Himself a captive, and his mockery
Acted again. Lo! to his holy lip
The vinegar and gall once more applied;
And he 'twixt living robbers doom'd to bleed.
Lo! the new Pilate, of whose cruelty
Such violence cannot fill the measure up,
With no decree to sanction, pushes on
Into the temple[16] his yet eager sails.

"O sovran Master! when shall I rejoice
To see the vengeance, which Thy wrath, well-pleased,
In secret silence broods?—While daylight lasts,
So long what thou didst hear of her, sole spouse
Of the Great Spirit, and on which thou turn'dst
To me for comment, is the general theme
Of all our prayers; but, when it darkens, then
A different strain we utter; then record
Pygmalion, whom his gluttonous thirst of gold
Made traitor, robber, parricide: the woes
Of Midas, which his greedy wish ensued,
Mark'd for derision to all future times:
And the fond Achan,[17] how he stole the prey,
That yet he seems by Joshua's ire pursued.
Sapphira with her husband next we blame;
And praise the forefeet, that with furious ramp

---

[15] "The flower-de-luce." Boniface VIII
was seized at Alagna in Campagna, by
the order of Philip IV, in the year 1303,
and soon after died of grief. G. Villani,
lib. viii. cap. lxiii. "As it pleased God,
the heart of Boniface being petrified with
grief, through the injury he had sustained,
when he came to Rome, he fell into a
strange malady, for he gnawed himself
as one frantic, and in this state expired."
His character is strongly drawn by the
annalist in the next chapter. Thus, says
Landino, was verified the prophecy of
Celestine respecting him, that he should
enter on the popedom like a fox, reign
like a lion, and die like a dog.

[16] It is uncertain whether our Poet
alludes still to the event mentioned in
the preceding note, or to the destruction
of the order of the Templars in 1310,
but the latter appears more probable.

[17] "Achan." Joshua vii.

Spurn'd Heliodorus.[18]   All the mountain round
Rings with the infamy of Thracia's king,[19]
Who slew his Phrygian charge: and last a shout
Ascends: 'Declare, O Crassus![20] for thou know'st,
The flavour of thy gold.'   The voice of each
Now high, now low, as each his impulse prompts,
Is led through many a pitch, acute or grave.
Therefore, not singly, I erewhile rehearsed
That blessedness we tell of in the day:
But near me, none, beside, his accent raised."

From him we now had parted, and essay'd
With utmost efforts to surmount the way;
When I did feel, as nodding to its fall,
The mountain tremble; whence an icy chill
Seized on me, as on one to death convey'd.
So shook not Delos, when Latona there
Couch'd to bring forth the twin-born eyes of Heaven.

Forthwith from every side a shout arose
So vehement, that suddenly my guide
Drew near, and cried: "Doubt not, while I conduct thee."
"Glory!" all shouted (such the sounds mine ear
Gather'd from those, who near me swell'd the sounds),
"Glory in the highest be to God." We stood
Immovably suspended, like to those,
The shepherds, who first heard in Bethlehem's field
That song: till ceased the trembling, and the song
Was ended: then our hallow'd path resumed,
Eying the prostrate shadows, who renew'd
Their custom'd mourning. Never in my breast
Did ignorance so struggle with desire   .
Of knowledge, if my memory do not err,
As in that moment; nor through haste dared I
To question, nor myself could aught discern.
So on I fared, in thoughtfulness and dread.

---

[18] "Heliodorus." "For there appeared unto them an horse, with a terrible rider upon him, and adorned with a very fair covering, and he ran fiercely and smote at Heliodorus with his fore feet." 2 Maccabees iii. 25.

[19] "Thracia's king." Polymnestor, the murderer of Polydorus. Hell, Canto xxx. 19.

[20] "Crassus." Marcus Crassus, who fell miserably in the Parthian war.

CANTO XXI

ARGUMENT.—The two Poets are overtaken by the spirit of Statius, who, being cleansed, is on his way to Paradise, and who explains the cause of the mountain shaking, and of the hymn; his joy at beholding Virgil.

THE natural thirst, ne'er quench'd but from the well[1],
Whereof the woman of Samaria craved,
Excited; haste, along the cumber'd path,
After my guide, impell'd; and pity moved
My bosom for the 'vengeful doom though just.
When lo! even as Luke[2] relates, that Christ
Appear'd unto the two upon their way,
New-risen from His vaulted grave; to us
A shade appear'd, and after us approach'd,
Contemplating the crowd beneath its feet.
We were not ware of it; so first it spake,
Saying, "God give you peace, my brethren!" then
Sudden we turn'd: and Virgil such salute,
As fitted that kind greeting, gave; and cried:
"Peace in the blessed council be thy lot,
Awarded by that righteous court which me
To everlasting banishment exiles."

"How!" he exclaim'd, nor from his speed meanwhile
Desisting; "If that ye be spirits whom God
Vouchsafes not room above; who up the height
Has been thus far your guide?" To whom the bard:
"If thou observe the tokens,[3] which this man,
Traced by the finger of the Angel, bears;
'Tis plain that in the kingdom of the just
He needs must share. But sithence she,[4] whose wheel
Spins day and night, for him not yet had drawn
That yarn, which on the fatal distaff piled,
Clotho apportions to each wight that breathes;
His soul, that sister is to mine and thine,
Not of herself could mount; for not like ours

---

[1] "The well." "The woman saith unto him, Sir, give me this water, that I thirst not."—John, iv. 15.

[2] "Luke." Chapter xxiv. 13.

[3] "The tokens." The letter P for Peccata, sins, inscribed upon his forehead by the Angel, in order to his being cleared of them in his passage through Purgatory to Paradise.

[4] "She." Lachesis, one of the three fates.

Her ken: whence I, from forth the ample gulf
Of Hell, was ta'en, to lead him, and will lead
Far as my lore avails. But, if thou know,
Instruct us for what cause, the mount erewhile
Thus shook, and trembled: wherefore all at once
Seem'd shouting, even from his wave-wash'd foot."
　　That questioning so tallied with my wish,
The thirst did feel abatement of its edge
E'en from expectance. He forthwith replied:
"In its devotion, nought irregular
This mount can witness, or by punctual rule
Unsanction'd; here from every change exempt,
Other than that, which Heaven in itself
Doth of itself receive, no influence
Can reach us. Tempest none, shower, hail, or snow,
Hoar frost, or dewy moistness, higher falls
Than that brief scale of threefold steps: thick clouds,
Nor scudding rack, are ever seen: swift glance
Ne'er lightens; nor Thaumantian Iris gleams,
That yonder often shifts on each side Heaven.
Vapour adust doth never mount above
The highest of the trinal stairs, whereon
Peter's vicegerent stands. Lower perchance,
With various motion rock'd, trembles the soil:
But here, through wind in earth's deep hollow pent,
I know not how, yet never trembled: then
Trembles, when any spirit feels itself
So purified, that it may rise, or move
For rising; and such loud acclaim ensues.
Purification, by the will alone,
Is proved, that free to change society
Seizes the soul rejoicing in her will.
Desire of bliss is present from the first;
But strong propension hinders, to that wish
By the just ordinance of Heaven opposed;
Propension now as eager to fulfill
The allotted torment, as erewhile to sin.
And I, who in this punishment had lain
Five hundred years and more, but now have felt
Free wish for happier clime. Therefore thou felt'st

The mountain tremble; and the spirits devout
Heard'st, over all his limits, utter praise
To that liege Lord, whom I entreat their joy
To hasten." Thus he spake: and, since the draught
Is grateful ever as the thirst is keen,
No words may speak my fullness of content.

"Now," said the instructor sage, "I see the net
That takes ye here; and how the toils are loosed;
Why rocks the mountain, and why ye rejoice.
Vouchsafe, that from thy lips I next may learn
Who on the earth thou wast; and wherefore here,
So many an age, wert prostrate."—"In that time,
When the good Titus,[5] with Heaven's King to help,
Avenged those piteous gashes, whence the blood
By Judas sold did issue; with the name[6]
Most lasting and most honor'd, there, was I
Abundantly renown'd," the shade replied,
"Not yet with faith endued. So passing sweet
My vocal spirit; from Tolosa, Rome
To herself drew me, where I merited
A myrtle garland to inwreathe my brow.
Statius they name me still. Of Thebes I sang,
And next of great Achilles; but i' the way
Fell with the second burden. Of my flame
Those sparkles were the seeds, which I derived
From the bright fountain of celestial fire
That feeds unnumber'd lamps; the song I mean
Which sounds Æneas' wanderings: that the breast
I hung at; that the nurse, from whom my veins
Drank inspiration: whose authority
Was ever sacred with me. To have lived
Coeval with the Mantuan, I would bide
The revolution of another sun
Beyond my stated years in banishment."

The Mantuan, when he heard him, turn'd to me;
And holding silence,by his countenance
Enjoin'd me silence: but the power, which wills,

---

[5] "When the good Titus." When it was so ordered by the divine Providence that Titus, by the destruction of Jeru-salem, should avenge the death of our Saviour on the Jews.

[6] "The name." The name of Poet.

Bears not supreme control: laughter and tears
Follow so closely on the passion prompts them,
They wait not for the motions of the will
In natures most sincere. I did but smile,
As one who winks; and thereupon the shade
Broke off, and peer'd into mine eyes, where best
Our looks interpret. "So to good event
Mayst thou conduct such great emprise," he cried,
"Say, why across thy visage beam'd, but now,
The lightning of a smile." On either part
Now am I straiten'd; one conjures me speak,
The other to silence binds me: whence a sigh
I utter, and the sigh is heard. "Speak on,"
The teacher cried: "and do not fear to speak;
But tell him what so earnestly he asks."
Whereon I thus: "Perchance, O ancient spirit!
Thou marvel'st at my smiling. There is room
For yet more wonder. He, who guides my ken
On high, he is that Mantuan, led by whom
Thou didst presume of men and gods to sing.
If other cause thou deem'dst for which I smiled,
Leave it as not the true one: and believe
Those words, thou spakest of him, indeed the cause."

    Now down he bent to embrace my teacher's feet;
But he forbade him: "Brother! do it not:
Thou art a shadow, and behold'st a shade."
He, rising, answer'd thus: "Now hast thou proved
The force and ardour of the love I bear thee,
When I forget we are but things of air,
And, as a substance, treat an empty shade."

CANTO XXII

ARGUMENT.—Dante, Virgil, and Statius mount to the sixth cornice, where the sin of gluttony is cleansed, the two Latin Poets discoursing by the way. Turning to the right, they find a tree hung with sweet-smelling fruit, and watered by a shower that issues from the rock. Voices are heard to proceed from among the leaves, recording examples of temperance.

NOW we had left the Angel, who had turn'd
To the sixth circle our ascending step;
One gash from off my forehead razed; while
they,
Whose wishes tend to justice, shouted forth,
"Blessed!"[1] and ended with "I thirst"; and I,
More nimble than along the other straits,
So journey'd, that, without the sense of toil,
I follow'd upwards the swift-footed shades;
When Virgil thus began: "Let its pure flame
From virtue flow, and love can never fail
To warm another's bosom, so the light
Shine manifestly forth. Hence, from that hour,
When, 'mongst us in the purlieus of the deep,
Came down the spirit of Aquinum's bard,
Who told of thine affection, my good will
Hath been for thee of quality as strong
As ever link'd itself to one not seen.
Therefore these stairs will now seem short to me.
But tell me: and, if too secure, I loose
The rein with a friend's licence, as a friend
Forgive me, and speak now as with a friend:
How chanced it covetous desire could find
Place in that bosom, 'midst such ample store
Of wisdom, as thy zeal had treasured there?"
First somewhat moved to laughter by his words,
Statius replied: "Each syllable of thine
Is a dear pledge of love. Things oft appear,
That minister false matter to our doubts,
When their true causes are removed from sight.
Thy question doth assure me, thou believest
I was on earth a covetous man; perhaps

[1] "Blessed." "Blessed are they which do hunger and thirst after righteousness, for they shall be filled."—Matt. v. 6.

Because thou found'st me in that circle placed.
Know then I was too wide of avarice:
And e'en for that excess, thousands of moons
Have wax'd and waned upon my sufferings.
And were it not that I with heedful care
Noted, where thou exclaim'st, as if in ire,
With human nature, 'Why, thou cursed thirst
Of gold! dost not with juster measure guide
The appetite of mortals?' I had met
The fierce encounter of the voluble rock.
Then was I ware that, with too ample wing,
The hands may haste to lavishment; and turn'd,
As from my other evil, so from this,
In penitence. How many from their grave
Shall with shorn locks[2] arise, who living, ay,
And at life's last extreme, of this offence,
Through ignorance, did not repent! And know,
The fault, which lies direct from any sin
In level opposition, here, with that,
Wastes its green rankness on one common heap.
Therefore, if I have been with those, who wail
Their avarice, to cleanse me; through reverse
Of their transgression, such hath been my lot."
     To whom the sovran of the pastoral song:
"While thou didst sing that cruel warfare waged
By the twin sorrow of Jocasta's womb[3]
From thy discourse with Clio there, it seems
As faith had not been thine; without the which,
Good deeds suffice not. And if so, what sun
Rose on thee, or what candle pierced the dark,
That thou didst after see to hoise the sail,
And follow where the fisherman had led?"
     He answering thus: "By thee conducted first,
I enter'd the Parnassian grots, and quaff'd
Of the clear spring: illumined first by thee,
Open'd mine eyes to God. Thou didst, as one
Who, journeying through the darkness, bears a light
Behind, that profits not himself, but makes

[2] "With shorn locks." See Hell, Canto
vii, 58.

[3] "The twin sorrow of Jocasta's womb."
Eteocles and Polynices.

His followers wise, when thou exclaimed'st, 'Lo!
A renovated world, Justice return'd,
Times of primeval innocence restored,
And a new race descended from above.'
Poet and Christian both to thee I owed.
That thou mayst mark more clearly what I trace,
My hand shall stretch forth to inform the lines
With livelier colouring. Soon o'er all the world,
By messengers from Heaven, the true belief
Teem'd now prolific; and that word of thine,
Accordant, to the new instructors chimed.
Induced by which agreement, I was wont
Resort to them; and soon their sanctity
So won upon me, that, Domitian's rage
Pursuing them, I mix'd my tears with theirs;
And, while on earth I stay'd, still succor'd them;
And their most righteous customs made me scorn
All sects besides. Before I led the Greeks,
In tuneful fiction, to the streams of Thebes,
I was baptized; but secretly, through fear,
Remain'd a Christian, and conform'd long time
To Pagan rites. Four centuries and more,
I, for that lukewarmness, was fain to pace
Round the fourth circle. Thou then, who hast raised
The covering which did hide such blessing from me,
Whilst much of this ascent is yet to climb,
Say, if thou know, where our old Terence bides,
Cæcilius, Plautus, Varro: if condemn'd
They dwell, and in what province of the deep."
"These," said my guide, "with Persius and myself,
And others many more, are with that Greek,[4]
Of mortals, the most cherish'd by the Nine,
In the first ward[5] of darkness. There, oft-times,
We of that mount hold converse, on whose top
For aye our nurses live. We have the bard
Of Pella,[6] and the Teian,[7] Agatho,
Simonides, and many a Grecian else
Ingarlanded with laurel. Of thy train,

---

[4] "That Greek." Homer.
[5] "In the first ward." In Limbo.
[6] Euripides.
[7] "The Teian." Anacreon.

Antigone is there, Deïphile,
Argia, and as sorrowful as erst
Ismene, and who show'd Langia's wave:[8]
Deïdamia with her sisters there,
And blind Tiresias' daughter,[9] and the bride
Sea-born of Peleus." [10] Either poet now
Was silent; and no longer by the ascent
Or the steep walls obstructed, round them cast
Inquiring eyes. Four handmaids of the day
Had finish'd now their office, and the fifth
Was at the chariot-beam, directing still
Its flamy point aloof; when thus my guide:
"Methinks, it well behoves us to the brink
Bend the right shoulder, circuiting the mount,
As we have ever used." So custom there
Was usher to the road; the which we chose
Less doubtful, as that worthy shade[11] complied.

They on before me went: I sole pursued,
Listening their speech, that to my thoughts convey'd
Mysterious lessons of sweet poesy.
But soon they ceased; for midway of the road
A tree we found, with goodly fruitage hung,
And pleasant to the smell: and as a fir,
Upward from bough to bough, less ample spreads;
So downward this less ample spread; that none,
Methinks, aloft may climb. Upon the side,
That closed our path, a liquid crystal fell
From the steep rock, and through the sprays above
Stream'd showering. With associate step the bards
Drew near the plant; and, from amidst the leaves,
A voice was heard: "Ye shall be chary of me;"
And after added: "Mary took more thought
For joy and honour of the nuptial feast,
Than for herself, who answers now for you.

[8] Hypsipile.
[9] "Tiresias' daughter." Dante, as some have thought, had forgotten that he had placed Manto, the daughter of Tiresias, among the sorcerers. See Hell, Canto xx. Vellutello endeavors to reconcile the apparent inconsistency, by observing, that although she was placed there as a sinner, yet, as one of famous memory, she had also a place among the worthies in Limbo.
[10] Thetis.
[11] "That worthy shade." Statius.

The women of old Rome were satisfied
With water for their beverage. Daniel[12] fed
On pulse, and wisdom gain'd. The primal age
Was beautiful as gold: and hunger then
Made acorns tasteful; thirst, each rivulet
Run nectar. Honey and locusts were the food,
Whereon the Baptist in the wilderness
Fed, and that eminence of glory reach'd
And greatness, which the Evangelist records."

CANTO XXIII

ARGUMENT.—They are overtaken by the spirit of Forese, who had been a friend
of our Poet's on earth, and who now inveighs bitterly against the immodest dress of
their countrywomen at Florence.

O N the green leaf mine eyes were fix'd, like his
Who throws away his days in idle chase
Of the diminutive birds, when thus I heard
The more than father warn me: "Son! our time
Asks thriftier using. Linger not: away!"

Thereat my face and steps at once I turn'd
Toward the sages, by whose converse cheer'd
I journey'd on, and felt no toil: and lo!
A sound of weeping, and a song: "My lips,[1]
O Lord!" and these so mingled, it gave birth
To pleasure and to pain. "O Sire beloved!
Say what is this I hear." Thus I inquired.

"Spirits," said he, "who, as they go, perchance,
Their debt of duty pay." As on their road
The thoughtful pilgrims, overtaking some
Not known unto them, turn to them, and look,
But stay not; thus, approaching from behind
With speedier motion, eyed us, as they pass'd,
A crowd of spirits, silent and devout.

[12] "Daniel." "Then said Daniel to Melzar, whom the prince of the eunuchs had
set over Daniel, Hananiah, Michael, and
Azariah, 'Prove thy servants, I beseech
thee, ten days; and let them give us pulse
to eat, and water to drink.'"—Dan. i. 11,
12. "Thus Melzar took away the portion
of their meat, and the wine that they
should drink: and gave them pulse. As
for these four children, God gave them
knowledge and skill in all learning and
wisdom: and Daniel had understanding
in all visions and dreams."—Ibid. 16, 17.
[1] "O Lord, open thou my lips; and my
mouth shall show forth thy praise."—
Psalm li. 15.

The eyes of each were dark and hollow; pale
Their visage, and so lean withal, the bones
Stood staring through the skin. I do not think
Thus dry and meagre Erisichthon show'd,
When pinch'd by sharp-set famine to the quick.
   "Lo!" to myself I mused, "the race, who lost
Jerusalem, when Mary with dire beak
Prey'd on her child." The sockets seem'd as rings,
From which the gems were dropt. Who reads the name[2]
Of man upon his forehead, there the M
Had traced most plainly. Who would deem, that scent
Of water and an apple could have proved
Powerful to generate such pining want,
Not knowing how it wrought? While now I stood,
Wondering what thus could waste them, (for the cause
Of their gaunt hollowness and scaly rind
Appear'd not,) lo! a spirit turn'd his eyes
In their deep-sunken cells, and fasten'd them
On me, then cried with vehemence aloud:
"What grace is this vouchsafed me?" By his looks
I ne'er had recognized him: but the voice
Brought to my knowledge what his cheer conceal'd.
Remembrance of his alter'd lineaments
Was kindled from that spark; and I agnized
The visage of Forese.[3] "Ah! respect
This wan and leprous-wither'd skin," thus he
Suppliant implored, "this macerated flesh.
Speak to me truly of thyself. And who
Are those twain spirits, that escort thee there?
Be it not said thou scorn'st to talk with me."
   "That face of thine," I answer'd him, "which dead
I once bewail'd, disposes me not less
For weeping, when I see it thus transform'd.
Say then, by Heaven, what blasts ye thus? The whilst
I wonder, ask not speech from me: unapt
Is he to speak, whom other will employs."

[2] The temples, nose, and forehead are supposed to represent this letter [of the Latin word (H)OMO—man], and the eyes the two O's.

[3] A brother of Piccarda. See also Canto xxiv. and Paradise, Canto iii. Cionacci is referred to by Lombardi, in order to show that Forese was also the brother of Corso Donati, our author's political enemy.

He thus: "The water and the plant, we pass'd,
With power are gifted, by the eternal will
Infused; the which so pines me. Every spirit,
Whose song bewails his gluttony indulged
Too grossly, here in hunger and in thirst
Is purified. The odour, which the fruit,
And spray that showers upon the verdure, breathe,
Inflames us with desire to feed and drink.
Nor once alone, encompassing our route,
We come to add fresh fuel to the pain:
Pain, said I? solace rather: for that will,
To the tree, leads us, by which Christ was led
To call on Eli, joyful, when he paid
Our ransom from his vein." I answering thus:
"Forese! from that day, in which the world
For better life thou changedst, not five years
Have circled. If the power of sinning more
Were first concluded in thee, ere thou knew'st
That kindly grief which re-espouses us
To God, how hither art thou come so soon?
I thought to find thee lower,[4] there, where time
Is recompense for time." He straight replied:
"To drink up the sweet wormwood of affliction
I have been brought thus early, by the tears
Stream'd down my Nella's[5] cheeks. Her prayers devout,
Her sighs have drawn me from the coast, where oft
Expectance lingers; and have set me free
From the other circles. In the sight of God
So much the dearer is my widow prized,
She whom I loved so fondly, as she ranks
More singly eminent for virtuous deeds.
The tract, most barbarous of Sardinia's isle,[6]
Hath dames more chaste, and modester by far,
Than that wherein I left her. O sweet brother!
What wouldst thou have me say? A time to come
Stands full within my view, to which this hour
Shall not be counted of an ancient date,

---

[4] In the Ante-Purgatory. See Canto ii.
[5] The wife of Forese.
[6] The Barbagia is a part of Sardinia, to which that name was given, on account of the uncivilized state of its inhabitants, who are said to have gone nearly naked.

When from the pulpit shall be loudly warn'd
The unblushing dames of Florence, lest they bare
Unkerchief'd bosoms to the common gaze.
What savage women hath the world e'er seen,
What Saracens,[7] for whom there needed scourge
Of spiritual or other discipline,
To force them walk with covering on their limbs?
But did they see, the shameless ones, what Heaven
Wafts on swift wing toward them while I speak,
Their mouths were oped for howling: they shall taste
Of sorrow (unless foresight cheat me here),
Or e'er the cheek of him be clothed with down,
Who is now rock'd with lullaby asleep.
Ah! now, my brother, hide thyself no more:
Thou seest how not I alone, but all,
Gaze, where thou veil'st the intercepted sun."
Whence I replied: "If thou recall to mind
What we were once together, even yet
Remembrance of those days may grieve thee sore.
That I forsook that life, was due to him
Who there precedes me, some few evenings past,
When she was round, who shines with sister lamp
To his that glisters yonder," and I show'd
The sun. "'Tis he, who through profoundest night
Of the true dead has brought me, with this flesh
As true, that follows. From that gloom the aid
Of his sure comfort drew me on to climb,
And, climbing, wind along this mountain-steep,
Which rectifies in you whate'er the world
Made crooked and depraved. I have his word,
That he will bear me company as far
As till I come where Beatrice dwells:
But there must leave me. Virgil is that spirit,
Who thus hath promised," and I pointed to him;
"The other is that shade, for whom so late
Your realm, as he arose, exulting, shook
Through every pendent cliff and rocky bound."

[7] "Saracens." This word, during the
Middle Ages, was applied to all nations
(except the Jews) who did not profess
Christianity.

CANTO XXIV

ARGUMENT.—Forese points out several others by name who are here, like himself,
purifying themselves from the vice of gluttony; and amongst the rest, Buonaggiunta
of Lucca, with whom our Poet converses. Forese then predicts the violent end of
Dante's political enemy, Corso Donati; and, when he has quitted them, the Poet, in
company with Statius and Virgil, arrives at another tree, from whence issue voices
that record ancient examples of gluttony; and proceeding forward, they are directed
by an Angel which way to ascend to the next cornice of the mountain.

OUR journey was not slacken'd by our talk,
  Nor yet our talk by journeying. Still we spake,
  And urged our travel stoutly, like a ship
When the wind sits astern. The shadowy forms,
That seem'd things dead and dead again, drew in
At their deep-delved orbs rare wonder of me,
Perceiving I had life; and I my words
Continued, and thus spake: "He journeys up
Perhaps more tardily than else he would,
For others' sake. But tell me, if thou know'st,
Where is Piccarda? Tell me, if I see
Any of mark, among this multitude
Who eye me thus."—"My sister (she for whom,
'Twixt beautiful and good, I cannot say
Which name was fitter) wears e'en now her crown,
And triumphs in Olympus." Saying this,
He added: "Since spare diet hath so worn
Our semblance out, 'tis lawful here to name
Each one. This," and his finger then he raised,
"Is Buonaggiunta,[1]—Buonaggiunta, he
Of Lucca: and that face beyond him, pierced
Unto a leaner fineness than the rest,
Had keeping of the Church; he was of Tours,[2]
And purges by wan abstinence away
Bolsena's eels and cups of muscadel."
  He show'd me many others, one by one:
And all, as they were named, seem'd well content;
For no dark gesture I discern'd in any.
I saw, through hunger, Ubaldino[3] grind

[1] "Buonaggiunta." Buonaggiunta Urbi-
ciani, of Lucca.
[2] "He was of Tours." Simon of Tours

became Pope with the title of Martin IV
in 1281, and died in 1285.
[3] Ubaldino degli Ubaldini, of Pila, in
the Florentine territory.

His teeth on emptiness; and Boniface,[4]
That waved the crozier o'er a numerous flock.
I saw the Marquis, who had time erewhile
To swill at Forli with less drought; yet so,
Was one ne'er sated. I howe'er, like him
That, gazing 'midst a crowd, singles out one,
So singled him of Lucca; for methought
Was none amongst them took such note of me.
Somewhat I heard him whisper of Gentucca:
The sound was indistinct, and murmur'd there,
Where justice, that so strips them, fix'd her sting.

"Spirit!" said I, "it seems as thou wouldst fain
Speak with me. Let me hear thee. Mutual wish
To converse prompts, which let us both indulge."

He, answering, straight began: "Woman is born,
Whose brow no wimple shades yet, that shall make
My city please thee, blame it as they may.
Go then with this forewarning. If aught false
My whisper too implied, the event shall tell.
But say, if of a truth I see the man
Of that new lay the inventor, which begins
With 'Ladies, ye that con the lore of love.' "

To whom I thus: "Count of me but as one,
Who am the scribe of love; that, when he breathes,
Take up my pen, and, as he dictates, write."

"Brother!" said he, "the hindrance, which once held
The notary, with Guittone and myself,
Short of that new and sweeter style I hear,
Is now disclosed: I see how ye your plumes
Stretch, as the inditer guides them; which, no question,
Ours did not. He that seeks a grace beyond,
Sees not the distance parts one style from other."
And, as contented, here he held his peace.

Like as the birds, that winter near the Nile,
In squared regiment direct their course,
Then stretch themselves in file for speedier flight;
Thus all the tribe of spirits, as they turn'd

---

[4] "Boniface." Archbishop of Ravenna. By Venturi he is called Bonifazio de' Fieschi, a Genoese; by Vellutello, the son of the above-mentioned Ubaldini; and by Landino, Francioso, a Frenchman.

Their visage, faster fled, nimble alike
Through leanness and desire. And as a man,
Tired with the motion of a trotting steed,
Slacks pace, and stays behind his company,
Till his o'erbreathed lungs keep temperate time;
E'en so Forese let that holy crew
Proceed, behind them lingering at my side,
And saying: "When shall I again behold thee?"

   "How long my life may last," said I, "I know not:
This know, how soon soever I return,
My wishes will before me have arrived:
Sithence the place,[5] where I am set to live,
Is, day by day, more scoop'd of all its good;
And dismal ruin seems to threaten it."

   "Go now," he cried: "lo! he,[6] whose guilt is most,
Passes before my vision, dragg'd at heels
Of an infuriate beast. Toward the vale,
Where guilt hath no redemption, on its speeds,
Each step increasing swiftness on the last;
Until a blow it strikes, that leaveth him
A corse most vilely shatter'd. No long space
Those wheels have yet to roll," (therewith his eyes
Look'd up to Heaven,) "ere thou shalt plainly see
That which my words may not more plainly tell.
I quit thee: time is precious here: I lose
Too much, thus measuring my pace with thine."

   As from a troop of well-rank'd chivalry,
One knight, more enterprising than the rest,
Pricks forth at gallop, eager to display
His prowess in the first encounter proved;
So parted he from us, with lengthen'd strides;
And left me on the way with those twain spirits,
Who were such mighty marshals of the world.

---

[5] "The place." Florence.

[6] "He."   Corso Donati was suspected of aiming at the sovereignty of Florence. To escape the fury of his fellow-citizens, he fled away on horseback, but falling, was overtaken and slain, A. D. 1308. The contemporary annalist, after relating at length the circumstances of his fate, adds, "that he was one of the wisest and most valorous knights, the best speaker, the most expert statesman, the most renowned and enterprising man of his age in Italy, a comely knight and of graceful carriage, but very worldly, and in his time had formed many conspiracies in Florence, and entered into many scandalous practices for the sake of attaining state and lordship." G. Villani, lib. v.

When he beyond us had so fled, mine eyes
No nearer reach'd him, than my thoughts his words,
The branches of another fruit, thick hung,
And blooming fresh, appear'd. E'en as our steps
Turn'd thither; not far off, it rose to view.
Beneath it were a multitude, that raised
Their hands, and shouted forth I know not what
Unto the boughs; like greedy and fond brats,
That beg, and answer none obtain from him,
Of whom they beg; but more to draw them on,
He, at arm's length, the object of their wish
Above them holds aloft, and hides it not.
    At length, as undeceived, they went their way:
And we approach the tree, whom vows and tears
Sue to in vain; the mighty tree. "Pass on,
And come not near. Stands higher up the wood,
Whereof Eve tasted: and from it was ta'en
This plant." Such sounds from midst the thickets came
Whence I, with either bard, close to the side
That rose, pass'd forth beyond. "Remember," next
We heard, "those unblest creatures of the clouds,[7]
How they their twyfold bosoms, overgorged,
Opposed in fight to Theseus: call to mind
The Hebrews, how, effeminate, they stoop'd
To ease their thirst; whence Gideon's ranks were thinn'd,
As he to Midian[8] march'd adown the hills."
    Thus near one border coasting, still we heard
The sins of gluttony, with woe erewhile
Reguerdon'd. Then along the lonely path,
Once more at large, full thousand paces on
We travel'd, each contemplative and mute.
    "Why pensive journey so ye three alone?"
Thus suddenly a voice exclaim'd: whereat
I shook, as doth a scared and paltry beast;
Then raised my head, to look from whence it came.
    Was ne'er, in furnace, glass, or metal, seen
So bright and glowing red, as was the shape
I now beheld. "If ye desire to mount,"
He cried; "here must ye turn. This way he goes,

[7] The Centaurs.   [8] Judges, vii.

Who goes in quest of peace." His countenance
Had dazzled me; and to my guides I faced
Backward, like one who walks as sound directs.

As when, to harbinger the dawn, springs up
On freshen'd wing the air of May, and breathes
Of fragrance, all impregn'd with herb and flowers;
E'en such a wind I felt upon my front
Blow gently, and the moving of a wing
Perceived, that, moving, shed ambrosial smell;
And then a voice: "Blessed are they, whom grace
Doth so illume, that appetite in them
Exhaleth no inordinate desire,
Still hungering as the rule of temperance wills."

CANTO XXV

ARGUMENT.—Virgil and Statius resolve some doubts that have arisen in the mind
of Dante from what he had just seen. They all arrive on the seventh and last cornice,
where the sin of incontinence is purged in fire; and the spirits of those suffering
therein are heard to record illustrious instances of chastity.

I T was an hour, when he who climbs, had need
To walk uncrippled: for the sun[1] had now
To Taurus the meridian circle left,
And to the Scorpion left the night. As one,
That makes no pause, but presses on his road,
Whate'er betide him, if some urgent need
Impel; so enter'd we upon our way,
One before other; for, but singly, none
That steep and narrow scale admits to climb.

E'en as the young stork lifteth up his wing
Through wish to fly, yet ventures not to quit
The nest, and drops it; so in me desire
Of questioning my guide arose, and fell,
Arriving even to the act that marks
A man prepared for speech. Him all our haste
Restrain'd not; but thus spake the sire beloved:
"Fear not to speed the shaft, that on thy lip

---

[1] "The sun." The sun had passed the
meridian two hours, and that meridian
was now occupied by the constellation of
Taurus, to which as the Scorpion is opposite, the latter constellation was consequently at the meridian of night.

Stands trembling for its flight." Encouraged thus,
I straight began: "How there can leanness come,
Where is no want of nourishment to feed?"
   "If thou," he answer'd, "hadst remember'd thee,
How Meleager[2] with the wasting brand
Wasted alike, by equal fires consumed;
This would not trouble thee: and hadst thou thought,
How in the mirror[3] your reflected form
With mimic motion vibrates; what now seems
Hard, had appear'd no harder than the pulp
Of summer-fruit mature. But that thy will
In certainty may find its full repose,
Lo Statius here! on him I call, and pray
That he would now be healer of thy wound."
   "If, in thy presence, I unfold to him
The secrets of Heaven's vengeance, let me plead
Thine own injunction to exculpate me."
So Statius answer'd, and forthwith began:
"Attend my words, O son, and in thy mind
Receive them; so shall they be light to clear
The doubt thou offer'st. Blood, concocted well,
Which by the thirsty veins is ne'er imbibed,
And rests as food superfluous, to be ta'en
From the replenish'd table, in the heart
Derives effectual virtue, that informs
The several human limbs, as being that
Which passes through the veins itself to make them.
Yet more concocted it descends, where shame
Forbids to mention: and from thence distils
In natural vessel on another's blood.
There each unite together; one disposed
To endure, to act the other, through that power
Derived from whence it came; and being met,
It 'gins to work, coagulating first;
Then vivifies what its own substance made

---

[2] Virgil reminds Dante that, as Meleager was wasted away by the decree of the fates, and not through want of blood; so by the divine appointment, there may be leanness where there is no need of nourishment.

[3] As the reflection of a form in a mirror is modified with the modification of the form itself; so the soul, separated from the earthly body, impresses the ghost of that body with its own affections.

Consist. With animation now indued,
The active virtue (differing from a plant
No further, than that this is on the way,
And at its limit that) continues yet
To operate, that now it moves, and feels,
As sea-sponge clinging to the rock: and there
Assumes the organic powers its seed convey'd.
This is the moment, son! at which the virtue,
That from the generating heart proceeds,
Is pliant and expansive; for each limb
Is in the heart by forgetful nature plann'd.
How babe of animal becomes, remains
For thy considering. At this point, more wise,
Than thou, has err'd, making the soul disjoin'd
From passive intellect, because he saw
No organ for the latter's use assign'd.

"Open thy bosom to the truth that comes.
Know, soon as in the embryo, to the brain
Articulation is complete, then turns
The primal Mover with a smile of joy
On such great work of nature; and imbreathes
New spirit replete with virtue, that what here
Active it finds, to its own substance draws;
And forms an individual soul, that lives,
And feels, and bends reflective on itself.
And that thou less may'st marvel at the word,
Mark the sun's heat; how that to wine doth change,
Mix'd with the moisture filter'd through the vine.

"When Lachesis hath spun the thread,[4] the soul
Takes with her both the human and divine,
Memory, intelligence, and will, in act
Far keener than before; the other powers
Inactive all and mute. No pause allow'd,
In wondrous sort self-moving, to one strand
Of those, where the departed roam, she falls:
Here learns her destined path. Soon as the place
Receives her, round the plastic virtue beams,
Distinct as in the living limbs before:
And as the air, when saturate with showers,

4 "When Lachesis hath spun the thread." When a man's life on earth is at an end.

The casual beam refracting, decks itself
With many a hue; so here the ambient air
Weareth that form, which influence of the soul
Imprints on it: and like the flame, that where
The fire moves, thither follows; so, henceforth,
The new form on the spirit follows still:
Hence hath it semblance, and is shadow call'd,
With each sense, even to the sight, indued:
Hence speech is ours, hence laughter, tears, and sighs,
Which thou mayst oft have witness'd on the mount.
The obedient shadow fails not to present
Whatever varying passion moves within us.
And this the cause of what thou marvel'st at."

   Now the last flexure of our way we reach'd;
And to the right hand turning, other care
Awaits us. Here the rocky precipice
Hurls forth redundant flames; and from the rim
A blast up-blown, with forcible rebuff
Driveth them back, sequester'd from its bound.

   Behoved us, one by one, along the side,
That border'd on the void, to pass; and I
Fear'd on one hand the fire, on the other fear'd
Headlong to fall: when thus the instructor warn'd:
"Strict rein must in this place direct the eyes.
A little swerving and the way is lost."

   Then from the bosom of the burning mass,
"O God of mercy!"[5] heard I sung, and felt
No less desire to turn. And when I saw
Spirits along the flame proceeding, I
Between their footsteps and mine own was fain
To share by turns my view. At the hymn's close
They shouted loud, "I do not know a man;"[6]
Then in low voice again took up the strain;
Which once more ended, "To the wood," they cried,
"Ran Dian, and drave forth Callisto stung
With Cytherea's poison"; then return'd
Unto their song; then many a pair extoll'd,

[5] "Summæ Deus clementiæ." The beginning of the hymn sung on the Sabbath
at matins, as in the ancient breviaries; in

the modern it is "summæ parens clementiæ."
[6] Luke, i. 34.

Who lived in virtue chastely and the bands
Of wedded love. Nor from that task, I ween,
Surcease they; whilesoe'er the scorching fire
Enclasps them. Of such skill appliance needs,
To medicine the wound that healeth last.

CANTO XXVI

ARGUMENT.—The spirits wonder at seeing the shadow cast by the body of Dante
on the flame as he passes it. This moves one of them to address him. It proves to
be Guido Guinicelli, the Italian poet, who points out to him the spirit of Arnault
Daniel, the Provençal, with whom he also speaks.

WHILE singly thus along the rim we walk'd,
        Oft the good master warn'd me: "Look thou
        Avail it that I caution thee." The sun   [well.
Now all the western clime irradiate changed
From azure tint to white; and, as I pass'd,
My passing shadow made the umber'd flame
Burn ruddier. At so strange a sight I mark'd
That many a spirit marvel'd on his way.
    This bred occasion first to speak of me.
"He seems," said they, "no insubstantial frame:"
Then, to obtain what certainty they might,
Stretch'd tow'rd me, careful not to overpass
The burning pale. "O thou! who followest
The others, haply not more slow than they,
But moved by reverence; answer me, who burn
In thirst and fire: nor I alone, but these
All for thine answer do more thirst, than doth
Indian or Æthiop for the cooling stream.
Tell us, how is it that thou makest thyself
A wall against the sun, as thou not yet
Into the inextricable toils of death
Hadst enter'd?" Thus spake one; and I had straight
Declared me, if attention had not turn'd
To new appearance. Meeting these, there came,
Midway the burning path, a crowd, on whom
Earnestly gazing, from each part I view
The shadows all press forward, severally
Each snatch a hasty kiss, and then away.

E'en so the emmets, 'mid their dusky troops,
Peer closely one at other, to spy out
Their mutual road perchance, and how they thrive.
   That friendly greeting parted, ere despatch
Of the first onward step, from either tribe
Loud clamour rises: those, who newly come,
Shout "Sodom and Gomorrah!" these, "The cow
Pasiphaë enter'd, that the beast she woo'd
Might rush unto her luxury." Then as cranes,
That part toward the Riphæan mountains fly,
Part toward the Lybic sands, these to avoid
The ice, and those the sun; so hasteth off
One crowd, advances the other; and resume
Their first song, weeping, and their several shout.
   Again drew near my side the very same,
Who had erewhile besought me; and their looks
Mark'd eagerness to listen. I, who twice
Their will had noted, spake: "O spirits! secure,
Whene'er the time may be, of peaceful end;
My limbs, nor crude, nor in mature old age,
Have I left yonder: here they bear me, fed
With blood, and sinew-strung. That I no more
May live in blindness, hence I tend aloft.
There is a Dame on high, who wins for us
This grace, by which my mortal through your realm
I bear. But may your utmost wish soon meet
Such full fruition, that the orb of heaven,
Fullest of love, and of most ample space,
Receive you; as ye tell (upon my page
Henceforth to stand recorded) who ye are;
And what this multitude, that at your backs
Have pass'd behind us." As one, mountain-bred,
Rugged and clownish, if some city's walls
He chance to enter, round him stares agape,
Confounded and struck dumb; e'en such appear'd
Each spirit. But when rid of that amaze,
(Not long the inmate of a noble heart,)
He, who before had question'd, thus resumed:
"O blessed! who, for death preparing, takest
Experience of our limits, in thy bark;

Their crime, who not with us proceed, was that
For which, as he did triumph, Cæsar heard
The shout of 'queen,' to taunt him. Hence their cry
Of 'Sodom,' as they parted; to rebuke
Themselves, and aid the burning by their shame.
Our sinning was hermaphrodite: but we,
Because the law of human kind we broke,
Following like beasts our vile concupiscence,
Hence parting from them, to our own disgrace
Record the name of her, by whom the beast
In bestial tire was acted. Now our deeds
Thou know'st, and how we sinn'd. If thou by name
Wouldst haply know us, time permits not now
To tell so much, nor can I. Of myself
Learn what thou wishest. Guinicelli I;
Who having truly sorrow'd ere my last,
Already cleanse me." With such pious joy,
As the two sons upon their mother gazed
From sad Lycurgus[1] rescued; such my joy
(Save that I more repress'd it) when I heard
From his own lips the name of him pronounced,
Who was a father to me, and to those
My betters, who have ever used the sweet
And pleasant rhymes of love. So naught I heard,
Nor spake; but long time thoughtfully I went,
Gazing on him; and, only for the fire,
Approached not nearer. When my eyes were fed
By looking on him; with such solemn pledge,
As forces credence, I devoted me
Unto his service wholly. In reply
He thus bespake me: "What from thee I hear
Is graved so deeply on my mind, the waves
Of Lethe shall not wash it off, nor make
A whit less lively. But as now thy oath
Has seal'd the truth, declare what cause impels

[1] Hypsipile had left her infant charge, the son of Lycurgus, on a bank, where it was destroyed by a serpent, when she went to show the Argive army the river of Langia; and on her escaping the effects of Lycurgus's resentment, the joy her own children felt at the sight of her was such as our Poet felt on beholding his predecessor Guinicelli

That love, which both thy looks and speech bewray."
  "Those dulcet lays," I answer'd; "which, as long
As of our tongue the beauty does not fade,
Shall make us love the very ink that traced them."
  "Brother!" he cried, and pointed at the shade
Before him, "there is one, whose mother speech
Doth owe to him a fairer ornament.
He[2] in love ditties, and the tales of prose,
Without a rival stands; and lets the fools
Talk on, who think the songster of Limoges[3]
O'ertops him. Rumour and the popular voice
They look to, more than truth; and so confirm
Opinion, ere by art or reason taught.
Thus many of the elder time cried up
Guittone, giving him the prize, till truth
By strength of numbers vanquish'd. If thou own
So ample privilege, as to have gain'd
Free entrance to the cloister, whereof Christ
Is Abbot of the college; say to him
One paternoster for me, far as needs
For dwellers in this world, where power to sin
No longer tempts us." Haply to make way
For one that follow'd next, when that was said,
He vanish'd through the fire, as through the wave
A fish, that glances diving to the deep.
  I, to the spirit he had shown me, drew
A little onward, and besought his name,
For which my heart, I said, kept gracious room.
He frankly thus began: "Thy courtesy[4]
So wins on me, I have nor power nor will
To hide me. I am Arnault; and with songs,
Sorely waymenting for my folly past,
Thorough this ford of fire I wade, and see
The day, I hope for, smiling in my view.
I pray ye by the worth that guides ye up

---

[2] Dante and Petrarch place Arnault Daniel first among Provençal poets.

[3] Giraud de Borneil, of Sideuil, a castle in Limoges. He was a Troubadour, much admired and caressed in his day, and appears to have been in favor with the monarchs of Castile, Leon, Navarre, and Arragon.

[4] Arnault is here made to speak in his own tongue, the Provençal.

Unto the summit of the scale, in time
Remember ye my sufferings." With such words
He disappear'd in the refining flame.

CANTO XXVII

ARGUMENT.—An Angel sends them forward through the fire to the last ascent, which leads to the terrestrial Paradise, situated on the summit of the mountain. They have not proceeded many steps on their way upward, when the fall of night hinders them from going further; and our Poet, who has lain down with Virgil and Statius to rest, beholds in a dream two females, figuring the active and contemplative life. With the return of morning, they reach the height; and here Virgil gives Dante full liberty to use his own pleasure and judgment in the choice of his way, till he shall meet with Beatrice.

NOW was the sun[1] so station'd, as when first
His early radiance quivers on the heights,
Where stream'd his Maker's blood; while Libra
          hangs
Above Hesperian Ebro; and new fires,
Meridian, flash on Ganges' yellow tide.
      So day was sinking, when the Angel of God
Appear'd before us. Joy was in his mien.
Forth of the flame he stood upon the brink;
And with a voice, whose lively clearness far
Surpass'd our human, "Blessed[2] are the pure
In heart," he sang: then near him as we came,
"Go ye not further, holy spirits!" he cried,
"Ere the fire pierce you: enter in; and list
Attentive to the song ye hear from thence."
      I, when I heard his saying, was as one
Laid in the grave. My hands together clasp'd,
And upward stretching, on the fire I look'd;
And busy fancy conjured up the forms
Erewhile beheld alive consumed in flames.
      The escorting spirits turn'd with gentle looks
Toward me; and the Mantuan spake: "My son,
Here torment thou mayst feel, but canst not death.
Remember thee, remember thee, if I
Safe e'en on Geryon brought thee; now I come
More near to God, wilt thou not trust me now?

---

[1] "The sun." At Jerusalem it was dawn, in Spain midnight, and in India noonday, in Purgatory sunset.   [2] "Blessed."—Matt. v. 8.

Of this be sure; though in its womb that flame
A thousand years contain'd thee, from thy head
No hair should perish. If thou doubt my truth,
Approach; and with thy hand thy vesture's hem
Stretch forth, and for thyself confirm belief.
Lay now all fear, oh! lay all fear aside.
Turn hither, and come onward undismay'd."
    I still, though conscience urged, no step advanced.
    When still he saw me fix'd and obstinate.
Somewhat disturb'd he cried: "Mark now, my son,
From Beatrice thou art by this wall
Divided." As at Thisbe's name the eye
Of Pyramus was open'd, (when life ebb'd
Fast from his veins), and took one parting glance,
While vermeil dyed the mulberry; thus I turn'd
To my sage guide, relenting, when I heard
The name that springs forever in my breast.
    He shook his forehead; and, "How long," he said,
"Linger we now?" then smiled, as one would smile
Upon a child that eyes the fruit and yields.
Into the fire before me then he walk'd;
And Statius, who erewhile no little space
Had parted us, he pray'd to come behind.
    I would have cast me into molten glass
To cool me, when I enter'd; so intense
Raged the conflagrant mass. The sire beloved,
To comfort me, as he proceeded, still
Of Beatrice talk'd. "Her eyes," saith he,
"E'en now I seem to view." From the other side
A voice, that sang, did guide us; and the voice
Following, with heedful ear, we issued forth,
There where the path led upward. "Come," [3] we heard,
"Come, blessed of my Father." Such the sounds,
That hail'd us from within a light, which shone
So radiant, I could not endure the view.
"The sun," it added, "hastes: and evening comes.
Delay not: ere the western sky is hung
With blackness, strive ye for the pass." Our way
Upright within the rock arose, and faced
Such part of heaven, that from before my steps

[3] "Come."—Matt. xxv. 34.

The beams were shrouded of the sinking sun.
    Nor many stairs were overpast, when now
By fading of the shadow we perceived
The sun behind us couch'd; and ere one face
Of darkness o'er its measureless expanse
Involved the horizon, and the night her lot
Held individual, each of us had made
A stair his pallet; not that will, but power,
Had fail'd us, by the nature of that mount
Forbidden further travel. As the goats,
That late have skipt and wanton'd rapidly
Upon the craggy cliffs, ere they had ta'en
Their supper on the herb, now silent lie
And ruminate beneath the umbrage brown,
While noon-day rages; and the goatherd leans
Upon his staff, and leaning watches them:
And as the swain, that lodges out all night
In quiet by his flock, lest beast of prey
Disperse them: even so all three abode,
I as a goat, and as the shepherds they,
Close pent on either side by shelving rock.
    A little glimpse of sky was seen above;
Yet by that little I beheld the stars,
In magnitude and lustre shining forth
With more than wonted glory. As I lay,
Gazing on them, and in that fit of musing
Sleep overcame me, sleep, that bringeth oft
Tidings of future hap. About the hour,
As I believe, when Venus from the east
First lighten'd on the mountain, she whose orb
Seems always glowing with the fire of love,
A lady young and beautiful, I dream'd,
Was passing o'er a lea; and, as she came,
Methought I saw her ever and anon
Bending to cull the flowers; and thus she sang:
"Know ye, whoever of my name would ask,
That I am Leah:[4] for my brow to weave

---

[4] Leah, the active life; Rachel, the contemplative; Michael Angelo has used these allegorical personages on his monument of Julius II in the church of S. Pietro in Vincolo.

A garland, these fair hands unwearied ply.
To please me at the crystal mirror, here
I deck me. But my sister Rachel, she
Before her glass abides the livelong day,
Her radiant eyes beholding, charm'd no less,
Than I with this delightful task. Her joy
In contemplation, as in labour mine."
    And now as glimmering dawn appear'd, that breaks
More welcome to the pilgrim still, as he
Sojourns less distant on his homeward way,
Darkness from all sides fled, and with it fled
My slumber; whence I rose, and saw my guide
Already risen. "That delicious fruit,
Which through so many a branch the zealous care
Of mortals roams in quest of, shall this day
Appease thy hunger." Such the words I heard
From Virgil's lip; and never greeting heard,
So pleasant as the sounds. Within me straight
Desire so grew upon desire to mount,
Thenceforward at each step I felt the wings
Increasing for my flight. When we had run
O'er all the ladder to its topmost round,
As there we stood, on me the Mantuan fix'd
His eyes, and thus he spake: "Both fires, my son,
The temporal and eternal, thou hast seen;
And art arrived, where of itself my ken
No further reaches. I, with skill and art,
Thus far have drawn thee. Now thy pleasure take
For guide. Thou hast o'ercome the steeper way,
O'ercome the straiter. Lo! the sun, that darts
His beam upon my forehead: lo! the herb,
The arborets and flowers, which of itself
This land pours forth profuse. Till those bright eyes[5]
With gladness come, which, weeping, made me haste
To succour thee, thou mayst or seat thee down,
Or wander where thou wilt. Expect no more
Sanction of warning voice or sign from me,
Free of thy own arbitrement to chuse,
Discreet, judicious. To distrust thy sense

[5] The eyes of Beatrice.

Were henceforth error. I invest thee then
With crown and mitre, sovereign o'er thyself."

CANTO XXVIII

ARGUMENT.—Dante wanders through the forest of the terrestrial Paradise, till he
is stopped by a stream, on the other side of which he beholds a fair lady, culling
flowers. He speaks to her; and she, in reply, explains to him certain things touching
the nature of that place, and tells that the water, which flows between them, is here
called Lethe, and in another place has the name of Eunoe.

THROUGH that celestial forest, whose thick shade
With lively greenness the new-springing day
Attemper'd, eager now to roam, and search
Its limits round, forthwith I left the bank;
Along the champain leisurely my way
Pursuing, o'er the ground, that on all sides
Delicious odour breathed. A pleasant air,
That intermitted never, never veer'd,
Smote on my temples, gently, as a wind
Of softest influence: at which the sprays,
Obedient all, lean'd trembling to that part[1]
Where first the holy mountain casts his shade;
Yet were not so disorder'd, but that still
Upon their top the feather'd quiristers
Applied their wonted art, and with full joy
Welcomed those hours of prime, and warbled shrill
Amid the leaves, that to their jocund lays
Kept tenour; even as from branch to branch,
Along the piny forests on the shore
Of Chiassi, rolls the gathering melody,
When Eolus hath from his cavern loosed
The dripping south. Already had my steps,
Though slow, so far into that ancient wood
Transported me, I could not ken the place
Where I had enter'd; when, behold! my path
Was bounded by a rill, which, to the left,
With little rippling waters bent the grass
That issued from its brink. On earth no wave
How clean soe'er, that would not seem to have

[1] "To that part." The west.

Some mixture in itself, compared with this,
Transpicuous clear; yet darkly on it roll'd,
Darkly beneath perpetual gloom, which ne'er
Admits or sun or moon-light there to shine.
    My feet advanced not; but my wondering eyes
Pass'd onward, o'er the streamlet to survey
The tender May-bloom, flush'd through many a hue,
In prodigal variety: and there,
As object, rising suddenly to view,
That from our bosom every thought beside
With the rare marvel chases, I beheld
A lady[2] all alone, who, singing, went,
And culling flower from flower, wherewith her way
Was all o'er painted. "Lady beautiful!
Thou, who (if looks, that use to speak the heart,
Art worthy of our trust) with love's own beam
Dost warm thee," thus to her my speech I framed;
"Ah! please thee hither toward the streamlet bend
Thy steps so near, that I may list thy song.
Beholding thee and this fair place, methinks,
I call to mind where wander'd and how look'd
Proserpine, in that season, when her child
The mother lost, and she the bloomy spring."
    As when a lady, turning in the dance,
Doth foot it featly, and advances scarce
One step before the other to the ground:
Over the yellow and vermilion flowers,
Thus turn'd she at my suit, most maiden-like
Valing her sober eyes; and came so near,
That I distinctly caught the dulcet sound.
Arriving where the limpid waters now
Laved the greensward, her eyes she deign'd to raise,
That shot such splendour on me, as I ween
Ne'er glanced from Cytherea's, when her son
Had sped his keenest weapon to her heart.
Upon the opposite bank she stood and smiled;
As through her graceful fingers shifted still

[2] Most of the commentators suppose that this lady, who in the last Canto is called Matilda, is the Countess Matilda, who endowed the Holy See with the estates called the Patrimony of St. Peter, and died in 1115. But it seems more probable that she should be intended for an allegorical personage.

The intermingling dyes, which without seed
That lofty land unbosoms. By the stream
Three paces only were we sunder'd: yet,
The Hellespont, where Xerxes pass'd it o'er,
(A curb for ever to the pride of man,[3])
Was by Leander not more hateful held
For floating, with inhospitable wave,
'Twixt Sestos and Abydos, than by me
That flood, because it gave no passage thence.

   "Strangers ye come; and haply in this place,
That cradled human nature in its birth,
Wondering, ye not without suspicion view
My smiles: but that sweet strain of psalmody,
'Thou, Lord! hast made me glad,'[4] will give ye light,
Which may uncloud your minds. And thou, who stand'st
The foremost, and didst make thy suit to me,
Say if aught else thou wish to hear: for I
Came prompt to answer every doubt of thine."

   She spake; and I replied: "I know not how
To reconcile this wave, and rustling sound
Of forest leaves, with what I late have heard
Of opposite report." She answering thus:
"I will unfold the cause, whence that proceeds,
Which makes thee wonder; and so purge the cloud
That hath enwrapt thee. The First Good, whose joy
Is only in Himself, created man,
For happiness; and gave this goodly place,
His pledge and earnest of eternal peace.
Favour'd thus highly, through his own defect
He fell; and here made short sojourn; he fell,
And, for the bitterness of sorrow, changed
Laughter unblamed and ever-new delight.
That vapours none, exhaled from earth beneath,
Or from the waters, (which, wherever heat
Attracts them, follow), might ascend thus far
To vex man's peaceful state, this mountain rose
So high toward the Heaven, nor fears the rage

[3] Because Xerxes had been so humbled, when he was compelled to repass the Hellespont in one small bark, after having a little before crossed with a prodigious army, in the hopes of subduing Greece.

[4] "Thou, Lord! hast made me glad."— Psalm xcii. 4.

Of elements contending; from that part
Exempted, where the gate his limit bars.
Because the circumambient air, throughout,
With its first impulse circles still, unless
Aught interpose to check or thwart its course;
Upon the summit, which on every side
To visitation of the impassive air
Is open, doth that motion strike, and makes
Beneath its sway the umbrageous wood resound:
And in the shaken plant such power resides,
That it impregnates with its efficacy
The voyaging breeze, upon whose subtle plume
That, wafted, flies abroad; and the other land,[5]
Receiving, (as 'tis worthy in itself,
Or in the clime, that warms it,) doth conceive;
And from its womb produces many a tree
Of various virtue. This when thou hast heard,
The marvel ceases, if in yonder earth
Some plant, without apparent seed, be found
To fix its fibrous stem. And further learn,
That with prolific foison of all seeds
This holy plain is fill'd, and in itself
Bears fruit that ne'er was pluck'd on other soil.

"The water, thou behold'st, springs not from vein,
Restored by vapour, that the cold converts;
As stream that intermittently repairs
And spends his pulse of life; but issues forth
From fountain, solid, undecaying, sure:
And, by the Will Omnific, full supply
Feeds whatsoe'er on either side it pours;
On this, devolved with power to take away
Remembrance of offence; on that, to bring
Remembrance back of every good deed done.
From whence its name of Lethe on this part;
On the other, Eunoë: both of which must first

[5] The continent, inhabited by the living, and separated from Purgatory by the ocean, is affected (and that diversely, according to the nature of the soil, or the climate) by a virtue, conveyed to it by the winds from plants growing in the terrestrial Paradise, which is situated on the summit of Purgatory; and this is the cause why some plants are found on earth without any apparent seed to produce them.

Be tasted, ere it work; the last exceeding
All flavours else. Albeit thy thirst may now
Be well contented, if I here break off,
No more revealing; yet a corollary
I freely give beside: nor deem my words
Less grateful to thee, if they somewhat pass
The stretch of promise. They, whose verse of yore
The golden age recorded and its bliss,
On the Parnassian mountain, of this place
Perhaps had dream'd. Here was man guiltless; here
Perpetual spring, and every fruit; and this
The far-famed nectar." Turning to the bards,
When she had ceased, I noted in their looks
A smile at her conclusion; then my face
Again directed to the lovely dame.

CANTO XXIX

ARGUMENT.—The lady, who in a following Canto is called Matilda, moves along
the side of the stream in a contrary direction to the current, and Dante keeps equal
pace with her on the opposite bank. A marvellous sight, preceded by music, appears
in view.

SINGING, as if enamour'd, she resumed
And closed the song, with "Blessed they[1] whose sins
Are cover'd." Like the wood-nymphs then, that
Singly across the sylvan shadows; one   [tripp'd
Eager to view, and one to escape the sun;
So moved she on, against the current, up
The verdant rivage. I, her mincing step
Observing, with as tardy step pursued.
    Between us not an hundred paces trod,
The bank, on each side bending equally,
Gave me to face the orient. Nor our way
Far onward brought us, when to me at once
She turn'd, and cried: "My brother! look, and hearken."
And lo! a sudden lustre ran across
Through the great forest on all parts, so bright,
I doubted whether lightning were abroad;
But that, expiring ever in the spleen

[1] "Blessed they."—Psalm xxxii. 1.

That doth unfold it, and this during still,
And waxing still in splendour, made me question
What it might be: and a sweet melody
Ran through the luminous air. Then did I chide,
With warrantable zeal, the hardihood
Of our first parent; for that there, where earth
Stood in obedience to the Heavens, she only,
Woman, the creature of an hour, endured not
Restraint of any veil, which had she borne
Devoutly, joys, ineffable as these,
Had from the first, and long time since, been mine.

    While, through that wilderness of primy sweets
That never fade, suspense I walk'd, and yet
Expectant of beatitude more high;
Before us, like a blazing fire, the air
Under the green boughs glow'd; and, for a song,
Distinct the sound of melody was heard.

    O ye thrice holy virgins! for your sakes
If e'er I suffer'd hunger, cold, and watching,
Occasion calls on me to crave your bounty.
Now through my breast let Helicon his stream
Pour copious, and Urania[2] with her choir
Arise to aid me; while the verse unfolds
Things, that do almost mock the grasp of thought.

    Onward a space, what seem'd seven trees of gold
The intervening distance to mine eye
Falsely presented; but, when I was come
So near them, that no lineament was lost
Of those, with which a doubtful object, seen
Remotely, plays on the misdeeming sense;
Then did the faculty, that ministers
Discourse to reason, these for tapers of gold[3]
Distinguish; and i' the singing trace the sound
"Hosanna!" Above, their beauteous garniture
Flamed with more ample lustre, than the moon
Through cloudless sky at midnight, in her noon.

[2] "Urania." Landino observes, that intending to sing of heavenly things, he rightly invokes Urania. Thus Milton:
"Descend from Heaven, Urania, by that name

If rightly thou art call'd."
            Paradise Lost, b. vii. 1.
[3] See Rev. i. 12.

I turn'd me, full of wonder, to my guide;
And he did answer with a countenance
Charged with no less amazement: whence my view
Reverted to those lofty things, which came
So slowly moving toward us, that the bride
Would have outstript them on her bridal day.

The lady call'd aloud: "Why thus yet burns
Affection in thee for these living lights,
And dost not look on that which follows them?"

I straightway mark'd a tribe behind them walk,
As if attendant on their leaders, clothed
With raiment of such whiteness, as on earth
Was never. On my left, the watery gleam
Borrow'd, and gave me back, when there I look'd,
As in a mirror, my left side portray'd.

When I had chosen on the river's edge
Such station, that the distance of the stream
Alone did separate me; there I stay'd
My steps for clearer prospect, and beheld
The flames go onward, leaving, as they went,
The air behind them painted as with trail
Of liveliest pencils; so distinct were mark'd
All those seven listed colours, whence the sun
Maketh his bow, and Cynthia her zone.
These streaming gonfalons did flow beyond
My vision; and ten paces, as I guess,
Parted the outermost. Beneath a sky
So beautiful, came four and twenty elders,[4]
By two and two, with flower-de-luces crown'd.
All sang one song: "Blessed be thou[5] among
The daughters of Adam! and thy loveliness
Blessed forever!" After that the flowers,
And the fresh herblets, on the opposite brink,
Were free from that elected race; as light
In heaven doth second light, came after them
Four[6] animals, each crown'd with verdurous leaf.
With six wings each was plumed; the plumage full

---

[4] "Upon the seats I saw four and twenty elders sitting."—Rev. iv. 4.

[5] "Blessed art thou among women, and blessed is the fruit of thy womb."—Luke i. 42.

[6] "Four." The four evangelists.

Of eyes; and the eyes of Argus would be such,
Were they endued with life. Reader! more rhymes
I will not waste in shadowing forth their form:
For other need so straitens, that in this
I may not give my bounty room. But read
Ezekiel;[7] for he paints them, from the north
How he beheld them come by Chebar's flood,
In whirlwind, cloud, and fire; and even such
As thou shalt find them character'd by him,
Here were they; save as to the pennons: there,
From him departing, John[8] accords with me.

The space, surrounded by the four, enclosed
A car triumphal:[9] on two wheels it came,
Drawn at a Gryphon's[10] neck; and he above
Stretch'd either wing uplifted, 'tween the midst
And the three listed hues, on each side, three;
So that the wings did cleave or injure none;
And out of sight they rose. The members, far
As he was bird, were golden; white the rest,
With vermeil intervein'd. So beautiful
A car, in Rome, ne'er graced Augustus' pomp,
Or Africanus': e'en the sun's itself
Were poor to this; that chariot of the sun,
Erroneous, which in blazing ruin fell
At Tellus' prayer devout, by the just doom
Mysterious of all-seeing Jove. Three nymphs,[11]
At the right wheel, came circling in smooth dance:
The one so ruddy, that her form had scarce
Been known within a furnace of clear flame;

[7] "Ezekiel." "And I looked, and be-hold, a whirlwind came out of the north, a great cloud, and a fire infolding itself, and a brightness was about it, and out of the midst thereof as the color of amber, out of the midst of fire. Also out of the midst thereof came the likeness of four living creatures. And this was their appearance; they had the likeness of a man. And every one had four faces, and every one had four wings."—Ezekiel, i. 4, 5, 6.
[8] "John." "And the four beasts had each of them six wings about him."—Rev. iv. 8.

[9] Either the Christian Church or per-haps the papal chair.
[10] Under the griffin (gryphon), an im-aginary creature, the fore-part of which is an eagle, and the hinder a lion, is shadowed forth the union of the divine and the human nature in Jesus Christ.
[11] The three evangelical virtues: Char-ity, Hope, and Faith. Faith may be pro-duced by charity, or charity by faith, but the inducements to hope must arise either from one or other of these.

The next did look, as if the flesh and bones
Were emerald; snow new-fallen seem'd the third.
Now seem'd the white to lead, the ruddy now;
And from her song who led, the others took
Their measure, swift or slow. At the other wheel,
A band quaternion,[12] each in purple clad,
Advanced with festal step, as, of them, one
The rest conducted;[13] one, upon whose front
Three eyes were seen. In rear of all this group,
Two old men[14] I beheld, dissimilar
In raiment, but in port and gesture like,
Solid and mainly grave; of whom, the one
Did show himself some favor'd counsellor
Of the great Coan,[15] him, whom nature made
To serve the costliest creature of her tribe:
His fellow mark'd an opposite intent;
Bearing a sword, whose glitterance and keen edge,
E'en as I viewed it with the flood between,
Appall'd me. Next, four others[16] I beheld
Of humble seeming: and, behind them all,
One single old man,[17] sleeping as he came,
With a shrewd visage. And these seven, each
Like the first troop were habited; but wore
No braid of lilies on their temples wreathed.
Rather, with roses and each vermeil flower,
A sight, but little distant, might have sworn,
That they were all on fire above their brow.

    Whenas the car was o'er against me, straight
Was heard a thundering, at whose voice it seem'd
The chosen multitude were stay'd; for there,
With the first ensigns, made they solemn halt.

---

[12] The four moral virtues, of whom Prudence directs the others.

[13] Prudence, described with three eyes, because she regards the past, the present, and the future.

[14] "Two old men." St. Luke, the physician, characterized as the writer of the Acts of the Apostles, and St. Paul, represented with a sword, on account, as it should seem, of the power of his style.

[15] Hippocrates, "whom nature made for the benefit of her favorite creature, man."

[16] "The commentators," says Venturi, "suppose these four to be the four evangelists; but I should rather take them to be four principal doctors of the Church." Yet both Landino and Vellutello expressly call them the authors of the epistles, James, Peter, John, and Jude.

[17] As some say, St. John, under the character of the author of the Apocalypse.

CANTO XXX

ARGUMENT.—Beatrice descends from Heaven, and rebukes the Poet.

SOON as that polar light,[1] fair ornament
    Of the first Heaven, which hath never known
    Setting nor rising, nor the shadowy veil
Of other cloud than sin, to duty there
Each one convoying, as that lower doth
The steersman to his port, stood firmly fix'd;
Forthwith the saintly tribe, who in the van
Between the Gryphon and its radiance came,
Did turn them to the car, as to their rest:
And one, as if commission'd from above,
In holy chant thrice shouted forth aloud;
"Come,[2] spouse! from Libanus:" and all the rest
Took up the song.—At the last audit, so
The blest shall rise, from forth his cavern each
Uplifting lightly his new-vested flesh;
As, on the sacred litter, at the voice
Authoritative of that elder, sprang
A hundred ministers and messengers
Of life eternal. "Blessed[3] thou, who comest!"
And, "Oh!" they cried, "from full hands scatter ye
Unwithering lilies": and, so saying, cast
Flowers overhead and round them on all sides.
    I have beheld, ere now, at break of day,
The eastern clime all roseate; and the sky
Opposed, one deep and beautiful serene;
And the sun's face so shaded, and with mists
Attemper'd, at his rising, that the eye
Long while endured the sight: thus, in a cloud
Of flowers, that from those hands angelic rose,
And down within and outside of the car
Fell showering, in white veil with olive wreathed,
A virgin in my view appear'd, beneath

---

[1] The seven candlesticks of gold, which he calls the polar light of Heaven itself, because they perform the same office for Christians that the polar star does for mariners, in guiding them to their port.

[2] "Come with me from Lebanon, my spouse, with me, from Lebanon."—Song of Solomon, iv. 8.

[3] "Blessed is he that cometh in the name of the Lord."—Matt. xxi. 9.

Green mantle, robed in hue of living flame:
And o'er my spirit, that so long a time
Had from her presence felt no shuddering dread,
Albeit mine eyes discern'd her not, there moved
A hidden virtue from her, at whose touch
The power of ancient love was strong within me.
   No sooner on my vision streaming, smote
The heavenly influence, which, years past, and e'en
In childhood, thrill'd me, than towards Virgil I
Turn'd me to leftward; panting, like a babe,
That flees for refuge to his mother's breast,
If aught have terrified or work'd him woe:
And would have cried, "There is no dram of blood,
That doth not quiver in me. The old flame
Throws out clear tokens of reviving fire."
But Virgil had bereaved us of himself;
Virgil, my best-loved father, Virgil, he
To whom I gave me up for safety: nor
All, our prime mother lost, avail'd to save
My undew'd cheeks from blur of soiling tears.
   "Dante! weep not that Virgil leaves thee; nay,
Weep thou not yet: behoves thee feel the edge
Of other sword; and thou shalt weep for that."
   As to the prow or stern, some admiral
Paces the deck, inspiriting his crew,
When 'mid the sail-yards all hands ply aloof;
Thus, on the left side of the car, I saw
(Turning me at the sound of mine own name,
Which here I am compell'd to register)
The virgin station'd, who before appear'd
Veil'd in that festive shower angelical.
   Towards me, across the stream, she bent her eyes;
Though from her brow the veil descending, bound
With foliage of Minerva, suffer'd not
That I beheld her clearly: then with act
Full royal, still insulting o'er her thrall,
Added, as one who, speaking, keepeth back
The bitterest saying, to conclude the speech:
"Observe me well. I am, in sooth, I am
Beatrice. What! and hast thou deign'd at last

Approach the mountain?   Knewest not, O man!
Thy happiness is here?"   Down fell mine eyes
On the clear fount; but there, myself espying,
Recoil'd, and sought the greensward; such a weight
Of shame was on my forehead. With a mien
Of that stern majesty, which doth surround
A mother's presence to her awe-struck child,
She look'd; a flavor of such bitterness
Was mingled in her pity. There her words
Brake off; and suddenly the angels sang,
"In thee, O gracious Lord! my hope hath been":
But[4] went no further than, "Thou, Lord! hast set
My feet in ample room." As snow, that lies,
Amidst the living rafters on the back
Of Italy, congeal'd, when drifted high
And closely piled by rough Sclavonian blasts;
Breathe but the land whereon no shadow falls,
And straightway melting it distils away,
Like a fire-wasted taper: thus was I,
Without a sigh or tear, or ever these
Did sing, that, with the chiming of Heaven's sphere,
Still in their warbling chime: but when the strain
Of dulcet symphony express'd for me
Their soft compassion, more than could the words,
"Virgin! why so consumest him?" then, the ice
Congeal'd about my bosom, turn'd itself
To spirit and water; and with anguish forth
Gush'd, through the lips and eyelids, from the heart.
     Upon the chariot's same edge still she stood,
Immovable; and thus address'd her words
To those bright semblances with pity touch'd:
"Ye in the eternal day your vigils keep;
So that nor night nor slumber, with close stealth,
Conveys from you a single step, in all
The goings on of time: thence, with more heed
I shape mine answer, for his ear intended,
Who there stands weeping; that the sorrow now
May equal the transgression. Not alone

[4] "But." They sang the thirty-first   What follows would not have suited the
Psalm, to the end of the eighth verse.   place or the occasion.

Through operation of the mighty orbs,
That mark each seed to some predestined aim,
As with aspect or fortunate or ill
The constellations meet; but through benign
Largess of heavenly graces, which rain down
From such a height as mocks our vision, this **man**
Was, in the freshness of his being, such,
So gifted virtually, that in him
All better habits wondrously had thrived
The more of kindly strength is in the soil,
So much doth evil seed and lack of culture
Mar it the more, and make it run to wildness.
These looks sometime upheld him; for I show'd
My youthful eyes, and led him by their light
In upright walking. Soon as I had reach'd
The threshold of my second age, and changed
My mortal for immortal; then he left me,
And gave himself to others. When from flesh
To spirit I had risen, and increase
Of beauty and of virtue circled me,
I was less dear to him, and valued less.
His steps were turn'd into deceitful ways,
Following false images of good, that make
No promise perfect. Nor avail'd me aught
To sue for inspirations, with the which,
I, both in dreams of night, and otherwise,
Did call him back; of them, so little reck'd him.
Such depth he fell, that all device was short
Of his preserving, save that he should view
The children of perdition. To this end
I visited the purlieus of the dead:
And one, who hath conducted him thus high,
Received my supplications urged with weeping.
It were a breaking of God's high decree,
If Lethe should be pass'd, and such food[5] tasted,
Without the cost of some repentant tear."

[5] The oblivion of sins.

CANTO XXXI

ARGUMENT.—Beatrice continues her reprehension of Dante, who confesses his error, and falls to the ground; coming to himself again, he is by Matilda drawn through the waters of Lethe, and presented first to the four virgins who figure the cardinal virtues; these in their turn lead him to the Gryphon, a symbol of our Saviour; and the three virgins, representing the evangelical virtues, intercede for him with Beatrice, that she would display to him her second beauty.

"O THOU!" her words she thus without delay
    Resuming, turn'd their point on me, to whom
    They, with but lateral edge,[1] seem'd harsh before:
"Say thou, who stand'st beyond the holy stream,
If this be true. A charge, so grievous, needs
Thine own avowal." On my faculty
Such strange amazement hung, the voice expired
Imperfect, ere its organs gave it birth.
    A little space refraining, then she spake:
"What dost thou muse on? Answer me. The wave
On thy remembrances of evil yet
Hath done no injury." A mingled sense
Of fear and of confusion, from my lips
Did such a "Yea" produce, as needed help
Of vision to interpret. As when breaks,
In act to be discharged, a cross-bow bent
Beyond its pitch, both nerve and bow o'erstretch'd;
The flagging weapon feebly hits the mark:
Thus, tears and sighs forth gushing, did I burst,
Beneath the heavy load: and thus my voice
Was slacken'd on its way. She straight began:
"When my desire invited thee to love
The good, which sets a bound to our aspirings;
What bar of thwarting foss or linked chain
Did meet thee, that thou so shouldst quit the hope
Of further progress? or what bait of ease,
Or promise of allurement, led thee on
Elsewhere, that thou elsewhere shouldst rather wait?"
    A bitter sigh I drew, then scarce found voice
To answer; hardly to these sounds my lips

---

[1] "With but lateral edge." The words of Beatrice, when not addressed directly to himself, but spoken of him to the Angel, Dante had thought sufficiently harsh.

Gave utterance, wailing: "Thy fair looks withdrawn,
Things present, with deceitful pleasures, turn'd
My steps aside." She answering spake: "Hadst thou
Been silent, or denied what thou avow'st,
Thou hadst not hid thy sin the more; such eye
Observes it. But whene'er the sinner's cheek
Breaks forth into the precious-streaming tears
Of self-accusing, in our court the wheel
Of justice doth run counter to the edge.[2]
Howe'er, that thou mayst profit by thy shame
For errors past, and that henceforth more strength
May arm thee, when thou hear'st the Syren-voice;
Lay thou aside the motive to this grief,
And lend attentive ear, while I unfold
How opposite a way my buried flesh
Should have impell'd thee. Never didst thou spy,
In art or nature, aught so passing sweet,
As were the limbs that in their beauteous frame
Enclosed me, and are scatter'd now in dust.
If sweetest thing thus fail'd thee with my death,
What, afterward, of mortal, should thy wish
Have tempted? When thou first hadst felt the dart
Of perishable things, in my departing
For better realms, thy wing thou shouldst have pruned
To follow me; and never stoop'd again,
To 'bide a second blow, for a slight girl,[3]
Or other gaud as transient and as vain.
The new and inexperienced bird[4] awaits,
Twice it may be, or thrice, the fowler's aim;
But in the sight of one whose plumes are full,
In vain the net is spread, the arrow wing'd."

I stood, as children silent and ashamed
Stand, listening, with their eyes upon the earth,
Acknowledging their fault, and self-condemn'd.
And she resumed: "If, but to hear, thus pains thee,
Raise thou thy beard, and lo! what sight shall do."

---

[2] "The weapons of divine justice are blunted by the confession and sorrow of the offender."

[3] "For a slight girl." Daniello and Venturi say that this alludes to Gentucca of Lucca, mentioned in the twenty-fourth Canto.

[4] "Bird." "Surely in vain the net is spread in the sight of any bird."—Prov. i. 17.

With less reluctance yields a sturdy holm,
Rent from its fibres by a blast, that blows
From off the pole, or from Iarbas' land,[5]
Than I at her behest my visage raised:
And thus the face denoting by the beard,
I mark'd the secret sting her words convey'd.
    No sooner lifted I mine aspect up,
Than I perceived those primal creatures cease
Their flowery sprinkling; and mine eyes beheld
(Yet unassured and wavering in their view)
Beatrice; she, who toward the mystic shape,
That joins two natures in one form, had turn'd:
And, even under shadow of her veil,
And parted by the verdant rill that flow'd
Between, in loveliness she seem'd as much
Her former self surpassing, as on earth
All others she surpass'd. Remorseful goads
Shot sudden through me. Each thing else, the more
Its love had late beguiled me, now the more
Was loathsome. On my heart so keenly smote
The bitter consciousness, that on the ground
O'erpower'd I fell: and what my state was then,
She knows, who was the cause. When now my strength
Flow'd back, returning outward from the heart,
The lady,[6] whom alone I first had seen,
I found above me. "Loose me not," she cried:
"Loose not thy hold:" and lo! had dragg'd me high
As to my neck into the stream; while she,
Still as she drew me after, swept along,
Swift as a shuttle, bounding o'er the wave.
    The blessed shore approaching, then was heard
So sweetly, *"Tu asperges me,"* that I
May not remember, much less tell the sound.
    The beauteous dame, her arms expanding, clasp'd
My temples, and immerged me where 'twas fit
The wave should drench me: and, thence raising up,
Within the fourfold dance of lovely nymphs
Presented me so laved; and with their arm
They each did cover me. "Here are we nymphs,

[5] "From Iarbas' land." The south.   [6] "The lady." Matilda.

And in the heaven are stars. Or ever earth
Was visited of Beatrice, we,
Appointed for her handmaids, tended on her.
We to her eyes will lead thee: but the light
Of gladness, that is in them, well to scan,
Those yonder three, of deeper ken than ours,
Thy sight shall quicken." Thus began their song:
And then they led me to the Gryphon's breast,
Where, turn'd toward us, Beatrice stood.
"Spare not thy vision. We have station'd thee
Before the emeralds, whence love, erewhile,
Hath drawn his weapons on thee." As they spake,
A thousand fervent wishes riveted
Mine eyes upon her beaming eyes, that stood,
Still fix'd toward the Gryphon, motionless.
As the sun strikes a mirror, even thus
Within those orbs the twyfold being shone;
Forever varying, in one figure now
Reflected, now in other. Reader! muse
How wondrous in my sight it seem'd, to mark
A thing, albeit steadfast in itself,
Yet in its imaged semblance mutable.

    Full of amaze, and joyous, while my soul
Fed on the viand, whereof still desire
Grows with satiety; the other three,
With gesture that declared a loftier line,
Advanced: to their own carol, on they came
Dancing, in festive ring angelical.

    "Turn, Beatrice!" was their song: "Oh! turn
Thy saintly sight on this thy faithful one,
Who, to behold thee, many a wearisome pace
Hath measured. Gracious at our prayer, vouchsafe
Unveiled to him thy cheeks; that he may mark
Thy second beauty, now conceal'd." O splendour!
O sacred light eternal! who is he,
So pale with musing in Pierian shades,
Or with that fount so lavishly imbued,
Whose spirit should not fail him in the essay
To represent thee such as thou didst seem,

When under cope of the still-chiming Heaven
Thou gavest to open air thy charms reveal'd?

CANTO XXXII

ARGUMENT.—Dante is warned not to gaze too fixedly on Beatrice. The procession
moves on, accompanied by Matilda, Statius, and Dante, till they reach an exceeding
lofty tree, where divers strange chances befall.

MINE eyes with such an eager coveting
        Were bent to rid them of their ten years' thirst,[1]
        No other sense was waking: and e'en they
Were fenced on either side from heed of aught;
So tangled, in its custom'd toils, that smile
Of saintly brightness drew me to itself:
When forcibly, toward the left, my sight
The sacred virgins turn'd; for from their lips
I heard the warning sounds: "Too fix'd a gaze!"
    Awhile my vision labour'd; as when late
Upon the o'erstrained eyes the sun hath smote:
But soon, to lesser object, as the view
Was now recover'd, (lesser in respect
To that excess of sensible, whence late
I had perforce been sunder'd), on their right
I mark'd that glorious army wheel, and turn,
Against the sun and sevenfold lights, their front.
As when, their bucklers for protection raised,
A well-ranged troop, with portly banners curl'd,
Wheel circling, ere the whole can change their ground;
E'en thus the goodly regiment of Heaven
Proceeding, all did pass us, ere the car
Had sloped his beam. Attendant at the wheels
The damsels turn'd; and on the Gryphon moved
The sacred burden, with a pace so smooth,
No feather on him trembled. The fair dame,
Who through the wave had drawn me, companied
By Statius and myself, pursued the wheel,
Whose orbit, rolling, mark'd a lesser arch.

[1] "Their ten years' thirst." Beatrice had been dead ten years.

Through the high wood, now void, (the more her blame,
Who by the serpent was beguiled), I pass'd,
With step in cadence to the harmony
Angelic. Onward had we moved, as far,
Perchance, as arrow at three several flights
Full wing'd had sped, when from her station down
Descended Beatrice. With one voice
All murmur'd "Adam"; circling next a plant
Despoil'd of flowers and leaf, on every bough,
Its tresses, spreading more as more they rose,
Were such, as 'midst their forest wilds, for height,
The Indians might have gazed at. "Blessed thou,
Gryphon!² whose beak hath never pluck'd that tree
Pleasant to taste: for hence the appetite
Was warp'd to evil." Round the stately trunk
Thus shouted forth the rest, to whom return'd
The animal twice-gender'd: "Yea! for so
The generation of the just are saved."
And turning to the chariot-pole, to foot
He drew it of the widow'd branch, and bound
There, left unto the stock whereon it grew.

As when large floods of radiance from above
Stream, with that radiance mingled, which ascends
Next after setting of the scaly sign,
Our plants then burgeon, and each wears anew
His wonted colours, ere the sun have yoked
Beneath another star his flamy steeds;
Thus putting forth a hue more faint than rose,
And deeper than the violet, was renew'd
The plant, erewhile in all its branches bare.
Unearthly was the hymn, which then arose.
I understood it not, nor to the end
Endured the harmony. Had I the skill
To pencil forth how closed the unpitying eyes
Slumbering, when Syrinx warbled, (eyes that paid
So dearly for their watching), then, like painter,
That with a model paints, I might design

---

² "Gryphon." Our Saviour's submission to the Roman Empire appears to be intended, and particularly his injunction to "render unto Cæsar the things that are Cæsar's."

The manner of my falling into sleep.
But feign who will the slumber cunningly,
I pass it by to when I waked; and tell,
How suddenly a flash of splendour rent
The curtain of my sleep, and one cries out,
"Arise: what dost thou?" As the chosen three,
On Tabor's mount, admitted to behold
The blossoming of that fair tree,[3] whose fruit
Is coveted of Angels, and doth make
Perpetual feast in Heaven; to themselves
Returning, at the word whence deeper sleeps[4]
Were broken, they their tribe diminish'd saw;
Both Moses and Elias gone, and changed
The stole their Master wore; thus to myself
Returning, over me beheld I stand
The piteous one,[5] who, cross the stream, had brought
My steps. "And where," all doubting, I exclaim'd,
"Is Beatrice?"—"See her," she replied,
"Beneath the fresh leaf, seated on its root.
Behold the associate choir that circles her.
The others, with a melody more sweet
And more profound, journeying to higher realms,
Upon the Gryphon tend." If there her words
Were closed, I know not; but mine eyes had now
Ta'en view of her, by whom all other thoughts
Were barr'd admittance. On the very ground
Alone she sat, as she had there been left
A guard upon the wain, which I beheld
Bound to the twyform beast. The seven nymphs
Did make themselves a cloister round about her;
And, in their hands, upheld those lights[6] secure
From blast septentrion and the gusty south.
　　"A little while thou shalt be forester here;
And citizen shalt be, forever with me,
Of that true Rome,[7] wherein Christ dwells a Roman.

---

[3] "The blossoming of that fair tree."
Our Saviour's transfiguration. "As the
apple-tree among the trees of the wood,
so is my beloved among the sons."—Solomon's Song, ii. 3.

[4] "Deeper sleeps." The sleep of death,
in the instance of the ruler of the syna-
gogue's daughter and of Lazarus."

[5] "The piteous one." Matilda.

[6] "Those lights." The tapers of gold.

[7] "Of that true Rome." Of Heaven.

To profit the misguided world, keep now
Thine eyes upon the car; and what thou seest,
Take heed thou write, returning to that place."[8]
   Thus Beatrice: at whose feet inclined
Devout, at her behest, my thought and eyes
I, as she bade, directed. Never fire,
With so swift motion, forth a stormy cloud
Leap'd downward from the welkin's farthest bound,
As I beheld the bird of Jove[9] descend
Down through the tree; and, as he rush'd, the rind
Disparting crush beneath him; buds much more,
And leaflets. On the car, with all his might
He struck; whence, staggering, like a ship it reel'd,
At random driven, to starboard now, o'ercome,
And now to larboard, by the vaulting waves.
   Next, springing up into the chariot's womb,
A fox[10] I saw, with hunger seeming pined
Of all good food. But, for his ugly sins
The saintly maid rebuking him, away
Scampering he turn'd, fast as his hide-bound corpse
Would bear him. Next, from whence before he came,
I saw the eagle dart into the hull
O' the car, and leave it with his feathers lined:[11]
And then a voice, like that which issues forth
From heart with sorrow rived, did issue forth
From Heaven, and "O poor bark of mine!" it cried,
"How badly art thou freighted." Then it seem'd
That the earth open'd, between either wheel;
And I beheld a dragon[12] issue thence,
That through the chariot fix'd his forked train;
And like a wasp, that draggeth back the sting,
So drawing forth his baleful train, he dragg'd
Part of the bottom forth; and went his way,
Exulting. What remain'd, as lively turf

[8] "To that place." To the earth.
[9] "The bird of Jove." This, which is imitated from Ezekiel, xvii. 3, 4, is typical of the persecutions which the Church sustained from the Roman emperors.
[10] "A fox." By the fox probably is represented the treachery of the heretics.
[11] "With his feathers lined." In allusion to the donations made by Constantine to the Church.
[12] "A dragon." Probably Mohammed; for what Lombardi offers to the contrary is far from satisfactory.

With green herb, so did clothe itself with plumes,[13]
Which haply had, with purpose chaste and kind,
Been offer'd; and therewith were clothed the wheels,
Both one and other, and the beam, so quickly,
A sigh were not breathed sooner. Thus transform'd,
The holy structure, through its several parts,
Did put forth heads;[14] three on the beam, and one
On every side: the first like oxen horn'd;
But with a single horn upon their front,
The four. Like monster, sight hath never seen.
O'er it[15] methought there sat, secure as rock
On mountain's lofty top, a shameless whore,
Whose ken roved loosely round her. At her side,
As 't were that none might bear her off, I saw
A giant stand; and ever and anon
They mingled kisses. But, her lustful eyes
Chancing on me to wander, that fell minion
Scourged her from head to foot all o'er; then full
Of jealousy, and fierce with rage, unloosed
The monster, and dragg'd on,[16] so far across
The forest, that from me its shades alone
Shielded the harlot and the new-form'd brute.

[13] "With plumes." The increase of wealth and temporal dominion, which followed the supposed gift of Constantine.

[14] "Heads." By the seven heads, it is supposed with sufficient probability, are meant the seven capital sins: by the three with two horns, pride, anger, and avarice, injurious both to man himself and to his neighbor: by the four with one horn, gluttony, gloominess, concupiscence, and envy, hurtful, at least in their primary effects, chiefly to him who is guilty of them.

[15] "O'er it." The harlot is thought to represent the state of the Church under Boniface VIII, and the giant to figure Philip IV of France.

[16] "Dragg'd on." The removal of the Pope's residence from Rome to Avignon is pointed at.

CANTO XXXIII

ARGUMENT.—After a hymn sung, Beatrice leaves the tree, and takes with her the seven virgins, Matilda, Statius, and Dante. She then darkly predicts to our Poet some future events. Lastly, the whole band arrive at the fountain, from whence the two streams, Lethe and Eunoë, separating, flow different ways; and Matilda, at the desire of Beatrice, causes our Poet to drink of the latter stream.

"THE heathen,[1] Lord! are come:" responsive thus,
The trinal now, and now the virgin band
Quaternion, their sweet psalmody began,
Weeping; and Beatrice listen'd, sad
And sighing, to the song, in such a mood,
That Mary, as she stood beside the Cross,
Was scarce more changed. But when they gave her place
To speak, then, risen upright on her feet,
She, with a colour glowing bright as fire,
Did answer: "Yet a little while,[2] and ye
Shall see me not; and, my beloved sisters!
Again a little while, and ye shall see me."
   Before her then she marshal'd all the seven;
And, beckoning only, motion'd me, the dame,
And that remaining sage,[3] to follow her.
   So on she pass'd; and had not set, I ween,
Her tenth step to the ground, when, with mine eyes
Her eyes encounter'd; and, with visage mild,
"So mend thy pace," she cried, "that if my words
Address thee, thou mayst still be aptly placed
To hear them." Soon as duly to her side
I now had hasten'd: "Brother!" she began,
"Why makest thou no attempt at questioning,
As thus we walk together?" Like to those
Who, speaking with too reverent an awe
Before their betters, draw not forth the voice
Alive unto their lips, befel me then
That I in sounds imperfect thus began:
"Lady! what I have need of, that thou know'st;
And what will suit my need." She answering thus:

[1] "The heathen." "O God, the heathen are come into thine inheritance."—Psalm lxxix. 1.
[2] "Yet a little while." "A little while, and ye shall not see me; and again a little while, and ye shall see me."—John xvi. 16.
[3] "That remaining sage." Statius.

"Of fearfulness and shame, I will that thou
Henceforth do rid thee; that thou speak no more,
As one who dreams. Thus far be taught of me:
The vessel which thou saw'st the serpent break,
Was, and is not:[4] let him, who hath the blame,
Hope not to scare God's vengeance with a sop.[5]
Without an heir forever shall not be
That eagle,[6] he, who left the chariot plumed,
Which monster made it first and next a prey.
Plainly I view, and therefore speak, the stars
E'en now approaching, whose conjunction, free
From all impediment and bar, brings on
A season, in the which, one sent from God,
(Five hundred, five, and ten, do mark him out,)
That foul one, and the accomplice of her guilt,
The giant, both, shall slay. And if perchance
My saying, dark as Themis or as Sphinx,
Fail to persuade thee, (since like them it foils
The intellect with blindness), yet ere long
Events shall be the Naïads, that will solve
This knotty riddle; and no damage light
On flock or field. Take heed; and as these words
By me are utter'd, teach them even so
To those who live that life, which is a race
To death: and when thou writest them, keep in mind
Not to conceal how thou hast seen the plant,
That twice[7] hath now been spoil'd. This whoso robs,
This whoso plucks, with blasphemy of deed
Sins against God, who for His use alone
Creating hallow'd it. For taste of this,

---

[4] "Was, and is not." "The beast that was, and is not."—Rev. xvii. 11.

[5] "Hope not to scare God's vengeance with a sop." "Let not him who hath occasioned the destruction of the Church, that vessel which the serpent brake, hope to appease the anger of the Deity by any outward acts of religious, or rather superstitious, ceremony; such as was that, in our Poet's time, performed by a murderer at Florence, who imagined himself secure from vengeance, if he ate a sop of bread in wine upon the grave of the person murdered, within the space of nine days."

[6] "That eagle." He prognosticates that the Emperor of Germany will not always continue to submit to the usurpations of the Pope, and foretells the coming of Henry VII, Duke of Luxemburg, signified by the numerical figures DVX; or, as Lombardi supposes, of Can Grande della Scala, appointed the leader of the Ghibelline forces.

[7] "Twice." First by the eagle and next by the giant.

In pain and in desire, five thousand years
And upward, the first soul did yearn for him
Who punish'd in himself the fatal gust.

  "Thy reason slumbers. if it deem this height,
And summit thus inverted, of the plant,
Without due cause: and were not vainer thoughts,
As Elsa's numbing waters,[8] to thy soul,
And their fond pleasures had not dyed it dark
As Pyramus the mulberry; thou hadst seen,
In such momentous circumstance alone,
God's equal justice morally implied
In the forbidden tree. But since I mark thee,
In understanding, harden'd into stone,
And, to that hardness, spotted too and stain'd,
So that thine eye is dazzled at my word;
I will, that, if not written, yet at least
Painted thou take it in thee, for the cause,
That one brings home his staff inwreathed with palm."

  I thus: "As wax by seal, that changeth not
Its impress, now is stamp'd my brain by thee.
But wherefore soars thy wish'd-for speech so high
Beyond my sight, that loses it the more,
The more it strains to reach it?"—"To the end
That thou mayst know," she answer'd straight, "the school,
That thou hast follow'd; and how far behind,
When following my discourse, its learning halts:
And mayst behold your art, from the divine
As distant, as the disagreement is
'Twixt earth and Heaven's most high and rapturous orb."

  "I not remember," I replied, "that e'er
I was estranged from thee; nor for such fault
Doth conscience chide me." Smiling she return'd:
"If thou canst not remember, call to mind
How lately thou hast drunk of Lethe's wave;
And, sure as smoke doth indicate a flame,
In that forgetfulness itself conclude
Blame from thy alienated will incurr'd.

---

[8] "Elsa's numbing waters." The Elsa,   about twenty miles below Florence, is said
a little stream, which flows into the Arno   to possess a petrifying quality.

From henceforth, verily, my words shall be
As naked, as will suit them to appear
In thy unpractised view." More sparkling now,
And with retarded course, the sun possess'd
The circle of mid-day, that varies still
As the aspect varies of each several clime;
When, as one, sent in vaward of a troop
For escort, pauses, if perchance he spy
Vestige of somewhat strange and rare; so paused
The sevenfold band, arriving at the verge
Of a dun umbrage hoar, such as is seen,
Beneath green leaves and gloomy branches, oft
To overbrow a bleak and alpine cliff.
And, where they stood, before them, as it seem'd,
I, Tigris and Euphrates both, beheld
Forth from one fountain issue; and, like friends,
Linger at parting. "O enlightening beam!
O glory of our kind! beseech thee say
What water this, which, from one source derived,
Itself removes to distance from itself?"
     To such entreaty answer thus was made:
"Entreat Matilda, that she teach thee this."
     And here, as one who clears himself of blame
Imputed, the fair dame return'd: "Of me
He this and more hath learnt; and I am safe
That Lethe's water hath not hid it from him."
     And Beatrice: "Some more pressing care,
That oft the memory 'reaves, perchance hath made
His mind's eye dark. But lo, where Eunoe flows!
Lead thither; and, as thou art wont, revive
His fainting virtue." As a courteous spirit,
That proffers no excuses, but as soon
As he hath token of another's will,
Makes it his own; when she had ta'en me, thus
The lovely maiden moved her on, and call'd
To Statius, with an air most lady-like:
"Come thou with him." Were further space allow'd,
Then, Reader! might I sing, though but in part,
That beverage, with whose sweetness I had ne'er

Been sated. But, since all the leaves are full,
Appointed for this second strain, mine art
With warning bridle checks me. I return'd
From the most holy wave, regenerate,
E'en as new plants renew'd with foliage new,
Pure and made apt for mounting to the stars.

PARADISE

CANTO I

ARGUMENT.—The Poet ascends with Beatrice toward the first heaven; and is, by her, resolved of certain doubts which arise in his mind.

HIS glory, by whose might all things are moved,
Pierces the universe, and in one part
Sheds more resplendence, elsewhere less. In
That largeliest of His light partakes, was I,   [Heaven
Witness of things, which, to relate again,
Surpasseth power of him who comes from thence;
For that, so near approaching its desire,
Our intellect is to such depth absorb'd,
That memory cannot follow. Nathless all,
That in my thoughts I of that sacred realm
Could store, shall now be matter of my song.
  Benign Apollo! this last labour aid;
And make me such a vessel of thy worth,
As thy own laurel claims, of me beloved.
Thus far[1] hath one of steep Parnassus' brows
Sufficed me; henceforth, there is need of both
For my remaining enterprise. Do thou[2]
Enter into my bosom, and there breathe
So, as when Marsyas by thy hand was dragg'd
Forth from his limbs, unsheathed. O power divine!
If thou to me of thine impart so much,
That of that happy realm the shadow'd form
Traced in my thoughts I may set forth to view;
Thou shalt behold me of thy favour'd tree
Come to the foot, and crown myself with leaves:
For to that honour thou, and my high theme

---

[1] "Thus far." He appears to mean nothing more than that this part of his poem will require a greater exertion of his powers than the former.

[2] "Do thou." Make me thine instrument; and, through me, utter such sound as when thou didst contend with Marsyas.

Will fit me. If but seldom, mighty Sire!
To grace his triumph, gathers thence a wreath
Cæsar, or bard, (more shame for human wills
Depraved), joy to the Delphic god must spring
From the Peneian foliage, when one breast
Is with such thirst inspired. From a small spark
Great flame hath risen: after me, perchance,
Others with better voice may pray, and gain,
From the Cyrrhæan city, answer kind.

    Through divers passages, the world's bright lamp
Rises to mortals; but through that[3] which joins
Four circles with the threefold cross, in best
Course, and in happiest constellation[4] set,
He comes; and, to the worldly wax, best gives
Its temper and impression. Morning there,[5]
Here eve was well-nigh by such passage made;
And whiteness had o'erspread that hemisphere,
Blackness the other part; when to the left[6]
I saw Beatrice turn'd, and on the sun
Gazing, as never eagle fix'd his ken.
As from the first a second beam is wont
To issue, and reflected upward rise,
Even as a pilgrim bent on his return;
So of her act, that through the eyesight pass'd
Into my fancy, mine was form'd: and straight,
Beyond our mortal wont, I fix'd mine eyes
Upon the sun. Much is allow'd us there,
That here exceeds our power; thanks to the place
Made for the dwelling of the human kind.

    I suffer'd it not long; and yet so long,
That I beheld it bickering sparks around,
As iron that comes boiling from the fire.
And suddenly upon the day appear'd
A day new-risen; as he, who hath the power,

---

[3] "Where the four circles, the horizon, the zodiac, the equator, and the equinoctial colure join; the last three intersecting each other so as to form three crosses, as may be seen in the armillary sphere."

[4] Aries. Some understand the planet Venus by the "migliore stella."

[5] "Morning there." It was morning where he then was, and about eventide on the earth.

[6] "To the left." Being in the opposite hemisphere to ours, Beatrice, that she may behold the rising sun, turns herself to the left.

Had with another sun bedeck'd the sky.

Her eyes fast fix'd on the eternal wheels,
Beatrice stood unmoved; and I with ken
Fix'd upon her, from upward gaze removed,
At her aspect, such inwardly became
As Glaucus, when he tasted of the herb
That made him peer among the ocean gods:
Words may not tell of that trans-human change;
And therefore let the example serve, though weak,
For those whom grace hath better proof in store.

If I were only what thou didst create,
Then newly, Love! by whom the Heaven is ruled;
Thou know'st, who by Thy light didst bear me up.
Whenas the wheel which Thou dost ever guide,
Desired Spirit! with its harmony,
Temper'd of Thee and measured, charm'd mine ear,
Then seem'd to me so much of Heaven to blaze
With the sun's flame, that rain or flood ne'er made
A lake so broad. The newness of the sound,
And that great light, inflamed me with desire,
Keener than e'er was felt, to know their cause.

Whence she, who saw me, clearly as myself,
To calm my troubled mind, before I ask'd,
Open'd her lips, and gracious thus began:
"With false imagination thou thyself
Makest dull; so that thou seest not the thing,
Which thou hadst seen, had that been shaken off.
Thou art not on the earth as thou believest;
For lightning, scaped from its own proper place,
Ne'er ran, as thou hast hither now return'd."

Although divested of my first-raised doubt
By those brief words accompanied with smiles,
Yet in new doubt was I entangled more,
And said: "Already satisfied, I rest
From admiration deep; but now admire
How I above those lighter bodies rise."

Whence, after utterance of a piteous sigh,
She toward me bent her eyes, with such a look,
As on her frenzied child a mother casts;
Then thus began: "Among themselves all things

Have order; and from hence the form,[7] which makes
The universe resemble God. In this
The higher creatures see the printed steps
Of that eternal worth, which is the end
Whither the line is drawn.[8] All natures lean,
In this their order, diversly; some more,
Some less approaching to their primal source.
Thus they to different havens are moved on
Through the vast sea of being, and each one
With instinct given, that bears it in its course:
This to the lunar sphere directs the fire;
This moves the hearts of mortal animals;
This the brute earth together knits, and binds.
Nor only creatures, void of intellect,
Are aim'd at by this bow; but even those,
That have intelligence and love, are pierced.
That Providence, who so well orders all,
With her own light makes ever calm the Heaven,[9]
In which the substance, that hath greatest speed,[10]
Is turn'd: and thither now, as to our seat
Predestined, we are carried by the force
Of that strong cord, that never looses dart
But at fair aim and glad. Yet is it true,
That as, oft-times, but ill accords the form
To the design of art, through sluggishness
Or unreplying matter; so this course
Is sometimes quitted by the creature, who
Hath power, directed thus, to bend elsewhere:
As from a cloud the fire is seen to fall,
From its original impulse warp'd, to earth,
By vitious fondness. Thou no more admire
Thy soaring (if I rightly deem) than lapse
Of torrent downward from a mountain's height.
There would in thee for wonder be more cause,
If, free of hindrance, thou hadst stay'd below,

---

[7] This order it is, that gives to the universe the form of unity, and therefore resemblance to God.

[8] All things, as they have their beginning from the Supreme Being, so are they referred to Him again.

[9] "The Heaven." The empyrean, which is always motionless.

[10] "The substance, etc." The *primum mobile*.

As living fire unmoved upon the earth."
So said, she turn'd toward the Heaven her face.

CANTO II

ARGUMENT.—Dante and his celestial guide enter the moon. The cause of the spots or shadows, which appear in that body, is explained to him.

ALL ye, who in small bark have following sail'd,
    Eager to listen, on the adventurous track
    Of my proud keel, that singing cuts her way,
Backward return with speed, and your own shores
Revisit; nor put out to open sea,
Where losing me, perchance ye may remain
Bewilder'd in deep maze. The way I pass,
Ne'er yet was run: Minerva breathes the gale;
Apollo guides me; and another Nine,
To my rapt sight, the arctic beams reveal.
Ye other few who have outstretch'd the neck
Timely for food of angels, on which here
They live, yet never know satiety;
Through the deep brine ye fearless may put out
Your vessel; marking well the furrow broad
Before you in the wave, that on both sides
Equal returns. Those, glorious, who pass'd o'er
To Colchis, wonder'd not as ye will do,
When they saw Jason following the plough.
    The increate perpetual thirst, that draws
Toward the realm of God's own form, bore us
Swift almost as the Heaven ye behold.
    Beatrice upward gazed, and I on her;
And in such space as on the notch a dart
Is placed, then loosen'd flies, I saw myself
Arrived, where wonderous thing engaged my sight.
Whence she, to whom no care of mine was hid,
Turning to me, with aspect glad as fair,
Bespake me: "Gratefully direct thy mind
To God, through whom to this first star[1] we come."
    Meseem'd as if a cloud had cover'd us,

[1] "This first star." The moon.

Translucent, solid, firm, and polish'd bright,
Like adamant, which the sun's beam had smit.
Within itself the ever-during pearl
Received us; as the wave a ray of light
Receives, and rests unbroken. If I then
Was of corporeal frame, and it transcend
Our weaker thought, how one dimension thus
Another could endure, which needs must be
If body enter body; how much more
Must the desire inflame us to behold
That Essence, which discovers by what means
God and our nature join'd! There will be seen
That, which we hold through faith; not shown by proof,
But in itself intelligibly plain,
E'en as the truth that man at first believes.

   I answer'd: "Lady! I with thoughts devout,
Such as I best can frame, give thanks to Him,
Who hath removed me from the mortal world.
But tell, I pray thee, whence the gloomy spots
Upon this body, which below on earth
Give rise to talk of Cain in fabling quaint?"

   She somewhat smiled, then spake: "If mortals err
In their opinion, when the key of sense
Unlocks not, surely wonder's weapon keen
Ought not to pierce thee: since thou find'st, the wings
Of reason to pursue the senses' flight
Are short. But what thy own thought is, declare."

   Then I: "What various here above appears,
Is caused, I deem, by bodies dense or rare."

   She then resumed: "Thou certainly wilt see
In falsehood thy belief o'erwhelm'd, if well
Thou listen to the arguments which I
Shall bring to face it. The eighth sphere displays
Numberless lights, the which, in kind and size,
May be remark'd of different aspects:
If rare or dense of that were cause alone,
One single virtue then would be in all;
Alike distributed, or more, or less.
Different virtues needs must be the fruits
Of formal principles; and these, save one,

Will by thy reasoning be destroy'd. Beside,
If rarity were of that dusk the cause,
Which thou inquirest, either in some part
That planet must throughout be void, nor fed
With its own matter; or, as bodies share
Their fat and leanness, in like manner this
Must in its volume change the leaves.[2] The first,
If it were true, had through the sun's eclipse
Been manifested, by transparency
Of light, as through aught rare beside effused.
But this is not. Therefore remains to see
The other cause: and, if the other fall,
Erroneous so must prove what seem'd to thee.
If not from side to side this rarity
Pass through, there needs must be a limit, whence
Its contrary no further lets it pass.
And hence the beam, that from without proceeds,
Must be pour'd back; as colour comes, through glass
Reflected, which behind it lead conceals.
Now wilt thou say, that there of murkier hue,
Than, in the other part, the ray is shown,
By being thence refracted farther back.
From this perplexity will free thee soon
Experience, if thereof thou trial make,
The fountain whence your arts derive their streams.
Three mirrors shalt thou take, and two remove
From thee alike; and more remote the third,
Betwixt the former pair, shall meet thine eyes:
Then turn'd toward them, cause behind thy back
A light to stand, that on the three shall shine,
And thus reflected come to thee from all.
Though that, beheld most distant, do not stretch
A space so ample, yet in brightness thou
Wilt own it equaling the rest. But now,
As under snow the ground, if the warm ray
Smites it, remains dismantled of the hue
And cold, that cover'd it before; so thee,
Dismantled in thy mind, I will inform

[2] "Change the leaves." Would, like leaves of parchment, be darker in some parts than in others.

With light so lively, that the tremulous beam
Shall quiver where it falls. Within the Heaven,[3]
Where peace divine inhabits, circles round
A body, in whose virtue lies the being
Of all that it contains. The following Heaven,
That hath so many lights, this being divides,
Through different essences, from it distinct,
And yet contain'd within it. The other orbs
Their separate distinctions variously
Dispose, for their own seed and produce apt.
Thus do these organs of the world proceed,
As thou beholdest now, from step to step;
Their influences from above deriving,
And thence transmitting downward. Mark me well;
How through this passage to the truth I ford,
The truth thou lovest; that thou henceforth, alone,
Mayst know to keep the shallows, safe, untold.
    "The virtue and motion of the sacred orbs,
As mallet by the workman's hand, must needs
By blessed movers[4] be inspired. This Heaven,[5]
Made beauteous by so many luminaries,
From the deep spirit,[6] that moves its circling sphere,
Its image takes and impress as a seal:
And as the soul, that dwells within your dust,
Through members different, yet together form'd,
In different powers resolves itself; e'en so
The intellectual efficacy unfolds
Its goodness multiplied throughout the stars;
On its own unity revolving still.
Different virtue[7] compact different
Makes with the precious body it enlivens,
With which it knits, as life in you is knit.

[3] According to our Poet's system, there are ten Heavens. The Heaven, "where peace divine inhabits," is the empyrean; the body within it, that "circles round," is the *primum mobile;* "the following Heaven," that of the fixed stars; and "the other orbs," the seven lower Heavens, are Saturn, Jupiter, Mars, the Sun, Venus, Mercury, and the Moon. Thus Milton, "Paradise Lost" b. iii. 481.

[4] "By blessed movers." By Angels.
[5] "This Heaven." The Heaven of fixed stars.
[6] "The deep spirit." The moving Angel.
[7] "Different virtue." "There is one glory of the sun, and another glory of the moon, and another glory of the stars; for one star differeth from another star in glory."—1 Cor. xv. 41.

From its original nature full of joy,
The virtue mingled through the body shines,
As joy through pupil of the living eye.
From hence proceeds that which from light to light
Seems different, and not from dense or rare.
This is the formal cause, that generates,
Proportion'd to its power, the dusk or clear."

CANTO III

ARGUMENT.—In the moon Dante meets with Piccarda, the sister of Forese, who tells him that this planet is allotted to those, who, after having made profession of chastity and a religious life, had been compelled to violate their vows; and she then points out to him the spirit of the Empress Costanza.

THAT sun,[1] which erst with love my bosom
            warmed,
            Had of fair truth unveil'd the sweet aspect,
By proof of right, and of the false reproof;
And I, to own myself convinced and free
Of doubt, as much as needed, raised my head
Erect for speech. But soon a sight appear'd,
Which, so intent to mark it, held me fix'd
That of confession I no longer thought.

As through translucent and smooth glass, or wave
Clear and unmoved, and flowing not so deep
As that its bed is dark, the shape returns
So faint of our impictured lineaments,
That, on white forehead set, a pearl as strong
Comes to the eye; such saw I many a face,
All stretch'd to speak; from whence I straight conceived,
Delusion[2] opposite to that, which raised,
Between the man and fountain, amorous flame.

Sudden, as I perceived them, deeming these
Reflected semblances, to see of whom
They were, I turn'd mine eyes, and nothing saw;
Then turn'd them back, directed on the light
Of my sweet guide, who, smiling, shot forth beams
From her celestial eyes. "Wonder not thou,"

[1] "That sun." Beatrice.
[2] "Delusion." "An error the contrary to that of Narcissus; because he mistook a shadow for a substance; I, a substance for a shadow."

She cried, "at this my smiling, when I see
Thy childish judgment; since not yet on truth
It rests the foot, but, as it still is wont,
Makes thee fall back in unsound vacancy.
True substances are these, which thou behold'st,
Hither through failure of their vow exiled.
But speak thou with them; listen, and believe,
That the true light, which fills them with desire,
Permits not from its beams their feet to stray."

   Straight to the shadow, which for converse seem'd
Most earnest, I address'd me; and began
As one by over-eagerness perplex'd:
"O spirit, born for joy! who in the rays
Of life eternal, of that sweetness know'st
The flavour, which, not tasted, passes far
All apprehension; me it well would please,
If thou wouldst tell me of thy name, and this
Your station here." Whence she with kindness prompt
And eyes glist'ring with smiles: "Our charity,
To any wish by justice introduced,
Bars not the door; no more than She above,
Who would have all her court be like herself.
I was a virgin sister in the earth;
And if thy mind observe me well, this form,
With such addition graced of loveliness,
Will not conceal me long; but thou wilt know
Piccarda,[3] in the tardiest sphere thus placed,
Here 'mid these other blessed also blest.
Our hearts, whose high affections burn alone
With pleasure from the Holy Spirit conceived,
Admitted to His order, dwell in joy.
And this condition, which appears so low,
Is for this cause assign'd us, that our vows
Were, in some part, neglected and made void."

   Whence I to her replied: "Something divine .
Beams in your countenances wondrous fair;
From former knowledge quite transmuting you.

---

[3] "Piccarda." The sister of Corso Donati, and of Forese, whom we have seen in the Purgatory, Canto xxiv. Petrarch has been supposed to allude to this lady in his "Triumph of Chastity," v. 160, etc.

Therefore to recollect was I so slow.
But what thou say'st hath to my memory
Given now such aid, that to retrace your forms
Is easier. Yet inform me, ye, who here
Are happy; long ye for a higher place,
More to behold, and more in love to dwell?"

    She with those other spirits gently smiled;
Then answer'd with such gladness, that she seem'd
With love's first flame to glow: "Brother! our will
Is, in composure, settled by the power
Of charity, who makes us will alone
What we possess, and naught beyond desire:
If we should wish to be exalted more,
Then must our wishes jar with the high will
Of Him, who sets us here; which in these orbs
Thou wilt confess not possible, if here
To be in charity must needs befall,
And if her nature well thou contemplate.
Rather it is inherent in this state
Of blessedness, to keep ourselves within
The Divine Will, by which our wills with His
Are one. So that as we, from step to step,
Are placed throughout this kingdom, pleases all,
Even as our King, who in us plants His will;
And in His will is our tranquillity:
It is the mighty ocean, whither tends
Whatever it creates and Nature makes."

    Then saw I clearly how each spot in Heaven
Is Paradise, though with like gracious dew
The supreme virtue shower not over all.

    But as it chances, if one sort of food
Hath satiated, and of another still
The appetite remains, that this is ask'd,
And thanks for that return'd; e'en so did I,
In word and motion, bent from her to learn
What web it was,[4] through which she had not drawn
The shuttle to its point. She thus began:
"Exalted worth and perfectness of life

[4] "What vow of religious life it was that she had been hindered from completing,
had been compelled to break."

The Lady[5] higher up inshrine in Heaven,
By whose pure laws upon your nether earth
The robe and veil they wear; to that intent,
That e'en till death they may keep watch, or sleep,
With their great Bridegroom, who accepts each vow,
Which to His gracious pleasure love conforms.
I from the world, to follow her, when young
Escaped; and, in her vesture mantling me,
Made promise of the way her sect enjoins.
Thereafter men, for ill than good more apt,
Forth snatch'd me from the pleasant cloister's pale.
God knows[6] how, after that, my life was framed.
This other splendid shape, which thou behold'st
At my right side, burning with all the light
Of this our orb, what of myself I tell
May to herself apply. From her, like me
A sister, with like violence were torn
The saintly folds, that shaded her fair brows.
E'en when she to the world again was brought
In spite of her own will and better wont,
Yet not for that the bosom's inward veil
Did she renounce. This is the luminary
Of mighty Constance,[7] who from that loud blast,
Which blew the second[8] over Suabia's realm,
That power produced, which was the third and last."
    She ceased from further talk, and then began

[5] St. Clare, the foundress of the order called after her. She was born at Assisi, in 1193, and died in 1253.

[6] Rodolfo da Tossignano, Hist. Seraph. Relig., relates the following legend of Piccarda: "Her brother Corso, inflamed with rage against his virgin sister, having joined with him Farinata, an infamous assassin, and twelve other abandoned ruffians, entered the monastery by a ladder, and carried away his sister forcibly to his own house; and then tearing off her religious habit, compelled her to go in a secular garment to her nuptials. Before the spouse of Christ came together with her new husband, she knelt down before a crucifix and recommended her virginity to Christ. Soon after her whole body was smitten with leprosy; in a few days, through the divine disposal, she passed with a palm of virginity to the Lord.

[7] Daughter of Ruggieri, King of Sicily, who being taken by force out of a monastery was married to the Emperor Henry VI and by him was mother of Frederick II. She was fifty years old or more at the time, and "because it was not credited that she could have a child at that age, she was delivered in a pavilion, and it was given out that any lady, who pleased, was at liberty to see her."

[8] Henry VI, son of Frederick I, was the second emperor of the house of Suabia; and his son Frederick II "the third and last."

"Ave Maria" singing; and with that song
Vanish'd, as heavy substance through deep wave.
   Mine eye, that, far as it was capable,
Pursued her, when in dimness she was lost,
Turn'd to the mark where greater want impell'd
And bent on Beatrice all its gaze.
But she, as lightning, beam'd upon my looks;
So that the sight sustain'd it not at first.
Whence I to question her became less prompt.

CANTO IV

ARGUMENT.—While they still continue in the moon, Beatrice removes certain doubts which Dante had conceived respecting the place assigned to the blessed, and respecting the will absolute or conditional. He inquires whether it is possible to make satisfaction for a vow broken.

BETWEEN two kinds of food, both equally
     Remote and tempting, first a man might die
     Of hunger, ere he one could freely chuse.
E'en so would stand a lamb between the maw
Of two fierce wolves, in dread of both alike:
E'en so between two deer a dog would stand.
Wherefore, if I was silent, fault nor praise
I to myself impute; by equal doubts
Held in suspense; since of necessity
It happen'd. Silent was I, yet desire
Was painted in my looks; and thus I spake
My wish more earnestly than language could.
   As Daniel,[1] when the haughty king he freed
From ire, that spurr'd him on to deeds unjust
And violent; so did Beatrice then.
   "Well I discern," she thus her words address'd,
"How thou art drawn by each of these desires;[2]
So that thy anxious thought is in itself
Bound up and stifled, nor breathes freely forth.
Thou arguest: if the good intent remain;
What reason that another's violence

---

[1] "Daniel." See Dan. ii. Beatrice did for Dante what Daniel did for Nebuchadnezzar, when he freed the King from the uncertainty respecting his dream, which had enraged him against the Chaldeans. See Hell, Canto xiv.

[2] His desire to have each of the doubts, which Beatrice mentions, resolved.

Should stint the measure of my fair desert?

"Cause too thou find'st for doubt, in that it seems,
That spirits to the stars, as Plato[3] deem'd,
Return. These are the questions which thy will
Urge equally; and therefore I, the first,
Of that[4] will treat which hath the more of gall.[5]
Of Seraphim[6] he who is most enskied,
Moses and Samuel, and either John
Chuse which thou wilt, nor even Mary's self,
Have not in any other Heaven their seats,
Than have those spirits which so late thou saw'st;
Nor more or fewer years exist; but all
Make the first circle[7] beauteous, diversely
Partaking of sweet life, as more or less
Afflation of eternal bliss pervades them.
Here were they shown thee, not that fate assigns
This for their sphere, but for a sign to thee
Of that celestial furthest from the height.
Thus needs, that ye may apprehend, we speak:
Since from things sensible alone ye learn
That, which, digested rightly, after turns
To intellectual. For no other cause
The Scripture, condescending graciously
To your perception, hands and feet to God
Attributes, nor so means: and holy Church
Doth represent with human countenance
Gabriel, and Michäel, and him who made
Tobias whole. Unlike what here thou seest,
The judgment of Timæus, who affirms
Each soul restored to its particular star;
Believing it to have been taken thence,
When nature gave it to inform her mold:
Yet to appearance his intention is

---

[3] "Plato." Plato, Timæus, v. ix. p. 326. "The Creator, when he had framed the universe, distributed to the stars an equal number of souls, appointing to each soul its several star."

[4] "Of that." Plato's opinion.

[5] Which is the more dangerous.

[6] She first resolves his doubt whether souls do not return to their own stars, as he had read in the Timæus of Plato. Angels, then, and beatified spirits, she declares, dwell all and eternally together, only partaking more or less of the divine glory, in the empyrean; although, in condescension to human understanding, they appear to have different spheres allotted to them.

[7] "The first circle." The empyrean.

Not what his words declare: and so to shun
Derision, haply thus he hath disguised
His true opinion. If his meaning be,
That to the influencing of these orbs revert
The honour and the blame in human acts,
Perchance he doth not wholly miss the truth.
This principle, not understood aright,
Erewhile perverted well-nigh all the world;
So that it fell to fabled names of Jove,
And Mercury, and Mars. That other doubt,
Which moves thee, is less harmful; for it brings
No peril of removing thee from me.
"That, to the eye of man,[8] our justice seems
Unjust, is argument for faith, and not
For heretic declension. But, to the end
This truth[9] may stand more clearly in your view,
I will content thee even to thy wish.

    "If violence be, when that which suffers, nought
Consents to that which forceth, not for this
These spirits stood exculpate. For the will,
That wills not, still survives, unquench'd, and doth,
As nature doth in fire, though violence
Wrest it a thousand times; for, if it yield
Or more or less, so far it follows force.
And thus did these, when they had power to seek
The hallow'd place again. In them, had will
Been perfect, such as once upon the bars
Held Laurence[10] firm, or wrought in Scævola
To his own hand remorseless; to the path,
Whence they were drawn, their steps had hasten'd back,
When liberty return'd: but in too few,
Resolve, so stedfast, dwells. And by these words,
If duly weigh'd, that argument is void,
Which oft might have perplex'd thee still. But now

[8] "That the ways of divine justice are often inscrutable to man, ought rather to be a motive to faith than an inducement to heresy."

[9] "This truth." That it is no impeachment of God's justice, if merit be lessened through compulsion of others, without any failure of good intention on the part of the meritorious. After all, Beatrice ends by admitting that there was a defect in the will, which hindered Constance and the others from seizing the first opportunity of returning to the monastic life.

[10] Martyr of the third century.

Another question thwarts thee, which, to solve,
Might try thy patience without better aid.
I have, no doubt, instill'd into thy mind,
That blessed spirit may not lie; since near
The source of primal truth it dwells for aye:
And thou mightst after of Piccarda learn
That Constance held affection to the veil;
So that she seems to contradict me here.
Not seldom, brother, it hath chanced for men
To do what they had gladly left undone;
Yet, to shun peril, they have done amiss:
E'en as Alcmæon, at his father's[11] suit
Slew his own mother;[12] so made pitiless,
Not to lose pity. On this point bethink thee,
That force and will are blended in such wise
As not to make the offence excusable.
Absolute will agrees not to the wrong;
But inasmuch as there is fear of woe
From non-compliance, it agrees. Of will[13]
Thus absolute, Piccarda spake, and I
Of the other; so that both have truly said."
　　Such was the flow of that pure rill, that well'd
From forth the fountain of all truth; and such
The rest, that to my wandering thoughts I found.
　　"O thou, of primal love the prime delight,
Goddess!" I straight replied, "whose lively words
Still shed new heat and vigour through my soul;
Affection fails me to requite thy grace
With equal sum of gratitude: be His
To recompense, who sees and can reward thee.
Well I discern, that by that Truth[14] alone
Enlighten'd, beyond which no truth may roam,
Our mind can satisfy her thirst to know:
Therein she resteth, e'en as in his lair
The wild beast, soon as she hath reach'd that bound.
And she hath power to reach it; else desire

---

[11] "His father's." Amphiaräus.
[12] "His own mother." Eriphyle.
[13] "Of will." What Piccarda asserts of Constance, that she retained her affection to the monastic life, is said absolutely and without relation to circumstances; and that, which I affirm, is spoken of the will conditionally and respectively: so that "both have truly said."
[14] The light of divine truth.

Were given to no end. And thence doth doubt
Spring, like a shoot, around the stock of truth;
And it is nature which, from height to height,
On to the summit prompts us. This invites,
This doth assure me, Lady! reverently
To ask thee of another truth, that yet
Is dark to me. I fain would know, if man
By other works well done may so supply
The failure of his vows, that in your scale
They lack not weight." I spake; and on me straight
Beatrice look'd, with eyes that shot forth sparks
Of love celestial, in such copious stream,
That, virtue sinking in me overpower'd,
I turn'd; and downward bent, confused, my sight.

CANTO V

ARGUMENT.—The question proposed in the last Canto is answered. Dante ascends
with Beatrice to the planet Mercury, which is the second heaven; and here he finds
a multitude of spirits, one of whom offers to satisfy him of anything he may desire
to know from them.

"IF beyond earthly wont,[1] the flame of love
Illume me, so that I o'ercome thy power
Of vision, marvel not: but learn the cause
In that perfection of the sight, which, soon
As apprehending, hasteneth on to reach
The good it apprehends. I well discern,
How in thine intellect already shines
The light eternal, which to view alone
Ne'er fails to kindle love; and if aught else
Your love seduces, 'tis but that it shows
Some ill-mark'd vestige of that primal beam.

"This wouldst thou know: if failure of the vow
By other service may be so supplied,
As from self-question to assure the soul."

Thus she her words, not heedless of my wish,
Began; and thus, as one who breaks not off

---

[1] "If beyond earthly wont." Dante having been unable to sustain the splendor
of Beatrice, as we have seen at the end
of the last Canto, she tells him to attribute her increase of brightness to the
place in which they were.

Discourse, continued in her saintly strain.
"Supreme of gifts,[2] which God, creating, gave
Of His free bounty, sign most evident
Of goodness, and in His account most prized
Was liberty of will; the boon, wherewith
All intellectual creatures, and them sole,
He hath endow'd. Hence now thou mayst infer
Of what high worth the vow, which so is framed
That when man offers, God well-pleased accepts:
For in the compact between God and him,
This treasure, such as I describe it to thee,
He makes the victim; and of his own act.
What compensation therefore may he find?
If that, whereof thou hast oblation made,
By using well thou think'st to consecrate,
Thou wouldst of theft do charitable deed.
Thus I resolve thee of the greater point.

"But forasmuch as holy Church, herein
Dispensing, seems to contradict the truth
I have discover'd to thee, yet behoves
Thou rest a little longer at the board,
Ere the crude aliment which thou hast ta'en,
Digested fitly, to nutrition turn.
Open thy mind to what I now unfold;
And give it inward keeping. Knowledge comes
Of learning well retain'd, unfruitful else.

"This sacrifice, in essence, of two things
Consisteth: one is that, whereof 'tis made;
The covenant, the other.[3] For the last,

[2] "Supreme of gifts." So in the "De Monarchiâ," lib. i. pp. 107 and 108. "If then the judgment altogether move the appetite, and is in no wise prevented by it, it is free. But if the judgment be moved by the appetite in any way preventing it, it cannot be free: because it acts not of itself, but is led captive by another. And hence it is that brutes cannot have free judgment, because their judgments are always prevented by appetite. And hence it may also appear manifest that intellectual substances, whose wills are immutable, and likewise souls separated from the body, and departing from it well and holily, lose not the liberty of choice on account of the immutability of the will, but retain it most perfectly and powerfully. This being discerned, it is again plain that this liberty, or principle of all our liberty, is the greatest good conferred on human nature by God; because by this very thing we are here made happy, as men; by this we are elsewhere happy, as divine beings."

[3] The one, the substance of the vow, as of a single life, or of keeping fast; the other, the compact.

It ne'er is cancel'd, if not kept: and hence
I spake, erewhile, so strictly of its force.
For this it was enjoin'd the Israelites,[4]   [change
Though leave were given them, as thou know'st, to
The offering, still to offer. The other part,
The matter and the substance of the vow,
May well be such, as that, without offence,
It may for other substance be exchanged.
But, at his own discretion, none may shift
The burden on his shoulders; unreleased
By either key,[5] the yellow and the white.
Nor deem of any change, as less than vain,
If the last bond[6] be not within the new
Included, as the quatre in the six.
No satisfaction therefore can be paid
For what so precious in the balance weighs,
That all in counterpoise must kick the beam.
Take then no vow at random: ta'en, with faith
Preserve it; yet not bent, as Jephthah once,
Blindly to execute a rash resolve,
Whom better it had suited to exclaim,
'I have done ill,' than to redeem his pledge
By doing worse: or, not unlike to him
In folly, that great leader of the Greeks;
Whence, on the altar, Iphigenia mourn'd
Her virgin beauty, and hath since made mourn
Both wise and simple, even all, who hear
Of so fell sacrifice. Be ye more staid,
O Christians! not, like feather, by each wind
Removable; nor think to cleanse yourselves
In every water. Either testament,
The old and new, is yours: and for your guide,
The shepherd of the Church. Let this suffice
To save you. When by evil lust enticed,
Remember ye be men, not senseless beasts;
Nor let the Jew, who dwelleth in your streets,
Hold you in mockery. Be not, as the lamb,
That, fickle wanton, leaves its mother's milk,

[4] See Lev. c. xii. and xxvii.
[5] Purgatory, Canto ix. 108.
[6] If the thing substituted be not more precious than the thing released.

To dally with itself in idle play."
    Such were the words that Beatrice spake:
These ended, to that region, where the world
Is liveliest, full of fond desire she turn'd.
    Though mainly prompt new question to propose,
Her silence and changed look did keep me dumb.
And as the arrow, ere the cord is still,
Leapeth unto its mark; so on we sped
Into the second realm. There I beheld
The dame, so joyous, enter, that the orb
Grew brighter at her smiles; and, if the star
Were moved to gladness, what then was my cheer,
Whom nature hath made apt for every change!
    As in a quiet and clear lake the fish,
If aught approach them from without, do draw
Toward it, deeming it their food; so drew
Full more than thousand splendours toward us;
And in each one was heard: "Lo! one arrived
To multiply our loves!" and as each came,
The shadow, streaming forth effulgence new,
Witness'd augmented joy. Here, Reader! think,
If thou didst miss the sequel of my tale,
To know the rest how sorely thou wouldst crave;
And thou shalt see what vehement desire
Possess'd me, soon as these had met my view,
To know their state. "O born in happy hour!
Thou, to whom grace vouchsafes, or e'er thy close
Of fleshly warfare, to behold the thrones
Of that eternal triumph; know, to us
The light communicated, which through Heaven
Expatiates without bound. Therefore, if aught
Thou of our beams wouldst borrow for thine aid,
Spare not; and, of our radiance, take thy fill."
    Thus of those piteous spirits one bespake me;
And Beatrice next: "Say on; and trust
As unto gods."—"How in the light supreme
Thou harbour'st, and from thence the virtue bring'st,
That, sparkling in thine eyes, denotes thy joy,
I mark; but, who thou art, am still to seek;
Or wherefore, worthy spirit! for thy lot

This sphere[7] assign'd, that oft from mortal ken
Is veil'd by other's beams." I said; and turn'd
Toward the lustre, that with greeting kind
Erewhile had hail'd me. Forthwith, brighter far
Than erst, it wax'd: and, as himself the sun
Hides through excess of light, when his warm gaze[8]
Hath on the mantle of thick vapours prey'd;
Within its proper ray the saintly shape
Was, through increase of gladness, thus conceal'd;
And, shrouded so in splendour, answer'd me,
E'en as the tenour of my song declares.

CANTO VI

ARGUMENT.—The spirit, who had offered to satisfy the inquiries of Dante, declares himself to be the Emperor Justinian; and after speaking of his own actions, recounts the victories, before him, obtained under the Roman Eagle. He then informs our Poet that the soul of Romeo the pilgrim is in the same star.

"AFTER that Constantine the eagle turn'd[1]
        Against the motions of the Heaven, that roll'd
        Consenting with its course, when he of yore,
Lavinia's spouse, was leader of the flight;
A hundred years twice told and more,[2] his seat
At Europe's extreme point,[3] the bird of Jove
Held, near the mountains, whence he issued first;
There under shadow of his sacred plumes
Swaying the world, till through successive hands
To mine he came devolved. Cæsar I was
And am Justinian; destined by the will
Of that prime love, whose influence I feel.

[7] "This sphere." The planet Mercury, which being nearest to the sun, is oftenest hidden by that luminary.

[8] "When his warm gaze." When the sun has dried up the vapors that shaded his brightness.

[1] Constantine, in transferring the seat of empire from Rome to Byzantium, carried the eagle, the imperial ensign, from the west to the east. Æneas, on the contrary, had, with better augury, moved along with the sun's course, when he passed from Troy to Italy.

[2] "A hundred years twice told and more." The Emperor Constantine entered Byzantium in 324; and Justinian began his reign in 527.

[3] "At Europe's extreme point." Constantine being situated at the extreme of Europe, and on the borders of Asia, near those mountains in the neighborhood of Troy, from whence the first founders of Rome had emigrated.

From vain excess to clear the incumber'd laws.[4]
Or e'er that work engaged me, I did hold
In Christ one nature only;[5] with such faith
Contented. But the blessed Agapete,[6]
Who was chief shepherd, he with warning voice
To the true faith recall'd me. I believed
His words: and what he taught, now plainly see,
As thou in every contradiction seest
The true and false opposed. Soon as my feet
Were to the Church reclaim'd, to my great task,
By inspiration of God's grace impell'd,
I gave me wholly; and consign'd mine arms
To Belisarius, with whom Heaven's right hand
Was link'd in such conjointment, 'twas a sign
That I should rest. To thy first question thus
I shape mine answer, which were ended here,
But that its tendency doth prompt perforce
To some addition; that thou well mayst mark,
What reason on each side they have to plead,
By whom that holiest banner is withstood,
Both who pretend its power[7] and who oppose.[8]

"Beginning from that hour, when Pallas died
To give it rule, behold the valorous deeds
Have made it worthy reverence. Not unknown
To thee, how for three hundred years and more
It dwelt in Alba, up to those fell lists
Where, for its sake, were met the rival three;[9]
Nor aught unknown to thee, which it achieved
Down[10] from the Sabines' wrong to Lucrece' woe,
With its seven kings conquering the nations round;
Nor all it wrought, by Roman worthies borne
'Gainst Brennus and the Epirot prince,[11] and hosts
Of single chiefs, or states in league combined

[4] The code of laws was abridged and reformed by Justinian.

[5] Justinian is said to have been a follower of heretical opinions held by Eutyches, "who taught that in Christ there was but one nature, viz., that of the incarnate Word." Maclaine's Mosheim.

[6] "Agapète." "Agapetus, Bishop of Rome, whose Scheda Regia, addressed to the Emperor Justinian, procured him a place among the wisest and most judicious writers of this country." Ibid.

[7] The Ghibellines. [8] The Guelfs.
[9] The Horatii and Curiatii.
[10] "From the rape of the Sabine women to the violation of Lucretia."
[11] King Pyrrhus.

Of social warfare: hence, Torquatus stern,
And Quintius[12] named of his neglected locks,
The Decii, and the Fabii hence acquired
Their fame, which I with duteous zeal embalm.
By it the pride of Arab hordes[13] was quell'd,
When they, led on by Hannibal, o'erpass'd
The Alpine rocks, whence glide thy currents, Po!
Beneath its guidance, in their prime of days
Scipio and Pompey triumph'd; and that hill[14]
Under whose summit[15] thou didst see the light,
Rued its stern bearing. After, near the hour,[16]
When Heaven was minded that o'er all the world
His own deep calm should brood, to Cæsar's hand
Did Rome consign it; and what then it wrought[17]
From Var unto the Rhine, saw Isere's flood,
Saw Loire and Seine, and every vale, that fills
The torrent Rhone. What after that it wrought,
When from Ravenna it came forth, and leap'd
The Rubicon, was of so bold a flight,
That tongue nor pen may follow it. Toward Spain
It wheel'd its bands, then toward Dyrrachium smote,
And on Pharsalia, with so fierce a plunge,
E'en the warm Nile was conscious to the pang;
Its native shores Antandros, and the streams
Of Simois revisited, and there
Where Hector lies; then ill for Ptolemy
His pennons shook again; lightening thence fell
On Juba, and the next, upon your west,
At sound of the Pompeian trump, return'd.

   "What following, and in its next bearer's gripe,[18]
It wrought, is now by Cassius and Brutus
Bark'd of in Hell; and by Perugia's sons,
And Modena's, was mourn'd. Hence weepeth still

---

[12] Quintius Cincinnatus.
[13] The Arabians seem to be put for the barbarians in general.
[14] ."That hill." The city of Fiesole, which was sacked by the Romans after the defeat of Catiline.
[15] "Under whose summit." "At the foot of which is situated Florence, thy birth-place."

[16] "Near the hour." Of our Saviour's birth.
[17] "What then it wrought." In the following fifteen lines the Poet has comprised the exploits of Julius Cæsar, for which, and for the allusions in the greater part of this speech of Justinian's, I must refer my reader to the history of Rome.
[18] With Augustus Cæsar.

Sad Cleopatra, who, pursued by it,
Took from the adder black and sudden death.
With him it ran e'en to the Red Sea coast;
With him composed the world to such a peace,
That of his temple Janus barr'd the door.

    "But all the mighty standard yet had wrought,
And was appointed to perform thereafter,
Throughout the mortal kingdom which it sway'd,
Falls in appearance dwindled and obscured,
If one with steady eye and perfect thought
On the third Cæsar[19] look; for to his hands,
The living Justice, in whose breath I move,
Committed glory, e'en into his hands,
To execute the vengeance of its wrath.

    "Hear now, and wonder at, what next I tell.
After with Titus it was sent to wreak
Vengeance for vengeance of the ancient sin.
And, when the Lombard tooth, with fang impure,
Did gore the bosom of the holy Church,
Under its wings, victorious Charlemain[20]
Sped to her rescue. Judge then for thyself
Of those, whom I erewhile accused to thee,
What they are, and how grievous their offending,
Who are the cause of all your ills. The one[21]
Against the universal ensign rears
The yellow lilies;[22] and with partial aim,
That, to himself, the other[23] arrogates:
So that 'tis hard to see who most offends.
Be yours, ye Ghibellines, to veil your hearts
Beneath another standard: ill is this
Follow'd of him, who severs it and justice:
And let not with his Guelfs the new-crown'd Charles

---

[19]. "The third Cæsar." The eagle in the hand of Tiberius, the third of the Cæsars, outdid all its achievements, both past and future, by becoming the instrument of that mighty and mysterious act of satisfaction made to the divine justice in the crucifixion of our Lord.

[20] "Charlemain." Dante could not be ignorant that the reign of Justinian was long prior to that of Charlemagne; but the spirit of the former emperor is represented, both in this instance and in what follows, as conscious of the events that had taken place after his own time.

[21] "The one." The Guelf party.

[22] The French ensign.

[23] The Ghibelline party.

Assail it;[24] but those talons hold in dread,
Which from a lion of more lofty port
Have rent the casing. Many a time ere now
The sons have for the sire's transgression wail'd:
Nor let him trust the fond belief, that Heaven
Will truck its armour for his lilied shield.

"This little star is furnish'd with good spirits,
Whose mortal lives were busied to that end,
That honour and renown might wait on them:
And, when desires[25] thus err in their intention,
True love must needs ascend with slacker beam.
But it is part of our delight, to measure
Our wages with the merit; and admire
The close proportion. Hence doth heavenly justice
Temper so evenly affection in us,
It ne'er can warp to any wrongfulness.
Of diverse voices is sweet music made:
So in our life the different degrees
Render sweet harmony among these wheels.

"Within the pearl, that now encloseth us,
Shines Romeo's light,[26] whose goodly deed and fair
Met ill acceptance. But the Provençals,
That were his foes, have little cause for mirth.
Ill shapes that man his course, who makes his wrong
Of other's worth. Four daughters[27] were there born
To Raymond Berenger; and every one
Became a queen: and this for him did Romeo,
Though of mean state and from a foreign land.

[24] "Charles." The commentators explain this to mean Charles II, King of Naples and Sicily. Is it not more likely to allude to Charles of Valois, son of Philip III of France, who was sent for, about this time, into Italy by Pope Boniface, with the promise of being made Emperor? See G. Villani, lib. viii. cap. xlii.

[25] When honour and fame are the chief motives to action, the love for Heaven must become less fervent.

[26] After he had long been faithful steward to Raymond Berenger, Count of Provence, and last of the house of Barcelona, who died 1245, when an account was required from him of the revenues which his master had lavishly disbursed, he demanded the little mule, the staff, and the scrip, with which he had first entered into the Count's service, a stranger pilgrim from the shrine of St. James, in Galicia, and parted as he came.

[27] Of the four daughters of Raymond, Margaret, the eldest, was married to Louis IX of France; Eleanor to Henry III of England; Sancha to Richard, Henry's brother, and King of the Romans; and the youngest, Beatrix, to Charles I, King of Naples and Sicily, and brother to Louis.

Yet envious tongues incited him to ask
A reckoning of that just one, who return'd
Twelve fold to him for ten. Aged and poor
He parted thence: and if the world did know
The heart he had, begging his life by morsels,
'Twould deem the praise, it yields him, scantly dealt."

CANTO VII

ARGUMENT.—In consequence of what had been said by Justinian, who together
with the other spirits has now disappeared, some doubts arise in the mind of Dante
respecting the human redemption. These difficulties are fully explained by Beatrice.

"*HOSANNA*[1] *Sanctus Deus Sabaoth,*
Superillustrans claritate tuâ
Felices ignes horum malahoth."
Thus chanting saw I turn that substance bright,[2]
With fourfold lustre to its orb again,
Revolving; and the rest, unto their dance,
With it, moved also; and, like swiftest sparks,
In sudden distance from my sight were veil'd.
  Me doubt possess'd; and "Speak," it whisper'd me,
"Speak, speak unto thy lady; that she quench
Thy thirst with drops of sweetness." Yet blank awe,
Which lords it o'er me, even at the sound
Of Beatrice's name, did bow me down
As one in slumber held. Not long that mood
Beatrice suffer'd: she, with such a smile,
As might have made one blest amid the flames,[3]
Beaming upon me, thus her words began:
"Thou in thy thought art pondering (as I deem,
And what I deem is truth) how just revenge
Could be with justice punish'd: from which doubt
I soon will free thee; so thou mark my words;
For they of weighty matter shall possess thee.
Through suffering not a curb upon the power
That will'd in him, to his own profiting,
That man, who was unborn,[4] condemn'd himself;

1 "Hosanna." "Hosanna holy God of
Sabaoth, abundantly illumining with thy
brightness the blessed fires of these kingdoms."

2 Justinian.
3 So Giusto de' Conti.
4 Adam.

And, in himself, all, who since him have lived,
His offspring: whence, below, the human kind
Lay sick in grievous error many an age;
Until it pleased the Word of God to come
Amongst them down, to His own person joining
The nature from its Maker far estranged,
By the mere act of His eternal love.
Contemplate here the wonder I unfold:
The nature with its Maker thus conjoin'd,
Created first was blameless, pure and good;
But, through itself alone, was driven forth
From Paradise, because it had eschew'd
The way of truth and life, to evil turn'd.
Ne'er then was penalty so just as that
Inflicted by the Cross, if thou regard
The nature in assumption doom'd; ne'er wrong
So great, in reference to Him, who took
Such nature on Him, and endured the doom.
So different effects[5] flow'd from one act:
For by one death God and the Jews were pleased;
And Heaven was open'd, though the earth did quake.
Count it not hard henceforth, when thou dost hear
That a just vengeance[6] was, by righteous court,
Justly revenged. But yet I see thy mind,
By thought on thought arising, sore perplex'd;
And, with how vehement desire, it asks
Solution of the maze. What I have heard,
Is plain, thou sayst: but wherefore God this way
For our redemption chose, eludes my search.

"Brother! no eye of man not perfected,
Nor fully ripen'd in the flame of love,
May fathom this decree. It is a mark,
In sooth, much aim'd at, and but little kenn'd:
And I will therefore show thee why such way

---

[5] The death of Christ was pleasing to God, inasmuch as it satisfied the divine justice; and to the Jews, because it gratified their malignity; and while Heaven opened for joy at man's ransom, the earth trembled through compassion for its Maker.

[6] The punishment of Christ by the Jews, although just as far as regarded the human nature assumed by Him, and so a righteous vengeance of sin, yet being unjust as regards the divine nature, was itself justly revenged on the Jews by the destruction of Jerusalem.

Was worthiest. The celestial Love, that spurns
All envying in its bounty, in itself
With such effulgence blazeth, as sends forth
All beauteous things eternal. What distils
Immediate thence, no end of being knows;
Bearing its seal immutably imprest.
Whatever thence immediate falls, is free,
Free wholly, uncontrollable by power
Of each thing new: by such conformity
More grateful to its Author, whose bright beams,
Though all partake their shining, yet in those
Are liveliest, which resemble Him the most.
These tokens of pre-eminence[7] on man
Largely bestow'd, if any of them fail,
He needs must forfeit his nobility,
No longer stainless. Sin alone is that,
Which doth disfranchise him, and make unlike
To the Chief Good; for that its light in him
Is darken'd. And to dignity thus lost
Is no return; unless, where guilt makes void,
He for ill pleasure pay with equal pain.
Your nature, which entirely in its seed
Transgress'd, from these distinctions fell, no less
Than from its state in Paradise; nor means
Found of recovery (search all methods out
As strictly as thou may) save one of these,
The only fords were left through which to wade:
Either, that God had of His courtesy
Released him merely; or else, man himself
For his own folly by himself atoned.

"Fix now thine eye, intently as thou canst,
On the everlasting counsel; and explore,
Instructed by my words, the dread abyss.

"Man in himself had ever lack'd the means
Of satisfaction, for he could not stoop
Obeying, in humility so low,
As high, he, disobeying, thought to soar:

---

[7] The before-mentioned gifts of immediate creation by God, independence
on secondary causes, and consequent
similitude and agreeableness to the Divine
Being, all at first conferred on man.

And, for this reason, he had vainly tried,
Out of his own sufficiency to pay
The rigid satisfaction. Then behoved
That God should by His own ways lead him back
Unto the life, from whence he fell, restored;
By both His ways, I mean, or one alone.[8]
But since the deed is ever prized the more,
The more the doer's good intent appears;
Goodness celestial, whose broad signature
Is on the universe, of all its ways
To raise ye up, was fain to leave out none.
Nor aught so vast or so magnificent,
Either for Him who gave or who received,
Between the last night and the primal day,
Was or can be. For God more bounty show'd,
Giving Himself to make man capable
Of his return to life, than had the terms
Been mere and unconditional release.
And for His justice, every method else
Were all too scant, had not the Son of God
Humbled Himself to put on mortal flesh.

"Now, to content thee fully, I revert;
And further in some part[9] unfold my speech,
That thou mayst see it clearly as myself.

"I see, thou sayst, the air, the fire I see,
The earth and water, and all things of them
Compounded, to corruption turn, and soon
Dissolve. Yet these were also things create.
Because, if what were told me, had been true,
They from corruption had been therefore free.

"The Angels, O my brother! and this clime
Wherein thou art, impassable and pure,
I call created, even as they are

[8] Either by mercy and justice united or by mercy alone.

[9] She reverts to that part of her discourse where she had said that what proceeds immediately from God "no end of being knows." She then proceeds to tell him that the elements, which, though he knew them to be created, he yet saw dissolved, received their form not immediately from God, but from a virtue or power created by God; that the soul of brutes and plants is in like manner drawn forth by the stars with a combination of those elements meetly tempered, *"di complession potenziata";* but that the angels and the heavens may be said to be created in that very manner in which they exist, without any intervention of agency.

In their whole being. But the elements,
Which thou hast named, and what of them is made,
Are by created virtue inform'd: create,
Their substance; and create, the informing virtue
In these bright stars, that round them circling move.
The soul of every brute and of each plant,
The ray and motion of the sacred lights,
Draw from complexion with meet power endued.
But this our life the Eternal Good inspires
Immediate, and enamours of itself;
So that our wishes rest for ever here.

   "And hence thou mayst by inference conclude
Our resurrection certain, if thy mind
Consider how the human flesh was framed,
When both our parents at the first were made."

CANTO VIII

ARGUMENT.—The Poet ascends with Beatrice to the third heaven, the planet Venus; and here finds the soul of Charles Martel, King of Hungary, who had been Dante's friend on earth, and who now, after speaking of the realms to which he was heir, unfolds the cause why children differ in disposition from their parents.

THE world[1] was, in its day of peril dark,
   Wont to believe the dotage of fond love,
   From the fair Cyprian deity, who rolls
In her third epicycle, shed on men
By stream of potent radiance: therefore they
Of elder time, in their old error blind,
Not her alone with sacrifice adored
And invocation, but like honours paid
To Cupid and Dione, deem'd of them
Her mother, and her son, him whom they feign'd
To sit in Dido's bosom: and from her,
Whom I have sung preluding, borrow'd they
The appellation of that star, which views

---

[1] The Poet, on his arrival at the third Heaven, tells us that the world, in its days of heathen darkness, believed the influence of sensual love to proceed from the star, to which, under the name of Venus, they paid divine honors; as they worshipped the supposed mother and son of Venus, under the names of Dione and Cupid.

Now obvious, and now averse, the sun.
    I was not ware that I was wafted up
Into its orb; but the new loveliness,
That graced my lady, gave me ample proof
That we had enter'd there. And as in flame
A sparkle is distinct, or voice in voice
Discern'd, when one its even tenour keeps,
The other comes and goes; so in that light
I other luminaries saw, that coursed
In circling motion, rapid more or less,
As their eternal vision each impels.
    Never was blast from vapour charged with cold,
Whether invisible to eye or no,
Descended with such speed, it had not seem'd
To linger in dull tardiness, compared
To those celestial lights, that toward us came,
Leaving the circuit of their joyous ring,
Conducted by the lofty Seraphim.
And after them, who in the van appear'd,
Such an Hosanna sounded as hath left
Desire, ne'er since extinct in me, to hear
Renew'd the strain. Then, parting from the rest,
One near us drew, and sole began: "We all
Are ready at thy pleasure, well disposed
To do thee gentle service. We are they
To whom thou in the world erewhile didst sing;
'O ye! whose intellectual ministry
Moves the third Heaven:' and in one orb we roll,
One motion, one impulse, with those who rule
Princedoms in Heaven; yet are of love so full,
That to please thee 'twill be as sweet to rest."
    After mine eyes had with meek reverence
Sought the celestial guide, and were by her
Assured, they turn'd again unto the light,
Who had so largely promised; and with voice
That bare the lively pressure of my zeal,
"Tell who ye are," I cried. Forthwith it grew
In size and splendour, through augmented joy;
And thus it answer'd: "A short date, below,

The world possess'd me.[2] Had the time been more,
Much evil, that will come, had never chanced.
My gladness hides thee from me, which doth shine
Around, and shroud me, as an animal
In its own silk enswathed. Thou lovedst me well,[3]
And hadst good cause; for had my sojourning
Been longer on the earth, the love I bare thee
Had put forth more than blossoms. The left bank,[4]
That Rhone, when he hath mix'd with Sorga, laves,
In me its lord expected, and that horn
Of fair Ausonia,[5] with its boroughs old,
Bari, and Croton, and Gaeta piled,
From where the Trento disembogues his waves
With Verde mingled, to the salt-sea flood.
Already on my temples beam'd the crown,
Which gave me sovereignty over the land[6]
By Danube wash'd, whenas he strays beyond
The limits of his German shores. The realm,
Where, on the gulf by stormy Eurus lash'd,
Betwixt Pelorus and Pachynian heights,
The beautiful Trinacria[7] lies in gloom,
(Not through Typhœus,[8] but the vapoury cloud
Bituminous upsteam'd), that too did look
To have its sceptre wielded by a race   [Rodolph,[9]
Of monarchs, sprung through me from Charles and
Had not ill-lording,[10] which doth desperate make

[2] The spirit now speaking is Charles Martel, crowned King of Hungary, and son of Charles II, King of Naples and Sicily, to which throne, dying in his father's lifetime, he did not succeed. The evil, that would have been prevented by the longer life of Charles Martel, was that resistance which his brother Robert, King of Sicily, who succeeded him, made to the Emperor Henry VII.

[3] Charles Martel might have been known to our Poet at Florence, whither he came to meet his father in 1259, the year of his death. G. Villani says that "he remained more than twenty days in Florence, waiting for his father, King Charles, and his brothers." Lib. vii. cap. xiii. His brother Robert, King of Naples, was the friend of Petrarch.

[4] "The left bank." Provence.

[5] The kingdom of Naples.

[6] "The land." Hungary.

[7] Sicily; so called from its three promontories of which Pachynus and Pelorus, here mentioned, are two.

[8] The giant, whom Jupiter overwhelmed under Mount Ætna, whence he vomited forth smoke and flame.

[9] "Sicily would be still ruled by monarchs, descended through me from Charles I and Rodolph I, the former my grandfather, King of Naples and Sicily; the latter, Emperor of Germany, my father-in-law;" both celebrated in the "Purgatory," Canto vii.

[10] If the ill-conduct of our governors in Sicily had not excited the people to that dreadful massacre at the Sicilian vespers

The people ever, in Palermo raised
The shout of 'death,' re-echoed loud and long.
Had but my brother's foresight[11] kenn'd as much,
He had been warier, that the greedy want
Of Catalonia might not work his bale.
And truly need there is that he forecast,
Or other for him, lest more freight be laid
On his already over-laden bark.
Nature in him, from bounty fallen to thrift,
Would ask the guard of braver arms, than such
As only care to have their coffers fill'd."

　　"My liege! it doth enhance the joy thy words
Infuse into me, mighty as it is,
To think my gladness manifest to thee,
As to myself, who own it, when thou look'st
Into the source and limit of all good,
There, where thou markest that which thou dost speak,
Thence prized of me the more. Glad thou hast made
Now make intelligent, clearing the doubt   [me:
Thy speech hath raised in me; for much I muse,
How bitter can spring up,[12] when sweet is sown."

　　I thus inquiring; he forthwith replied:
"If I have power to show one truth, soon that
Shall face thee, which thy questioning declares
Behind thee now conceal'd. The Good,[13] that guides

in consequence of which the kingdom fell into the hands of Peter III of Arragon, in 1282.

[11] He seems to tax his brother Robert with employing necessitous and greedy Catalonians to administer the affairs of his kingdom.

[12] "How a covetous son can spring from a liberal father." Yet that father has himself been accused of avarice in the "Purgatory," Canto xx. 78; though his general character was that of a bounteous prince.

[13] The Supreme Being uses these spheres as the intelligent instruments of His providence in the conduct of terrestrial natures; so that these natures cannot but be conducted aright, unless these heavenly bodies should themselves fail from not having been made perfect at first, or the Creator of them should fail. To this Dante replies, that Nature, he is satisfied, thus directed must do her part. Charles Martel then reminds him that he had learned from Aristotle that human society requires a variety of conditions, and consequently a variety of qualifications in its members. Accordingly, men are born with different powers and capacities, caused by the influence of the heavenly bodies at the time of their nativity; on which influence, and not on their parents, those powers and capacities depend. Charles Martel adds, by way of corollary, that the want of observing their natural bent, in the destination of men to their several offices in life, is the occasion of much of the disorder that prevails in the world.

And blessed makes this realm which thou dost mount,
Ordains its providence to be the virtue
In these great bodies: nor the natures only
The all-perfect Mind provides for, but with them
That which preserves them too; for naught, that lies
Within the range of that unerring bow,
But is as level with the destined aim,
As ever mark to arrow's point opposed.
Were it not thus, these Heavens, thou dost visit,
Would their effect so work, it would not be
Art, but destruction; and this may not chance,
If the intellectual powers, that move these stars,
Fail not, and who, first faulty made them, fail.
Wilt thou this truth more clearly evidenced?"

To whom I thus: "It is enough: no fear,
I see, lest nature in her part should tire."

He straight rejoin'd: "Say, were it worse for man,
If he lived not in fellowship on earth?"

"Yea," answer'd I; "nor here a reason needs."

"And may that be, if different estates
Grow not of different duties in your life?
Consult your teacher,[14] and he tells you 'no.'"

Thus did he come, deducing to this point,
And then concluded: "For this cause behoves,
The roots, from whence your operations come,
Must differ. Therefore one is Solon born;
Another, Xerxes; and Melchisedec
A third; and he a fourth, whose airy voyage
Cost him his son.[15] In her circuitous course,
Nature, that is the seal to mortal wax,
Doth well her art, but no distinction owns
'Twixt one or other household. Hence befals
That Esau is so wide of Jacob: hence
Quirinus[16] of so base a father springs,

14 Aristotle, De Rep., lib. iii. cap. 4: Since a state is made up of members differing from one another (for even as an animal, in the first instance, consists of soul and body; and the soul, of reason and desire; and a family, of man and woman; and property, of master and slave; in like manner a state consists both of all these, and besides these of other dissimilar kinds); it necessarily follows that the excellence of all the members of the state cannot be one and the same.

15 Dædalus.

16 "Quirinus." Romulus, born of so obscure a father that his parentage was attributed to Mars.

He dates from Mars his lineage. Were it not
That Providence celestial overruled,
Nature, in generation, must the path
Traced by the generator still pursue
Unswervingly. Thus place I in thy sight
That, which was late behind thee. But, in sign
Of more affection for thee, 'tis my will
Thou wear this corollary. Nature ever,
Finding discordant fortune, like all seed
Out of its proper climate, thrives but ill.
And were the world below content to mark
And work on the foundation nature lays,
I would not lack supply of excellence.
But ye perversely to religion strain
Him, who was born to gird on him the sword,
And of the fluent phraseman make your king:
Therefore your steps have wander'd from the path."

CANTO IX

ARGUMENT.—The next spirit who converses with our Poet in the planet Venus
is the amorous Cunizza. To her succeeds Folco, or Folques, the Provençal bard, who
declares that the soul of Rahab the harlot is there also; and then, blaming the Pope
for his neglect of the Holy Land, prognosticates some reverse to the papal power.

AFTER solution of my doubt, thy Charles,
O fair Clemenza,[1] of the treachery[2] spake,
That must befal his seed; but, "Tell it not,"
Said he, "and let the destined years come round."
Nor may I tell thee more, save that the meed
Of sorrow well-deserved shall quit your wrongs.
   And now the visage of that saintly light[3]
Was to the sun, that fills it, turn'd again,
As to the good, whose plenitude of bliss
Sufficeth all. O ye misguided souls!
Infatuate, who from such a good estrange
Your hearts, and bend your gaze on vanity,
Alas for you!—And lo! toward me, next,

[1] Daughter of Charles Martel, and second wife of Louis X of France.
[2] "The treachery." He alludes to the occupation of the Kingdom of Sicily by Robert, in exclusion of his brother's son Carobert, or Charles Robert, the rightful heir.
[3] Charles Martel.

Another of those splendent forms approach'd,
That, by its outward brightening, testified
The will it had to pleasure me. The eyes
Of Beatrice, resting, as before,
Firmly upon me, manifested forth
Approval of my wish. "And O," I cried,
"Blest spirit! quickly be my will perform'd;
And prove thou to me,[4] that my inmost thoughts
I can reflect on thee." Thereat the light,
That yet was new to me, from the recess,
Where it before was singing, thus began,
As one who joys in kindness: "In that part[5]
Of the depraved Italian land, which lies
Between Rialto and the fountain springs
Of Brenta and of Piava, there doth rise,
But to no lofty eminence, a hill,
From whence erewhile a firebrand did descend,
That sorely shent the region. From one root
I and it sprang; my name on earth Cunizza:[6]
And here I glitter, for that by its light
This star o'ercame me. Yet I naught repine,[7]
Nor grudge myself the cause of this my lot:
Which haply vulgar hearts can scarce conceive.

"This[8] jewel, that is next me in our Heaven,
Lustrous and costly, great renown hath left,
And not to perish, ere these hundred years

[4] The thoughts of all created minds being seen by the Deity, and all that is in the Deity being the object of vision to beatified spirits, such spirits must consequently see the thoughts of all created minds. Dante, therefore, requests of the spirit, who now approaches him, a proof of this truth with regard to his own thoughts. See v. 70.

[5] Between Rialto in the Venetian territory, and the sources of the rivers Brenta and Piava, is situated a castle called Romano, the birthplace of the famous tyrant Ezzolino or Azzolino, the brother of Cunizza, who is now speaking. See Hell, Canto xii. v. 110.

[6] "Cunizza." The adventures of Cunizza, overcome by the influence of her star, are related by the chronicler Rolandino.

of Padua. She eloped from her first husband, Richard of St. Boniface, in the company of Sordello, with whom she is supposed to have cohabited before her marriage: then lived with a soldier of Trevigi, whose wife was living at the same time in the same city; and, on his being murdered by her brother the tyrant, was by her brother married to a nobleman of Braganzo: lastly, when he also had fallen by the same hand, she after her brother's death, was again wedded in Verona.

[7] "I am not dissatisfied that I am not allotted a higher place."

[8] "This." Folco of Genoa, a celebrated Provençal poet, commonly termed Folques of Marseilles, of which place he was perhaps bishop.

Five times[9] absolve their round. Consider thou,
If to excel be worthy man's endeavour,
When such life may attend the first.[10] Yet they
Care not for this, the crowd[11] that now are girt
By Adice and Tagliamento, still
Impenitent, though scourged. The hour is near[12]
When for their stubbornness, at Padua's marsh
The water shall be changed, that laves Vicenza.
And where Cagnano meets with Sile, one[13]
Lords it, and bears his head aloft, for whom
The web[14] is now a-warping. Feltro[15] too
Shall sorrow for its godless shepherd's fault,
Of so deep stain, that never, for the like,
Was Malta's[16] bar unclosed. Too large should be
The skillet[17] that would hold Ferrara's blood,
And wearied he, who ounce by ounce would weigh it,
The which this priest,[18] in show of party-zeal,
Courteous will give; nor will the gift ill suit
The country's custom. We descry above
Mirrors, ye call them Thrones, from which to us
Reflected shine the judgments of our God:
Whence these our sayings we avouch for good."
    She ended; and appear'd on other thoughts

[9] The 500 years are elapsed.

[10] When the mortal life of man may be attended by so lasting and glorious a memory, which is a kind of second life.

[11] The people who inhabited the country bounded by the Tagliamento to the east and Adice to the west.

[12] Cunizza foretells the defeat of Giacopo da Carrara and the Paduans, by Can Grande, at Vicenza, on September 18, 1314.

[13] "One." She predicts also the fate of Riccardo da Camino, who is said to have been murdered at Trevigi (where the rivers Sile and Cagnano meet) where he was engaged in playing at chess.

[14] "The web." The net, or snare, into which he is destined to fall.

[15] The Bishop of Feltro having received a number of fugitives from Ferrara, who were in opposition to the Pope, under a promise of protection, afterward gave them up; so that they were reconducted to that city, and the greater part of them there put to death.

[16] "Malta's." A tower, either in the citadel of Padua, which, under the tyranny of Ezzolino, had been "with many a foul and midnight murder fed"; or (as some say) near a river of the same name, that falls into the Lake of Bolsena, in which the Pope was accustomed to imprison such as had been guilty of an irremissible sin.

[17] "The skillet." The blood shed could not be contained in such a vessel, if it were of the usual size.

[18] The bishop, who, to show himself a zealous partisan of the Pope, had committed the above-mentioned act of treachery. The commentators are not agreed as to his name. Troya calls him Alessandro Novello, and relates the circumstances at full.

Intent, re-entering on the wheel she late
Had left. That other joyance meanwhile wax'd
A thing to marvel at, in splendour glowing,
Like choicest ruby stricken by the sun.
For, in that upper clime, effulgence[19] comes
Of gladness, as here laughter: and below,
As the mind saddens, murkier grows the shade.

"God seeth all: and in Him is thy sight,"
Said I, "blest spirit! Therefore will of His
Cannot to thee be dark. Why then delays
Thy voice to satisfy my wish untold;
That voice, which joins the inexpressive song,
Pastime of Heaven, the which those Ardours sing,
That cowl them with six shadowing wings[20] outspread?
I would not wait thy asking, wert thou known
To me, as throughly I to thee am known."

He, forthwith answering, thus his words began:
"The valley of waters,[21] widest next to that[22]
Which doth the earth engarland, shapes its course,
Between discordant shores,[23] against the sun
Inward so far, it makes meridian[24] there,
Where was before the horizon. Of that vale
Dwelt I upon the shore, 'twixt Ebro's stream
And Macra's,[25] that divides with passage brief
Genoan bounds from Tuscan. East and west
Are nearly one to Begga[26] and my land
Whose haven[27] erst was with its own blood warm.
Who knew my name, were wont to call me Folco;
And I did bear impression of this Heaven,[28]

[19] As joy is expressed by laughter on earth, so is it by an increase of splendor in Paradise; and, on the contrary, grief is betokened in Hell by augmented darkness.

[20] "Above it stood the seraphims; each one had six wings."—Is. vi. 2.

[21] The Mediterranean Sea.

[22] "That." The great ocean.

[23] Europe and Africa.

[24] "Meridian." Extending to the east, the Mediterranean at last reaches the coast of Palestine, which is on its horizon when it enters the Straits of Gibraltar.

[25] Ebro, a river to the west, and Macra, a river to the east, of Genoa, where Folco was born; others think that Marseilles, and not Genoa, is here described; and then Ebro must be understood of the river in Spain.

[26] "Begga." A place in Africa.

[27] Alluding to the slaughter of the Genoese by the Saracens in 936.

[28] The planet Venus, by which Folco declares himself to have been formerly influenced.

That now bears mine: for not with fiercer flame
Glow'd Belus' daughter,[29] injuring alike
Sichæus and Creusa, than did I,
Long as it suited the unripen'd down
That fledged my cheek; nor she of Rhodope,[30]
That was beguiled of Demophoon;
Nor Jove's son,[31] when the charms of Iole
Were shrined within his heart. And yet there bides
No sorrowful repentance here, but mirth,
Not for the fault, (that doth not come to mind,)
But for the virtue, whose o'erruling sway
And providence have wrought thus quaintly. Here
The skill is look'd into, that fashioneth
With such effectual working, and the good
Discern'd, accruing to the lower world
From this above. But fully to content
Thy wishes all that in this sphere have birth,
Demands my further parle. Inquire thou wouldst,
Who of this light is denizen, that here
Beside me sparkles, as the sunbeam doth
On the clear wave. Know then, the soul of Rahab[32]
Is in that gladsome harbour; to our tribe
United, and the foremost rank assign'd.
She to this Heaven,[33] at which the shadow ends
Of your sublunar world, was taken up,
First, in Christ's triumph, of all souls redeem'd:
For well behoved, that, in some part of Heaven,
She should remain a trophy, to declare
The mighty conquest won with either palm;[34]
For that she favour'd first the high exploit
Of Joshua on the Holy Land, whereof
The Pope[35] recks little now. Thy city, plant
Of him,[36] that on his Maker turn'd the back,
And of whose envying so much woe hath sprung,

---

[29] "Belus' daughter." Dido.
[30] "She of Rhodope." Phyllis.
[31] "Jove's son." Hercules.
[32] "Rahab." Heb. xi. 31.
[33] "This planet of Venus, at which the shadow of the earth ends (Almagest) writes Ptolemy."—Vellutello.
[34] By both hands nailed to the cross.
[35] "Who cares not that the Holy Land is in the possession of the Saracens."
[36] "Of him." Of Satan.

Engenders and expands the cursed flower,[37]
That hath made wander both the sheep and lambs,
Turning the shepherd to a wolf. For this,
The Gospel and great teachers laid aside,
The decretals,[38] as their stuft margins show,
Are the sole study. Pope and Cardinals,
Intent on these, ne'er journey but in thought
To Nazareth, where Gabriel oped his wings.
Yet it may chance, ere long, the Vatican,[39]
And other most selected parts of Rome,
That were the grave of Peter's soldiery,
Shall be deliver'd from the adulterous bond."

CANTO X

ARGUMENT.—Their next ascent carries them into the sun, which is the fourth heaven. Here they are encompassed with a wreath of blessed spirits, twelve in number. Thomas Aquinas, who is one of these, declares the names and endowments of the rest.

LOOKING into His First-Born with the Love,
　　　Which breathes from both eternal, the first Might
　　　Ineffable, wherever eye or mind
Can roam, hath in such order all disposed,
As none may see and fail to enjoy. Raise, then,
O reader! to the lofty wheels, with me,
Thy ken directed to the point,[1] whereat
One motion strikes on the other. There begin
Thy wonder of the mighty Architect,

[37] The coin of Florence, the florin; the covetous desire of which has excited the Pope to so much evil.

[38] "The decretals." The canon law. So in the "De Monarchiâ," lib. iii. p. 137: "There are also a third set, whom they call Decretalists. These, alike ignorant of theology and philosophy, relying wholly on their decretals (which I indeed esteem not unworthy of reverence), in the hope I suppose of obtaining for them a paramount influence, derogate from the authority of the empire. Nor is this to be wondered at, when I have heard one of them impudently maintaining, that traditions are the foundation of the faith of the Church."

[39] He alludes either to the death of Pope Boniface VIII or to the coming of the Emperor Henry VII into Italy; or else to the transfer of the Holy See from Rome to Avignon, which took place in the pontificate of Clement V.

[1] To that part of heaven where the equinoctial circle and the Zodiac intersect each other, where the common motion of the heavens from east to west may be said to strike with greatest force against the motion proper to the planets, and this repercussion, as it were, is here the strongest, because the velocity of each is increased to the utmost by their respective distances from the poles.

Who loves His work so inwardly, His eye
Doth ever watch it. See, how thence oblique[2]
Brancheth the circle, where the planets roll
To pour their wished influence on the world;
Whose path not bending thus, in Heaven above[3]
Much virtue would be lost, and here on earth
All power well-nigh extinct: or, from direct
Were its departure distant more or less,
I' the universal order, great defect
Must, both in Heaven and here beneath, ensue.

  Now rest thee, reader! on thy bench, and muse
Anticipative of the feast to come;
So shall delight make thee not feel thy toil.
Lo! I have set before thee; for thyself
Feed now: the matter I indite, henceforth
Demands entire my thought. Join'd with the part,[4]
Which late we told of, the great minister[5]
Of nature, that upon the world imprints
The virtue of the Heaven, and doles out
Time for us with his beam, went circling on
Along the spires,[6] where[7] each hour sooner comes;
And I was with him, weetless of ascent,
But as a man,[8] that weets his thought, ere thinking.

  For Beatrice, she who passeth on
So suddenly from good to better, time
Counts not the act, oh then how great must needs
Have been her brightness! What there was i' th' sun,
(Where I had enter'd,) not through change of hue,
But light transparent—did I summon up
Genius, art, practice—I might not so speak,
It should be e'er imagined: yet believed

---

[2] "Oblique." The Zodiac.

[3] If the planets did not preserve that order in which they move, they would not receive nor transmit their due influences; and if the Zodiac were not thus oblique; if toward the north it either passed or went short of the tropic of Cancer, or else toward the south it passed, or went short of the tropic of Capricorn, it would not divide the seasons as it now does.

[4] The intersection of the equinoctial circle and the Zodiac.

[5] "Minister." The sun.

[6] According to Dante, as the earth is motionless, the sun passes by a spiral motion, from one tropic to another.

[7] "Where." In which the sun rises earlier every day after the vernal equinox.

[8] "But as a man." That is, he was quite insensible of it.

It may be, and the sight be justly craved.
And if our fantasy fail of such height,
What marvel, since no eye above the sun
Hath ever travel'd? Such are they dwell here,
Fourth family[9] of the Omnipotent Sire,
Who of His Spirit and of His Offspring[10] shows;
And holds them still enraptured with the view.
And thus to me Beatrice: "Thank, oh thank
The Sun of Angels, Him, who by His grace
To this perceptible hath lifted thee."

    Never was heart in such devotion bound,
And with complacency so absolute
Disposed to render up itself to God,
As mine was at those words: and so entire
The love for Him, that held me, it eclipsed
Beatrice in oblivion. Nought displeased
Was she, but smiled thereat so joyously,
That of her laughing eyes the radiance brake
And scatter'd my collected mind abroad.

    Then saw I a bright band, in liveliness
Surpassing, who themselves did make the crown,
And us their centre: yet more sweet in voice,
Than, in their visage, beaming. Cinctured thus,
Sometime Latona's daughter we behold,
When the impregnate air retains the thread
That weaves her zone. In the celestial court,
Whence I return, are many jewels found,
So dear and beautiful, they cannot brook
Transporting from that realm: and of these lights
Such was the song.[11] Who doth not prune his wing
To soar up thither, let him[12] look from thence
For tidings from the dumb. When, singing thus,
Those burning suns had circled round us thrice,
As nearest stars around the fixed pole;
Then seem'd they like to ladies, from the dance
Not ceasing, but suspense, in silent pause,

---

[9] "Fourth family." The inhabitants of the sun, the fourth planet.

[10] The procession of the third and the generation of the second person in the Trinity.

[11] The song of these spirits was like a jewel so highly prized that the exportation of it is prohibited by law.

[12] Let him not expect intelligence of that place, for it surpasses description.

Listening, till they have caught the strain anew:
Suspended so they stood: and, from within,
Thus heard I one, who spake: "Since with its beam
The Grace, whence true love lighteth first his flame,
That after doth increase by loving, shines
So multiplied in thee, it leads thee up
Along this ladder, down whose hallow'd steps
None e'er descend, and mount them not again;
Who from his phial should refuse thee wine
To slake thy thirst, no less constrained[13] were,
Than water flowing not unto the sea.
Thou fain wouldst hear, what plants are these, that bloom
In the bright garland, which, admiring, girds
This fair dame round, who strengthens thee for Heaven.
I, then,[14] was of the lambs, that Dominic
Leads, for his saintly flock, along the way
Where well they thrive, not swoln with vanity.
He, nearest on my right hand, brother was,
And master to me: Albert of Cologne[15]
Is this; and, of Aquinum, Thomas[16] I.
If thou of all the rest wouldst be assured,
Let thine eye, waiting on the words I speak,
In circuit journey round the blessed wreath.
That next resplendence issues from the smile
Of Gratian,[17] who to either forum[18] lent

[13] "The rivers might as easily cease to flow toward the sea, as we could deny thee thy request."

[14] "I was of the Dominican order."

[15] Albertus Magnus was born at Laugingen, in Thuringia, in 1193, and studied at Paris and at Padua; at the latter place he entered into the Dominican order. He then taught theology in various parts of Germany, and particularly at Cologne. Thomas Aquinas was his favorite pupil. In 1260 he reluctantly accepted the bishopric of Ratisbon, and in two years after resigned it, and returned to his cell in Cologne, where the remainder of his life was passed in superintending the school, and in composing his voluminous works on divinity and natural science. He died in 1280.

[16] Thomas Aquinas, of whom Bucer is reported to have said, "Take but Thomas away, and I will overturn the Church of Rome"; and whom Hooker terms "the greatest among the school divines"— ("Eccl. Pol." b. iii. § 9), was born of noble parents, who anxiously but vainly endeavored to divert him from a life of celibacy and study. He died in 1274, at the age of forty-seven.

[17] "Gratian." Gratian, a Benedictine monk belonging to the convent of St. Felix and Nabor, at Bologna, and by birth a Tuscan, composed, about the year 1130, for the use of the schools, an abridgement or epitome of canon law, drawn from the letters of the pontiffs, the decrees of councils and the writings of the ancient doctors.

[18] "To either forum." By reconciling the civil with the canon law.

Such help, as favour wins in Paradise.
The other, nearest, who adorns our quire,
Was Peter,[19] he that with the widow gave
To holy Church his treasure. The fifth light,[20]
Goodliest of all, is by such love inspired,
That all your world craves tidings of his doom:[21]
Within, there is a lofty light, endow'd
With sapience so profound, if truth be truth,
That with a ken of such wide amplitude
No second hath arisen. Next behold
That taper's radiance,[22] to whose view was shown,
Clearliest, the nature and the ministry
Angelical, while yet in flesh it dwelt.
In the other little light serenely smiles
That pleader [23] for the Christian temples, he,
Who did provide Augustin of his lore.
Now, if thy mind's eye pass from light to light,
Upon my praises following, of the eighth[24]
Thy thirst is next. The saintly soul, that shows
The world's deceitfulness, to all who hear him,
Is, with the sight of all the good that is,
Blest there. The limbs, whence it was driven, lie

[19] "Peter." Pietro Lombardo was of obscure origin, nor is the place of his birth in Lombardy ascertained. With a recommendation from the Bishop of Lucca to St. Bernard, he went into France to continue his studies; and for that purpose remained some time at Rheims, whence he proceeded to Paris. Here his reputation was so great that Philip, brother of Louis VII, being chosen Bishop of Paris, resigned that dignity to Pietro, whose pupil he had been. He held his bishopric only one year, and died 1160. His "Liber Sententiarum" is highly esteemed. It contains a system of scholastic theology, much more complete than any which had been yet seen.

[20] "The fifth light." Solomon.

[21] "His doom." It was a common question, it seems, whether Solomon were saved or no.

[22] St. Dionysius, the Areopagite. "The famous Grecian fanatic, who gave himself out for Dionysius the Areopagite, disciple of St. Paul, and who, under the protection of this venerable name, gave laws and instructions to those that were desirous of raising their souls above all human things, in order to unite them to their great source by sublime contemplation, lived most probably in the fourth century." Maclaine's Mosheim.

[23] "That pleader." In the fifth century, Paulus Orosius "acquired a considerable degree of reputation by the history he wrote to refute the cavils of the Pagans against Christianity, and by his books against the Pelagians and Priscillianists." Ibid.

[24] Boëtius, whose book "de Consolatione Philosophiæ," excited so much attention during the Middle Ages, was born about 470. "In 524 he was cruelly put to death by Theodoric, either on real or pretended suspicion of his being engaged in a conspiracy." Della Lett. Ital.

Down in Cieldauro;[25] and from martyrdom
And exile came it here. Lo! further on,
Where flames the arduous spirit of Isidore;[26]
Of Bede;[27] and Richard,[28] more than man, erewhile,
In deep discernment. Lastly this, from whom
Thy look on me reverteth, was the beam
Of one, whose spirit, on high musings bent,
Rebuked the lingering tardiness of death.
It is the eternal light of Sigebert[29]
Who 'scaped not envy, when of truth he argued,
Reading in the straw-litter'd street."[30] Forthwith,
As clock, that calleth up the spouse of God[31]
To win her Bridegroom's love at matin's hour,
Each part of other fitly drawn and urged,
Sends out a tinkling sound, of note so sweet,
Affection springs in well-disposed breast;
Thus saw I move the glorious wheel; thus heard
Voice answering voice, so musical and soft,
It can be known but where day endless shines.

CANTO XI

ARGUMENT.—Thomas Aquinas enters at large into the life and character of St. Francis; and then solves one of two difficulties, which he perceived to have risen in Dante's mind from what he had heard in the last Canto.

O FOND anxiety of mortal men!
   How vain and inconclusive arguments
   Are those, which make thee beat thy wings below.
For statutes one, and one for aphorisms[1]

[25] "Cieldauro." Boëtius was buried at Pavia, in the monastery of St. Pietro in Ciel d'Oro.

[26] He was Archbishop of Seville during forty years, and died in 635.

[27] "Bede." Bede, whose virtues obtained him the appellation of the Venerable, was born in 672, at Wearmouth and Jarrow in the bishopric of Durham, and died at Jarrow in 735. Invited to Rome by Pope Sergius I, he preferred passing almost the whole of his life in the seclusion of a monastery.

[28] Richard of St. Victor, a native either of Scotland or Ireland, was canon and prior of the monastery of that name at Paris; and died in 1173. "He was at the head of the Mystics in this century; and his treatise, entitled the "Mystical Ark," which contains as it were the marrow of this kind of theology, was received with the greatest avidity." Maclaine's Mosheim.

[29] A monk of the Abbey of Gemblours, in high repute at the end of the eleventh, and beginning of the twelfth century.

[30] The name of a street in Paris; the "Rue de Fouarre."

[31] The Church.

[1] The study of medicine.

Was hunting; this the priesthood follow'd; that,
By force or sophistry, aspired to rule;
To rob, another; and another sought,
By civil business, wealth; one, moiling, lay
Tangled in net of sensual delight;
And one to wistless indolence resign'd;
What time from all these empty things escaped,
With Beatrice, I thus gloriously
Was raised aloft, and made the guest of Heaven.

They of the circle to that point, each one,
Where erst it was, had turn'd; and steady glow'd,
As candle in his socket. Then within
The lustre,[2] that erewhile bespake me, smiling
With merer gladness, heard I thus begin:
"E'en as His beam illumes me, so I look
Into the Eternal Light, and clearly mark
Thy thoughts, from whence they rise. Thou art in doubt,
And wouldst, that I should bolt my words afresh
In such plain open phrase, as may be smooth
To thy perception, where I told thee late
That 'well they thrive';[3] and that 'no second such[4]
Hath risen,' which no small distinction needs.

"The Providence, that governeth the world,
In depth of counsel by created ken
Unfathomable, to the end that she,[5]
Who with loud cries was 'spoused in precious blood,
Might keep her footing toward her well-beloved,[6]
Safe in herself and constant unto Him,
Hath two ordain'd, who should on either hand
In chief escort her: one,[7] seraphic all
In fervency; for wisdom upon earth,
The other,[8] splendour of cherubic light.
I but of one will tell: he tells of both,
Who one commendeth, which of them soe'er
Be taken: for their deeds were to one end.

"Between Tupino,[9] and the wave that falls

[2] The spirit of Thomas Aquinas.
[3] See the last Canto, v. 93.
[4] See the last Canto, v. 111.
[5] "She." The Church.
[6] Jesus Christ.

[7] "One." St. Francis.
[8] "The other." St. Dominic.
[9] Thomas Aquinas describes the birth-place of St. Francis, between Tupino, a rivulet near Assisi, or Ascesi, where the

From blest Ubaldo's chosen hill, there hangs
Rich slope of mountain high, whence heat and cold[10]
Are wafted through Perugia's eastern gate:
And Nocera with Gualdo, in its rear,
Mourn for their heavy yoke.[11] Upon that side,
Where it doth break its steepness most, arose
A sun upon the world, as duly this
From Ganges doth: therefore let none, who speak
Of that place, say Ascesi; for its name
Were lamely so deliver'd; but the East,
To call things rightly, be it henceforth styled.
He was not yet much distant from his rising,
When his good influence 'gan to bless the earth.
A dame,[12] to whom none openeth pleasure's gate
More than to death, was, 'gainst his father's will,[13]
His stripling choice: and he did make her his,
Before the spiritual court,[14] by nuptial bonds,
And in his father's sight: from day to day,
Then loved her more devoutly. She, bereaved
Of her first Husband,[15] slighted and obscure,
Thousand and hundred years and more, remain'd
Without a single suitor, till he came.
Nor aught avail'd, that, with Amyclas,[16] she
Was found unmoved at rumour of his voice,
Who shook the world: nor aught her constant boldness,
Whereby with Christ she mounted on the Cross,
When Mary stay'd beneath. But not to deal

saint was born in 1182, and Chiasciò, a stream that rises in a mountain near Agobbio, chosen by St. Ubaldo for his retirement.

[10] Cold from the snow, and heat from the reflection of the sun.

[11] Vellutello understands this of the vicinity of the "mountain" to Nocera and Gualdo; and Venturi of the heavy impositions laid on those places by the Perugians.

[12] In the under church of St. Francis, Assisi, is a picture painted by Giotto from this subject. It is considered one of the artist's best works. See Kugler's "Handbook of the History of Painting, translated by a lady." Lond. 1842, p. 48.

[13] In opposition to the wishes of his natural father.

[14] He made a vow of poverty in the presence of the bishop and of his natural father.

[15] "Her first Husband." Christ.

[16] Lucan makes Cæsar exclaim, on witnessing the secure poverty of the fisherman Amyclas:—

"O happy poverty! thou greatest good
  Bestow'd by Heaven, but seldom understood!
Here nor the cruel spoiler seeks his
  prey,
Nor ruthless armies take their dreadful
  way." etc.—Rowe.

Thus closely with thee longer, take at large
The lovers' titles—Poverty and Francis.
Their concord and glad looks, wonder and love,
And sweet regard gave birth to holy thoughts,
So much, that venerable Bernard[17] first
Did bare his feet, and, in pursuit of peace
So heavenly, ran, yet deem'd his footing slow.
O hidden riches! O prolific good!
Egidius[18] bares him next, and next Sylvester,[19]
And follow, both, the bridegroom: so the bride
Can please them. Thenceforth goes he on his way,
The father and the master, with his spouse,
And with that family, whom now the cord[20]
Girt humbly: nor did abjectness of heart
Weigh down his eyelids, for that he was son
Of Pietro Bernardone,[21] and by men
In wondrous sort despised. But royally
His hard intention he to Innocent[22]
Set forth; and, from him, first received the seal
On his religion. Then, when numerous flock'd
The tribe of lowly ones, that traced his steps,
Whose marvellous life deservedly were sung
In heights empyreal; through Honorius'[23] hand
A second crown, to deck their Guardian's virtues,
Was by the eternal Spirit inwreathed: and when
He had, through thirst of martyrdom, stood up
In the proud Soldan's presence,[24] and there preach'd
Christ and His followers, but found the race
Unripen'd for conversion; back once more
He hasted (not to intermit his toil)
And reap'd Ausonian lands. On the hard rock,[25]

---

[17] Of Quintavalle; one of the first followers of the saint.

[18] "Egidius." The third of his disciples, who died in 1262. His work, entitled "Verba Aurea," was published in 1534, at Antwerp.

[19] Another of his earliest associates.

[20] "Whom now the cord." St. Francis bound his body with a cord, in sign that it required, like a beast, to be led by a halter.

[21] A man in an humble station of life at Assisi.

[22] Pope Innocent III.

[23] "Honorius." His successor Honorius III, who granted certain privileges to the Franciscans.

[24] The Soldan of Egypt, before whom St. Francis is said to have preached.

[25] Mt. Alverna in the Apennines.

'Twixt Arno and the Tiber, he from Christ
Took the last signet,[26] which his limbs two years
Did carry. Then, the season come that He,
Who to such good had destined him, was pleased
To advance him to the meed, which he had earn'd
By his self-humbling; to his brotherhood,
As their just heritage, he gave in charge
His dearest lady:[27] and enjoin'd their love
And faith to her; and, from her bosom, will'd
His goodly spirit should move forth, returning
To its appointed kingdom; nor would have
His body[28] laid upon another bier.

   "Think now of one, who were a fit colleague
To keep the bark of Peter, in deep sea,
Helm'd to right point; and such our Patriarch[29] was.
Therefore who follow him as he enjoins,
Thou mayst be certain, take good lading in.
But hunger of new viands tempts his flock;[30]
So that they needs into strange pastures wide
Must spread them: and the more remote from him
The stragglers wander, so much more they come
Home, to the sheep-fold, destitute of milk.
There are of them, in truth, who fear their harm,
And to the shepherd cleave; but these so few,
A little stuff may furnish out their cloaks.

   "Now, if my words be clear; if thou have ta'en
Good heed; if that, which I have told, recall
To mind; thy wish may be in part fulfill'd:
For thou wilt see the plant from whence they split;[31]
And he shall see, who girds him, what that means,
'That well they thrive, not swoln with vanity.'"

---

[26] "The last signet." Alluding to the *stigmata,* or marks resembling the wounds of Christ, said to have been found on the saint's body.

[27] "His dearest lady." Poverty.

[28] He forbade any funeral pomp to be observed at his burial; and, as it is said, ordered that his remains should be deposited in a place where criminals were executed and interred.

[29] St. Dominic, to whose order Thomas Aquinas belonged.

[30] "His flock." The Dominicans.

[31] "The rule of their order, which the Dominicans neglect to observe."

CANTO XII

ARGUMENT.—A second circle of glorified souls encompasses the first. Buonaventura, who is one of them, celebrates the praises of St. Dominic, and informs Dante who the other eleven are, that are in this second circle or garland.

SOON as its final word the blessed flame[1]
    Had raised for utterance, straight the holy mill[2]
    Began to wheel; nor yet had once revolved,
Or e'er another, circling, compass'd it,
Motion to motion, song to song, conjoining;
Song, that as much our muses doth excel,
Our Syrens with their tuneful pipes, as ray
Of primal splendour doth its faint reflex.

    As when, if Juno bid her handmaid forth,
Two arches parallel, and trick'd alike,
Span the thin cloud, the outer taking birth
From that within (in manner of that voice[3]
Whom love did melt away, as sun the mist),
And they who gaze, presageful call to mind
The compact, made with Noah, of the world
No more to be o'erflow'd; about us thus,
Of sempiternal roses, bending, wreathed
Those garlands twain; and to the innermost
E'en thus the external answer'd. When the footing,
And other great festivity, of song,
And radiance, light with light accordant, each
Jocund and blythe, had at their pleasure still'd,
(E'en as the eyes, by quick volition moved,
Are shut and raised together), from the heart
Of one[4] amongst the new lights[5] moved a voice,

---

[1] Thomas Aquinas.

[2] The circle of spirits.

[3] One rainbow giving back the image of the other, as sound is reflected by Echo, that nymph, who was melted away by her fondness for Narcissus, as vapor is melted by the sun. The reader will observe in the text not only a second and third simile within the first, but two mythological and one sacred allusion bound up together with the whole. Even after this accumulation of imagery, the two circles of spirits, by whom Beatrice and Dante were encompassed, are by a bold figure termed two garlands of never-fading roses.

[4] "One." St. Buonaventura, general of the Franciscan order, in which he effected some reformation; and one of the most profound divines of his age. "He refused the archbishopric of York, which was offered him by Clement IV, but afterward was prevailed on to accept the bishopric of Albano and a cardinal's hat. He was born at Bagnoregio or Bagnorea, in Tuscany, A. D. 1221, and died in

That made me seem[6] like needle to the star,
In turning to its whereabout; and thus
Began: "The love,[7] that makes me beautiful,
Prompts me to tell of the other guide, for whom
Such good of mine is spoken. Where one is,
The other worthily should also be;
That as their warfare was alike, alike
Should be their glory. Slow, and full of doubt,
And with thin ranks, after its banner moved
The army of Christ, (which it so dearly cost
To reappoint), when its imperial Head
Who reigneth ever, for the drooping host
Did make provision, through grace alone,
And not through its deserving. As thou heard'st,[8]
Two champions to the succour of His spouse
He sent, who by their deeds and words might join
Again His scatter'd people. In that clime[9]
Where springs the pleasant west-wind to unfold
The fresh leaves, with which Europe sees herself
New-garmented; nor from those billows[10] far,
Beyond whose chiding, after weary course,
The sun doth sometimes[11] hide him; safe abides
The happy Callaroga,[12] under guard
Of the great shield, wherein the lion lies
Subjected and supreme. And there was born
The loving minion of the Christian faith,[13]
The hallow'd wrestler, gentle to his own,

1274." Dict. Histor. par Chaudon et Delandine, Ed. Lyon. 1804.

[5] In the circle that had newly surrounded the first.

[6] " 'That made me turn to it, as the needle does to the pole."

[7] "The love." By an act of mutual courtesy, Buonaventura, a Franciscan, is made to proclaim the praises of St. Dominic, as Thomas Aquinas, a Dominican, has celebrated those of St. Francis; and in like manner each blames the irregularities, not of the other's order, but of that to which himself belonged. Even Macchiavelli, no great friend to the Church, attributes the revival of Christianity to the influence of these two saints.

[8] See the last Canto, v. 33.

[9] "In that clime." Spain.

[10] "Those billows." The Atlantic.

[11] During the summer solstice.

[12] "Callaroga." Between Osma and Aranda, in Old Castile designated by the royal coat-of-arms.

[13] Dominic was born April 5, 1170, and died August 6, 1221. His birthplace Callaroga; his father and mother's names, Felix, and Joanna; his mother's dream; his name of Dominic, given him in consequence of a vision by his godmother, are all told in an anonymous life of the saint, said to have been written in the thirteenth century.

And to his enemies terrible. So replete
His soul with lively virtue, that when first
Created, even in the mother's womb,[14]
It prophesied. When, at the sacred font,
The spousals were complete 'twixt faith and him,
Where pledge of mutual safety was exchanged,
The dame,[15] who was his surety, in her sleep
Beheld the wondrous fruit, that was from him
And from his heirs to issue. And that such
He might be construed, as indeed he was,
She was inspired to name him of his owner,
Whose he was wholly; and so call'd him Dominic.
And I speak of him, as the labourer,
Whom Christ in His own garden chose to be
His help-mate. Messenger he seem'd, and friend
Fast-knit to Christ; and the first love he show'd,
Was after the first counsel[16] that Christ gave.
Many a time[17] his nurse, at entering, found
That he had risen in silence, and was prostrate,
As who should say, 'My errand was for this.'
O happy father! Felix[18] rightly named.
O favour'd mother! rightly named Joanna;
If that do mean, as men interpret it.[19]
Not for the world's sake, for which now they toil
Upon Ostiense[20] and Taddeo's[21] lore;
But for the real manna, soon he grew
Mighty in learning; and did set himself

---

[14] His mother, when pregnant with him, is said to have dreamt that she should bring forth a white and black dog with a lighted torch in his mouth, which were signs of the habit to be worn by his order, and of his fervent zeal.

[15] His godmother's dream was, that he had one star in his forehead and another in the nape of his neck, from which he communicated light to the east and the west.

[16] "Jesus said unto him, If thou wilt be perfect, go and sell that thou hast, and give to the poor, and thou shalt have treasure in heaven; and come and follow me."—Matt. xix. 21. Dominic is said to have followed this advice.

[17] His nurse, when she returned to him, often found that he had left his bed, and was prostrate, and in prayer.

[18] "Felix." Felix Gusman.

[19] Grace or gift of the Lord.

[20] Arrigo (about 1250 A. D.), a native of Susa, and cardinal of Ostia and Velletri, hence his name of Ostiense, was celebrated for his lectures on the Decretals.

[21] "Taddeo." Either the physician or the lawyer of that name. The former, T. d' Alderotto, a Florentine, called the Hippocratean, translated the Ethics of Aristotle into Latin; and died toward the end of the thirteenth century. The other, of Bologna, left no writings behind him.

To go about the vineyard, that soon turns
To wan and wither'd, if not tended well:
And from the see[22] (whose bounty to the just
And needy is gone by, not through its fault,
But his who fills it basely), he besought,
No dispensation[23] for commuted wrong,
Nor the first vacant fortune,[24] nor the tenths
That to God's paupers rightly appertain,
But, 'gainst an erring and degenerate world,
License to fight, in favour of that seed[25]
From which the twice twelve cions gird thee round.
Then, with sage doctrine and good will to help,
Forth on his great apostleship he fared,
Like torrent bursting from a lofty vein;
And, dashing 'gainst the stocks of heresy,
Smote fiercest, where resistance was most stout.
Thence many rivulets have since been turn'd,
Over the garden catholic to lead
Their living waters, and have fed its plants.

  "If such, one wheel[26] of that two-yoked car,
Wherein the holy Church defended her,
And rode triumphant through the civil broil;
Thou canst not doubt its fellow's excellence,
Which Thomas,[27] ere my coming, hath declared
So courteously unto thee. But the track,[28]
Which its smooth fellies made, is now deserted:
That, mouldy mother is, where late were lees.
His family, that wont to trace his path,
Turn backward, and invert their steps; erelong
To rue the gathering in of their ill crop,
When the rejected tares[29] in vain shall ask

---

[22] "The apostolic see, which no longer continues its wonted liberality toward the indigent and deserving; not indeed through its own fault, as its doctrines are still the same, but through the fault of the pontiff, who is seated in it."

[23] Dominic did not ask for license to compound for the use of unjust acquisitions by dedicating a part of them to pious purposes.

[24] The first benefice that fell vacant.

[25] "For that seed of the divine Word, from which have sprung up these four-and-twenty plants, these holy spirits that now environ thee."

[26] Dominic; as the other wheel is Francis.

[27] "Thomas." Thomas Aquinas.

[28] "But the track." "But the rule of St. Francis is already deserted; and the lees of the wine are turned into mouldiness."

[29] "Tares." He adverts to the parable of the tares and the wheat.

Admittance to the barn.   I question not[30]
But he, who search'd our volume, leaf by leaf,
Might still find page with this inscription on't,
'I am as I was wont.'   Yet such were not
From Acquasparta nor Casale, whence,
Of those who come to meddle with the text,
One stretches and another cramps its rule.
Bonaventura's life in me behold,
From Bagnoregio; one, who, in discharge
Of my great offices, still laid aside
All sinister aim.   Illuminato here,
And Agostino[31] join me: two they were,
Among the first of those barefooted meek ones,
Who sought God's friendship in the cord: with
    them
Hugues of Saint Victor;[32] Pietro Mangiadore;[33]
And he of Spain[34] in his twelve volumes shining;
Nathan the prophet; Metropolitan
Chrysostom;[35] and Anselmo;[36] and, who deign'd
To put his hand to the first art, Donatus.

[30] "I question not."   "Some indeed might be found, who still observe the rule of the order; but such would come neither from Casale nor Acquasparta."   At Casale, in Monferrat, the discipline had been enforced by Uberto with unnecessary rigor; and at Acquasparta, in the territory of Todi, it had been equally relaxed by the Cardinal Matteo, general of the order.

[31] Two among the earliest followers of St. Francis.

[32] "Hugues of Saint Victor."   He was of the monastery of St. Victor at Paris, and died in 1142, at the age of forty-four. His ten books, illustrative of the celestial hierarchy of Dionysius the Areopagite, according to the translation of Joannes Scotus, are inscribed to King Louis, son of Louis le Gros, by whom the monastery had been founded.

[33] "Pietro Mangiadore."   Petrus Comestor, or the Eater, born at Troyes, was canon and dean of that church, and afterward chancellor of the church of Paris.   He relinquished these benefices to become a regular canon of St. Victor at Paris, where he died in 1198.

[34] To Pope Adrian V succeeded John XXI, a native of Lisbon; a man of great genius and extraordinary acquirements, especially in logic and in medicine, as his books, written in the name of Peter of Spain, (by which he was known before he became Pope), may testify.   He was killed at Viterbo, by the falling in of the roof of his chamber, after he had been pontiff only eight months and as many days, A. D. 1277.

[35] "Chrysostom."   The eloquent Patriarch of Constantinople.

[36] Anselm, Archbishop of Canterbury, was born at Aosta, about 1034, and studied under Lanfranc, at the monastery of Bec in Normandy, where he afterward devoted himself to a religious life, in his twenty-seventh year.   In three years he was made prior, and then abbot of that monastery; from whence he was taken, in 1093, to succeed to the archbishopric, vacant by the death of Lanfranc.   He enjoyed this dignity till his death in 1109, though it was disturbed by many dissensions with William II and Henry I respecting immunities and investitures.

Raban[37] is here; and at my side there shines
Calabria's abbot, Joachim,[38] endow'd
With soul prophetic. The bright courtesy
Of friar Thomas and his goodly lore,
Have moved me to the blazon of a peer[39]
So worthy; and with me have moved this throng."

CANTO XIII

ARGUMENT.—Thomas Aquinas resumes his speech. He solves the other of those doubts which he discerned in the mind of Dante, and warns him earnestly against assenting to any proposition without having duly examined it.

LET him,[1] who would conceive what now I saw,
Imagine, (and retain the image firm
As mountain rock, the whilst he hears me speak,)
Of stars, fifteen, from midst the ethereal host
Selected that, with lively ray serene,
O'ercome the massiest air: thereto imagine
The wain, that, in the bosom of our sky,
Spins ever on its axle night and day,
With the bright summit of that horn, which swells
Due from the pole, round which the first wheel rolls,
To have ranged themselves in fashion of two signs
In Heaven, such as Ariadne made,
When death's chill seized her; and that one of them
Did compass in the other's beam; and both
In such sort whirl around, that each should tend
With opposite motion; and, conceiving thus,
Of that true constellation, and the dance
Twofold, that circled me, he shall attain
As 'twere the shadow; for things there as much
Surpass our usage, as the swiftest Heaven
Is swifter than the Chiana.[2] There was sung

[37] Rabanus Maurus, Archbishop of Mentz, 847, is placed at the head of the Latin writers of this age.

[38] Abbot of Flora in Calabria; whom the multitude revered as divinely inspired, and equal to the most illustrious prophets of ancient times.

[39] "A peer." St. Dominic.

[1] "Let him." "Whoever would conceive the sight that now presented itself to me, must imagine to himself fifteen of the brightest stars in heaven, together with seven stars of Arcturus Major and two of Arcturus Minor, ranged in two circles, one within the other, each resembling the crown of Ariadne, and moving round in opposite directions."

[2] See Hell, Canto xxix. 45.

No Bacchus, and no Io Pæan, but
Three Persons in the Godhead, and in one
Person that nature and the human join'd.
   The song and round were measured: and to us
Those saintly lights attended, happier made
At each new ministering. Then silence brake
Amid the accordant sons of Deity,
That luminary,[3] in which the wondrous life
Of the meek man of God[4] was told to me;
And thus it spake: "One ear[5] o' the harvest thresh'd,
And its grain safely stored, sweet charity
Invites me with the other to like toil.
   "Thou know'st, that in the bosom,[6] whence the rib
Was ta'en to fashion that fair cheek, whose taste
All the world pays for; and in that, which pierced
By the keen lance, both after and before
Such satisfaction offer'd as outweighs
Each evil in the scale; whate'er of light
To human nature is allow'd, must all
Have by His virtue been infused, who form'd
Both one and other: and thou thence admirest
In that I told thee, of beatitudes,
A second there is none to him enclosed
In the fifth radiance. Open now thine eyes
To what I answer thee; and thou shalt see
Thy deeming and my saying meet in truth,
As centre in the round. That[7] which dies not,
And that which can die, are but each the beam
Of that idea, which our Sovereign Sire
Engendereth loving; for that lively light,[8]

---

[3] Thomas Aquinas.

[4] St. Francis. See Canto xi. 25.

[5] "Having solved one of thy questions, I proceed to answer the other. Thou thinkest then that Adam and Christ were both endued with all the perfection of which the human nature is capable; and therefore wonderest at what has been said concerning Solomon."

[6] "Thou knowest that in the breast of Adam, whence the rib was taken to make that fair cheek of Eve, which, by tasting the apple, brought death into the world;

and also in the breast of Christ, which, being pierced by the lance, made satisfaction for the sins of the whole world; as much wisdom resided, as human nature was capable of: and thou dost therefore wonder that I should have spoken of Solomon as the wisest." See Canto x. 105.

[7] "That." Things, corruptible and incorruptible, are only emanations from the archetypal idea residing in the Divine Mind.

[8] The Word; the Son of God.

Which passeth from His splendour, not disjoin'd
From Him, nor from His love triune with them,[9]
Doth, through His bounty, congregate itself,
Mirror'd, as 'twere, in new existences;[10]
Itself unalterable, and ever one.

"Descending hence unto the lowest powers,[11]
Its energy so sinks, at last it makes
But brief contingencies; for so I name
Things generated, which the heavenly orbs
Moving, with seed or without seed, produce.
Their wax, and that which moulds it,[12] differ much:
And thence with lustre, more or less, it shows
The ideal stamp imprest: so that one tree,
According to his kind, hath better fruit,
And worse: and, at your birth, ye, mortal men,
Are in your talents various. Were the wax
Moulded with nice exactness, and the heaven[13]
In its disposing influence supreme,
The brightness of the seal[14] should be complete:
But nature renders it imperfect ever;
Resembling thus the artist, in his work,
Whose faltering hand is faithless to his skill.
Therefore,[15] if fervent Love dispose, and mark
The lustrous Image of the primal Virtue,
There all perfection is vouchsafed; and such
The clay[16] was made, accomplish'd with each gift,
That life can teem with; such the burden fill'd
The Virgin's bosom: so that I commend
Thy judgment, that the human nature ne'er
Was, or can be, such as in them it was.

"Did I advance no further than this point;
'How then had he no peer?' thou might'st reply.
But, that what now appears not, may appear

[9] "His love triune with them."
The Holy Ghost.
[10] Angels and human souls.
[11] Irrational life and brute matter.
[12] "Their wax, and that which moulds it." Matter, and the virtue or energy that acts on it.
[13] "The heaven." The influence of the planetary bodies.

[14] The brightness of the Divine idea before spoken of.
[15] "Therefore." Daniello remarks that our Poet intends this for a brief description of the Trinity: the primal virtue signifying the Father; the lustrous image, the Son; the fervent love, the Holy Ghost.
[16] "The clay." Adam.

Right plainly, ponder, who he was, and what
(When he was bidden 'Ask') the motive, sway'd
To his requesting. I have spoken thus,
That thou mayst see, he was a king, who ask'd[17]
For wisdom, to the end he might be king
Sufficient: not, the number to search out
Of the celestial movers; or to know,
If necessary with contingent e'er
Have made necessity; or whether that
Be granted, that first motion[18] is; or if,
Of the mid-circle,[19] can by art be made
Triangle, with its corner blunt or sharp.

"Whence, noting that, which I have said, and this,
Thou kingly prudence and that ken mayst learn,
At which the dart of my intention aims.
And, marking clearly, that I told thee, 'Risen,'
Thou shalt discern it only hath respect
To kings, of whom are many, and the good
Are rare. With this distinction take my words;
And they may well consist with that which thou
Of the first human father dost believe,
And of our well-beloved. And let this
Henceforth be lead unto thy feet, to make
Thee slow in motion, as a weary man,
Both to the 'yea' and to the 'nay' thou seest not.
For he among the fools is down full low,
Whose affirmation, or denial, is
Without distinction, in each case alike.
Since it befalls, that in most instances
Current opinion leans to false: and then
Affection bends the judgment to her ply.

"Much more than vainly doth he loose from shore,

[17] "Who ask'd." "He did not desire to know the number of the celestial intelligences, or to pry into the subtleties of logical, metaphysical, or mathematical science: but asked for that wisdom which might fit him for his kingly office."

[18] "That first motion." "If we must allow one first motion, which is not caused by other motion; a question resolved affirmatively by metaphysics, according to that principle, *repugnant in causis processus in infinitum*." Lombardi.

[19] "Of the mid-circle." "If in the half of the circle a rectilinear triangle can be described, one side of which shall be the diameter of the same circle, without its forming a right angle with the other two sides; which geometry shows to be impossible." Lombardi.

Since he returns not such as he set forth,
Who fishes for the truth and wanteth skill.
And open proofs of this unto the world
Have been afforded in Parmenides,
Melissus, Bryso,[20] and the crowd beside,
Who journey'd on, and knew not whither: so did
Sabellius, Arius,[21] and the other fools,
Who, like to scimitars,[22] reflected back
The scripture-image by distortion marr'd.

"Let not the people be too swift to judge;
As one who reckons on the blades in field,
Or e'er the crop be ripe. For I have seen
The thorn frown rudely all the winter long,
And after bear the rose upon its top;
And bark, that all her way across the sea
Ran straight and speedy, perish at the last
E'en in the haven's mouth. Seeing one steal,
Another bring his offering to the priest,
Let not[23] Dame Birtha and Sir Martin[24] thence
Into Heaven's counsels deem that they can pry;
For one of these may rise, the other fall."

[20]   "——Parmenides,
    Melissus, Bryso."
For the singular opinions entertained by
the two former of these heathen philosophers, see Diogenes Laertius, lib. ix.
[21] "Sabellius, Arius."   Well-known
heretics.
[22] "Scimitars."   Bertradon de la Broc-
quière, who wrote before Dante, informs
us that the wandering Arabs used their
scimitars as mirrors.

[23] "Let not."   "Let not shortsighted
mortals presume to decide on the future
doom of any man, from a consideration
of his present character and actions." This
is meant as an answer to the doubts
entertained respecting the salvation of
Solomon. See Canto x. 107.
[24] "Dame Birtha and Sir Martin."
Names put generally for persons who
have more curiosity than discretion.

CANTO XIV

ARGUMENT.—Solomon, who is one of the spirits in the inner circle, declares what the appearance of the blest will be after the resurrection of the body. Beatrice and Dante are translated into the fifth heaven, which is that of Mars; and here behold the souls of those, who had died fighting for the true faith, ranged in the sign of the cross, athwart which the spirits move to the sound of a melodious hymn.

FROM centre to the circle, and so back
From circle to the centre, water moves
In the round chalice, even as the blow
Impels it, inwardly, or from without.
Such was the image[1] glanced into my mind,
As the great spirit of Aquinum ceased;
And Beatrice, after him, her words
Resumed alternate: "Need there is (though yet
He tells it to you not in words, nor e'en
In thought) that he should fathom to its depth
Another mystery.   Tell him, if the light,
Wherewith your substance blooms, shall stay with you
Eternally, as now; and, if it doth,
How, when[2] ye shall regain your visible forms,
The sight may without harm endure the change,
That also tell."   As those, who in a ring
Tread the light measure, in their fitful mirth
Raise loud the voice, and spring with gladder bound;
Thus, at the hearing of that pious suit,
The saintly circles, in their tourneying
And wondrous note, attested new delight.
    Whoso laments, that we must doff this garb
Of frail mortality, thenceforth to live
Immortally above; he hath not seen
The sweet refreshing of that heavenly shower.[3]
    Him, who lives ever, and forever reigns
In mystic union of the three in one,
Unbounded, bounding all, each spirit thrice
Sang, with such melody, as, but to hear,
For highest merit were an ample meed.

[1] The voice of Thomas Aquinas proceeding from the circle to the centre; and that of Beatrice, from the centre to the circle.

[2] "When." When ye shall be again clothed with your bodies at the resurrection.

[3] That effusion of beatific light.

And from the lesser orb the goodliest light,[4]
With gentle voice and mild, such as perhaps
The Angel's once to Mary, thus replied:
"Long as the joy of Paradise shall last,
Our love shall shine around that raiment, bright
As fervent; fervent as, in vision, blest;
And that as far, in blessedness, exceeding,
As it hath grace, beyond its virtue, great.
Our shape, regarmented with glorious weeds
Of saintly flesh, must, being thus entire,
Show yet more gracious. Therefore shall increase
Whate'er, of light, gratuitous imparts
The Supreme Good; light, ministering aid,
The better to disclose His glory: whence,
The vision needs increasing, must increase
The fervour, which it kindles; and that too
The ray, that comes from it. But as the gleed
Which gives out flame, yet in its whiteness shines
More livelily than that, and so preserves
Its proper semblance; thus this circling sphere
Of splendour shall to view less radiant seem,
Than shall our fleshly robe, which yonder earth
Now covers. Nor will such excess of light
O'erpower us, in corporeal organs made
Firm, and susceptible of all delight."
    So ready and so cordial an "Amen"
Follow'd from either choir, as plainly spoke
Desire of their dead bodies; yet perchance
Not for themselves, but for their kindred dear,
Mothers and sires, and those whom best they loved,
Ere they were made imperishable flame.
    And lo! forthwith there rose up round about
A lustre, over that already there;
Of equal clearness, like the brightening up
Of the horizon. As at evening hour
Of twilight, new appearances through Heaven
Peer with faint glimmer, doubtfully descried;
So, there, new substances, methought, began
To rise in view beyond the other twain,

----

[4] "The goodliest light."   Solomon.

And wheeling, sweep their ampler circuit wide.
  O genuine glitter of eternal Beam!
With what a sudden whiteness did it flow,
O'erpowering vision in me. But so fair,
So passing lovely, Beatrice show'd,
Mind cannot follow it, nor words express
Her infinite sweetness. Thence mine eyes regain'd
Power to look up; and I beheld myself,
Sole with my lady, to more lofty bliss[5]
Translated: for the star, with warmer smile
Impurpled, well denoted our ascent.
  With all the heart, and with that tongue which speaks
The same in all, an holocaust I made
To God, befitting the new grace vouchsafed.
And from my bosom had not yet upsteam'd
The fuming of that incense, when I knew
The rite accepted. With such mighty sheen
And mantling crimson, in two listed rays
The splendours shot before me, that I cried,
"God of Sabaoth! that dost prank them thus!"
  As leads the galaxy from pole to pole,
Distinguish'd into greater lights and less,
Its pathway, which the wisest fail to spell;
So thickly studded, in the depth of Mars,
Those rays described the venerable sign,
That quadrants in the round conjoining frame.
  Here memory mocks the toil of genius. Christ
Beam'd on that cross; and pattern fails me now.
But whoso takes his cross, and follows Christ,
Will pardon me for that I leave untold,
When in the flecker'd dawning he shall spy
The glitterance of Christ. From horn to horn,
And 'tween the summit and the base, did move
Lights, scintillating, as they met and pass'd.
Thus oft are seen with ever-changeful glance,
Straight or athwart, now rapid and now slow,
The atomies of bodies, long or short,
To move along the sunbeam, whose slant line
Checkers the shadow interposed by art

    5 "To more lofty bliss." To the planet Mars.

Against the noontide heat. And as the chime
Of minstrel music, dulcimer, and harp
With many strings, a pleasant dinning makes
To him, who heareth not distinct the note;
So from the lights, which there appear'd to me,
Gather'd along the cross a melody,
That, indistinctly heard, with ravishment
Possess'd me. Yet I mark'd it was a hymn
Of lofty praises; for there came to me
"Arise," and "Conquer," as to one who hears
And comprehends not. Me such ecstasy
O'ercame, that never, till that hour, was thing
That held me in so sweet imprisonment.
  Perhaps my saying overbold appears,
Accounting less the pleasure of those eyes,
Whereon to look fulfilleth all desire.
But he, who is aware those living seals
Of every beauty work with quicker force,
The higher they are risen; and that there
I had not turn'd me to them; he may well
Excuse me that, whereof in my excuse
I do accuse me, and may own my truth;
That holy pleasure here not yet reveal'd,
Which grows in transport as we mount aloof.

CANTO XV

ARGUMENT.—The spirit of Cacciaguida, our Poet's ancestor, glides rapidly to the
foot of the cross; tells who he is; and speaks of the simplicity of the Florentines in his
days, since then much corrupted.

TRUE love, that ever shows itself as clear
     In kindness, as loose appetite in wrong,
     Silenced that lyre harmonious, and still'd
The sacred cords, that are by Heaven's right hand
Unwound and tighten'd. How to righteous prayers
Should they not hearken, who, to give me will
For praying, in accordance thus were mute?
He hath in sooth good cause for endless grief,
Who, for the love of thing that lasteth not,
Despoils himself forever of that love.

As oft along the still and pure serene,
At nightfall, glides a sudden trail of fire,
Attracting with involuntary heed
The eye to follow it, erewhile at rest;
And seems some star that shifted place in Heaven,
Only that, whence it kindles, none is lost,
And it is soon extinct: thus from the horn,
That on the dexter of the cross extends,
Down to its foot, one luminary ran
From mid the cluster shone there; yet no gem
Dropp'd from its foil: and through the beamy list,
Like flame in alabaster, glow'd its course.
 So forward stretch'd him (if of credence aught
Our greater muse may claim) the pious ghost
Of old Anchises, in the Elysian bower,
When he perceived his son. "O thou, my blood!
O most exceeding grace divine! to whom,
As now to thee, hath twice the heavenly gate
Been e'er unclosed?" So spake the light: whence I
Turn'd me toward him; then unto my dame
My sight directed: and on either side
Amazement waited me; for in her eyes
Was lighted such a smile, I thought that mine
Had dived unto the bottom of my grace
And of my bliss in Paradise. Forthwith,
To hearing and to sight grateful alike,
The spirit to his proem added things
I understood not, so profound he spake:
Yet not of choice, but through necessity,
Mysterious; for his high conception soar'd
Beyond the mark of mortals. When the flight
Of holy transport had so spent its rage,
That nearer to the level of our thought
The speech descended; the first sounds I heard
Were, "Blest be thou, Triunal Deity!
That hast such favour in my seed vouchsafed."
Then follow'd. "No unpleasant thirst, though long,
Which took me reading in the sacred book,
Whose leaves or white or dusky never change,
Thou hast allay'd, my son! within this light,

From whence my voice thou hear'st: more thanks to her,
Who, for such lofty mounting, has with plumes
Begirt thee. Thou dost deem thy thoughts to me
From Him transmitted, who is first of all,
E'en as all numbers ray from unity;
And therefore dost not ask me who I am,
Or why to thee more joyous I appear,
Than any other in this gladsome throng.
The truth is as thou deem'st; for in this life
Both less and greater in that Mirror look,
In which thy thoughts, or e'er thou think'st, are shown.
But, that the love, which keeps me wakeful ever,
Urging with sacred thirst of sweet desire,
May be contented fully; let thy voice,
Fearless, and frank, and jocund, utter forth
Thy will distinctly, utter forth the wish,
Whereto my ready answer stands decreed."
    I turn'd me to Beatrice; and she heard
Ere I had spoken, smiling an assent,
That to my will gave wings; and I began:
"To each among your tribe, what time ye kenn'd
The nature, in whom naught unequal dwells,
Wisdom and love were in one measure dealt;
For that they are so equal in the Sun,
From whence ye drew your radiance and your heat,
As makes all likeness scant. But will and means,
In mortals, for the cause ye well discern,
With unlike wings are fledged. A mortal, I
Experience inequality like this;
And therefore give no thanks, but in the heart,
For thy paternal greeting. This howe'er
I pray thee, living topaz! that ingemm'st
This precious jewel; let me hear thy name."
    "I am thy root,[1] O leaf! whom to expect
Even, hath pleased me." Thus the prompt reply
Prefacing, next it added: "He, of whom[2]

---

[1] "I am thy root." Cacciaguida, father to Alighieri, of whom our Poet was the great-grandson.

[2] "He, of whom." "Thy great-grand-father, Alighieri, has been in the first round of Purgatory more than a hundred years; and it is fit that thou by thy good deserts shouldst endeavor to shorten the time of his remaining there." His son Bellincione was living in 1266; and of

Thy kindred appellation comes, and who,
These hundred years and more, on its first ledge
Hath circuited the mountain, was my son,
And thy great-grandsire. Well befits, his long
Endurance should he shorten'd by thy deeds.

"Florence, within her ancient limit-mark,
Which calls her still[3] to matin prayers and noon,
Was chaste and sober, and abode in peace.
She had no armlets and no head-tires then;
No purfled dames; no zone, that caught the eye
More than the person did. Time was not yet,
When[4] at his daughter's birth the sire grew pale,
For fear the age and dowry should exceed,
On each side, just proportion. House was none
Void[5] of its family: nor yet had come
Sardanapalus,[6] to exhibit feats
Of chamber prowess. Montemalo[7] yet
O'er our suburban turret[8] rose; as much
To be surpast in fall, as in its rising.
I saw Bellincion Berti[9] walk abroad
In leathern girdle, and a clasp of bone;
And, with no artful colouring on her cheeks,

him was born the father of our Poet,
whom Benvenuto da Imola calls a lawyer
by profession.
  [3] The public clock being still within
the circuit of the ancient walls.
  [4] When the women were not married
at too early an age, and did not expect
too large a portion.
  [5] Through the civil wars and banish-
ments. Or he may mean that houses
were not formerly built merely for show,
nor of greater size than was necessary for
containing the families that inhabited
them.
  [6] The luxurious monarch of Assyria.
  [7] Either an elevated spot between Rome
and Viterbo; or Monte Mario, the site of
the villa Mellini, commanding a view of
Rome.
  [8] Uccellatojo, near Florence, whence
that city was discovered. Florence had
not yet vied with Rome in the grandeur
of her public buildings.
  [9] "Bellincion Berti." Hell, Canto xvi.

38, and notes. "And observe that in the
time of the said people (A. D. 1259),
and before and for a long time after, the
citizens of Florence lived soberly, on
coarse viands, and at little cost, and in
many customs and courtesies of life were
rude and unpolished; and dressed themselves and their women in coarse cloths:
many wore plain leather, without cloth
over it; bonnets on their heads; and all,
boots on the feet; and the Florentine women were without ornament; the better
sort content with a close gown of scarlet
cloth of Ypres or of camlet, bound with a
girdle in the ancient mode, and a mantle
lined with fur, and a hood to it, which
was worn on the head; the common sort
of women were clad in a coarse gown of
Cambrai in like manner . . . and with
their coarse way of living and poverty
[the Florentines] did greater and more
virtuous deeds than have been done in
our times with greater refinement and
wealth."—G. Villani, lib. vi. c. lxxi.

His lady leave the glass. The sons I saw
Of Nerli, and of Vecchio,[10] well content
With unrobed jerkin; and their good dames handling
The spindle and the flax: O happy they!
Each[11] sure of burial in her native land,
And none left desolate a-bed for France.
One waked to tend the cradle, hushing it
With sounds that lull'd the parent's infancy:
Another, with her maidens, drawing off
The tresses from the distaff, lectured them
Old tales of Troy, and Fesole, and Rome.
A Salterello and Cianghella[12] we
Had held as strange a marvel, as ye would
A Cincinnatus or Cornelia now.

"In such composed and seemly fellowship,
Such faithful and such fair equality,
In so sweet household, Mary[13] at my birth
Bestow'd me, call'd on with loud cries; and there,
In your old baptistery, I was made
Christian at once and Cacciaguida; as were
My brethren, Eliseo and Moronto.

"From Valdipado[14] came to me my spouse;
And hence thy surname grew. I follow'd then
The Emperor Conrad:[15] and his knighthood he
Did gird on me; in such good part he took
My valiant service. After him I went
To testify against that evil law,
Whose people,[16] by the Shepherd's fault, possess
Your right usurp'd. There I by that foul crew
Was disentangled from the treacherous world

[10] Two opulent families in Florence.
[11] "Each." "None fearful either of dying in banishment, or of being deserted by her husband on a scheme of traffic in France."
[12] The latter a shameless woman of the family of Tosa, married to Lito degli Alidosi of Imola: the former Lapo Salterello, a lawyer, with whom Dante was at variance. "We should have held an abandoned character, like these, as a great wonder, as ye would the contrary now."
[13] "Mary." The Virgin was invoked in the pains of child-birth. Purgatory, Canto xx. 21.
[14] Cacciaguida's wife, whose family name was Alighieri, came from Ferrara, called Val di Pado, from its being watered by the Po.
[15] "Conrad." The Emperor Conrad III, who died in 1152.
[16] The Mohammedans, who were left in the possession of the Holy Land, through the supineness of the Pope. See Canto iv. 123.

Whose base affection many a spirit soils;
And from the martyrdom came to this peace."

CANTO XVI

ARGUMENT.—Cacciaguida relates the time of his birth; and, describing the extent
of Florence when he lived there, recounts the names of the chief families who then
inhabited it. Its degeneracy, and subsequent disgrace, he attributes to the introduction
of families from the neighboring country and villages, and to their mixture with the
primitive citizens.

O SLIGHT respect of man's nobility!
 I never shall account it marvellous,
  That our infirm affection here below
Thou movest to boasting; when I could not chuse,
E'en in that region of unwarp'd desire,
In Heaven itself, but make my vaunt in thee.
Yet cloak thou art soon shorten'd; for that Time,
Unless thou be eked out from day to day,
Goes round thee with his shears. Resuming then,
With greeting[1] such as Rome was first to bear,
But since hath disaccustom'd, I began:
And Beatrice, that a little space
Was sever'd, smiled; reminding me of her,
Whose cough embolden'd (as the story holds)
To first offence the doubting Guenever.[2]
 "You are my sire," said I: "you give me heart
Freely to speak my thought: above myself
You raise me. Through so many streams with joy
My soul is fill'd, that gladness wells from it;
So that it bears the mighty tide, and bursts not.
Say then, my honour'd stem! what ancestors
Were those you sprang from, and what years were mark'd
In your first childhood? Tell me of the fold,[3]
That hath Saint John for guardian, what was then
Its state, and who in it were highest seated!"

[1] "With greeting." The Poet, who had
addressed the spirit, not knowing him to
be his ancestor, with a plain "Thou,"
now uses more ceremony, and calls him
"You," according to a custom of the
Romans in the latter times of the empire.

[2] Beatrice's smile reminded him of the
female servant who, by her coughing,
emboldened Queen Guenever to encour-
age Lancelot. See Hell, Canto v. 124.

[3] Florence, of which John the Baptist
was the patron saint.

As embers, at the breathing of the wind,
Their flame enliven; so that light I saw
Shine at my blandishments; and, as it grew
More fair to look on, so with voice more sweet,
Yet not in this our modern phrase, forthwith
It answer'd: "From the day,[4] when it was said
'Hail Virgin!' to the throes by which my mother,
Who now is sainted, lighten'd her of me
Whom she was heavy with, this fire had come
Five hundred times and fourscore, to relume
Its radiance underneath the burning foot
Of its own lion. They, of whom I sprang,
And I, had there our birth-place, where the last[5]
Partition of our city first is reach'd
By him that runs her annual game. Thus much
Suffice of my forefathers: who they were,
And whence they hither came, more honourable
It is to pass in silence than to tell.
All those, who at that time were there, betwixt
Mars and the Baptist, fit to carry arms,
Were but the fifth of them this day alive.
But then the citizen's blood, that now is mix'd
From Campi and Certaldo and Fighine,[6]
Ran purely through the last mechanic's veins.
O how much better were it, that these people[7]
Were neighbours to you; and that at Galluzzo
And at Trespiano ye should have your boundary;
Than to have them within, and bear the stench
Of Aguglione's hind, and Signa's,[8] him,
That hath his eye already keen for bartering.
Had not the people,[9] which of all the world

[4] From the incarnation of our Lord to the birth of Cacciaguida, the planet Mars had returned 580 times to the constellation of Leo, with which it is supposed to have a congenial influence. As Mars then completed his revolution in a period of forty-three days short of two years, Cacciaguida was born about 1090.

[5] The city was divided into four compartments. The Elisei, the ancestors of Dante, resided near the entrance of that named from the Porta S. Piero, which was the last reached by the competitor in the annual race at Florence.

[6] Country places near Florence.

[7] "That the inhabitants of the above-mentioned places had not been mixed with the citizens; nor the limits of Florence extended beyond Galluzzo and Trespiano."

[8] Baldo of Aguglione, and Bonifazio of Signa.

[9] If Rome had continued in her allegiance to the Emperor, and the Guelfi-

Degenerates most, been stepdame unto Cæsar,
But, as a mother to her son, been kind,
Such one, as hath become a Florentine,
And trades and traffics, hath been turn'd adrift
To Simifonte,[10] where his grandsire plied
The beggar's craft: the Conti were possest
Of Montemurlo[11] still: the Cerchi still
Were in Acone's parish: nor had haply
From Valdigreve passed the Buondelmonti.
The city's malady hath ever source
In the confusion of its persons, as
The body's, in variety of food:
And the blind bull falls with a steeper plunge,
Than the blind lamb: and oftentimes one sword
Doth more and better execution,
Than five. Mark Luni; Urbisaglia[12] mark;
How they are gone; and after them how go
Chiusi and Sinigaglia![13] and 't will seem
No longer new, or strange to thee, to hear
That families fail, when cities have their end.
All things that appertain to ye, like yourselves,
Are mortal: but mortality in some
Ye mark not; they endure so long, and you
Pass by so suddenly. And as the moon
Doth, by the rolling of her heavenly sphere,
Hide and reveal the strand unceasingly;
So fortune deals with Florence. Hence admire not
At what of them I tell thee, whose renown
Time covers, the first Florentines. I saw
The Ughi, Catilini, and Filippi,
The Alberichi, Greci, and Ormanni,
Now in their wane, illustrious citizens;
And great as ancient, of Sannella him,
With him of Arca saw, and Soldanieri,

Ghibelline factions had thus been prevented, Florence would not have been
polluted by a race of upstarts, nor lost
her best element.
   [10] A castle dismantled by the Florentines. The person here alluded to is not
known.

[11] The Conti Guidi, unable to defend
their castle from the Pistoians, sold it to
the state of Florence.
   [12] Cities formerly of importance, but
then fallen to decay.
   [13] The same.

And Ardinghi, and Bostichi. At the poop[14]
That now is laden with new felony
So cumbrous it may speedily sink the bark,
The Ravignani sat, of whom is sprung
The County Guido, and whoso hath since
His title from the famed Bellincion ta'en.

Fair governance was yet an art well prized
By him of Pressa: Galigaio show'd
The gilded hilt and pommel,[15] in his house;
The column, clothed with verrey,[16] still was seen
Unshaken; the Sacchetti still were great,
Giuochi, Fifanti, Galli, and Barucci,
With them[17] who blush to hear the bushel named.
Of the Calfucci still the branchy trunk
Was in its strength: and, to the curule chairs,
Sizii and Arrigucci[18] yet were drawn.

How mighty them[19] I saw, whom, since, their pride
Hath undone! And in all their goodly deeds
Florence was, by the bullets of bright gold,[20]
O'erflourish'd. Such the sires of those,[21] who now,
As surely as your church is vacant, flock
Into her consistory, and at leisure
There stall them and grow fat. The o'erweening broad,[22]
That plays the dragon after him that flees,
But unto such as turn and show the tooth,
Ay or the purse, is gentle as a lamb,
Was on its rise, but yet so slight esteem'd,
That Ubertino of Donati grudged
His father-in-law should yoke him to its tribe.

[14] The Cerchi, Dante's enemies, had succeeded to the houses over the gate of St. Peter.

[15] The symbols of knighthood.

[16] The arms of the Pigli, or as some wrote it, the Billi.

[17] Either the Chiaramontesi, or the Tosinghi; one of which had committed a fraud in measuring out the wheat from the public granary. See Purgatory, Canto xii. 99.

[18] "These families still obtained the magistracies."

[19] "Them." The Uberti.

[20] The arms of the Abbati, or of the Lamberti.

[21] Of the Visdomini, the Tosinghi, and the Cortigiani, who, being sprung from the founders of the bishopric of Florence, are the curators of its revenues, which they do not spare, whenever it becomes vacant.

[22] This family was so little esteemed that Ubertino Donato, of the same stock as his wife, was offended with his father-in-law, Bellincion Berti, for giving another daughter to one of them.

Already Caponsacco[23] had descended
Into the mart from Fesole: and Giuda
And Infangato[24] were good citizens.
A thing incredible I tell, though true:
The gateway, named from those of Pera, led
Into the narrow circuit of your wells.
Each one, who bears the sightly quarterings
Of the great Baron,[25] (he whose name and worth
The festival of Thomas still revives,)
His knighthood and his privilege retain'd;
Albeit one,[26] who borders them with gold,
This day is mingled with the common herd.
In Borgo yet the Gualterotti dwelt,
And Importuni;[27] well for its repose,
Had it still lack'd of newer neighbourhood.[28]
The house,[29] from whence your tears have had their spring,
Through the just anger, that hath murder'd ye
And put a period to your gladsome days,
Was honour'd; it, and those consorted with it.
O Buondelmonte! what ill counselling
Prevail'd on thee to break the plighted bond?
Many, who now are weeping, would rejoice,
Had God to Ema[30] given thee, the first time
Thou near our city camest. But so was doom'd:

23 The Caponsacchi, who had removed
from Fiesole.
24 Guida Guidi and the family of In-
fangati.
25 The Marchese Ugo, who resided at
Florence as lieutenant of the Emperor
Otho III, gave many of the chief families
license to bear his arms. A vision is related, in consequence of which he sold
all his possessions in Germany, and
founded seven abbeys, in one whereof his
memory was celebrated at Florence on
St. Thomas's day. "The marquis, when
hunting, strayed away from his people,
and, wandering through a forest, came to
a smithy, where he saw black and deformed men tormenting others with fire
and hammers; and, asking the meaning
of this, he was told that they were condemned souls, who suffered this punishment, and that the soul of the Mar-

chese Ugo was doomed to suffer the same,
if he did not repent. Struck with horror,
he commended himself to the Virgin
Mary; and soon after founded the seven
religious houses."
26 Giano della Bella, of one of the
families thus distinguished, who no longer
retained his place among the nobility,
and had yet added to his arms a bordure
or.
27 Two families in the compartment of
the city called Borgo.
28 Some understand this of the Bardi;
and others, of the Buondelmonti.
29 "The house." Of Amidei.
30 "To Ema." "It had been well for
the city if thy ancestor had been drowned
in the Ema when he crossed that stream
on his way from Montebuono to Florence."

Florence! on that maim'd stone[31] which guards the bridge
The victim, when thy peace departed, fell.
"With these and others like to them, I saw
Florence in such assured tranquillity,
She had no cause at which to grieve: with these
Saw her so glorious and so just, that ne'er
The lily[32] from the lance had hung reverse,
Or through division been with vermeil dyed."

CANTO XVII

ARGUMENT.—Cacciaguida predicts to our Poet his exile and the calamities he had
to infer; and, lastly, exhorts him to write the present poem.

SUCH as the youth,[1] who came to Clymene,
    To certify himself of that reproach
    Which had been fasten'd on him, (he whose end,
Still makes the fathers chary to their sons),
E'en such was I; nor unobserved was such
Of Beatrice, and that saintly lamp,[2]
Who had erewhile for me his station moved;
When thus my lady: "Give thy wish free vent,
That it may issue, bearing true report
Of the mind's impress: not that aught thy words
May to our knowledge add, but to the end
That thou mayst use thyself to own thy thirst,[3]
And men may mingle for thee when they hear."
    "O plant, from whence I spring! revered and loved!
Who soar'st so high a pitch, that thou as clear,[4]
As earthly thought determines two obtuse
In one triangle not contain'd, so clear
Dost see contingencies, ere in themselves
Existent, looking at the point[5] whereto

[31] Near the remains of the statue of Mars, Buondelmonti was slain, as if he had been a victim to the god; and Florence had not since known the blessing of peace.

[32] The arms of Florence had never hung reversed on the spear of her enemies; nor been changed from argent to gules; as they afterward were, when the Guelfi gained the predominance.

[1] Phaëton, who came to his mother Clymene, to inquire if he were indeed the son of Apollo.

[2] Cacciaguida.

[3] "That thou mayst obtain from others a solution of any doubt that may occur to thee."

[4] "Thou beholdest future events with the same clearness of evidence that we discern the simplest mathematical demonstrations."

[5] The divine nature.

All times are present; I, the whilst I scaled
With Virgil the soul-purifying mount
And visited the nether world of woe,
Touching my future destiny have heard
Words grievous, though I feel me on all sides
Well squared to fortune's blows. Therefore my will
Were satisfied to know the lot awaits me;
The arrow, seen beforehand, slacks his flight."
    So said I to the brightness, which erewhile
To me had spoken; and my will declared,
As Beatrice will'd, explicitly.
Nor with oracular response obscure,
Such as, or e'er the Lamb of God was slain,
Beguiled the credulous nations: but, in terms
Precise, and unambiguous lore, replied
The spirit of paternal love, enshrined,
Yet in his smile apparent; and thus spake:
"Contingency,[6] whose verge extendeth not
Beyond the tablet of your mortal mold,
Is all depictured in the eternal sight;
But hence deriveth not necessity,[7]
More than the tall ship, hurried down the flood,
Is driven by the eye that looks on it.
From thence,[8] as to the ear sweet harmony
From organ comes, so comes before mine eye
The time prepared for thee. Such as driven out
From Athens, by his cruel stepdame's[9] wiles,
Hippolytus departed; such must thou
Depart from Florence. This they wish, and this
Contrive, and will ere long effectuate, there,[10]
Where gainful merchandize is made of Christ
Throughout the live-long day. The common cry,[11]
Will, as 'tis ever wont, affix the blame

---

[6] "Contingency." Contingency, which
has no place beyond the limits of the
material world.

[7] "The evidence with which we see
casual events portrayed in the source of
all truth, no more necessitates those
events, than does the image, reflected in
the sight by a ship sailing down a stream,
necessitate the motion of the vessel."

[8] From the view of the Deity Himself.

[9] Phædra.

[10] "There." At Rome, where the expulsion of Dante's party from Florence
was then plotting, in 1300.

[11] The multitude will, as usual, be ready
to blame those who are sufferers, whose
cause will at last be vindicated by the
overthrow of their enemies.

Unto the party injured: but the truth
Shall, in the vengeance it dispenseth, find
A faithful witness. Thou shalt leave each thing
Beloved most dearly: this is the first shaft
Shot from the bow of exile. Thou shalt prove
How salt the savour is of other's bread;
How hard the passage, to descend and climb
By other's stairs. But that shall gall thee most,
Will be the worthless and vile company,
With whom thou must be thrown into these straits.
For all ungrateful, impious all, and mad,
Shall turn 'gainst thee: but in a little while,
Theirs,[12] and not thine, shall be the crimson'd brow.
Their course shall so evince their brutishness,
To have ta'en thy stand apart shall well become thee.
    "First refuge thou must find, first place of rest,
In the great Lombard's[13] courtesy, who bears,
Upon the ladder perch'd, the sacred bird.
He shall behold thee with such kind regard,
That 'twixt ye two, the contrary to that
Which 'falls 'twixt other men, the granting shall
Forerun the asking. With him shalt thou see
That mortal,[14] who was at his birth imprest
So strongly from this star, that of his deeds
The nations shall take note. His unripe age
Yet holds him from observance; for these wheels
Only nine years have compasst him about.
But, ere the Gascon[15] practise on great Harry,[16]
Sparkles of virtue shall shoot forth in him,
In equal scorn of labours and of gold
His bounty shall be spread abroad so widely,
As not to let the tongues, e'en of his foes,
Be idle in its praise. Look thou to him,
And his beneficence: for he shall cause
Reversal of their lot to many people;

[12] "They shall be ashamed of the part they have taken against thee."

[13] Either Bartolommeo della Scala or Alboino his brother. Their coat-of-arms was a ladder and an eagle.

[14] "That mortal." Can Grande della Scala, born under the influence of Mars, but at this time only nine years old. He was a son of Alberto della Scala.

[15] "The Gascon." Pope Clement V.

[16] The Emperor Henry VII.

Rich men and beggars interchanging fortunes.
And thou shalt bear this written in thy soul,
Of him, but tell it not:" and things he told
Incredible to those who witness them;
Then added: "So interpret thou, my son,
What hath been told thee.—Lo! the ambushment
That a few circling seasons hide for thee.
Yet envy not thy neighbours: time extends
Thy span beyond their treason's chastisement."

Soon as the saintly spirit, by silence, mark'd
Completion of that web, which I had stretch'd
Before it, warp'd for weaving; I began,
As one, who in perplexity desires
Counsel of other, wise, benign and friendly:
"My father! well I mark how time spurs on
Toward me, ready to inflict the blow,
Which falls most heavily on him who most
Abandoneth himself. Therefore 'tis good
I should forecast, that, driven from the place[17]
Most dear to me, I may not lose myself [18]
All other by my song. Down through the world
Of infinite mourning; and along the mount,
From whose fair height my lady's eyes did lift me;
And, after, through this Heaven, from light to
        light;
Have I learnt that, which if I tell again,
It may with many wofully disrelish:
And, if I am a timid friend to truth,
I fear my life may perish among those,
To whom these days shall be of ancient date."

The brightness, where enclosed the treasure[19] smiled,
Which I had found there, first shone glisteringly,
Like to a golden mirror in the sun;
Next answer'd: "Conscience, dimm'd or by its own
Or other's shame, will feel thy saying sharp.
Thou, notwithstanding, all deceit removed,

---

[17] "The place." Our poet here discovers both that Florence, much as he inveighs against it, was still the dearest object of his affections, and that it was not without some scruple he indulged his satirical vein.

[18] "That being driven out of my country, I may not deprive myself of every other place by the boldness with which I expose in my writings the vices of mankind."

[19] "The treasure." Cacciaguida.

See the whole vision be made manifest;
And let them wince, who have their withers wrung.
What though, when tasted first, thy voice shall prove
Unwelcome: on digestion, it will turn
To vital nourishment. The cry thou raisest,
Shall, as the wind doth, smite the proudest summits;
Which is of honour no light argument.
For this, there only have been shown to thee,
Throughout these orbs, the mountain, and the deep,
Spirits, whom fame hath note of. For the mind
Of him, who hears, is loth to acquiesce
And fix its faith, unless the instance brought
Be palpable, and proof apparent urge."

CANTO XVIII

ARGUMENT.—Dante sees the souls of many renowned warriors and crusaders in the planet Mars; and then ascends with Beatrice to Jupiter, the sixth heaven, in which he finds the souls of those who had administered justice rightly in the world, so disposed, as to form the figure of an eagle. The Canto concludes with an invective against the avarice of the clergy, and especially of the pope.

NOW in his word, sole, ruminating, joy'd
That blessed spirit: and I fed on mine,
Tempering the sweet with bitter. She mean-
    while,
Who led me unto God, admonish'd: "Muse
On other thoughts: bethink thee, that near Him
I dwell, who recompenseth every wrong."
   At the sweet sounds of comfort straight I turn'd;
And, in the saintly eyes what love was seen,
I leave in silence here, nor through distrust
Of my words only, but that to such bliss
The mind remounts not without aid. Thus much
Yet may I speak; that, as I gazed on her,
Affection found no room for other wish.
While the everlasting pleasure, that did full
On Beatrice shine, with second view
From her fair countenance my gladden'd soul
Contented; vanquishing me with a beam
Of her soft smile, she spake: "Turn thee, and list.
These eyes are not thy only Paradise."
   As here, we sometimes in the looks may see

The affection mark'd, when that its sway hath ta'en
The spirit wholly; thus the hallow'd light,[1]
To whom I turn'd, flashing, bewray'd its will
To talk yet further with me, and began:
"On this fifth lodgment of the tree,[2] whose life
Is from its top, whose fruit is ever fair
And leaf unwithering, blessed spirits abide,
That were below, ere they arrived in Heaven,
So mighty in renown, as every muse
Might grace her triumph with them. On the horns
Look, therefore, of the cross: he whom I name,
Shall there enact, as doth in summer cloud
Its nimble fire." Along the cross I saw,
At the repeated name of Joshua,
A splendour gliding; nor, the word was said,
Ere it was done: then, at the naming, saw,
Of the great Maccabee,[3] another move
With whirling speed; and gladness was the scourge
Unto that top. The next for Charlemain
And for the peer Orlando, two my gaze
Pursued, intently, as the eye pursues
A falcon flying. Last, along the cross,
William, and Renard,[4] and Duke Godfrey[5] drew
My ken, and Robert Guiscard.[6] And the soul
Who spake with me, among the other lights
Did move away, and mix; and with the quire
Of heavenly songsters proved his tuneful skill.

To Beatrice on my right I bent,
Looking for intimation, or by word
Or act, what next behoved; and did descry
Such mere effulgence in her eyes, such joy,
It pass'd all former wont. And, as by sense
Of new delight, the man, who perseveres
In good deeds, doth perceive, from day to day,

---

[1] In which the spirit of Cacciaguida was enclosed.

[2] Mars, the fifth of the heavens.

[3] Judas Maccabæus.

[4] Probably not William II of Orange, and his kinsman Raimbaud, two of the crusaders under Godfrey of Bouillon, but rather the two more celebrated heroes in the age of Charlemain. The former, William I of Orange, supposed to have been the founder of the present illustrious family of that name, died about 808. The latter has been celebrated by Ariosto, under the name of Rinaldo.

[5] Godfrey of Bouillon.

[6] See Hell, Canto xxviii. 12.

His virtue growing; I e'en thus perceived,
Of my ascent, together with the Heaven,
The circuit widen'd; noting the increase
Of beauty in that wonder. Like the change
In a brief moment on some maiden's cheek,
Which, from its fairness, doth discharge the weight
Of pudency, that stain'd it; such in her,
And to mine eyes so sudden was the change,
Through silvery whiteness of that temperate star,
Whose sixth orb now enfolded us. I saw,
Within that Jovial cresset, the clear sparks
Of love, that reign'd there, fashion to my view
Our language. And as birds, from river banks
Arisen, now in round, now lengthen'd troop,
Array them in their flight, greeting, as seems,
Their new-found pastures; so, within the lights,
The saintly creatures flying, sang; and made
Now D, now I, now L, figured i' the air.
First singing to their notes they moved; then, one
Becoming of these signs, a little while
Did rest them, and were mute. O nymph divine
Of Pegasean race! who souls, which thou
Inspirest, makest glorious and long-lived, as they
Cities and realms by thee; thou with thyself
Inform me; that I may set forth the shapes,
As fancy doth present them: be thy power
Display'd in this brief song. The characters,
Vocal and consonant, were five-fold seven.
In order, each, as they appear'd, I mark'd.
Diligite Justitiam, the first,
Both verb and noun all blazon'd; and the extreme,
Qui judicatis terram. In the M
Of the fifth word they held their station;
Making the star seem silver streak'd with gold.
And on the summit of the M, I saw
Descending other lights, that rested there,
Singing, methinks, their bliss and primal good.
Then, as at shaking of a lighted brand,
Sparkles innumerable on all sides
Rise scatter'd, source of augury to the unwise;

Thus more than thousand twinkling lustres hence
Seem'd reascending; and a higher pitch
Some mounting, and some less, e'en as the sun,
Which kindleth them, decreed. And when each one
Had settled in his place; the head and neck
Then saw I of an eagle, livelily
Graved in that streaky fire. Who painteth there,[7]
Hath none to guide Him: of Himself He guides:
And every line and texture of the nest
Doth own from Him the virtue fashions it.
The other bright beatitude,[8] that seem'd
Erewhile, with lilied crowning, well content
To over-canopy the M, moved forth,
Following gently the impress of the bird.

   Sweet star; what glorious and thick-studded gems
Declared to me our justice on the earth
To be the effluence of that Heaven, which thou,
Thyself a costly jewel, dost inlay.
Therefore I pray the Sovran Mind, from whom
Thy motion and thy virtue are begun,
That He would look from whence the fog doth rise,
To vitiate thy beam; so that once more[9]
He may put forth his hand 'gainst such, as drive
Their traffic in that sanctuary, whose walls
With miracles and martyrdoms were built.
   Ye host of Heaven, whose glory I survey!
O beg ye grace for those, that are, on earth,
All after ill example gone astray.
War once had for his instrument the sword:
But now 'tis made, taking the bread away,[10]
Which the good Father locks from none.—And thou,
That writest but to cancel,[11] think, that they,
Who for the vineyard, which thou wastest, died,
Peter and Paul, live yet, and mark thy doings.

---

[7] "Who painteth there." The Deity himself.

[8] The band of spirits.

[9] That he may again drive out those who buy and sell in the temple.

[10] "Taking the bread away." Excommunication, or interdiction of the Eucharist, is now employed as a weapon of warfare.

[11] "That writest but to cancel." "And thou, Pope Boniface, who writest thy ecclesiastical censures for no other purpose than to be paid for revoking them."

Thou hast good cause to cry, "My heart so cleaves
To him,[12] that lived in solitude remote,
And for a dance was dragg'd to martyrdom,
I wist not of the Fisherman nor Paul."

CANTO XIX

ARGUMENT.—The eagle speaks as with one voice proceeding from a multitude of spirits, that compose it; and declares the cause for which it is exalted to that state of glory. It then solves a doubt, which our Poet had entertained, respecting the possibility of salvation without belief in Christ; exposes the inefficacy of a mere profession of such belief; and prophesies the evil appearance that many Christian potentates will make at the day of judgment.

BEFORE my sight appear'd, with open wings,
The beauteous image; in fruition sweet,
Gladdening the thronged spirits. Each did seem
A little ruby, whereon so intense
The sun-beam glow'd, that to mine eyes it came
In clear refraction. And that, which next
Befalls me to portray, voice hath not utter'd,
Nor hath ink written, nor in fantasy
Was e'er conceived. For I beheld and heard
The beak discourse; and, what intention form'd
Of many, singly as of one express,
Beginning: "For that I was just and piteous,
I am exalted to this height of glory,
The which no wish exceeds: and there on earth
Have I my memory left, e'en by the bad
Commended, while they leave its course untrod."
Thus is one heat from many embers felt;
As in that image many were the loves,
And one the voice, that issued from them all:
Whence I address'd them: "O perennial flowers
Of gladness everlasting! that exhale
In single breath your odours manifold;
Breathe now: and let the hunger be appeased,
That with great craving long hath held my soul,
Finding no food on earth. This well I know;

---

[12] "To him." The coin of Florence was stamped with the impression of John the Baptist: and, for this, the avaricious Pope is made to declare that he felt more devotion, than either for Peter or Paul.

That if there be in Heaven a realm, that shows
In faithful mirror the celestial Justice,
Yours without veil reflects it. Ye discern
The heed, wherewith I do prepare myself
To hearken; ye, the doubt, that urges me
With such inveterate craving." Straight I saw,
Like to a falcon issuing from the hood,
That rears his head, and claps him with his wings,
His beauty and his eagerness bewraying;
So saw I move that stately sign, with praise
Of grace divine inwoven, and high song
Of inexpressive joy. "He," it began,
"Who turn'd His compass on the world's extreme,
And in that space so variously hath wrought,
Both openly and in secret; in such wise
Could not, through all the universe, display
Impression of His glory, that the Word
Of His omniscience should not still remain
In infinite excess. In proof whereof,
He first through pride supplanted, who was sum
Of each created being, waited not
For light celestial; and abortive fell.
Whence needs each lesser nature is but scant
Receptacle unto that Good, which knows
No limit, measured by itself alone.
Therefore your sight, of the omnipresent Mind
A single beam, its origin must own
Surpassing far its utmost potency.
The ken, your world is gifted with, descends
In the everlasting Justice as low down,
As eye doth in the sea; which, though it mark
The bottom from the shore, in the wide main
Discerns it not; and ne'ertheless it is;
But hidden through its deepness. Light is none,
Save that which cometh from the pure serene
Of ne'er disturbed ether: for the rest,
'Tis darkness all; or shadow of the flesh,
Or else its poison. Here confess reveal'd
That covert, which hath hidden from thy search
The living justice, of the which thou madest

Such frequent question; for thou said'st—'A man
Is born on Indus' banks, and none is there
Who speaks of Christ, nor who doth read nor write;
And all his inclinations and his acts,
As far as human reason sees, are good;
And he offendeth not in word or deed:
But unbaptized he dies, and void of faith.
Where is the justice that condemns him? where
His blame, if he believeth not?'—What then,
And who art thou, that on the stool wouldst sit
To judge at distance of a thousand miles
With the short-sighted vision of a span?
To him, who subtilizes thus with me,
There would assuredly be room for doubt
Even to wonder, did not the safe word
Of Scripture hold supreme authority.
  "O animals of clay! O spirits gross!
The Primal Will,[1] that in itself is good,
Hath from itself, the chief Good, ne'er been moved.
Justice consists in consonance with it,
Derivable by no created good,
Whose very cause depends upon its beam."

  As on her nest the stork, that turns about
Unto her young, whom lately she hath fed,
Whiles they with upward eyes do look on her;
So lifted I my gaze; and, bending so,
The ever-blessed image waved its wings,
Labouring with such deep counsel. Wheeling round
It warbled, and did say: "As are my notes
To thee, who understand'st them not; such is
The eternal judgment unto mortal ken."

  Then still abiding in that ensign ranged,
Wherewith the Romans overawed the world,
Those burning splendours of the Holy Spirit
Took up the strain; and thus it spake again:
"None ever hath ascended to this realm,
Who hath not a believer been in Christ,
Either before or after the blest limbs
Were nail'd upon the wood. But lo! of those

            [1] The divine will.

Who call 'Christ, Christ,'[2] there shall be many found,
In judgment, further off from Him by far,
Than such to whom His name was never known.
Christians like these the Æthiop[3] shall condemn:
When that the two assemblages shall part;
One rich eternally, the other poor.

"What may the Persians say unto your kings,
When they shall see that volume,[4] in the which
All their dispraise is written, spread to view?
There amidst Albert's[5] works shall that be read,
Which will give speedy motion to the pen,
When Prague[6] shall mourn her desolated realm.
There shall be read the woe, that he[7] doth work
With his adulterate money on the Seine,
Who by the tusk will perish; there be read
The thirsting pride, that maketh fool alike
The English and Scot,[8] impatient of their bound.
There shall be seen the Spaniard's luxury;[9]
The delicate living there of the Bohemian,[10]
Who still to worth has been a willing stranger.
The halter of Jerusalem[11] shall see
A unit for his virtue; for his vices,
No less a mark than million. He,[12] who guards

[2] "Not every one that saith unto me, Lord, Lord, shall enter into the kingdom of heaven."—Matt. vii. 21.

[3] "The Æthiop." "The men of Nineveh shall rise in judgment with this generation, and shall condemn it."—Matt. xii. 41.

[4] "That volume." "And I saw the dead, small and great, stand before God; and the books were opened: and another book was opened, which is the book of life; and the dead were judged out of those things which were written in the books, according to their works."—Rev. xx. 12.

[5] "Albert." Purgatory, Canto vi. 98.

[6] "Prague." The eagle predicts the devastation of Bohemia by Albert, which happened soon after this time, when that Emperor obtained the kingdom for his eldest son Rodolph.

[7] "He." Philip IV of France, after the battle of Courtrai, 1302, in which the French were defeated by the Flemings, raised the nominal value of the coin. This King died in consequence of his horse being thrown to the ground by a wild boar, in 1314.

[8] "The English and Scot." He adverts to the disputes between John Baliol and Edward I, the latter of whom is commended in the Purgatory, Canto vii. 130.

[9] "The Spaniard's luxury." It seems probable that the allusion is to Ferdinand IV, who came to the crown in 1295, and died in 1312, at the age of twenty-four, in consequence, as it was supposed, of his extreme intemperance.

[10] "The Bohemian." Wenceslaus II. Purgatory, Canto vii. 99.

[11] "The halter of Jerusalem." Charles II of Naples and Jerusalem, who was lame.

[12] "He." Frederick of Sicily, son of Peter III of Arragon. Purgatory, Canto vii. 117. The isle of fire is Sicily, where was the tomb of Anchises.

The isle of fire by old Anchises honour'd,
Shall find his avarice there and cowardice;
And better to denote his littleness,
The writing must be letters maim'd, that speak
Much in a narrow space. All there shall know
His uncle[13] and his brother's [14] filthy doings,
Who so renown'd a nation and two crowns
Have bastardized. And they, of Portugal[15]
And Norway,[16] there shall be exposed, with him
Of Ratza,[17] who hath counterfeited ill
The coin of Venice. O blest Hungary![18]
If thou no longer patiently abidest
Thy ill-entreating: and, O blest Navarre![19]
If with thy mountainous girdle[20] thou wouldst arm thee.
In earnest of that day, e'en now are heard
Wailings and groans in Famagosta's streets
And Nicosia's,[21] grudging at their beast,
Who keepeth even footing with the rest."

[13] "His uncle." James, King of Majorca and Minorca, brother to Peter III.

[14] "His brother." James II of Arragon, who died in 1327. See Purgatory, Canto vii. 117.

[15] "Of Portugal." In the time of Dante, Dionysius was King of Portugal. He died in 1325, after a reign of nearly forty-six years, and does not seem to have deserved the stigma here fastened on him. Perhaps the rebellious son of Dionysius may be alluded to.

[16] "Norway." Haquin, King of Norway, is probably meant; who having given refuge to the murderers of Eric VII, King of Denmark, A. D. 1288, commenced a war against his successor, Eric VIII, "which continued for nine years, almost to the utter ruin and destruction of both kingdoms."

[17]   "————— him
           Of Ratza."
One of the dynasty of the house of Nemagna, which ruled the Kingdom of Rassia or Ratza, in Sclavonia, from 1161

to 1371, and whose history may be found in Mauro Orbino. Uladislaus appears to have been the sovereign in Dante's time; but the disgraceful forgery, adverted to in the text, is not recorded by the historian.

[18] "Hungary." The kingdom of Hungary was about this time disputed by Carobert, son of Charles Martel, and Wenceslaus, prince of Bohemia, son of Wenceslaus II.

[19] "Navarre." Navarre was now under the yoke of France. It soon after (in 1328) followed the advice of Dante, and had a monarch of its own.

[20] "Mountainous girdle." The Pyrenees.

[21]   "————— Famagosta's streets
          And Nicosia's."
Cities in the Kingdom of Cyprus, at that time ruled by Henry VII, a pusillanimous prince. The meaning appears to be, that the complaints made by those cities of their weak and worthless governor may be regarded as an earnest of his condemnation at the last doom.

CANTO XX

ARGUMENT.—The eagle celebrates the praise of certain kings, whose glorified spirits form the eye of the bird. In the pupil is David; and, in the circle round it, Trajan, Hezekiah, Constantine, William II of Sicily, and Ripheus. It explains to our Poet how the souls of those whom he supposed to have had no means of believing in Christ, came to be in Heaven; and concludes with an admonition against presuming to fathom the counsels of God.

WHEN, disappearing from our hemisphere,
    The world's enlightener vanishes, and day
    On all sides wasteth; suddenly the sky,
Erewhile irradiate only with his beam,
Is yet again unfolded, putting forth
Innumerable lights wherein one shines.
Of such vicissitude in Heaven I thought;
As the great sign,[1] that marshaleth the world
And the world's leaders, in the blessed beak
Was silent: for that all those living lights,
Waxing in splendour, burst forth into songs,
Such as from memory glide and fall away.
    Sweet Love, that doth apparel thee in smiles!
How lustrous was thy semblance in those sparkles,
Which merely are from holy thoughts inspired.
    After[2] the precious and bright beaming stones,
That did ingem the sixth light, ceased the chiming
Of their angelic bells; methought I heard
The murmuring of a river, that doth fall
From rock to rock transpicuous, making known
The richness of his spring-head: and as sound
Of cittern, at the fret-board, or of pipe,
Is, at the wind-hole, modulate and tuned;
Thus up the neck, as it were hollow, rose
That murmuring of the eagle; and forthwith
Voice there assumed; and thence along the beak
Issued in form of words, such as my heart
Did look for, on whose tables I inscribed them.
    "The part in me, that sees and bears the sun
In mortal eagles," it began, "must now

[1] The eagle, the imperial ensign.
[2] "After." "After the spirits in the sixth planet (Jupiter) had ceased their singing."

Be noted steadfastly: for, of the fires
That figure me, those, glittering in mine eye,
Are chief of all the greatest. This, that shines
Midmost for pupil, was the same who[3] sang
The Holy Spirit's song, and bare about
The ark from town to town: now doth he know
The merit of his soul-impassion'd strains
By their well-fitted guerdon. Of the five,
That make the circle of the vision, he,[4]
Who to the beak is nearest, comforted
The widow for her son: now doth he know,
How dear it costeth not to follow Christ;
Both from experience of this pleasant life,
And of its opposite. He next,[5] who follows
In the circumference, for the over-arch,
By true repenting slack'd the pace of death:
Now knoweth he, that the decrees of Heaven[6]
Alter not, when, through pious prayer below,
To-day is made to-morrow's destiny.
The other following,[7] with the laws and me,
To yield the Shepherd room, pass'd o'er[8] to Greece;
From good intent, producing evil fruit:
Now knoweth he, how all the ill, derived
From his well doing, doth not harm him aught;
Though it have brought destruction on the world.
That, which thou seest in the under bow,
Was William,[9] whom that land bewails, which weeps
For Charles and Frederick living: now he knows,
How well is loved in Heaven the righteous king;
Which he betokens by his radiant seeming.
Who, in the erring world beneath, would deem

[3] "Who." David.
[4] Trajan. See Purgatory, x. 68.
[5] "He next." Hezekiah.
[6] The eternal counsels of God are indeed immutable, though they appear to us men to be altered by the prayers of the pious.
[7] Constantine. No passage in which Dante's opinion of the evil that had arisen from the mixture of the civil with the ecclesiastical power is more unequivocally declared.

[8] Left the Roman State to the Pope, and transferred the seat of the empire to Constantinople.
[9] William II, called "the Good," King of Sicily, at the latter part of the twelfth century. He was of the Norman line of sovereigns. His loss was as much the subject of regret in his dominions, as the presence of Charles II of Anjou, and Frederick of Arragon, was of sorrow.

That Trojan Ripheus,[10] in this round, was set,
Fifth of the saintly splendours? now he knows
Enough of that, which the world cannot see;
The grace divine: albeit e'en his sight
Reach not its utmost depth." Like to the lark,
That warbling in the air expatiates long,
Then, trilling out his last sweet melody,
Drops, satiate with the sweetness; such appear'd
That image, stampt by the everlasting pleasure,
Which fashions, as they are, all things that be.

I, though my doubting were as manifest,
As is through glass the hue that mantles it,
In silence waited not; for to my lips
"What things are these?" involuntary rush'd,
And forced a passage out: whereat I mark'd
A sudden lightening and new revelry.
The eye was kindled; and the blessed sign,
No more to keep me wondering and suspense,
Replied: "I see that thou believest these things,
Because I tell them, but discern'st not how;
So that thy knowledge waits not on thy faith:
As one, who knows the name of thing by rote,
But is a stranger to its properties,
Till other's tongue reveal them. Fervent love,
And lively hope, with violence assail
The Kingdom of the Heavens, and overcome
The will of the Most High; not in such sort
As man prevails o'er man; but conquers it,
Because 'tis willing to be conquer'd; still,
Though conquer'd, by its mercy, conquering.

"Those, in the eye who live the first and fifth,
Cause thee to marvel, in that thou behold'st
The region of the Angels deck'd with them.
They quitted not their bodies, as thou deem'st,
Gentiles, but Christians; in firm rooted faith,
This,[11] of the feet in future to be pierced,
That,[12] of feet nail'd already to the Cross.

[10] "Then Ripheus fell, the justest far of all the sons of Troy."—Virgil, Æneid. lib. ii. 427.

[11] "This."   Ripheus.
[12] "That."   Trajan.

One from the barrier of the dark abyss,
Where never any with good will returns,
Came back unto his bones. Of lively hope
Such was the meed; of lively hope, that wing'd
The prayers[13] sent up to God for his release,
And put power into them to bend his will.
The glorious Spirit, of whom I speak to thee;
A little while returning to the flesh,
Believed in Him, who had the means to help;
And, in believing, nourish'd such a flame
Of holy love, that at the second death
He was made sharer in our gamesome mirth.
The other, through the riches of that grace,
Which from so deep a fountain doth distil,
As never eye created saw its rising,
Placed all his love below on just and right:
Wherefore, of grace, God oped in him the eye
To the redemption of mankind to come;
Wherein believing, he endured no more
The filth of Paganism, and for their ways
Rebuked the stubborn nations. The three nymphs,[14]
Whom at the right wheel thou beheld'st advancing,
Were sponsors for him, more than thousand years
Before baptizing. O how far removed,
Predestination! is thy root from such
As see not the First Cause entire: and ye,
O mortal men! be wary how ye judge:
For we, who see our Maker, know not yet
The number of the chosen; and esteem
Such scantiness of knowledge our delight:
For all our good is, in that Primal Good,
Concentrate; and God's will and ours are one."
    So, by that form divine, was given to me
Sweet medicine to clear and strengthen sight.
And, as one handling skilfully the harp,
Attendant on some skilful songster's voice
Bids the chord vibrate; and therein the song
Acquires more pleasure: so the whilst it spake.

---

[13] The prayers of St. Gregory.   [14] "The three nymphs." Faith, Hope, and Charity. Purgatory, Canto xxix. 116.

It doth remember me, that I beheld
The pair[15] of blessed luminaries move,
Like the accordant twinkling of two eyes,
Their beamy circlets, dancing to the sounds.

CANTO XXI

ARGUMENT.—Dante ascends with Beatrice to the seventh heaven, which is the
planet Saturn; wherein is placed a ladder, so lofty, that the top of it is out of his sight.
Here are the souls of those who had passed their life in holy retirement and contemplation. Piero Damiano comes near them, and answers questions put to him by
Dante; then declares who he was on earth; and ends by declaiming against the
luxury of pastors and prelates in those times.

AGAIN mine eyes were fix'd on Beatrice;
     And, with mine eyes, my soul that in her looks
     Found all contentment. Yet no smile she wore:
And, "Did I smile," quoth she, "thou wouldst be straight
Like Semele when into ashes turn'd;
For, mounting these eternal palace-stairs,
My beauty, which the loftier it climbs,
As thou hast noted, still doth kindle more,
So shines, that, were no tempering interposed,
Thy mortal puissance would from its rays
Shrink, as the leaf doth from the thunderbolt.
Into the seventh splendour[1] are we wafted,
That, underneath the burning lion's breast,[2]
Beams, in this hour, commingled with his might.
Thy mind be with thine eyes; and, in them, mirror'd[3]
The shape, which in this mirror shall be shown."
    Whoso can deem, how fondly I had fed
My sight upon her blissful countenance,
May know, when to new thoughts I changed, what joy
To do the bidding of my heavenly guide;
In equal balance,[4] poising either weight.
    Within the crystal, which records the name
(As its remoter circle girds the world)

15 Ripheus and Trajan.
1 The planet Saturn.
2 The constellation Leo.
3 "In them, mirror'd." "Let the
form which thou shalt now behold in
this mirror," the planet, that is, of
Saturn (soon after, v. 22, called the
crystal), "be reflected in the mirror of
thy sight."
4 "My pleasure was as great in com-
plying with her will, as in beholding
her countenance."

Of that loved monarch,[5] in whose happy reign
No ill had power to harm, I saw rear'd up,
In colour like to sun-illumined gold,
A ladder, which my ken pursued in vain,
So lofty was the summit; down whose steps
I saw the splendours in such multitude
Descending, every light in Heaven, methought,
Was shed thence. As the rooks, at dawn of day,
Bestirring them to dry their feathers chill,
Some speed their way a-field; and homeward some,
Returning, cross their flight; while some abide,
And wheel around their airy lodge: so seem'd
That glitterance,[6] wafted on alternate wing,
As upon certain stair it came, and clash'd
Its shining. And one, lingering near us, wax'd
So bright, that in my thought I said: "The love,
Which this betokens me, admits no doubt."
    Unwillingly from question I refrain;
To her, by whom my silence and my speech
Are order'd, looking for a sign: whence she,
Who in the sight of Him, that seeth all,
Saw wherefore I was silent, prompted me
To indulge the fervent wish; and I began:
"I am not worthy, of my own desert,
That thou shouldst answer me: but for her sake,
Who hath vouchsafed my asking, spirit blest,
That in thy joy art shrouded! say the cause,
Which bringeth thee so near: and wherefore, say,
Doth the sweet symphony of Paradise
Keep silence here, pervading with such sounds
Of rapt devotion every lower sphere?"
"Mortal art thou in hearing, as in sight;"
Was the reply: "and what forbade the smile[7]
Of Beatrice interrupts our song.
Only to yield thee gladness of my voice,
And of the light that vests me, I thus far
Descend these hallow'd steps; not that more love

[5] Saturn. Compare Hell, Canto xiv. 91.

[6] That multitude of shining spirits, who, coming to a certain point of the ladder, made those different movements, as of birds.

[7] Because it would have overcome thee.

Invites me; for, lo! there aloft,[8] as much
Or more of love is witness'd in those flames:
But such my lot by charity assign'd,
That makes us ready servants, as thou seest,
To execute the counsel of the Highest."

   "That in this court," said I, "O sacred lamp!
Love no compulsion needs, but follows free
The eternal Providence, I well discern:
This harder find to deem: why, of thy peers,
Thou only, to this office wert foredoom'd."

   I had not ended, when, like rapid mill,
Upon its centre whirl'd the light; and then
The love that did inhabit there, replied:
"Splendour eternal, piercing through these folds,
Its virtue to my vision knits; and thus
Supported, lifts me so above myself,
That on the sovran Essence, which it wells from,
I have the power to gaze: and hence the joy,
Wherewith I sparkle, equaling with my blaze
The keenness of my sight. But not the soul,[9]
That is in Heaven most lustrous, nor the Seraph,
That hath his eyes most fix'd on God, shall solve
What thou hast ask'd: for in the abyss it lies
Of th' everlasting statute sunk so low,
That no created ken may fathom it.
And, to the mortal world when thou return'st,
Be this reported: that none henceforth dare
Direct his footsteps to so dread a bourn.
The mind, that here is radiant, on the earth
Is wrapt in mist. Look then if she may do
Below, what passeth her ability
When she is ta'en to Heaven." By words like these
Admonish'd, I the question urged no more;
And of the spirit humbly sued alone
To instruct me of its state. " 'Twixt either shore[10]
Of Italy, nor distant from thy land,
A stony ridge[11] ariseth; in such sort,

[8] "There aloft." Where the other souls were.

[9] "Not the soul." The particular ends of Providence being concealed from the very Angels themselves.

[10] Between the Adriatic Gulf and the Mediterranean Sea.

[11] A part of the Apennines.

The thunder doth not lift his voice so high.
They call it Catria:[12] at whose foot, a cell
Is sacred to the lonely Eremite;
For worship set apart and holy rites."
A third time thus it spake; then added: "There
So firmly to God's service I adhered,
That with no costlier viands than the juice
Of olives, easily I pass'd the heats
Of summer and the winter frosts; content
In heaven-ward musings. Rich were the returns
And fertile, which that cloister once was used
To render to these Heavens: now 'tis fallen
Into a waste so empty, that ere long
Detection must lay bare its vanity.
Pietro Damiano[13] there was I y-clept:
Pietro the sinner, when before I dwelt,
Beside the Adriatic,[14] in the house
Of our blest Lady. Near upon my close
Of mortal life, through much importuning
I was constrain'd to wear the hat,[15] that still
From bad to worse is shifted.—Cephas[16] came:
He came, who was the Holy Spirit's vessel;[17]
Barefoot and lean; eating their bread, as chanced,
At the first table. Modern Shepherds need

---

[12] Now the Abbey of Santa Croce, in the Duchy of Urbino, about half way between Gubbio and La Pergola. Here Dante is said to have resided for some time.

[13] "Pietro Damiano." "S. Pietro Damiano obtained a great and well-merited reputation by the pains he took to correct the abuses among the clergy. Ravenna is supposed to have been the place of his birth, about 1007. He was employed in several important missions, and rewarded by Stephen IX with the dignity of cardinal, and the bishopric of Ostia, to which, however, he preferred his former retreat in the monastery of Fonte Avellana, and prevailed on Alexander II to permit him to retire thither. Yet he did not long continue in this seclusion, before he was sent on other embassies. He died at Faenza in 1072. His letters throw much light on the obscure history of these times. Besides them, he has left several treatises on sacred and ecclesiastical subjects. His eloquence is worthy of a better age." Tiraboschi, Storia della Lett. Ital.

[14] Some editions and manuscripts have "fu," instead of "fui." According to the former of these readings, S. Pietro Damiano is made to distinguish himself from S. Pietro degli Onesti, surnamed "Il Peccator," founder of the monastery of S. Maria del Porto, on the Adriatic coast, near Ravenna, who died in 1119, at about eighty years of age.

[15] "The hat." The cardinal's hat.

[16] "Cephas." St. Peter.

[17] St. Paul. See Hell, Canto ii. 30.

Those who on either hand may prop and lead them,
So burly are they grown; and from behind,
Others to hoist them. Down the palfrey's sides
Spread their broad mantles, so as both the beasts
Are cover'd with one skin. O patience! thou
That look'st on this, and dost endure so long."
    I at those accents saw the splendours down
From step to step alight, and wheel, and wax,
Each circuiting, more beautiful. Round this[18]
They came, and stay'd them; utter'd then a shout
So loud, it hath no likeness here: nor I
Wist what it spake, so deafening was the thunder.

CANTO XXII

ARGUMENT.—He beholds many other spirits of the devout and contemplative; and among these is addressed by St. Benedict, who, after disclosing his own name and the names of certain of his companions in bliss, replies to the request made by our Poet that he might look on the form of the saint, without that covering of splendor, which then invested it; and then proceeds, lastly, to inveigh against the corruption of the monks. Next Dante mounts with his heavenly conductress to the eighth heaven, or that of the fixed stars, which he enters at the constellation of the Twins; and thence looking back, reviews all the space he has passed between his present station and the earth.

ASTOUNDED, to the guardian of my steps
    I turn'd me, like the child, who always runs
    Thither for succour, where he trusteth most:
And she was like the mother, who her son
Beholding pale and breathless, with her voice
Soothes him, and he is cheer'd; for thus she spake,
Soothing me: "Know'st not thou, thou art in Heaven?
And know'st not thou, whatever is in Heaven,
Is holy; and that nothing there is done,
But is done zealously and well? Deem now,
What change in thee the song, and what my smile
Had wrought, since thus the shout had power to move
      thee;
In which, couldst thou have understood their prayers,
The vengeance[1] were already known to thee,
Which thou must witness ere thy mortal hour.

[18] "Round this." Round the spirit of Pietro Damiano.

[1] "The vengeance. " Beatrice, it is sup- posed, intimates the approaching fate of Boniface VIII. See Purgatory, Canto xx. 86.

The sword of Heaven is not in haste to smite,
Nor yet doth linger; save unto his seeming,
Who, in desire or fear, doth look for it.
But elsewhere now I bid thee turn thy view;
So shalt thou many a famous spirit behold."

Mine eyes directing, as she will'd, I saw
A hundred little spheres, that fairer grew
By interchange of splendour. I remain'd,
As one, who fearful of o'er-much presuming,
Abates in him the keenness of desire,
Nor dares to question; when, amid those pearls,
One largest and most lustrous onward drew,
That it might yield contentment to my wish;
And, from within it, these the sounds I heard.

"If thou, like me, beheld'st the charity
That burns amongst us; what thy mind conceives
Were utter'd. But that, ere the lofty bound
Thou reach, expectance may not weary thee;
I will make answer even to the thought,
Which thou hast such respect of. In old days,
That mountain, at whose side Cassino[2] rests,
Was, on its height, frequented by a race
Deceived and ill-disposed: and I it was,[3]
Who thither carried first the name of Him,
Who brought the soul-subliming truth to man.
And such a speeding grace shone over me,
That from their impious worship I reclaim'd
The dwellers round about, who with the world
Were in delusion lost. These other flames,
The spirits of men contemplative, were all
Enliven'd by that warmth, whose kindly force
Gives birth to flowers and fruits of holiness.
Here is Macarius;[4] Romoaldo[5] here;

[2] A castle in the Terra di Lavoro.

[3] "A new order of monks, which in a manner absorbed all the others that were established in the west, was instituted, 529, by Benedict of Nursia, a man of piety and reputation for the age he lived in." Maclaine's Mosheim, Eccles. Hist.

[4] "Macarius, an Egyptian monk, deserves the first rank among the practical writers of the fourth century, as his works displayed, some few things excepted, the brightest and most lovely portraiture of sanctity and virtue." Ibid.

[5] S. Romoaldo, a native of Ravenna, and the founder of the order of Camaldoli, died in 1027. He was the author of a commentary on the Psalms.

And here my brethren, who their steps refrain'd
Within the cloisters, and held firm their heart."
   I answering thus: "Thy gentle words and kind,
And this the cheerful semblance I behold,
Not unobservant, beaming in ye all,
Have raised assurance in me; wakening it
Full-blossom'd in my bosom, as a rose
Before the sun, when the consummate flower
Has spread to utmost amplitude. Of thee
Therefore intreat I, father, to declare
If I may gain such favour, as to gaze
Upon thine image by no covering veil'd."
   "Brother!" he thus rejoin'd, "in the last sphere[6]
Expect completion of thy lofty aim:
For there on each desire completion waits,
And there on mine; where every aim is found
Perfect, entire, and for fulfilment ripe.
There all things are as they have ever been:
For space is none to bound; nor pole divides.
Our ladder reaches even to that clime;
And so, at giddy distance, mocks thy view.
Thither the patriarch Jacob[7] saw it stretch
Its topmost round; when it appear'd to him
With Angels laden. But to mount it now
None lifts his foot from earth: and hence my rule
Is left a profitless stain upon the leaves;
The walls, for abbey rear'd, turn'd into dens;
The cowls, to sacks choak'd up with musty meal.
Foul usury doth not more lift itself
Against God's pleasure, than that fruit, which makes,
The hearts of monks so wanton: for whate'er
Is in the Church's keeping, all pertains
To such, as sue for Heaven's sweet sake; and not
To those, who in respect of kindred claim,
Or on more vile allowance. Mortal flesh

---

[6] "In the last sphere." The Empyrean, where he afterward sees St. Benedict, Canto xxxii. 30. Beatified spirits, though they have different heavens allotted them, have all their seats in that higher sphere.
[7] "The patriarch Jacob." "And he dreamed, and behold, a ladder set upon the earth, and the top of it reached to heaven: and behold the angels of God ascending and descending on it."—Gen. xxviii. 12.

Is grown so dainty, good beginnings last not
From the oak's birth unto the acorn's setting.
His convent Peter founded without gold
Or silver; I, with prayers and fasting, mine;
And Francis, his in meek humility.
And if thou note the point, whence each proceeds,
Then look what it hath err'd to; thou shalt find
The white grown murky. Jordan was turn'd back:
And a less wonder, than the refluent sea,
May, at God's pleasure, work amendment here."
   So saying, to his assembly back he drew:
And they together cluster'd into one;
Then all roll'd upward, like an eddying wind.
   The sweet dame beckon'd me to follow them:
And, by that influence only, so prevail'd
Over my nature, that no natural motion,
Ascending or descending here below,
Had, as I mounted, with my pennon vied.
   So, reader, as my hope is to return
Unto the holy triumph, for the which
I oft-times wail my sins, and smite my breast;
Thou hadst been longer drawing out and thrusting
Thy finger in the fire, than I was, ere
The sign,[8] that followeth Taurus, I beheld,
And enter'd its precinct. O glorious stars!
O light impregnate with exceeding virtue!
To whom whate'er of genius lifteth me
Above the vulgar, grateful I refer;
With ye the parent[9] of all mortal life
Arose and set, when I did first inhale
The Tuscan air; and afterward, when grace
Vouchsafed me entrance to the lofty wheel[10]
That in its orb impels ye, fate decreed
My passage at your clime. To you my soul
Devoutly sighs, for virtue, even now,
To meet the hard emprise that draws me on.
   "Thou art so near the sum of blessedness,"

---

[8] "The sign." The constellation of Gemini.

[9] "The parent." The sun was in the constellation of the Twins at the time of Dante's birth.

[10] "The lofty wheel." The eighth heaven; that of the fixed stars.

Said Beatrice, "that behoves thy ken
Be vigilant and clear. And, to this end,
Or ever thou advance thee further, hence
Look downward, and contemplate, what a world
Already stretch'd under our feet there lies:
So as thy heart may, in its blithest mood,
Present itself to the triumphal throng,
Which, through the ethereal concave, comes rejoicing."
    I straight obey'd; and with mine eye return'd
Through all the seven spheres; and saw this globe
So pitiful of semblance, that perforce
It moved my smiles: and him in truth I hold
For wisest, who esteems it least; whose thoughts
Elsewhere are fix'd, him worthiest call and best.
I saw the daughter of Latona shine
Without the shadow,[11] whereof late I deem'd
That dense and rare were cause. Here I sustain'd
The visage, Hyperion, of thy son;[12]
And mark'd, how near him with their circles, round
Move Maia and Dione;[13] here discern'd
Jove's tempering 'twixt his sire and son;[14] and hence,
Their changes and their various aspects,
Distinctly scann'd. Nor might I not descry
Of all the seven, how bulky each, how swift;
Nor, of their several distances, not learn.
This petty area, (o'er the which we stride
So fiercely), as along the eternal Twins
I wound my way, appear'd before me all,
Forth from the havens stretch'd unto the hills.
Then, to the beauteous eyes, mine eyes return'd.

[11] "Without the shadow." See Canto ii. 71.
[12] "Of thy son." The sun.
[13] "Maia and Dione." The planets Mercury and Venus, Dione being the mother of the latter, and Maia of the former deity.
[14] " 'Twixt his sire and son." Betwixt Saturn and Mars.

CANTO XXIII

ARGUMENT.—He sees Christ triumphing with his Church. The Saviour ascends followed by his Virgin Mother. The others remain with St. Peter.

E'EN as the bird, who midst the leafy bower
   Has, in her nest, sat darkling through the night,
   With her sweet brood; impatient to descry
Their wished looks, and to bring home their food,
In the fond quest unconscious of her toil:
She, of the time prevenient, on the spray,
That overhangs their couch, with wakeful gaze
Expects the sun; nor ever, till the dawn,
Removeth from the east her eager ken:
So stood the dame erect, and bent her glance
Wistfully on that region,[1] where the sun
Abateth most his speed; that, seeing her
Suspense and wondering, I became as one,
In whom desire is waken'd, and the hope
Of somewhat new to come fills with delight.

   Short space ensued; I was not held, I say,
Long in expectance, when I saw the Heaven
Wax more and more resplendent; and, "Behold,"
Cried Beatrice, "the triumphal hosts
Of Christ, and all the harvest gather'd in,
Made ripe by these revolving spheres." Meseem'd,
That, while she spake, her image all did burn;
And in her eyes such fulness was of joy,
As I am fain to pass unconstrued by.

   As in the calm full moon, when Trivia[2] smiles,
In peerless beauty, 'mid the eternal nymphs,[3]
That paint through all its gulfs the blue profound;
In bright pre-eminence so saw I there
O'er million lamps a Sun, from whom all drew
Their radiance, as from ours the starry train:
And, through the living light, so lustrous glow'd
The substance, that my ken endured it not.

---

[1] "That region." Toward the south, where the course of the sun appears less rapid, than when he is in the east or the west

[2] "Trivia." A name of Diana.

[3] "The eternal nymphs." The stars. Those starry nymphs which dance about the pole. Drummond Sonnet.

O Beatrice! sweet and precious guide,
Who cheer'd me with her comfortable words:
"Against the virtue, that o'erpowereth thee,
Avails not to resist. Here is the Might,[4]
And here the Wisdom, which did open lay
The path, that had been yearned for so long,
Betwixt the Heaven and earth." Like to the fire,
That, in a cloud imprison'd, doth break out
Expansive, so that from its womb enlarged,
It falleth against nature to the ground;
Thus, in that heavenly banqueting, my soul
Outgrew herself; and, in the transport lost,
Holds now remembrance none of what she was.
　　"Ope thou thine eyes, and mark me: thou hast seen
Things, that empower thee to sustain my smile."
　　I was as one, when a forgotten dream
Doth come across him, and he strives in vain
To shape it in his fantasy again:
Whenas that gracious boon was proffer'd me,
Which never may be cancel'd from the book
Wherein the past is written. Now were all
Those tongues to sound, that have, on sweetest milk
Of Polyhymnia and her sisters, fed
And fatten'd; not with all their help to boot,
Unto the thousandth parcel of the truth,
My song might shadow forth that saintly smile,
How merely, in her saintly looks, it wrought.
And, with such figuring of Paradise,
The sacred strain must leap, like one that meets
A sudden interruption to his road.
But he, who thinks how ponderous the theme,
And that 'tis laid upon a mortal shoulder,
May pardon, if it tremble with the burden.
The track, our venturous keel must furrow, brooks
No unribb'd pinnace, no self-sparing pilot.
　　"Why doth my face," said Beatrice, "thus
Enamour thee, as that thou dost not turn
Unto the beautiful garden, blossoming

4 "The Might." Our Saviour.

Beneath the rays of Christ? Here is the Rose,[5]
Wherein the Word Divine was made incarnate;
And here the lilies,[6] by whose odour known
The way of life was follow'd." Prompt I heard
Her bidding, and encounter'd once again
The strife of aching vision. As, erewhile,   [cloud,
Through glance of sun-light, stream'd through broken
Mine eyes a flower-besprinkled mead have seen;
Though veil'd themselves in shade: so saw I there
Legions of splendours, on whom burning rays
Shed lightnings from above; yet saw I not
The fountain whence they flow'd. O gracious Virtue
Thou, whose broad stamp is on them, higher up
Thou didst exalt Thy glory,[7] to give room
To my o'erlabour'd sight; when at the name
Of that fair flower,[8] whom duly I invoke
Both morn and eve, my soul with all her might
Collected, on the goodliest ardour fix'd.
And, as the bright dimensions of the star
In Heaven excelling, as once here on earth,
Were, in my eye-balls livelily pourtray'd;
Lo! from within the sky a cresset[9] fell,
Circling in fashion of a diadem;
And girt the star; and, hovering, round it wheel'd.
    Whatever melody sounds sweetest here,
And draws the spirit most unto itself,
Might seem a rent cloud, when it grates the thunder;
Compared unto the sounding of that lyre,[10]
Wherewith the goodliest sapphire,[11] that inlays
The floor of Heaven, was crown'd. "Angelic Love
I am, who thus with hovering flight enwheel

---

[5] "The rose." The Virgin Mary, who is termed by the Church, "Rosa Mystica." "I was exalted like a palm-tree in Engaddi, and as a rose-plant in Jericho."—Ecclesiasticus, xxiv. 14.

[6] "The lilies." The Apostles. "And give ye a sweet savour as frankincense, and flourish as a lily."—Ecclesiasticus, xxxix. 14.

[7] "Thou didst exalt thy glory." The divine light retired upward, to render the eyes of Dante more capable of enduring the spectacle which now presented itself.

[8] "—— the name
    Of that fair flower."
The name of the Virgin.

[9] "A cresset." The angel Gabriel.

[10] "That lyre." By synecdoche, the lyre is put for the angel.

[11] The Virgin.

The lofty rapture from that womb inspired,
Where our desire did dwell: and round thee so,
Lady of Heaven! will hover; long as thou
Thy Son shalt follow, and diviner joy
Shall from thy presence gild the highest sphere."
      Such close was to the circling melody:
And, as it ended, all the other lights
Took up the strain, and echoed Mary's name.
      The robe,[12] that with its regal folds enwraps
The world, and with the nearer breath of God
Doth burn and quiver, held so far retired
Its inner hem and skirting over us,
That yet no glimmer of its majesty
Had stream'd unto me: therefore were mine eyes
Unequal to pursue the crowned flame,[13]
That towering rose, and sought the seed[14] it bore.
And like to babe, that stretches forth its arms
For very eagerness toward the breast,
After the milk is taken; so outstretch'd
Their wavy summits all the fervent band,
Through zealous love to Mary: then, in view,
There halted; and "Regina Cœli"[15] sang
So sweetly, the delight hath left me never.
      Oh! what o'erflowing plenty is up-piled
In those rich-laden coffers,[16] which below
Sow'd the good seed, whose harvest now they keep.
Here are the treasures tasted, that with tears
Were in the Babylonian exile[17] won,
When gold had fail'd them. Here, in synod high
Of ancient council with the new convened,
Under the Son of Mary and of God,
Victorious he[18] his mighty triumph holds,
To whom the keys of glory were assign'd.

[12] "The robe." The ninth heaven, the *primum mobile,* that enfolds and moves the eight lower heavens.

[13] "The crowned flame." The Virgin, with the angel hovering over her.

[14] "The seed." Our Saviour.

[15] "Regina Cœli." "The beginning of an anthem, sung by the Church at Easter, in honor of Our Lady."

[16] "Those rich-laden coffers." Those spirits, who, having sown the seed of good works on earth, now contain the fruit of their pious endeavors.

[17] "In the Babylonian exile." During their abode in this world.

[18] "He." St. Peter, with the other holy men of the Old and New Testaments.

CANTO XXIV

ARGUMENT.—St. Peter examines Dante touching Faith, and is contented with his answers.

"O YE! in chosen fellowship advanced
    To the great supper of the blessed Lamb,
    Whereon who feeds hath every wish fulfill'd;
If to this man through God's grace be vouchsafed
Foretaste of that, which from your table falls,
Or ever death his fated term prescribe;
Be ye not heedless of his urgent will:
But may some influence of your sacred dews
Sprinkle him. Of the fount ye alway drink,
Whence flows what most he craves." Beatrice spake;
And the rejoicing spirits, like to spheres
On firm-set poles revolving, trail'd a blaze
Of comet splendour: and as wheels, that wind
Their circles in the horologe, so work
The stated rounds, that to the observant eye
The first seems still, and as it flew, the last;
E'en thus their carols weaving variously,
They, by the measure paced, or swift, or slow,
Made me to rate the riches of their joy.

    From that, which I did note in beauty most
Excelling, saw I issue forth a flame
So bright, as none was left more goodly there.
Round Beatrice thrice it wheel'd about,
With so divine a song, that fancy's ear
Records it not; and the pen passeth on,
And leaves a blank: for that our mortal speech,
Nor e'en the inward shaping of the brain,
Hath colours fine enough to trace such folds.

    "O saintly sister mine! thy prayer devout
Is with so vehement affection urged,
Thou dost unbind me from that beauteous sphere."
    Such were the accents towards my lady breathed
From that blest ardour, soon as it was stay'd;
To whom she thus: "O everlasting light
Of him, within whose mighty grasp our Lord
Did leave the keys, which of this wondrous bliss

He bare below! tent this man as thou wilt,
With lighter probe or deep, touching the faith,
By the which thou didst on the billows walk.
If he in love, in hope, and in belief,
Be steadfast, is not hid from thee: for thou
Hast there thy ken, where all things are beheld
In liveliest portraiture. But since true faith
Has peopled this fair realm with citizens;
Meet is, that to exalt its glory more,
Thou, in his audience, shouldst thereof discourse."
  Like to the bachelor, who arms himself,
And speaks not, till the master have proposed
The question, to approve, and not to end it;
So I, in silence, arm'd me, while she spake,
Summoning up each argument to aid;
As was behoveful for such questioner,
And such profession: "As good Christian ought,
Declare thee, what is faith?" Whereat I raised
My forehead to the light, whence this had breathed;
Then turn'd to Beatrice; and in her looks
Approval met, that from their inmost fount
I should unlock the waters. "May the grace,
That giveth me the captain of the Church
For confessor," said I, "vouchsafe to me
Apt utterance for my thoughts;" then added: "Sire!
E'en as set down by the unerring style
Of thy dear brother, who with thee conspired
To bring Rome in unto the way of life,
Faith of things hoped is substance, and the proof
Of things not seen; and herein doth consist
Methinks its essence."—"Rightly hast thou deem'd,"
Was answer'd; "if thou well discern, why first
He hath defined it substance, and then proof."
  "The deep things," I replied, "which here I scan
Distinctly, are below from mortal eye
So hidden, they have in belief alone
Their being; on which credence, hope sublime
Is built: and, therefore substance, it intends.
And inasmuch as we must needs infer

From such belief our reasoning, all respect
To other view excluded; hence of proof
The intention is derived." Forthwith I heard:
"If thus, whate'er by learning men attain,
Were understood; the sophist would want room
To exercise his wit." So breathed the flame
Of love; then added: "Current is the coin
Thou utter'st, both in weight and in alloy.
But tell me, if thou hast it in thy purse."

   "Even so glittering and so round," said I,
"I not a whit misdoubt of its assay."
Next issued from the deep-imbosom'd splendour:
"Say, whence the costly jewel, on the which
Is founded every virtue, came to thee."

   "The flood," I answer'd, "from the Spirit of God
Rain'd down upon the ancient bond and new,[1]—
Here is the reasoning that convinceth me
So feelingly, each argument beside
Seems blunt and forceless in comparison."
Then heard I: "Wherefore holdest thou that each,
The elder proposition and the new,
Which so persuade thee, are the voice of Heaven?"

   "The works, that follow'd, evidence their truth,"
I answer'd: "Nature did not make for these
The iron hot, or on her anvil mould them."

   "Who voucheth to thee of the works themselves,"
Was the reply, "that they in very deed
Are that they purport? None hath sworn so to thee."

   "That all the world," said I, "should have been
      turn'd
To Christian, and no miracle been wrought,
Would in itself be such a miracle,
The rest were not an hundredth part so great.
E'en thou went'st forth in poverty and hunger
To set the goodly plant, that, from the vine
It once was, now is grown unsightly bramble."

   That ended, through the high celestial court
Resounded all the spheres, "Praise we one God!"

[1] "The ancient bond and new." The Old and New Testaments.

In song of most unearthly melody.
And when that Worthy[2] thus, from branch to branch,
Examining, had led me, that we now
Approach'd the topmost bough; he straight resumed:
"The grace, that holds sweet dalliance with thy soul
So far discreetly hath thy lips unclosed;
That, whatsoe'er has past them, I commend.
Behoves thee to express, what thou believest,
The next; and, whereon, thy belief hath grown."

  "O saintly sire and spirit!" I began,
"Who seest that, which thou didst so believe,
As to outstrip feet younger than thine own,
Toward the sepulchre; thy will is here,
That I the tenour of my creed unfold;
And thou, the cause of it, hast likewise ask'd.
And I reply: I in one God believe;
One sole eternal Godhead, of whose love
All Heaven is moved, Himself unmoved the while.
Nor demonstration physical alone,
Or more intelligential and abstruse,
Persuades me to this faith: but from that truth
It cometh to me rather, which is shed
Through Moses; the rapt Prophets; and the Psalms;
The Gospel; and what ye yourselves did write,
When ye were gifted of the Holy Ghost.
In three eternal Persons I believe;
Essence threefold and one; mysterious league
Of union absolute, which, many a time,
The word of gospel lore upon my mind
Imprints: and from this germ, this firstling spark
The lively flame dilates; and, like Heaven's star,
Doth glitter in me." As the master hears,
Well pleased, and then enfoldeth in his arms
The servant, who hath joyful tidings brought,
And having told the errand keeps his peace;
Thus benediction uttering with song,
Soon as my peace I held, compass'd me thrice

---

[2] "Quel Baron." In the next Canto, Boccaccio, G. vi. N. 10, we find "Baron
St. James is called "Barone." So in Messer Santo Antonio."

The apostolic radiance, whose behest
Had oped my lips: so well their answer pleased.

CANTO XXV

ARGUMENT.—St. James questions our Poet concerning Hope. Next St. John appears; and, on perceiving that Dante looks intently on him, informs him that he, St. John, had left his body resolved into earth, upon the earth, and that Christ and the Virgin alone had come with their bodies into Heaven.

IF e'er the sacred poem, that hath made
Both Heaven and earth copartners in its toil,
And with lean abstinence, through many a year,
Faded my brow, be destined to prevail
Over the cruelty, which bars me forth
Of the fair sheep-fold,[1] where, a sleeping lamb,
The wolves set on and fain had worried me;
With other voice, and fleece of other grain,
I shall forthwith return; and, standing up
At my baptismal font, shall claim the wreath
Due to the poet's temples: for I there
First enter'd on the faith, which maketh souls
Acceptable to God: and, for its sake,[2]
Peter had then circled my forehead thus.
   Next from the squadron, whence had issued forth
The first fruit of Christ's vicars on the earth,
Toward us moved a light, at view whereof
My Lady, full of gladness, spake to me:
"Lo! lo! behold the peer of mickle might,
That makes Galicia throng'd with visitants."[3]
   As when the ring-dove by his mate alights;
In circles, each about the other wheels,
And, murmuring, coos his fondness; thus saw I

---

[1] Florence, whence he was banished.
[2] For the sake of that faith.
[3] "At the time that the sepulchre of the apostle St. James was discovered, the devotion for that place extended itself not only over all Spain, but even round about to foreign nations. Multitudes from all parts of the world came to visit it. Many others were deterred by the difficulty of the journey, by the roughness and barrenness of those parts, and by the incursions of the Moors, who made captives many of the pilgrims. The canons of St. Eloy, afterward (the precise time is not known), with a desire of remedying these evils, built, in many places along the whole road, which reached as far as to France, hospitals for the reception of the pilgrims."

One, of the other[4] great and glorious prince,
With kindly greeting, hail'd; extolling, both,
Their heavenly banqueting: but when an end
Was to their gratulation, silent, each,
Before me sat they down, so burning bright,
I could not look upon them. Smiling then,
Beatrice spake: "O life in glory shrined!
Who[5] didst the largess of our kingly court
Set down with faithful pen, let now thy voice,
Of hope the praises, in this height resound.
For well thou know'st, who figurest it as oft,
As Jesus, to ye three, more brightly shone."

   "Lift up thy head; and be thou strong in trust:
For that, which hither from the mortal world
Arriveth, must be ripen'd in our beam."

   Such cheering accents from the second flame[6]
Assured me; and mine eyes I lifted up[7]
Unto the mountains, that had bow'd them late
With over-heavy burden. "Sith our Liege
Wills of His grace, that thou, or e'er thy death,
In the most secret council with His lords
Shouldst be confronted, so that having view'd
The glories of our court, thou mayest therewith
Thyself, and all who hear, invigorate
With hope, that leads to blissful end; declare,
What is that hope? how it doth flourish in thee?
And whence thou hadst it?" Thus, proceeding still,
The second light: and she, whose gentle love
My soaring pennons in that lofty flight
Escorted, thus preventing me, rejoin'd:
"Among her sons, not one more full of hope,
Hath the Church Militant: so 'tis of him
Recorded in the Sun, whose liberal orb
Enlightened all our tribe: and ere his term
Of warfare, hence permitted he is come,

---

[4] "One, of the other." St. Peter and St. James.

[5] "Who." The Epistle of St. James is here attributed to the elder apostle of that name, whose shrine was at Compostella, in Galicia.

[6] "The second flame." St. James.

[7] "I lifted up." "I looked up to the apostles." "I will lift up mine eyes unto the hills, from whence cometh my help." —Psalm cxxi. 1.

From Egypt to Jerusalem,[8] to see.
The other points, both which[9] thou hast inquired,
Not for more knowledge, but that he may tell
How dear thou hold'st the virtue; these to him
Leave I: for he may answer thee with ease,
And without boasting, so God give him grace."

  Like to the scholar, practised in his task,
Who, willing to give proof of diligence,
Seconds his teacher gladly; "Hope," said I,
"Is of the joy to come a sure expectance,
The effect of grace divine and merit preceding.
This light from many a star, visits my heart;
But flow'd to me, the first, from him who sang
The songs of the Supreme; himself supreme
Among his tuneful brethren. 'Let all hope
In thee,' so spake his anthem, 'who have known
Thy name;' and, with my faith, who knows not that?
From thee, the next, distilling from his spring,
In thine epistle, fell on me the drops
So plenteously, that I on others shower
The influence of their dew." Whileas I spake,
A lamping, as of quick and volley'd lightning,
Within the bosom of that mighty sheen[10]
Play'd tremulous; then forth these accents breathed:
"Love for the virtue, which attended me
E'en to the palm, and issuing from the field,
Glows vigorous yet within me; and inspires
To ask of thee, whom also it delights,
What promise thou from hope, in chief, dost win."

  "Both scriptures, new and ancient," I replied,
"Propose the mark (which even now I view)
For souls beloved of God. Isaias[11] saith,
'That, in their own land, each one must be clad
In two-fold vesture;' and their proper land
Is this delicious life. In terms more full,

---

[8] From the lower world to Heaven.

[9] One point Beatrice has herself answered: "how that hope flourishes in him." The other two remain for Dante to resolve.

[10] "That mighty sheen." The spirit of St. James.

[11] "Isaias." "He hath clothed me with the garments of salvation, he hath covered me with the robe of righteousness.'—Chap. lxi. 10.

And clearer far, thy brother[12] hath set forth
This revelation to us, where he tells
Of the white raiment destined to the saints."
And, as the words were ending, from above,
"They hope in Thee!" first heard we cried: whereto
Answer'd the carols all. Amidst them next,
A light of so clear amplitude emerged,
That winter's month were but a single day,
Were such a crystal in the Cancer's sign.

   Like as a virgin riseth up, and goes,
And enters on the mazes of the dance;
Though gay, yet innocent of worse intent,
Than to do fitting honour to the bride:
So I beheld the new effulgence come
Unto the other two, who in a ring
Wheel'd, as became their rapture. In the dance,
And in the song, it mingled. And the dame
Held on them fix'd her looks; e'en as the spouse,
Silent, and moveless. "This[13] is he, who lay
Upon the bosom of our Pelican:
This he, into whose keeping, from the Cross,
The mighty charge was given." Thus she spake:
Yet therefore naught the more removed her sight
From marking them: or e'er her words began,
Or when they closed. As he, who looks intent,
And strives with searching ken, how he may see
The sun in his eclipse, and, through desire
Of seeing, loseth power of sight; so I[14]
Peer'd on that last resplendence, while I heard:
"Why dazzlest thou thine eyes in seeking that,
Which here abides not? Earth my body is,
In earth; and shall be, with the rest, so long,
As till our number equal the decree
Of the Most High. The two[15] that have ascended,

---

[12] "Thy brother." St. John in the Rev. vii. 9.

[13] St. John, who reclined on the bosom of our Saviour, and to whose charge Jesus recommended his mother.

[14] "So I." He looked so earnestly, to descry whether St. John were present

there in body, or in spirit only; having had his doubts raised by that saying of our Saviour's: "If I will, that he tarry till I come, what is that to thee?"

[15] Christ and Mary, decribed in Canto xxiii. as rising above his sight.

In this our blessed cloister, shine alone
With the two garments. So report below."
  As when, for ease of labour, or to shun
Suspected peril, at a whistle's breath,
The oars, erewhile dash'd frequent in the wave,
All rest: the flamy circle at that voice
So rested; and the mingling sound was still,
Which from the trinal band, soft-breathing, rose.
I turn'd, but ah! how trembled in my thought,
When, looking at my side again to see
Beatrice, I descried her not; although,
Not distant, on the happy coast she stood.

CANTO XXVI

ARGUMENT.—St. John examines our Poet touching Charity. Afterward Adam tells when he was created, and placed in the terrestrial Paradise; how long he remained in that state; what was the occasion of his fall; when he was admitted into Heaven; and what language he spake.

WITH dazzled eyes, whilst wondering I remain'd;
    Forth of the beamy flame,[1] which dazzled me,
    Issued a breath, that in attention mute
Detain'd me; and these words it spake: " 'Twere well
That, long as till thy vision, on my form
O'erspent, regain its virtue, with discourse
Thou compensate the brief delay. Say then,
Beginning, to what point thy soul aspires:
And meanwhile rest assured, that sight in thee
Is but o'erpower'd a space, not wholly quench'd;
Since thy fair guide and lovely, in her look
Hath potency, the like to that, which dwelt
In Ananias' hand."[2] I answering thus:
"Be to mine eyes the remedy, or late
Or early, at her pleasure; for they were
The gates, at which she enter'd, and did light
Her never-dying fire. My wishes here
Are centred: in this palace is the weal,
That Alpha and Omega is, to all

[1] "The beamy flame." St. John.
[2] "Ananias' hand." Who, by putting his hand on St. Paul, restored his sight. Acts, ix. 17.

The lessons love can read me." Yet again
The voice, which had dispersed my fear when dazed
With that excess, to converse urged, and spake:
"Behoves thee sift more narrowly thy terms;
And say, who level'd at this scope thy bow."
  "Philosophy," said I, "hath arguments,
And this place hath authority enough,
To imprint in me such love: for, of constraint,
Good, inasmuch as we perceive the good,
Kindles our love; and in degree the more,
As it comprises more of goodness in 't.
The essence then, where such advantage is,
That each good, found without it, is naught else
But of His light the beam, must needs attract
The soul of each one, loving, who the truth
Discerns, on which this proof is built. Such truth
Learn I from Him, who shows me the first love
Of all intelligential substances
Eternal: from His voice I learn, whose word
Is truth; that of Himself to Moses saith,
'I will make all My good before thee pass:'
Lastly, from thee I learn, who chief proclaim'st,
E'en at the outset[3] of thy heralding,
In mortal ears the mystery of Heaven."
  "Through human wisdom, and the authority
Therewith agreeing," heard I answer'd, "keep
The choicest of thy love for God. But say,
If thou yet other cords within thee feel'st,
That draw thee towards Him; so that thou report
How many are the fangs, with which this love
Is grappled to thy soul." I did not miss,
To what intent the eagle of our Lord[4]
Had pointed his demand; yea, noted well
The avowal which he led to; and resumed:
"All grappling bonds, that knit the heart to God,
Confederate to make fast our charity.
The being of the world; and mine own being;
The death which He endured, that I should live;
And that, which all the faithful hope, as I do;

---

[3] "At the outset." John i. 1. etc.   [4] "The eagle of our Lord." St. John.

To the foremention'd lively knowledge join'd;
Have from the sea of ill love saved my bark,
And on the coast secured it of the right.
As for the leaves,[5] that in the garden bloom,
My love for them is great, as is the good
Dealt by the eternal hand, that tends them all."
   I ended: and therewith a song most sweet
Rang through the spheres; and "Holy, holy, holy,"
Accordant with the rest, my lady sang.
And as a sleep is broken and dispersed
Through sharp encounter of the nimble light,
With the eye's spirit running forth to meet
The ray, from membrane on to membrane urged;
And the upstartled wight loathes that he sees;
So, at his sudden waking, he misdeems
Of all around him, till assurance waits
On better judgment: thus the saintly dame
Drove from before mine eyes the motes away,
With the resplendence of her own, that cast
Their brightness downward, thousand miles below.
Whence I my vision, clearer than before,
Recover'd; and well nigh astounded, ask'd
Of a fourth light, that now with us I saw.
   And Beatrice: "The first living soul,[6]
That ever the first Virtue framed, admires
Within these rays his Maker." Like the leaf,
That bows its lithe top till the blast is blown;
By its own virtue rear'd, then stands aloof:
So I, the whilst she said, awe-stricken bow'd.
Then eagerness to speak embolden'd me;
And I began: "O fruit! that wast alone
Mature, when first engender'd; ancient father!
That doubly seest in every wedded bride
Thy daughter, by affinity and blood;
Devoutly as I may, I pray thee hold
Converse with me: my will thou seest: and I,
More speedily to hear thee, tell it not."
   It chanceth oft some animal bewrays,
Through the sleek covering of his furry coat,

[5] "The leaves." Created beings.   [6] "The first living soul." Adam

The fondness, that stirs in him, and conforms
His outside seeming to the cheer within:
And in like guise was Adam's spirit moved
To joyous mood, that through the covering shone,
Transparent, when to pleasure me it spake:
"No need thy will be told, which I untold
Better discern, than thou whatever thing
Thou hold'st most certain: for that will I see
In Him, who is truth's mirror; and Himself,
Parhelion unto all things, and naught else,
To Him. This wouldst thou hear: how long since, God
Placed me in that high garden, from whose bounds
She led thee up this ladder, steep and long;
What space endured my season of delight;
Whence truly sprang the wrath that banish'd me;
And what the language, which I spake and framed.
Not that I tasted of the tree, my son,
Was in itself the cause of that exile,
But only my transgressing of the mark
Assign'd me. There, whence[7] at thy lady's hest
The Mantuan moved him, still was I debarr'd
This council, till the sun had made complete,
Four thousand and three hundred rounds and twice,
His annual journey; and, through every light
In his broad pathway, saw I him return,
Thousand save seventy times, the whilst I dwelt
Upon the earth. The language I did use
Was worn away, or ever Nimrod's race
Their unaccomplishable work began.
For naught, that man inclines to, e'er was lasting;
Left by his reason free, and variable
As is the sky that sways him. That he speaks,
Is nature's prompting: whether thus, or thus,
She leaves to you, as ye do most affect it.
Ere I descended into Hell's abyss,
El was the name on earth of the Chief Good,
Whose joy enfolds me: Eli then 'twas call'd.

---

[7] "Whence." That is, from Limbo. See Hell, Canto ii. 53. Adam says that 5,232 years elapsed from his creation to the time of his deliverance, which followed the death of Christ.

And so beseemeth: for, in mortals, use
Is as the leaf upon the bough: that goes,
And other comes instead. Upon the mount
Most high above the waters, all my life,
Both innocent and guilty, did but reach
From the first hour, to that which cometh next
(As the sun changes quarter) to the sixth."

CANTO XXVII

ARGUMENT.—St. Peter bitterly rebukes the covetousness of his successors in the
Apostolic See, while all the heavenly host sympathize in his indignation; they then
vanish upward. Beatrice bids Dante again cast his view below. Afterward they are
borne into the ninth heaven, of which she shows him the nature and properties;
blaming the perverseness of man, who places his will on low and perishable things.

THEN "Glory to the Father, to the Son,
And to the Holy Spirit," rang aloud
Throughout all Paradise; that with the song
My spirit reel'd, so passing sweet the strain.
And what I saw was equal ecstasy:
One universal smile it seem'd of all things;
Joy past compare; gladness unutterable;
Imperishable life of peace and love;
Exhaustless riches, and unmeasured bliss.
    Before mine eyes stood the four torches[1] lit:
And that,[2] which first had come, began to wax
In brightness; and, in semblance, such became,
As Jove might be, if he and Mars were birds,
And interchanged their plumes. Silence ensued,
Through the blest quire; by Him, who here appoints
Vicissitude of ministry, enjoin'd;
When thus I heard: "Wonder not, if my hue
Be changed; for, while I speak, these shalt thou see
All in like manner change with me. My place
He[3] who usurps on earth, (my place, ay, mine,
Which in the presence of the Son of God
Is void,) the same hath made my cemetery
A common sewer of puddle and of blood:

---

[1] "Four torches." St. Peter, St. James,
St. John, and Adam.
[2] "That." St. Peter, who looked as the
planet Jupiter would, if it assumed the
sanguine appearance of Mars.
[3] "He." Boniface VIII.

The more below his triumph, who from hence
Malignant fell." Such colour, as the sun,
At eve or morning, paints an adverse cloud,
Then saw I sprinkled over all the sky.
And as the unblemish'd dame, who, in herself
Secure of censure, yet at bare report
Of other's failing, shrinks with maiden fear;
So Beatrice, in her semblance, changed:
And such eclipse in Heaven, methinks, was seen,
When the Most Holy suffer'd. Then the words
Proceeded, with voice, alter'd from itself
So clean, the semblance did not alter more.
"Not to this end was Christ's spouse with my blood,
With that of Linus, and of Cletus,[4] fed;
That she might serve for purchase of base gold:
But for the purchase of this happy life,
Did Sextus, Pius, and Callixtus bleed,
And Urban;[5] they, whose doom was not without
Much weeping seal'd. No purpose was of ours,[6]
That on the right hand of our successors,
Part of the Christian people should be set,
And part upon their left; nor that the keys,
Which were vouchsafed me, should for ensign serve
Unto the banners, that do levy war
On the baptized; nor I, for sigil-mark,
Set upon sold and lying privileges:
Which makes me oft to bicker and turn red.
In shepherd's clothing, greedy wolves[7] below
Range wide o'er all the pastures. Arm of God!
Why longer sleep'st thou? Cahorsines and Gascons[8]
Prepare to quaff our blood. O good beginning!
To what a vile conclusion must thou stoop.
But the high Providence, which did defend,

---

[4] Bishops of Rome in the first century.

[5] The former two, bishops of the same see, in the second; and the others, in the fourth century.

[6] "We did not intend that our successors should take any part in the political divisions among Christians; or that my figure (the seal of St. Peter) should serve as a mark to authorize iniquitous grants and privileges."

[7] "Wolves shall succeed to teachers, grievous wolves." — Milton, "Paradise Lost," b. xii. 508.

[8] He alludes to Jacques d'Ossa, a native of Cahors, pope, as John XXII, in 1316, after the chair had been two years vacant, and to Clement V, a Gascon.

Through Scipio, the world's empery for Rome,
Will not delay its succour: and thou, son,
Who through thy mortal weight shalt yet again
Return below, open thy lips, nor hide
What is by me not hidden." As a flood
Of frozen vapours streams adown the air,
What time the she-goat[9] with her skiey horn
Touches the sun; so saw I there stream wide
The vapours, who with us had linger'd late,
And with glad triumph deck the ethereal cope.
Onward my sight their semblances pursued;
So far pursued, as till the space between
From its reach sever'd them: whereat the guide
Celestial, marking me no more intent
On upward gazing, said, "Look down, and see
What circuit thou hast compast." From the hour[10]
When I before had cast my view beneath,
All the first region overpast I saw,
Which from the midmost to the boundary winds;
That onward, thence, from Gades,[11] I beheld
The unwise passage of Laertes' son;
And hitherward the shore,[12] where thou, Europa,
Madest thee a joyful burden; and yet more
Of this dim spot had seen, but that the sun,[13]
A constellation off and more, had ta'en
His progress in the zodiac underneath.

Then by the spirit, that doth never leave
Its amorous dalliance with my lady's looks,
Back with redoubled ardour were mine eyes
Led unto her: and from her radiant smiles,
Whenas I turn'd me, pleasure so divine
Did lighten on me, that whatever bait
Or art or nature in the human flesh,
Or in its limn'd resemblance, can combine

[9] When the sun is in Capricorn.

[10] "From the hour." Since he had last looked (see Canto xxii) he perceived that he had passed from the meridian circle to the eastern horizon; the half of our hemisphere, and a quarter of the heaven.

[11] See Hell, Canto xxvi. 106.

[12] Phœnicia, where Europa, daughter of Agenor, mounted on the back of Jupiter, in his shape of a bull.

[13] "The sun." Dante was in the constellation of Gemini, and the sun in Aries. There was, therefore, part of those two constellations, and the whole of Taurus, between them.

Through greedy eyes to take the soul withal,
Were, to her beauty, nothing. Its boon influence
From the fair nest of Leda[14] rapt me forth,
And wafted on into the swiftest Heaven.

  What place for entrance Beatrice chose,
I may not say; so uniform was all,
Liveliest and loftiest. She my secret wish
Divined; and, with such gladness, that God's love
Seem'd from her visage shining, thus began:
"Here is the goal, whence motion on his race
Starts: motionless the centre, and the rest
All moved around. Except the soul divine,
Place in this Heaven is none; the soul divine,
Wherein the love, which ruleth o'er its orb,
Is kindled, and the virtue, that it sheds:
One circle, light and love, enclasping it,
As this doth clasp the others; and to Him,
Who draws the bound, its limit only known.
Measured itself by none, it doth divide
Motion to all, counted unto them forth,
As by the fifth or half ye count forth ten.
The vase, wherein time's roots are plunged, thou seest:
Look elsewhere for the leaves. O mortal lust!
That canst not lift thy head above the waves
Which whelm and sink thee down. The will in man
Bears goodly blossoms; but its ruddy promise
Is, by the dripping of perpetual rain,
Made mere abortion: faith and innocence
Are met with but in babes; each taking leave,
Ere cheeks with down are sprinkled: he, that fasts
While yet a stammerer, with his tongue let loose
Gluts every food alike in every moon:
One, yet a babbler, loves and listens to
His mother; but no sooner hath free use
Of speech, than he doth wish her in her grave.
So suddenly doth the fair child of him,
Whose welcome is the morn and eve his parting,
To negro blackness change her virgin white.

---

14 "The fair nest of Leda." From the Gemini; thus called, because Leda was the
    mother of the twins, Castor and Pollux.

"Thou, to abate thy wonder, note, that none
Bears rule in earth; and its frail family
Are therefore wanderers. Yet before the date,
When through the hundredth in his reckoning dropt,
Pale January must be shoved aside
From winter's calendar, these heavenly spheres
Shall roar so loud, that fortune shall be fain[15]
To turn the poop, where she hath now the prow;
So that the fleet run onward: and true fruit,
Expected long, shall crown at last the bloom."

CANTO XXVIII

ARGUMENT.—Still in the ninth heaven, our Poet is permitted to behold the divine
essence; and then sees, in three hierarchies, the nine choirs of angels. Beatrice clears
some difficulties which occur to him on this occasion.

SO she, who doth imparadise my soul,
    Had drawn the veil from off our present life,
    And bared the truth of poor mortality:
When lo! as one who, in a mirror, spies
The shining of a flambeau at his back,
Lit sudden ere he deem of its approach,
And turneth to resolve him, if the glass
Have told him true, and sees the record faithful
As note is to its metre; even thus,
I well remember, did befal to me,
Looking upon the beauteous eyes, whence love
Had made the leash to take me. As I turn'd:
And that which none, who in that volume looks,
Can miss of, in itself apparent, struck
My view; a point I saw, that darted light
So sharp, no lid, unclosing, may bear up
Against its keenness. The least star we ken
From hence, had seem'd a moon; set by its side,
As star by side of star. And so far off,
Perchance, as is the halo from the light
Which paints it, when most dense the vapour spreads;

[15] "Fortune shall be fain." The commentators in general suppose that our
Poet here augurs that great reform which
he vainly hoped would follow on the
arrival of the Emperor Henry VII in Italy.

There wheel'd about the point a circle of fire,
More rapid than the motion which surrounds,
Speediest, the world. Another this enring'd;
And that a third; the third a fourth, and that
A fifth encompass'd; which a sixth next bound;
And over this, a seventh, following, reach'd
Circumference so ample, that its bow,
Within the span of Juno's messenger,
Had scarce been held entire. Beyond a seventh,
Ensued yet other two. And every one,
As more in number distant from the first,
Was tardier in motion: and that glow'd
With flame most pure, that to the sparkle of truth,
Was nearest; as partaking most, methinks,
Of its reality. The guide beloved
Saw me in anxious thought suspense, and spake:
"Heaven, and all nature, hangs upon that point.
The circle thereto most conjoin'd observe;
And know, that by intenser love its course
Is, to this swiftness, wing'd." To whom I thus:
"It were enough; nor should I further seek,
Had I but witness'd order, in the world
Appointed, such as in these wheels is seen.
But in the sensible world such difference is,
That in each round shows more divinity,
As each is wider from the centre. Hence,
If in this wondrous and angelic temple,
That hath, for confine, only light and love,
My wish may have completion, I must know,
Wherefore such disagreement is between
The exemplar and its copy: for myself,
Contemplating, I fail to pierce the cause."

"It is no marvel, if thy fingers foil'd
Do leave the knot untied: so hard 'tis grown
For want of tenting." Thus she said: "But take,"
She added, "if thou wish thy cure, my words,
And entertain them subtly. Every orb,
Corporeal, doth proportion its extent
Unto the virtue through its parts diffused.
The greater blessedness preserves the more,

The greater is the body (if all parts
Share equally) the more is to preserve.
Therefore the circle, whose swift course enwheels
The universal frame, answers to that
Which is supreme in knowledge and in love.
Thus by the virtue, not the seeming breadth
Of substance, measuring, thou shalt see the Heavens,
Each to the intelligence that ruleth it,
Greater to more, and smaller unto less,
Suited in strict and wondrous harmony."
   As when the north blows from his milder cheek
A blast, that scours the sky, forthwith our air,
Clear'd of the rack that hung on it before,
Glitters; and, with his beauties all unveil'd,
The firmament looks forth serene, and smiles:
Such was my cheer, when Beatrice drove
With clear reply the shadows back, and truth
Was manifested, as a star in Heaven.
And when the words were ended, not unlike
To iron in the furnace, every cirque,
Ebullient, shot forth scintillating fires:
And every sparkle shivering to new blaze,
In number[1] did outmillion the account
Reduplicate upon the chequer'd board.
Then heard I echoing on, from choir to choir,
"Hosanna," to the fixed point, that holds,
And shall for ever hold them to their place,
From everlasting, irremovable.
   Musing awhile I stood: and she, who saw
My inward meditations, thus began:
"In the first circles, they, whom thou beheld'st
Are Seraphim and Cherubim. Thus swift
Follow their hoops, in likeness to the point,
Near as they can, approaching; and they can
The more, the loftier their vision. Those
That round them fleet, gazing the Godhead next,
Are Thrones; in whom the first trine ends. And all

---

[1] "In number." The sparkles exceeded the number which would be produced by the sixty-four squares of a chess-board, if for the first we reckoned one; for the next, two; for the third, four; and so went on doubling to the end of the account.

Are blessed, even as their sight descends
Deeper into the Truth, wherein rest is
For every mind. Thus happiness hath root
In seeing, not in loving, which of sight
Is aftergrowth. And of the seeing such
The meed, as unto each, in due degree,
Grace and good-will their measure have assign'd.
The other trine, that with still opening buds
In this eternal springtide blossom fair,
Fearless of bruising from the nightly ram,[2]
Breathe up in warbled melodies threefold
Hosannas, blending ever; from the three,
Transmitted, hierarchy of gods, for aye
Rejoicing; dominations first; next them,
Virtues; and powers the third; the next to whom
Are princedoms and archangels, with glad round
To tread their festal ring; and last, the band
Angelical, disporting in their sphere.
All, as they circle in their orders, look
Aloft; and, downward, with such sway prevail,
That all with mutual impulse tend to God.
These once a mortal view beheld. Desire
In Dionysius,[3] so intensely wrought,
That he, as I have done, ranged them; and named,
Their orders, marshal'd in his thought. From him,
Dissentient, one refused his sacred read.
But soon as in this Heaven his doubting eyes
Were open'd, Gregory[4] at his error smiled.
Nor marvel, that a denizen of earth
Should scan such secret truth; for he had learnt[5]

2 Not injured, like spring products, by
the influence of autumn, when the constellation Aries rises at sunset.
  3 The Areopagite, in his book "De
Cœlesti Hierarchiâ."
  4 "Gregory." Gregory the Great.
  5 "He had learnt." Dionysius, he says,
had learnt from St. Paul. The book
above referred to, which goes under his
name, was the production of a later age.
In Bishop Bull's seventh sermon, which
treats of the different degrees of beatitude
in Heaven, there is much that resembles
what is said on the same subject by our
Poet. The learned prelate, however, appears a little inconsistent, when, after
having blamed Dionysius the Areopagite,
"for reckoning up exactly the several
orders of the angelical hierarchy, as if he
had seen a muster of the heavenly host
before his eyes" (v. i. p. 313), he himself
speaks more particularly of the several
orders in the celestial hierarchy than Holy
Scripture warrants.

Both this and much beside of these our orbs,
From an eye-witness to Heaven's mysteries."

CANTO XXIX

ARGUMENT.—Beatrice beholds, in the mirror of divine truth, some doubts which had entered the mind of Dante. These she resolves; and then digresses into a vehement reprehension of certain theologians and preachers in those days, whose ignorance or avarice induced them to substitute their own inventions for the pure word of the Gospel.

NO longer, than what time Latona's twins
 Cover'd of Libra and the fleecy star,
 Together both, girding the horizon hang;
In even balance, from the zenith poised;
Till from that verge, each, changing hemisphere,
Part the nice level; e'en so brief a space
Did Beatrice's silence hold. A smile
Sat painted on her cheek; and her fix'd gaze
Bent on the point, at which my vision fail'd:
When thus, her words resuming, she began:
"I speak, nor what thou wouldst inquire demand;
For I have mark'd it, where all time and place
Are present. Not for increase to Himself
Of good, which may not be increased, but forth
To manifest His glory by its beams;
Inhabiting His own eternity,
Beyond time's limit or what bound soe'er
To circumscribe His being; as He will'd,
Into new natures, like unto Himself,
Eternal Love unfolded. Nor before,
As if in dull inaction, torpid, lay.
For, not in process of before or aft,
Upon these waters moved the Spirit of God.
Simple and mix'd, both form and substance, forth
To perfect being started, like three darts
Shot from a bow three-corded. And as ray
In crystal, glass, and amber, shines entire,
E'en at the moment of its issuing; thus
Did, from the eternal Sovran, beam entire
His threefold operation, at one act

Produced coeval. Yet, in order, each
Created his due station knew: those highest,
Who pure intelligence were made; mere power,
The lowest; in the midst, bound with strict league,
Intelligence and power, unsever'd bond.
Long tract of ages by the Angels past,
Ere the creating of another world,
Described on Jerome's pages,[1] thou hast seen.
But that what I disclose to thee is true,
Those penmen,[2] whom the Holy Spirit moved
In many a passage of their sacred book,
Attest; as thou by diligent search shalt find:
And reason,[3] in some sort, discerns the same,
Who scarce would grant the heavenly ministers,
Of their perfection void, so long a space.
Thus when and where these spirits of love were made,
Thou know'st, and how: and, knowing, hast allay'd
Thy thirst, which from the triple question[4] rose.
Ere one had reckon'd twenty, e'en so soon,
Part of the Angels fell: and in their fall,
Confusion to your elements ensued.
The others kept their station: and this task,
Whereon thou look'st, began, with such delight,
That they surcease not ever, day nor night,
Their circling. Of that fatal lapse the cause
Was the curst pride of him, whom thou hast seen
Pent with the world's incumbrance. Those, whom here
Thou seest, were lowly to confess themselves
Of His free bounty, who had made them apt
For ministeries so high: therefore their views
Were, by enlightening grace and their own merit
Exalted; so that in their will confirm'd
They stand, nor fear to fall. For do not doubt,
But to receive the grace, which Heaven vouchsafes

---

[1] St. Jerome had described the Angels as created long before the rest of the universe; an opinion which Thomas Aquinas controverted.

[2] As in Gen. i. 1, and Eccles. xviii. 1.

[3] "Reason." The heavenly ministers ("*motori*") would have existed to no purpose if they had been created before the corporeal world, which they were to govern.

[4] He had wished to know where, when, and how the Angels had been created, and these three questions had been resolved.

Is meritorious, even as the soul
With prompt affection welcometh the guest.
Now, without further help, if with good heed
My words thy mind have treasured, thou henceforth
This consistory round about mayst scan,
And gaze thy fill. But, since thou hast on earth
Heard vain disputers, reasoners in the schools,
Canvass the angelic nature, and dispute
Its powers of apprehension, memory, choice;
Therefore, 'tis well thou take from me the truth,
Pure and without disguise; which they below,
Equivocating, darken and perplex.

"Know thou, that, from the first, these substances,
Rejoicing in the countenance of God,
Have held unceasingly their view, intent
Upon the glorious vision, from the which
Nought absent is nor hid: where then no change
Of newness, with succession, interrupts,
Remembrance, there, needs none to gather up
Divided thought and images remote.

"So that men, thus at variance with the truth,
Dream, though their eyes be open; reckless some
Of error; others well aware they err,
To whom more guilt and shame are justly due.
Each the known track of sage philosophy
Deserts, and has a bye-way of his own:
So much the restless eagerness to shine,
And love of singularity prevail.
Yet this, offensive as it is, provokes
Heaven's anger less, than when the Book of God
Is forced to yield to man's authority,
Or from its straightness warp'd: no reckoning made
What blood the sowing of it in the world
Has cost; what favour for himself he wins,
Who meekly clings to it. The aim of all
Is how to shine: e'en they, whose office is
To preach the Gospel, let the Gospel sleep,
And pass their own inventions off instead.
One tells, how at Christ's suffering the wan moon
Bent back her steps, and shadow'd o'er the sun

With intervenient disk, as she withdrew:
Another, how the light shrouded itself
Within its tabernacle, and left dark
The Spaniard, and the Indian, with the Jew.
Such fables Florence in her pulpit hears,
Bandied about more frequent, than the names
Of Bindi and of Lapi[5] in her streets.
The sheep, meanwhile, poor witless ones, return
From pasture, fed with wind: and what avails
For their excuse, they do not see their harm?
Christ said not to His first conventicle,
'Go forth and preach impostures to the world,'
But gave them truth to build on; and the sound
Was mighty on their lips: nor needed they,
Beside the Gospel, other spear or shield,
To aid them in their warfare for the faith.
The preacher now provides himself with store
Of jests and gibes; and, so there be no lack
Of laughter, while he vents them, his big cowl
Distends, and he has won the meed he sought:
Could but the vulgar catch a glimpse the while
Of that dark bird which nestles in his hood,
They scarce would wait to hear the blessing said,
Which now the dotards hold in such esteem,
That every counterfeit, who spreads abroad
The hands of holy promise, finds a throng
Of credulous fools beneath. Saint Anthony
Fattens with this his swine,[6] and others worse
Than swine, who diet at his lazy board,
Paying with unstampt metal[7] for their fare,
  "But (for we far have wander'd) let us seek
The forward path again; so as the way
Be shorten'd with the time. No mortal tongue,
Nor thought of man, hath ever reach'd so far,
That of these natures he might count the tribes.
What Daniel[8] of their thousands hath reveal'd,

[5] Common names at Florence.
[6] On the sale of these blessings, the brothers of St. Anthony supported themselves and their paramours. From behind the swine of St. Anthony, our Poet levels a blow at Boniface VIII, from whom, in 1297, they obtained the privileges of an independent congregation.
[7] With false indulgences.
[8] "Daniel." "Thousand thousands min-

With finite number, infinite conceals.
The fountain, at whose source these drink their beams,
With light supplies them in as many modes,
As there are splendours that it shines on: each
According to the virtue it conceives,
Differing in love and sweet affection.
Look then how lofty and how huge in breadth
The eternal Might, which, broken and dispersed
Over such countless mirrors, yet remains
Whole in itself and one, as at the first."

CANTO XXX

ARGUMENT.—Dante is taken up with BEATRICE into the empyrean; and there having his sight strengthened by her aid, and by the virtue derived from looking on the river of light, he sees the triumph of the Angels and of the souls of the blessed.

NOON'S fervid hour perchance six thousand miles[1]
From hence is distant; and the shadowy cone
Almost to level on our earth declines;
When, from the midmost of this blue abyss,
By turns some star is to our vision lost.
And straightway as the handmaid of the sun
Puts forth her radiant brow, all, light by light,
Fade; and the spangled firmament shuts in,
E'en to the loveliest of the glittering throng.
Thus vanish'd gradually from my sight
The triumph, which plays ever round the point,
That overcame me, seeming (for it did)
Engirt[2] by that it girdeth. Wherefore love,
With loss of other object, forced me bend
Mine eyes on Beatrice once again.
    If all, that hitherto is told of her,
Were in one praise concluded, 'twere too weak
To furnish out this turn. Mine eyes did look
On beauty, such, as I believe in sooth,

istered unto him, and ten thousand times ten thousand stood before him."—Dan. vii. 10.

[1] He compares the vanishing of the vision to the fading away of the stars at dawn, when it is noonday 6,000 miles off, and the shadow, formed by the earth over the part of it inhabited by the Poet, is about to disappear.

[2] "Appearing to be encompassed by these angelic bands, which are in reality encompassed by it."

Not merely to exceed our human; but,
That save its Maker, none can to the full
Enjoy it. At this point o'erpower'd I fail;
Unequal to my theme; as never bard
Of buskin or of sock hath fail'd before.
For as the sun doth to the feeblest sight,
E'en so remembrance of that witching smile
Hath dispossest my spirit of itself.
Not from that day, when on this earth I first
Beheld her charms, up to that view of them,
Have I with song applausive ever ceased
To follow; but now follow them no more;
My course here bounded, as each artist's is,
When it doth touch the limit of his skill.

　　She (such as I bequeath her to the bruit
Of louder trump than mine, which hasteneth on
Urging its arduous matter to the close)
Her words resumed, in gesture and in voice
Resembling one accustom'd to command:
"Forth[3] from the last corporeal are we come
Into the Heaven, that is unbodied light;
Light intellectual, replete with love;
Love of true happiness, replete with joy;
Joy, that transcends all sweetness of delight.
Here shalt thou look on either mighty host[4]
Of Paradise; and one in that array,
Which in the final judgment thou shalt see."

　　As when the lightning, in a sudden spleen
Unfolded, dashes from the blinding eyes
The visive spirits, dazzled and bedimm'd;
So, round about me, fulminating streams
Of living radiance play'd, and left me swathed
And veiled in dense impenetrable blaze.
Such weal is in the love, that stills this heaven;
For its own flame[5] the torch thus fitting ever.

　　No sooner to my listening ear had come

---

[3] From the ninth sphere to the empyrean, which is mere light.
[4] Of Angels, that remained faithful, and of beatified souls; the latter in the form they will have at the last day.
[5] Thus disposing the spirits to receive its own beatific light.

The brief assurance, than I understood
New virtue into me infused, and sight
Kindled afresh, with vigour to sustain
Excess of light however pure. I look'd;
And, in the likeness of a river, saw
Light flowing, from whose amber-seeming waves
Flash'd up effulgence, as they glided on
'Twixt banks, on either side, painted with spring,
Incredible how fair: and, from the tide,
There ever and anon, outstarting, flew
Sparkles instinct with life; and in the flowers
Did set them, like to rubies, chased in gold:
Then, as if drunk with odours, plunged again
Into the wondrous flood; from which, as one
Re-enter'd, still another rose. "The thirst
Of knowledge high, whereby thou art inflamed,
To search the meaning of what here thou seest,
The more it warms thee, pleases me the more,
But first behoves thee of this water drink,
Or e'er that longing be allay'd." So spake
The day-star of mine eyes: then thus subjoin'd:
"This stream; and these, forth issuing from its gulf,
And diving back, a living topaz each;
With all this laughter on its bloomy shores;
Are but a preface, shadowy of the truth
They emblem: not that, in themselves, the things
Are crude; but on thy part is the defect,
For that thy views not yet aspire so high."
    Never did babe, that had outslept his wont,
Rush, with such eager straining, to the milk,
As I toward the water; bending me,
To make the better mirrors of mine eyes
In the refining wave: and as the eaves
Of mine eyelids did drink of it, forthwith
Seem'd it unto me turn'd from length to round.
Then as a troop of maskers, when they put
Their vizors off, look other than before;
The counterfeited semblance thrown aside:
So into greater jubilee were changed
Those flowers and sparkles; and distinct I saw,

Before me, either court of Heaven display'd.
   O prime enlightener! thou who gavest me strength
On the high triumph of Thy realm to gaze;
Grant virtue now to utter what I kenn'd.
   There is in Heaven a light, whose goodly shine
Makes the Creator visible to all
Created, that in seeing Him alone
Have peace; and in a circle spreads so far,
That the circumference were too loose a zone
To girdle in the sun. All is one beam,
Reflected from the summit of the first,
That moves, which being hence and vigour takes.
And as some cliff, that from the bottom eyes
His image mirror'd in the crystal flood,
As if to admire his brave apparelling
Of verdure and of flowers; so, round about,
Eying the light, on more than million thrones,
Stood, eminent, whatever from our earth
Has to the skies return'd. How wide the leaves,
Extended to their utmost, of this rose,
Whose lowest step embosoms such a space
Of ample radiance! Yet, nor amplitude
Nor height impeded, but my view with ease
Took in the full dimensions of that joy.
Near or remote, what there avails, where God
Immediate rules, and Nature, awed, suspends
Her sway? Into the yellow of the rose
Perennial, which, in bright expansiveness,
Lays forth its gradual blooming, redolent
Of praises to the never-wintering sun,
As one, who fain would speak yet holds his peace,
Beatrice led me; and, "Behold," she said,
"This fair assemblage; stoles of snowy white,
How numberless. The city, where we dwell,
Behold how vast; and these our seats so throng'd,
Few now are wanting here. In that proud stall,
On which, the crown, already o'er its state
Suspended, holds thine eyes—or e'er thyself
Mayst at the wedding sup—shall rest the soul

Of the great Harry,[6] he who, by the world
Augustus hail'd, to Italy must come,
Before her day be ripe. But ye are sick,
And in your tetchy wantonness as blind,
As is the bantling, that of hunger dies,
And drives away the nurse. Nor may it be,
That he,[7] who in the sacred forum sways,
Openly or in secret, shall with him
Accordant walk: whom God will not endure
I' the holy office long; but thrust him down
To Simon Magus, where Alagna's priest[8]
Will sink beneath him: such will be his meed."

CANTO XXXI

ARGUMENT.—The Poet expatiates further on the glorious vision described in the
last Canto. On looking round for Beatrice, he finds that she has left him, and that
an old man is at his side. This proves to be St. Bernard, who shows him that Beatrice
has returned to her throne, and then points out to him the blessedness of the
Virgin Mother.

IN fashion, as a snow white rose, lay then
Before my view the saintly multitude,[1]
Which in His own blood Christ espoused. Meanwhile,
That other host,[2] that soar aloft to gaze
And celebrate His glory, whom they love,
Hover'd around; and, like a troop of bees,
Amid the vernal sweets alighting now,
Now, clustering, where their fragrant labour glows,
Flew downward to the mighty flower, or rose
From the redundant petals, streaming back
Unto the steadfast dwelling of their joy,
Faces had they of flame, and wings of gold:

[6] "Of the great Harry." The Emperor
Henry VII, who died in 1313. "Henry,
Count of Luxemburg, held the imperial
power three years, seven months and
eighteen days from his first coronation
to his death. He was a man wise, and
just, and gracious; brave and intrepid
in arms; a man of honor and a good
catholic; and although by his lineage
he was of no great condition, yet he
was of a magnanimous heart, much
feared and held in awe; and if he had
lived longer, would have done the greatest things." G. Villani.
[7] Clement V. See Canto xxvii. 53.
[8] "Alagna's priest." Pope Boniface
VIII. Hell, Canto xix. 79.
[1] Human souls, advanced to this state
of glory through the mediation of Christ.
[2] "That other host." The Angels.

The rest was whiter than the driven snow;
And, as they flitted down into the flower,
From range to range, fanning their plumy loins,
Whisper'd the peace and ardour, which they won
From that soft winnowing. Shadow none, the vast
Interposition of such numerous flight
Cast, from above, upon the flower, or view
Obstructed aught. For, through the universe,
Wherever merited, celestial light
Glides freely, and no obstacle prevents.

All there, who reign in safety and in bliss,
Ages long past or new, on one sole mark
Their love and vision fix'd. O trinal beam
Of individual star, that charm'st them thus!
Vouchsafe one glance to gild our storm below.[3]

If the grim brood,[4] from Arctic shores that roam'd,
(Where Helice[5] for ever, as she wheels,
Sparkles a mother's fondness on her son),
Stood in mute wonder 'mid the works of Rome,
When to their view the Lateran arose
In greatness more than earthly; I, who then
From human to divine had past, from time
Unto eternity, and out of Florence
To justice and to truth, how might I chuse
But marvel too? 'Twixt gladness and amaze,
In sooth no will had I to utter aught,
Or hear. And, as a pilgrim, when he rests
Within the temple of his vow, looks round
In breathless awe, and hopes some time to tell
Of all its goodly state; e'en so mine eyes
Coursed up and down along the living light,
Now low, and now aloft, and now around,
Visiting every step. Looks I beheld,
Where charity in soft persuasion sat;
Smiles from within, and radiance from above;
And, in each gesture, grace and honour high.
So roved my ken, and in its general form

---

[3] To guide us through the dangers of this tempestuous life.

[4] "If the grim brood." The northern hordes who invaded Rome.

[5] "Helice." Callistro, and her son Arcas, changed into the constellation of the Greater Bear and Arctophylax, or Boötes.

All Paradise survey'd: when round I turn'd
With purpose of my lady to inquire
Once more of things, that held my thought suspense.
But answer found from other than I ween'd;
For, Beatrice, when I thought to see,
I saw instead a senior, at my side,
Robed, as the rest, in glory. Joy benign
Glow'd in his eye, and o'er his cheek diffused,
With gestures such as spake a father's love.
And, "Whither is she vanish'd?" straight I ask'd.
    "By Beatrice summon'd," he replied,
"I come to aid thy wish. Looking aloft
To the third circle from the highest, there
Behold her on the throne, wherein her merit
Hath placed her." Answering not, mine eyes I raised,
And saw her, where aloof she sat, her brow
A wreath reflecting of eternal beams.
Not from the centre of the sea so far
Unto the region of the highest thunder,
As was my ken from hers; and yet the form
Came through that medium down, unmix'd and pure.
    "O Lady! thou in whom my hopes have rest;
Who, for my safety, hast not scorn'd, in Hell
To leave the traces of thy footsteps mark'd;
For all mine eyes have seen, I to thy power
And goodness, virtue owe and grace. Of slave
Thou hast to freedom brought me: and no means,
For my deliverance apt, hast left untried.
Thy liberal bounty still toward me keep:
That, when my spirit, which thou madest whole,
Is loosen'd from this body, it may find
Favour with thee." So I my suit preferr'd:
And she, so distant, as appear'd, look'd down,
And smiled; then toward the eternal fountain turn'd.
    And thus the senior, holy and revered:
"That thou at length mayst happily conclude
Thy voyage, (to which end I was despatch'd,
By supplication moved and holy love),
Let thy upsoaring vision range, at large,
This garden through: for so, by ray divine

Kindled, thy ken a higher flight shall mount;
And from Heaven's Queen, whom fervent I adore,
All gracious aid befriend us; for that I
Am her own faithful Bernard." [6] Like a wight,
Who haply from Croatia wends to see
Our Veronica,[7] and, the while 'tis shown,
Hangs over it with never-sated gaze,
And, all that he hath heard revolving, saith
Unto himself in thought: "And didst Thou look
E'en thus, O Jesus, my true Lord and God?
And was this semblance Thine?" So gazed I then
Adoring; for the charity of him,[8]
Who musing, in this world that peace enjoy'd,
Stood livelily before me. "Child of grace!"
Thus he began: "Thou shalt not knowledge gain
Of this glad being, if thine eyes are held
Still in this depth below. But search around
The circles, to the furthest, till thou spy
Seated in state, the Queen[9] that of this realm
Is sovran." Straight mine eyes I raised; and bright,
As, at the birth of morn, the eastern clime
Above the horizon, where the sun declines;
So to mine eyes, that upward, as from vale
To mountain sped, at the extreme bound, a part
Excell'd in lustre all the front opposed.
And as the glow burns ruddiest o'er the wave,
That waits the ascending team, which Phaëton
Ill knew to guide, and on each part the light
Diminish'd fades, intensest in the midst;
So burn'd the peaceful oriflame, and slack'd
On every side the living flame decay'd.

---

[6] "Bernard." St. Bernard, the venerable Abbot of Clairvaux, and the great promoter of the Second Crusade, who died A. D. 1153, in his sixty-third year. He has been termed the last of the fathers of the Church. That the part he acts in the present poem should be assigned to him, appears somewhat remarkable, when we consider that he severely censured the new festival established in honor of the Immaculate Conception of the Virgin, and "opposed the doctrine itself with the greatest vigor, as it supposed her being honored with a privilege which belonged to Christ alone."

[7] A copy in miniature of the picture of Christ, which is supposed to have been miraculously imprinted upon a handkerchief preserved in the church of St. Peter at Rome.

[8] "Him." St. Bernard.

[9] "The queen." The Virgin Mary.

And in that midst their sportive pennons waved
Thousands of Angels; in resplendence each
Distinct, and quaint adornment. At their glee
And carol, smiled the Lovely One of Heaven,
That joy was in the eyes of all the blest.

Had I a tongue in eloquence as rich,
As is the colouring in fancy's loom,
'Twere all too poor to utter the least part
Of that enchantment. When he saw mine eyes
Intent on her, that charm'd him; Bernard gazed
With so exceeding fondness, as infused
Ardour into my breast, unfelt before.

CANTO XXXII

ARGUMENT.—St. Bernard shows him, on their several thrones, the other blessed souls, of both the Old and New Testament; explains to him that their places are assigned them by grace, and not according to merit; and, lastly, tells him that if he would obtain power to descry what remained of the heavenly vision, he must unite with him in supplication to Mary.

FREELY the sage, though wrapt in musings high,
Assumed the teacher's part, and mild began:
"The wound, that Mary closed, she[1] open'd first,
Who sits so beautiful at Mary's feet.
The third in order, underneath her, lo!
Rachel with Beatrice: Sarah next;
Judith; Rebecca; and the gleaner-maid,
Meek ancestress[2] of him, who sang the songs
Of sore repentance in his sorrowful mood.
All, as I name them, down from leaf to leaf,
Are, in gradation, throned on the rose.
And from the seventh step, successively,
Adown the breathing tresses of the flower,
Still doth the file of Hebrew dames proceed.
For these are a partition wall, whereby
The sacred stairs are sever'd, as the faith
In Christ divides them. On this part, where blooms
Each leaf in full maturity, are set
Such as in Christ, or e'er He came, believed.
On the other, where an intersected space

----

[1] Eve.   [2] Ruth, the ancestress of David.

Yet shows the semicircle void, abide
All they, who look'd to Christ already come
And as our Lady on her glorious stool,
And they who on their stools beneath her sit,
This way distinction make; e'en so on his,
The mighty Baptist that way marks the line
(He who endured the desert, and the pains
Of martyrdom, and, for two years,[3] of Hell,
Yet still continued holy), and beneath,
Augustin;[4] Francis;[5] Benedict;[6] and the rest,
Thus far from round to round. So Heaven's decree
Forecasts, this garden equally to fill,
With faith in either view, past or to come.
Learn too, that downward from the step, which cleaves,
Midway, the twain compartments, none there are
Who place obtain for merit of their own,
But have through others' merit been advanced,
On set conditions; spirits all released,
Ere for themselves they had the power to chuse.
And, if thou mark and listen to them well,
Their childish looks and voice declare as much.

"Here, silent as thou art, I know thy doubt;
And gladly will I loose the knot, wherein
Thy subtile thoughts have bound thee. From this realm
Excluded, chance no entrance here may find;
No more than hunger, thirst, or sorrow can.
A law immutable hath stablish'd all;
Nor is there aught thou seest, that doth not fit,
Exactly, as the finger to the ring.
It is not, therefore, without cause, that these
O'erspeedy comers to immortal life,
Are different in their shares of excellence.
Our Sovran Lord, that settleth this estate
In love and in delight so absolute,
That wish can dare no further, every soul,
Created in His joyous sight to dwell,
With grace, at pleasure, variously endows.

[3] The time that elapsed between the death of the Baptist and his redemption by the death of Christ.

[4] Bishop of Hippo, fourth century. See also Canto x. 117.

[5] "Francis." See Canto xi.

[6] "Benedict." See Canto xxii.

And for a proof the effect may well suffice.
And 'tis moreover most expressly mark'd
In holy Scripture, where the twins are said
To have struggled in the womb. Therefore, as grace
Inweaves the coronet, so every brow
Weareth its proper hue of orient light.
And merely in respect to his prime gift,
Not in reward of meritorious deed,
Hath each his several degree assign'd.
In early times with their own innocence
More was not wanting than the parents' faith,
To save them: those first ages past, behoved
That circumcision in the males should imp
The flight of innocent wings: but since the day
Of grace hath come, without baptismal rites
In Christ accomplish'd, innocence herself
Must linger yet below. Now raise thy view
Unto the visage most resembling Christ:
For, in her splendour only, shalt thou win
The power to look on Him." Forthwith I saw
Such floods of gladness on her visage shower'd,
From holy spirits, winging that profound;
That, whatsoever I had yet beheld,
Had not so much suspended me with wonder,
Or shown me such similitude of God.
And he, who had to her descended, once,
On earth, now hail'd in Heaven; and on poised wing,
"Ave, Maria, Gratia Plena," sang:
To whose sweet anthem all the blissful court,
From all parts answering, rang: that holier joy
Brooded the deep serene. "Father revered!
Who deign'st, for me, to quit the pleasant place
Wherein thou sittest, by eternal lot;
Say, who that Angel is, that with such glee
Beholds our Queen, and so enamour'd glows
Of her high beauty, that all fire he seems."
So I again resorted to the lore
Of my wise teacher, he, whom Mary's charms
Embellish'd, as the sun the morning star;
Who thus in answer spake: "In him are summ'd,

Whate'er of buxomness and free delight
May be in spirit, or in Angel, met:
And so beseems: for that he bare the palm
Down unto Mary, when the Son of God
Vouchsafed to clothe Him in terrestrial weeds.
Now let thine eyes wait heedful on my words;
And note thou of this just and pious realm
The chiefest nobles. Those, highest in bliss,
The twain, on each hand next our Empress throned,
Are as it were two roots unto this rose:
He to the left, the parent, whose rash taste
Proves bitter to his seed; and, on the right,
That ancient father of the holy Church,
Into whose keeping Christ did give the keys
Of this sweet flower; near whom behold the seer,[7]
That, ere he died, saw all the grievous times
Of the fair bride, who with the lance and nails
Was won. And, near unto the other, rests
The leader, under whom, on manna, fed
The ungrateful nation, fickle and perverse.
On the other part, facing to Peter, lo!
Where Anna sits, so well content to look
On her loved daughter, that with moveless eye
She chants the loud hosanna: while, opposed
To the first father of your mortal kind,
Is Lucia,[8] at whose hest thy lady sped,
When on the edge of ruin closed thine eye.
    "But (for the vision hasteneth to an end)
Here break we off, as the good workman doth,
That shapes the cloak according to the cloth;
And to the Primal Love our ken shall rise;
That thou mayst penetrate the brightness, far
As sight can bear thee. Yet, alas! in sooth
Beating thy pennons, thinking to advance,
Thou backward fall'st. Grace then must first be gain'd;
Her grace, whose might can help thee. Thou in prayer
Seek her: and, with affection, whilst I sue,
Attend, and yield me all thy heart." He said;
And thus the saintly orison began.

[7] St. John.   [8] See Hell, Canto ii. 97, and Purgatory, Canto ix. 50.

CANTO XXXIII

ARGUMENT.—St. Bernard supplicates the Virgin Mary that Dante may have grace given him to contemplate the brightness of the Divine Majesty, which is accordingly granted; and Dante then himself prays to God for ability to show forth some part of the celestial glory in his writings. Lastly, he is admitted to a glimpse of the great mystery; the Trinity, and the Union of Man with God.

"O VIRGIN MOTHER, daughter of thy Son!
    Created beings all in lowliness
    Surpassing, as in height above them all;
Term by the eternal counsel pre-ordain'd;
Ennobler of thy nature, so advanced
In thee, that its great Maker did not scorn,
To make Himself his own creation;
For in thy womb rekindling shone the love
Reveal'd, whose genial influence makes now
This flower to germin in eternal peace:
Here thou to us, of charity and love,
Art, as the noon-day torch; and art, beneath,
To mortal men, of hope a living spring.
So mighty art thou, Lady, and so great,
That he, who grace desireth, and comes not
To thee for aidance, fain would have desire
Fly without wings. Not only him, who asks,
Thy bounty succours; but doth freely oft
Forerun the asking. Whatsoe'er may be
Of excellence in creature, pity mild,
Relenting mercy, large munificence,
Are all combined in thee. Here kneeleth one,
Who of all spirits hath review'd the state,
From the world's lowest gap unto this height.
Suppliant to thee he kneels, imploring grace
For virtue yet more high, to lift his ken
Toward the bliss supreme. And I, who ne'er
Coveted sight, more fondly, for myself,
Than now for him, my prayers to thee prefer,
(And pray they be not scant), that thou wouldst
Each cloud of his mortality away,   [drive
Through thine own prayers, that on the sovran joy
Unveil'd he gaze. This yet, I pray thee, Queen,

Who canst do what thou wilt; that in him thou
Wouldst, after all he hath beheld, preserve
Affection sound, and human passions quell.
Lo! where, with Beatrice, many a saint
Stretch their clasp'd hands, in furtherance of my suit."

    The eyes, that Heaven with love and awe regards,
Fix'd on the suitor, witness'd, how benign
She looks on pious prayers: then fasten'd they
On the everlasting light, wherein no eye
Of creature, as may well be thought, so far
Can travel inward. I, meanwhile, who drew
Near to the limit, where all wishes end,
The ardour of my wish (for so behoved)
Ended within me. Beckoning smiled the sage,
That I should look aloft: but, ere he bade,
Already of myself aloft I look'd;
For visual strength, refining more and more,
Bare me into the ray authentical
Of sovran light. Thenceforward, what I saw,
Was not for words to speak, nor memory's self
To stand against such outrage on her skill.

    As one, who from a dream awaken'd, straight,
All he hath seen forgets; yet still retains
Impression of the feeling in his dream;
E'en such am I: for all the vision dies,
As 'twere, away; and yet the sense of sweet,
That sprang from it, still trickles in my heart.
Thus in the sun-thaw is the snow unseal'd;
Thus in the winds on flitting leaves was lost
The Sibyl's sentence. O eternal beam!   [soar?)
(Whose height what reach of mortal thought may
Yield me again some little particle
Of what Thou then appearedst; give my tongue
Power, but to leave one sparkle of Thy glory,
Unto the race to come, that shall not lose
Thy triumph wholly, if Thou waken aught
Of memory in me, and endure to hear
The record sound in this unequal strain.

    Such keenness from the living ray I met,
That, if mine eyes had turn'd away, methinks,

I had been lost; but, so embolden'd, on
I pass'd, as I remember, till my view
Hover'd the brink of dread infinitude.

 O grace, unenvying of Thy boon! that gavest
Boldness to fix so earnestly my ken
On the everlasting splendour, that I look'd,
While sight was unconsumed, and, in that depth,
Saw in one volume clasp'd of love, whate'er
The universe unfolds; all properties
Of substance and of accident, beheld,
Compounded, yet one individual light
The whole. And of such bond methinks I saw
The universal form; for that whene'er
I do but speak of it, my soul dilates
Beyond her proper self; and, till I speak,
One moment seems a longer lethargy,
Than five-and-twenty ages had appear'd
To that emprize, that first made Neptune wonder
At Argo's shadow darkening on his flood.

 With fixed heed, suspense and motionless,
Wondering I gazed; and admiration still
Was kindled as I gazed. It may not be,
That one, who looks upon that light, can turn
To other object, willingly, his view.
For all the good, that will may covet, there
Is summ'd; and all, elsewhere defective found,
Complete. My tongue shall utter now, no more
E'en what remembrance keeps, than could the babe's
That yet is moisten'd at his mother's breast.
Not that the semblance of the living light
Was changed, (that ever as at first remain'd),
But that my vision quickening, in that sole
Appearance, still new miracles descried,
And toil'd me with the change. In that abyss
Of radiance, clear and lofty, seem'd, methought,
Three orbs of triple hue, clipt in one bound:[1]
And, from another, one reflected seem'd,

---

[1] "Three orbs of triple hue, clipt in one bound." The Trinity. This passage may be compared to what Plato, in his second Epistle, enigmatically says of a first, second, and third, and of the impossibility that the human soul should attain to what it desires to know of them, by means of anything akin to itself.

As rainbow is from rainbow: and the third
Seem'd fire, breathed equally from both. O speech!
How feeble and how faint art thou, to give
Conception birth. Yet this to what I saw
Is less than little. O eternal Light!
Sole in Thyself that dwell'st; and of Thyself
Sole understood, past, present, or to come;
Thou smiledst, on that circling,[2] which in Thee
Seem'd as reflected splendour, while I mused;
For I therein, methought, in its own hue
Beheld our image painted: steadfastly
I therefore pored upon the view. As one,
Who versed in geometric lore, would fain
Measure the circle; and, though pondering long
And deeply, that beginning, which he needs,
Finds not: e'en such was I, intent to scan
The novel wonder, and trace out the form,
How to the circle fitted, and therein
How placed: but the flight was not for my wing;
Had not a flash darted athwart my mind,
And, in the spleen, unfolded what it sought.

Here vigour fail'd the towering fantasy:
But yet the will roll'd onward, like a wheel
In even motion, by the Love impell'd,
That moves the sun in Heaven and all the stars.

[2] "That circling." The second of the circles, "Light of Light," in which he dimly beheld the mystery of the Incarnation.

GLOSSARY

Adveur, opposite.
Afflation, the act of blowing upon, or the state of being blown upon.
Agnized, acknowledged; recognized; learnt.

Backening, hindering.
Besteads, profits.
Bewraying, discovering, betraying.
Brachs, female hounds; dogs that pursue their prey by the scent.
Burgein, bud, put forth branches.

Champain, flat, open country.
Charlemain, Charlemagne: Charles the Great.
Chuses, chooses.
Cirque, a circle; an encircling cliff.
Cittern, a musical instrument, like a guitar, but strung with wire instead of gut.
Cloked, concealed; d i s g u i s e d; contradicted.
Cope, head-covering; summit; canopy.
Curule-chair, among the Romans a chair of state reserved under the Republic for officers of high dignity, hence called "curule magistrates."
Cyon, scion.

Doddered, overgrown with dodder, or slender, twining, leafless parasites, involving and destroying the whole plant on which they grow.
Dispred, expanded.

Empery, empire, sovereignty, dominion.
Emprize, undertaking of great import and risk.
Erst, formerly.

Featly, dexterously; nimbly.
Fardel, burden.
Foison, outpouring; abundance.
Foss, moat; ditch; depression; chasm.
Frore, frozen; frosty.

Germain, related.

Gleed, spark.
Governance, the art of governing.
Grot, grotto; crypt; hidden chamber.
Gyres, circles.

Hight, called; named.
Holm, holly; oak-holm.

Indurated, hardened; obdurate.

Jocund, cheerful; care-free.

Ken, *sub.* attention, understanding; *v.* recognize, apprehend.

Lea, meadow.
Limn'd, painted; drawn; illuminated.
List, Purg., c. 18, l. 59, please; Purg., c. 23, l. 48, listen to.
Losel, a lazy vagabond; a scoundrel.

Meed, reward, in both bad and good sense.
Mickle, much; great.

Nathless, none the less.

Omnific, all-creating.

Pallet, couch; resting place.
Practic, practical skill; *i. e.*, proof.
Primy, flourishing; in its prime.
Proem, preface; introduction.
Propension, inclination.

Quaternion, composed of four, as in Purg., c. 33, l. 3, the four virgins.
Quatre, four.
Quire, choir; company.
Quiresters, choristers; singing birds.

Ramp, leap; spring; bound.
Reaves, bereaves.
Rere, rear; backward.
Rereward, to the rear.
Rivage, river bank; shore; coast.

Sempiternal, having beginning, but no end; everlasting.

427

Septentrion, northern.
Sheret, hurt; damaged.
Sicklies, makes sick.
Sigil-mark, seal; signature; an occult sign, mark, or character.
Sith, since; afterwards.
Sithence, since; seeing that.
Swerd, sword.

Tent, prove; sound; tempt; try.
Tetchy, peevish; irritable.
Tilth, that which is tilled; or the act of tilling.
Tinct, tinged; colored.
Tourneying, competing (or turning, varying?).
Transpicuous, transparent.
Trinal, threefold.
Trine, threefold.
Twyfold, twofold.

Unweeting, unwitting; unconscious.

Vaward, vanward; to the front.
Vermeil dyed the mulberry, etc., the story as told by Ovid in his *Metamorphoses*, the blood of Pyramis dyed the white mulberry a dark tint or purple hue.
Vermeil-tinctured, vermilion-tinged or rosy colored.
Verrey, verry, same as *vairé*, a term in heraldry denoting green-tinctured.
Visive, visual.

Wain, sub. Charles's wain—churl's or farmer's wagon, the seven brightest stars of the constellation Great Bear, which has been called a wagon or "wain" since the time of Homer; *v.*, to carry.
Waymenting, bewailing; lamentation.
Whenas, when; whereas; while.
Whilom, once; formerly.
Wons, lives; dwells.